ISRAEL'S HISTORY
AND THE HISTORY OF ISRAEL

BibleWorld

Series Editors: James Crossley, University of Sheffield; Philip R. Davies, University of Sheffield

BibleWorld shares the fruits of modern (and postmodern) biblical scholarship not only among practitioners and students, but also with anyone interested in what academic study of the Bible means in the twenty-first century. It explores our ever-increasing knowledge and understanding of the social world that produced the biblical texts, but also analyses aspects of the bible's role in the history of our civilization and the many perspectives – not just religious and theological, but also cultural, political and aesthetic – which drive modern biblical scholarship.

Published

Sodomy:
A History of a Christian Biblical Myth
Michael Carden

Yours Faithfully:
Virtual Letters from the Bible
Edited by: Philip R. Davies

The Apostle Paul and His Letters
Edwin D. Freed

The Origins of the 'Second' Temple:
Persian Imperial Policy and the
Rebuilding of Jerusalem
Diana Edelman

An Introduction to the Bible
(Revised edition)
John Rogerson

The Morality of Paul's Converts
Edwin D. Freed

The Mythic Mind
Essays on Cosmology and Religion in
Ugaritic and Old Testament Literature
N. Wyatt

History, Literature and Theology in
the Book of Chronicles
Ehud Ben Zvi

Sectarianism in Early Judaism
Sciological Advances
Edited by David J. Chalcraft

Symposia
Dialogues Concerning the History
of Biblical Interpretation
Roland Boer

Jonah's World
Social Science and the Reading of
Prophetic Story
Lowell K. Handy

Uruk
The First City
Mario Liverani

Women Healing/Healing Women
The Genderisation of Healing in Early Christianity
Elaine Wainwright

ISRAEL'S HISTORY
AND THE HISTORY OF ISRAEL

MARIO LIVERANI

TRANSLATED BY CHIARA PERI AND PHILIP R. DAVIES

Routledge
Taylor & Francis Group

LONDON AND NEW YORK

First published in Italian in 2003 by Gius. Laterza & Figli Spa, Roma-Bari, entitled *Oltre la Bibbia: Storia Antica di Israele.* This translation is published by arrangement with Gius. Laterza & Figli Spa, Roma-Bari.

First published in English in hardback in 2005 and paperback edition published in 2007 by Equinox Publishing Ltd, an imprint of Acumen

Published 2014 by Routledge
2 Park Square, Milton Park, Abingdon, Oxon OX14 4RN
711 Third Avenue, New York, NY 10017, USA

Routledge is an imprint of the Taylor & Francis Group, an informa business

© 2003 Gius. Laterza & Figli Spa, Rome-Bari
This translation © Chiara Peri and Philip R. Davies 2005.

Notices
Practitioners and researchers must always rely on their own experience and knowledge in evaluating and using any information, methods, compounds, or experiments described herein. In using such information or methods they should be mindful of their own safety and the safety of others, including parties for whom they have a professional responsibility.

To the fullest extent of the law, neither the Publisher nor the authors, contributors, or editors, assume any liability for any injury and/or damage to persons or property as a matter of products liability, negligence or otherwise, or from any use or operation of any methods, products, instructions, or ideas contained in the material herein.

British Library Cataloguing-in-Publication Data
A catalogue record for this book is available from the British Library.

ISBN 978 1 84553 341 0 (paperback)

Typeset by CA Typesetting Ltd.

All kingdoms designated by the name of Assyria are so called because they enrich themselves at Israel's expense...all kingdoms designated by the name of Egypt are so called because they persecute Israel.

(Genesis Rabbah 16.4)*

CONTENTS

IMPRINTING

Part I
A NORMAL HISTORY

LIST OF TABLES AND ILLUSTRATIONS

1. Tables

2. Figures

FOREWORD

Another history of ancient Israel? Are there not enough of them already? And what if its author is not even a professional *Alttestamentler*, but a historian of the ancient Near East? It is true: we already have many (perhaps too many) histories of ancient Israel, but they are all so similar to each other because, inescapably, they are all too similar to the story we find in the Biblical text. They share its plot, its way of presenting facts, even when they question critically its historical reliability.

The history of ancient Israel has always been presented as a sort of paraphrase of the Biblical text. At first the theological relevance of the revealed word made it difficult to accept a rational critique that could, even at great pains, open the way to a secular approach. Even the archaeological discoveries in Palestine were not at first so sensational as to allow a complete rethinking of the history of the area on the basis of ancient and original sources, as was the case in Egypt, Mesopotamia and Hittite Anatolia. Indeed, towards the end of the nineteenth century, archaeology began to be used as 'proof' of the reliability of the Biblical text, while that text was already being questioned at the time by the literary criticism of German philologists.

During the last two centuries, Biblical criticism has progressively dismantled the historicity of creation and flood, then of the patriarchs, then (in chronological order) of the exodus and of the conquest, of Moses and Joshua, then the period of Judges and the 'twelve tribe league', stopping at the era of the 'United Monarchy' of David and Solomon, which was still considered substantially historical. The realization that foundational episodes of conquest and law-giving were in fact post-exilic retrojections, aiming to justify the national and religious unity and the possession of the land by groups of returnees from the Babylonian exile, implied a degree of rewriting of the history of Israel, but did not challenge the idea that Israel was a united (and powerful) state at the time of David and Solomon and that a 'First Temple' really existed. Hence the return from exile was understood as recreating an ethnic, political and religious reality that had existed in the past.

Recent criticism of the concept of the 'United Monarchy' has questioned the Biblical narrative from its very foundation, because it reduces the 'historical' Israel to one of several Palestinian kingdoms swept away by the Assyrian conquest. Any connection between Israel and Judah in the pre-exilic era (including the existence of a united Israel) is completely denied. At this point, a drastic rewriting of the history of Israel is needed.

The critical approach to Israelite history, however, has always produced *Prolegomena* (to use Wellhausen's expression) and brave theoretical manifestos (some of them very recent), but not yet a *narrated history* following the order of modern reconstructions instead of the traditional plot of the Biblical narrative. If the critical *de*construction of the Biblical text is accepted, why not also attempt a *re*construction, referring literary texts to the time in which they were written and not to the period they speak about? Some recent postmodernist critics have, however, denied the possibility of writing a history of ancient Israel and opened a gap between a narrated history of the traditional kind and a literary criticism that breaks any contact with a historical use of sources.

In the present work I have tried to write – at least in the form of a first draft – a new version of the history of Israel, starting from the results of textual and literary criticism as well as from data collected by archaeology and epigraphy. In doing this I have felt free to change the Biblical plot, while keeping a properly historical approach. This attempt, as obvious as it is, is nevertheless something new, and is attended by tremendous difficulties and very serious implications.

The result is a division of the history of Israel into two different phases. The first one is the 'normal' (i.e. not unique) and quite insignificant history of two kingdoms in Palestine, very similar to the other kingdoms destroyed by the Assyrian and then Babylonian conquests, with the consequent devastation, deportations and deculturation. This first phase is not particularly important, particularly interesting, nor consequential – just as the parallel histories of similar kingdoms (from Carchemish to Damascus, Tyre or Gaza) have importance only to the specialist. But the fact is that we cannot read the 'Bibles' of Carchemish, Damascus, Tyre or Gaza, and their traditions were lost forever under the advance of the empires.

In just one case a peculiar event occurred, prompted by the project of a king of Judah (Josiah) who planned to found a united kingdom of Judah-Israel in the decades between the collapse of Assyria and the rise of the Babylonian empire. Josiah's plan had a religious (Yahwistic monotheism, 'Mosaic' law) and historiographical element. The speedy return to Palestine of Judean exiles not fully assimilated to the imperial world, their attempt to create a temple-city (Jerusalem) on a Babylonian model and to gather around it a whole nation (Israel, in the broader sense) implied a huge and variegated rewriting of an 'ordinary' history with the aim of creating a suitable context for those archetypes that they intended to revitalize: united kingdom, monotheism and single temple, law, possession of the land, holy war, and so on. The whole history of Israel, therefore, had to be characterized by a very special calling.

While the real but normal history had no more than a local interest, the invented and exceptional one became the basis for the foundation of a nation (Israel) and of a religion (Judaism) that would have an influence on the subsequent history of the whole world.

Once again I have to express my gratitude to the Pontifical Biblical Institute of Rome for the kind hospitality of its library – one of the few places in the world where it is possible to realize a project like this – and for the efficiency and courtesy of all the staff. I am grateful to my friends Giovanni Garbini and Andrea Giardina for reading a first version of the book and discussing with me some of the problems; to my daughter Serena for the computerizing of the many maps; to my daughter Diletta and to Mrs Leonarda De Ninno for drawing some of the pictures. I am particularly grateful to my Italian publisher Giuseppe Laterza for his encouragement to write this book – a tremendous decision. I did it in a relatively short time (two years), conscious that a whole life would not be enough to achieve a more satisfactory work. I think this book will please neither more progressive scholars, who will not like the first part, as being too confidently historical, nor more traditional ones, who will dislike the second part, as too critically destructive. But when I conceived this division, I did not consider the reaction of any particular readers: I honestly thought that this was the only way to describe the existent contradiction between a real and commonplace history and an invented one that has become the basis and the location of a set of universal values.

Please note that all the dates are BCE if not differently specified. The chronological table (Table 1) is intended to help the reader with an initial diachronic orientation.

In the book reference is made to the redactional schools responsible for the historical books of the Old Testament, which biblical critics have tried, rather successfully, to place in their historical context. Occasionally allusions are made to the 'Elohist' and 'Yahwist' – once dated to the monarchic age and now dated to the exilic period. More frequent are references to 'Deuteronomic' works (named after the book of Deuteronomy), or the 'Deuteronomistic school' (or 'Deuteronomistic historiography'), which began in Judah towards the end of the seventh century and continued during the Babylonian exile in the sixth century. Finally, the 'Priestly' school (including the author of the Book of Chronicles) can be dated to the time of the Babylonian exile, in the sixth to fourth centuries. For a general reading of this book, no more information is needed, while anyone interested in the problems of Old Testament criticism will find useful references in the bibliography.

Transcription of personal names has proved very problematic, because a certain consistency is needed, but forms too different from those familiar to the reader should be avoided. The names of the main kings of Judah and Israel, the patriarchs, tribes, prophets and other well-known characters are cited in the form currently used in English. For other names, a simplified but correct transcription of the Hebrew form is used, without diacritics or vowel length markers. Aspirated forms of consonants, apart from p/f, are not indicated. The same is true for Biblical placenames: for those particularly well known the conventional form is used; for all the others a simplified transcription of the Hebrew name. Modern placenames (both Arabic and Hebrew) are written without diacritics.

In the index the correct transcription of personal and placenames is indicated. For placenames (both ancient and modern) of the Palestinian region, geographical co-ordinates according to the modern Israel grid (as in picture 1 and in the margins of other maps) are also indicated: this is not an unnecessary technicality, but facilitates quick and precise location of sites. For placenames in other areas, the historical region alone is indicated. The indexes include multiple cross-references between ancient and modern placenames and an annotated index of personal names, all intended to provide the reader with an effective means of reference.

ABBREVIATIONS

Collections of Ancient Near Eastern Texts

ABC	A.K. Grayson, *Assyrian and Babylonian Chronicles*, Locust Valley, NY: J.J. Augustin, 1975.
AEL	M. Lichtheim, *Ancient Egyptian Literaure*, I-III, Berkeley, CA: University of California Press, 1980.
ANEP	J.B. Pritchard, *The Ancient Near East in Pictures Relating to the Old Testament*, Princeton, NJ: Princeton University Press, 1954.
ANET	J.B. Pritchard (ed.), *Ancient Near Eastern Texts Relating to the Old Testament*, Princeton, NJ: Princeton University Press, 1955 (plus *Supplement*, 1969).
ARE	J.H. Breasted, *Ancient Records of Egypt*, I-V, Chicago, The University of Chicago Press, 1906.
AS	D.D. Luckenbill, *The Annals of Sennacherib*, Chicago: Univesity of Chicago Press, 1924.
BIA	R. Borger, *Beiträge zum Inschriftenwerk Assurbanipals*, Wiesbaden: Harrassowitz, 1996.
EA	*The Amarna Letters* (ed. and trans. W.L. Moran; Baltimore: The Johns Hopkins University Press, 1992).
Emar	D. Arnaud, *Recherches au pays d'Aštata. Emar*, Texte 3; Paris: Éditions Recherche sur les Civilisations, 1986.
HDT	G. Beckman, *Hittite Diplomatic Texts* (SBL Writings from the Ancient World, 7; Atlanta, GA: Scholars Press, 1996).
IAKA	R. Borger, *Die Inschriften Asarhaddons Königs von Assyrien*, Graz: E. Weidner, 1956.
ISK	A. Fuchs, *Die Inschriften Sargons II. aus Khorsabad*, Göttingen: Vandenhoeck & Ruprecht, 1993.
ITP	H. Tadmor, *The Inscriptions of Tiglath-pileser III King of Assyria*, Jerusalem: Israel Academy at Sciences and Humanities, 1994.
LA	M. Liverani, *Le lettere di el-Amarna*, I-II, Brescia: Paideia, 1998–1999.
LPAE	E. Bresciani, *Letteratura e poesia dell'antico Egitto*, Torino: G. Einaudi, 1990².
PRU	*Le palais royal d'Ugarit*, II-VI, Paris: Imprimerie Nationale, 1957–1970.
RIMA	*The Royal Inscriptions of Mesopotamia. Assyrian Periods*, I-III, Toronto: University of Toronto Press, 1987-1996.
RIMB	*The Royal Inscriptions of Mesopotamia. Babylonian Periods*, II, Toronto: University of Toronto Press, 1995.

RTU	N. Wyatt, *Religious Texts from Ugarit*, London: Sheffield Academic Press, 2002².
SAA	S. Parpola (ed.), *State Archives of Assyria*, I-XV, Helsinki: Helsinki University Press, 1987–2001.
SSI	J.C.L. Gibson, *Textbook of Syrian Semitic Inscriptions*. 1. *Hebrew and Moabite Inscriptions*; 2. *Aramaic Inscriptions*; 3. *Phoenician Inscriptions*, Oxford, Clarendon Press, 1971; 1975; 1982.
Ug.	*Ugaritica*, I-VI, Paris, Imprimerie Nationale, 1939-1969.

Classical Sources

Herod.	Herodotus, *Histories*
Ant.	Flavius Josephus, *Antiquitates Iudaicae*
C. Ap.	Flavius Josephus, *Contra Apionem*

Journals and Collections

BA	*Biblical Archaeologist*
BAR	*Biblical Archaelogy Review*
BASOR	*Bulletin of the American Schools of Oriental Research*
Bibl	*Biblica*
BZ	*Biblische Zeitschrift*
CBQ	*Catholic Biblical Quarterly*
EI	*Eretz-Israel*
HThR	*Harvard Theological Review*
IEJ	*Israel Exploration Journal*
JAOS	*Journal of the American Oriental Society*
JBL	*Journal of Biblical Literature*
JCS	*Journal of Cuneiform Studies*
JESHO	*Journal of the Economic and Social History of the Orient*
JSOT	*Journal for the Study of the Old Testament*
KS	A. Alt, *Kleine Schriften zur Geschichte des Volkes Israel*, I-III, München: Beck, 1959.
Lev	*Levant*
OA	*Oriens Antiquus*
Or	*Orientalia*
PEQ	*Palestine Exploration Quarterly*
RB	*Revue Biblique*
Sem	*Semitica*
SJOT	*Scandinavian Journal of the Old Testament*
Trans	*Transeuphratène*
UF	*Ugarit-Forschungen*
VT	*Vetus Testamentum*
ZABR	*Zeitschrift für altorientalische und biblische Rechtsgeschichte*
ZAW	*Zeitschrift für die alttestamentliche Wissenschaft*
ZDPV	*Zeitschrift des Deutschen Palästina-Vereins*

IMPRINTING

Chapter 1

PALESTINE IN THE LATE BRONZE AGE (FOURTEENTH–THIRTEENTH CENTURIES)

1. *Landscape and Resources*

Palestine is a humble and fascinating land. It is humble in its natural resources and its marginality within the region; it is fascinating because of the historical stratification of its human landscape and the symbolic stratification of its memories.

In the south-eastern extremity of the Mediterranean Sea, the Atlantic rainfall crashes against the mountains, which are fairly high only in the northern part (about 1,000m in Upper Galilee, about 700m in the central area) and receive adequate rainfall. Palestine is almost entirely in the semi-arid zone (rainfall between 400 and 250 mm per year) and its southern parts, the Negev and Sinai desert, and its inland parts, the Transjordanian plateau and Syrian-Arabian desert, are in the highly arid zone (around 100 mm or less). There is only one river worth mentioning, the Jordan, which is fed from the Lebanon and Anti-Lebanon ranges, with its perennial tributaries, the Yarmuk and the Jabbok, or Wadi Zarqa) filled from the eastern plateaux and ending in the closed and salty basin of the Dead Sea. Cultivation is therefore enabled not by irrigation (apart from little 'oases' near springs), but by rainfall: and it depends on the uncertain rains, regulated by inscrutable gods – sometimes generous and beneficent, sometimes punitive. The contrast with neighbouring Egypt, where water is a stable 'matter of fact', not a matter for anxiety, was abundantly clear:

> For the land that you are about to enter to occupy is not like the land of Egypt, from which you have come, where you sow your seed and irrigate by foot like a vegetable garden. But the land that you are crossing over to occupy is a land of hills and valleys, watered by rain from the sky, a land that the LORD your God looks after. The eyes of the LORD your God are always on it, from the beginning of the year to the end of the year (Deut. 11.10-12).

The contrast was noticed also by the Egyptians, as recorded in Amenhotep's *Great Hymn to Aten*:

> All distant foreign countries, thou makest their life (also),
> For thou hast set a Nile in heaven,
> That it may descend for them and make waves upon the mountains,
> Like the great green sea,
> To water their fields in their towns.
> How effective they are, thy plans, O Lord of eternity!
> The Nile in heaven, it is for the foreign peoples
> And for the beasts of every desert that go upon (their) feet;
> (While the true) Nile comes from the underworld for Egypt (*ANET*, 371).

The country is small: in Cisjordan, the area inhabited 'from Dan to Beersheba' is 200 km long (N–S) and 80 km wide (E–W); another 40 km area in Transjordan can be added. Altogether there are about 20,000 km^2 – less than an Italian region like Piedmont or Sicily. To think that such a density of memories and events of millennial and universal relevance is concentrated in such a small land!

Not all the territory can be used for agriculture. The only alluvial plains are in the central valley of the Jordan and in the plain of Jezreel; the costal strip is sandy and salty, but the low hills of the Shephelah are much more suitable. The rest is all hills and mountains, once covered with woods, then stripped by the action of men and goats, destined to a process of erosion contained only by the exhausting work of terracing. Such a setting is suitable for a transhumant sheep-rearing and to small-scale agriculture, restricted to valley 'niches' (or to the bottom of *wadis* in semi-arid zones), occupied only by family farms and minute villages.

With the aid of constant human labour, this Mediterranean landscape becomes capable of sustaining a diverse, even if small, population and a region where agricultural and pastoral resources (especially when compared with the desert) are sufficient to fulfil the necessities of human life in the ancient world. The description of a land 'flowing with milk and honey (Num. 13.27) is certainly exaggerated, but conveys the idea of a land that can sustain human habitation:

> a good land, a land with flowing streams, with springs and underground waters welling up in valleys and hills, a land of wheat and barley, of vines and fig trees and pomegranates, a land of olive trees and honey, a land where you may eat bread without scarcity, where you will lack nothing, a land whose stones are iron and from whose hills you may mine copper (Deut. 8.7-9).

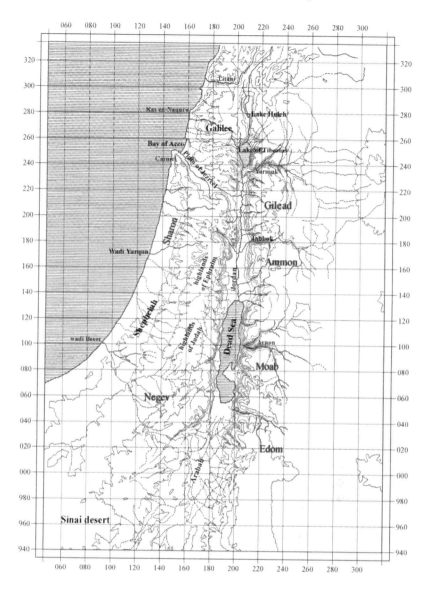

Figure 1. *Relief map of Palestine, with reference grid*

Actually, metals are very scarce (the copper of the 'Araba is not found in Palestine), there are no gemstones (the turquoise of Sinai lies even further away), and there is no valuable timber (as in Lebanon). The coast is mostly covered by dunes, with a few modest lagoons, and it does not afford secure harbours except in the extreme north, between the Carmel promontory and Ras en-Naqura on the Lebanese border. Caravans travelling along the

'Way of the Sea' from the Egyptian Delta to Syria were anxious as they traversed a poor and menacing land. Those travelling on the 'King's Highway' from Arabia to Damascus and the Middle Euphrates, passed along the edge of Palestine, almost preferring the clear spaces of the desert to the misery of the settled land.

Compared with other areas of the Near East, such as Egypt and Mesopotamia, Syria and Anatolia, which already in ancient times provided the seat of renowned civilizations, of extensive states centred on monumental cities, Palestine seems singularly unattractive. If the number of inhabitants is a valid indicator of the opportunities afforded to civilized communities for subsistence and development, the data are self-evident. In the Late Bronze Age, when Egypt and Mesopotamia hosted some millions of inhabitants, Palestine did not reach 250,000. Even at the summit of its development, during Iron Age II, its inhabitants numbered no more than 400,000.

If we focus on the internal configuration of Palestine, the narrowness of the landscape is striking: it is all fragmented into mountains and hills, and the view never meets an open horizon. Seen within a regional dimension, then, the marginality of the land appears with stark clarity: it lies to the extreme south of the 'Fertile Crescent', the semicircle of cultivated lands between the Syro-Arabian desert, the Iranian and Anatolian mountains and the Mediterranean sea. The role that geography dictates for this land, if any, is to serve as a connection (more for transit than for settlement) between Egypt and Western Asia: but this location seems to have brought the inhabitants of Palestine more misfortune than benefit.

Yet this country, so modest in natural resources and in population, has played a key role in the history of a large part of the world. The contradiction is due to the extraordinary ability of its inhabitants to bind together landscape and memory, conferring on their land a set of symbolic values that, through alternating episodes of dispersion and focalization, departure and return, spread widely beyond its borders.

It is not only the landscape that is thoroughly man-made, as is normal in all countries with a long cultural history. Not only its constitutive elements, even the smallest ones – a centuries-old oak, a well, a cave, some ancient ruins, an ancestral tomb – become sites of memory and tokens of legitimation. But the entire country, marked off from the surrounding diversity, is put at the centre of a complete mental history: as the object of a divine promise that makes it the selective heritage of certain groups, excluding others; and as the place of the physical presence of God in the world and therefore the setting of events whose value is universal and eternal. The terms 'Promised Land' and 'Holy Land' indicate how a specific region could become a symbol and a value, without even naming it, since everyone knows immediately which land it is.

2. Geopolitical Fragmentation

Topographical and ecologic characteristics, together with the technological capacity of the ancient world, determined to a great extent the geopolitical asset of Palestine over several millennia. The typical formation of ancient states is always conditioned by the relation between spatial factors, demographic density and productive potential. A state lives on what is produced locally: long distance terrestrial trade may provide raw materials (especially metals) and luxury products that are economically transportable, but it cannot bring cereals. Since the foundation of the first cities (i.e. settlements whose population is diversified in function and stratified in income, with a 'public' area – a temple, a palace, or both), territorial units are formed, simultaneously economic and political, comprising the city itself and an agricultural hinterland extending about 10 km in radius, together with a periphery of highlands or steppes suitable for transhumance.

We could define these configurations as city-states, if the term were not burdened with historiographical and ideological connotations. In fact this definition immediately reminds us of the Greek *polis* and its values of democracy, freedom and market economy – an image actually derived more from the individual case of Athens rather than from a general evaluation. It is therefore wiser to use a more neutral and merely descriptive term such as 'cantonal state', or the definition used at the time: 'little kingdom', as opposed to the 'great kingdom' of the imperial ruler. The centre is the city, whose dimension is related to the resources of the territory it is able to draw upon: in Palestine, which was economically poor, Bronze Age cities (about 2800-1200) have hardly more than 3,000-4,000 inhabitants and the situation does not change much in Iron Age II (about 900–600), following the crisis of Iron Age I that had reduced them to their minimum size. In the city stands the residence of the 'king' (the palace, a building of about 1,000 m^2), with a court for direct dependants: craftsmen, guards, servants/slaves (see below, §1.6).

The rural population is concentrated in villages, ranging from a few houses to about 50. Transhumant groups are linked with villages, and are quite limited in size. Further north, in northern Syria, where the state formations are bigger and richer, the texts allow to reconstruct a cantonal state (Ugarit) of about 25,000 people, 8,000 of whom resided in the city and the rest in villages. In Palestine, the average cantonal state would have been about half this size. Also in Northern Syria (Alalakh) we know that the population was broadly divided into 20 percent of palace dependants, 20 percent shepherds and 60 percent farmers: these figures (which are merely indicative, of course) may also be valid for Palestine.

Table 1. *Correlation of historical and biblical periodization*

Absolute Chronology	Archaeological Periods	Biblical Periods	Historical Periods
c. 3500–2800	Late Chalcolithic		
c. 2800–2000	Early Bronze Age		First urbanization
c. 2000–1550	Middle Bronze Age	Patriarchal Age	Independent city-states
c. 1550–1180	Late Bronze Age	Exodus and Conquest	Egyptian domination
c. 1180–900	Iron Age I	Judges United Monarchy	Period of national formation
c. 900–600	Iron Age II	Divided kingdoms	Divided kingdoms Assyrian domination
c. 600–330	Iron Age III	Exilic period Postexilic period	Neo-Babylonian period Persian period

This structure, the basic cell of political systems, remains unchanged for a long period. In other areas – Egypt, Mesopotamia – the presence of large rivers suitable for transport of bulky goods, and the necessity of coordinating irrigation systems that were initially local but later on a wide scale, necessitated the process of political unification, creating states that may be defined as 'regional'. These states nevertheless remained as agglomerations of 'cantonal' cells, each functioning as a economic unit, in the form of provinces, or 'nomes' as they are called in Egypt. Yet, political unification in areas where land productivity was higher and the population much denser gave rise to a corresponding sudden change in scale. While the average Late Bronze Palestinian kingdoms had about 15,000 inhabitants (and the larger Iron II kingdoms as a whole an average of 50,000), Egypt could count, at a moderate estimate, on 3 or 4 million subjects of the Pharaoh, while Babylon (even in decline) on a couple of million. This process of unification and corresponding change of scale (up to a 200-fold increase) was precluded in Palestine, mainly because of its geography and landscape.

3. *Discontinuity of Settlements*

The third point to take into consideration is Palestine's marginality, not in a strictly geographical sense, but rather from the socioeconomic and political point of view. Agricultural lands were in any case less rich than the alluvial plains of the Nile and Euphrates: light soils, with rain-fed agriculture and yields of 1:3 or 1:5 (the average yield in Egypt and Upper Mesopotamia was 1:10 and in Lower Mesopotamia 1:15 or more). Moreover, the cultivable land, and the great part of the population, were concentrated almost entirely in a few zones: the coast and the hills immediately behind it, the plain of Jezreel and the central and upper Jordan valley. This demographic concentration reached its peak during the Late Bronze Age. The rest of the land was mainly suitable for transhumant sheep-rearing and was thus occupied by quite small seasonal camps. Such was the case in the highlands (still covered with woods and Mediterranean scrub) of Judah, Samaria and Galilee, and of the steppe areas towards the east (Transjordan) and south (Negev) due to the decrease in rainfall. The Late Bronze Age political landscape reflects this disposition of settlements: thus the city-centred political units based on agriculture were concentrated along the coast, in the plain of Jezreel and in the Jordan valley, while they were extremely scarce in the highland zones and virtually absent to the east of the Jordan and in the south of Judah.

A typological diversity was established between the plain region, with close and self-intertwined city-states and the mountain region, where the cities were more scattered, free to expand their zone of influence and characterized by a stronger pastoral element (becoming exclusive in the steppe regions). A rough political map of fourteenth-century Palestine, as can be deduced from the Egyptian el-Amarna archive, shows a concentration of small states in the plains and then two fairly isolated towns, Jerusalem and Shechem, centres of the two most extensive cantonal states, one in the highlands of Judah and the other in the Ephraimite hill-country.

This settlement scheme, which can be reconstructed from archaeological and textual data, holds for the Late Bronze Age (fourteenth–thirteenth centuries), but did not always exist: it is the result of transformations in the demographical history of the country, perhaps caused ultimately by climatic factors. If we compare the settlement distribution of the Late Bronze Age with that of previous phases (Middle Bronze and, even more, Early Bronze) we notice a progressive shrinking of the frontier of settlements and a concentration of the population in the areas more suitable for agriculture. Semi-arid zones and highlands were gradually abandoned, so that in the Late Bronze Age there were no longer permanent settlements south of Hebron in Cisjordan, or of Madaba in Transjordan.

During the Late Bronze Age, the arid steppes and wooded mountains were left to seasonal usage by shepherds, who practised their seasonal transhumance of the 'vertical' type on the central plateaux, moving between summer pastures in the highlands and winter pastures on the plains; and of the 'horizontal' type in the semi-arid steppes, moving between winter pastures in the steppe and summer pastures in cultivated valleys. The well-known interaction between sheep-rearing and agriculture is very close and the rhythms of transhumance tend to respect the needs of agricultural use of the land. Farmers and shepherds live in the same villages, representing integrated, even if not fully homogeneous productive units. But such a general neglect of the less favoured zones inevitably created a certain marginalization (from the urban point of view) or autonomy (from the pastoral point of view) of human groups and spaces that, in other periods of history, were much more closely integrated.

4. *Egyptian Domination*

For about three centuries (c. 1460–c. 1170) Palestine was under the direct control of Egypt, though some degree of political (and cultural) influence existed before and afterwards. This long period of domination by a country whose ideological prestige was matched to a huge demographic, economic and military preponderance, naturally had a major impact on the political life of the region. This political imprinting of an imperial nature was probably as profound and significant as the more obvious influence of the geographical setting we considered earlier.

Egyptian control was mostly indirect, and the local 'little kings' preserved their autonomy (but not their independence) as 'servants' and vassals of the Pharaoh. The picture we get from the 'Amarna letters (1370–1350) shows that only three Syro-Palestinian towns were seats of Egyptian governors: Gaza, on the southern coast, Kumidi in the Lebanese Beq'a valley, and Sumura on the northern coast, beside the present Syro-Lebanese border. There were also Egyptian garrisons in other places: Jaffa (near modern Tel Aviv), Beth-Shean (between the plain of Jezreel and the Jordan valley) and Ullaza (where the route from the Orontes valley reaches the coast). Even if we count the small standing garrisons and the army that, as we shall see, made an annual 'tour' for the collection of tribute, we can calculate that Egypt in the Amarna Age employed no more than 700 people to run and control its Syro-Palestinian 'empire'.

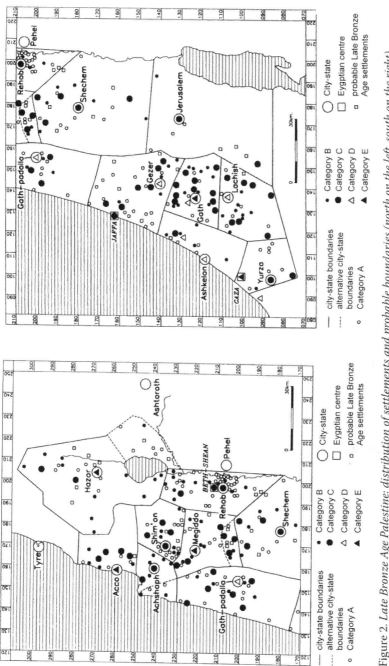

Figure 2. *Late Bronze Age Palestine: distribution of settlements and probable boundaries (north on the left, south on the right)*

It had not always been like that. The large campaigns of the fifteenth century had employed up to 10,000 soldiers, but had become unnecessary after the peace treaty and intermarriage between Egypt and Mitanni in about 1420. For the current administration, the initial plan established by Thutmose III – the Pharaoh who had finally conquered Palestine and most of Syria around 1470-1460 – tried to establish an extensive direct Egyptian control with the ports and the best agricultural land directly managed by the Egyptians. But such a project was difficult to realize and too expensive: similar results could be obtained by indirect administration, and thus we find the situation of the Amarna Age, just described. Later, during the thirteenth century, the Egyptian presence became more pervasive, as evidenced especially in the archaeological data. We know of several Egyptian 'residencies' in the period from Seti I to Ramses III: in Tel Afeq stratum IV (including the discovery of cuneiform texts), in Beth-Shean stratum VII, and in several other sites in the extreme south: Tell el-Far'a (south), Tel Sera' (stratum X), Tel Mor strata 8-7, Deir el-Balah strata 7-4, Tell Jemme (ancient Yursa) and Tell el-'Ajjul stratum V. These fortresses, significantly, were established to guard trade routes: the so-called 'Horus Road' from the Delta to Gaza, fortified by Seti I, and the transverse caravan routes to the Gulf of Aqaba and the Timna copper mines, directly exploited by Egypt during the entire Ramesside period. We will see later (§3.9) that these final elements of Egyptian presence left traces even after the collapse of the empire.

5. *Egyptian Ideology*

According to Egyptian religious ideology, the Pharaoh was an incarnated god and all the verbal and ceremonial imagery by which local kings addressed him shows that this ideology was known and accepted. Local kings called him 'Sun of all lands' and 'god' (or rather 'gods', since they use the plural form, as in Hebrew *'ĕlōhîm*), prostrated before him 'seven times and seven times', even specifying 'seven times on the back and seven times on the belly' (which was much harder...). They declared themselves 'ground on which he walked' and the 'stool under his feet', or 'under his sandals', in perfect coherence with the pharaonic iconography of the time: in the palace at el-'Amarna, the floor of the corridor to the throne room was decorated with standardized images of vanquished enemies, so that the Pharaoh could literally walk on them; the footstool of the throne and the sandals of Tutankhamun were also decorated with images of vanquished enemies, upon which the Pharaoh trampled while walking or seated on his throne.

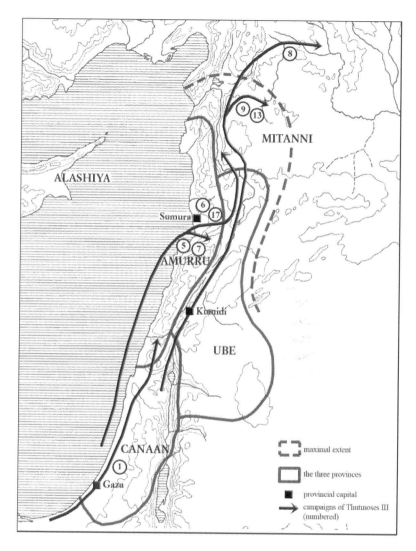

Figure 3. *Egyptian domination in the Levant: the campaigns of Thutmoses III and the 'provinces' of the Amarna Age*

The Pharaoh required a pledge of faithfulness which was short and absolute: 'We will never (again) rebel against His Majesty' (*ANET*, 238), in payment for that sort of original sin that consisted in being a foreigner, and therefore an inferior enemy – not 'wretched', as is sometimes translated, but rather one destined to defeat and total subjugation. The pledge was then made concrete by an annual tribute, by entertaining Egyptian messengers and caravans in transit, by providing goods on request and also (a real honour!) by providing princesses for the royal harem, together with their rich dowries. Another duty was what was called in the 'Amarna texts 'protecting' the town committed to them by the Pharaoh – protecting it against external enemies, but especially keeping it in good order, ready to answer to Egyptian requests. Local kings were very worried about performing their task of 'protecting' (*naṣāru*) the town, and 'listening' or 'observing' (again *naṣāru*) Pharaoh's word:

> I have heard the orders of the king, my lord and my Sun, and I am indeed protecting Megiddo, the city of the king my lord, day and night. By day I protect (it) from the fields with chariots, and by night on I protect the walls of the king my lord. But the hostility of the enemies (*ḫabiru*) in the land is severe. May the king, my lord, take cognizance of his land (*LA* 88 = *EA* 243.8-22, from Megiddo).

> Whatever proceeds from the mouth of the king, my lord, I indeed observe it day and night (*LA* 12 = *EA* 326.20-24, from Ashkelon).

Figure 4. *Egyptian domination: forms of homage*

In exchange for all this, Pharaoh gave 'life' (Egypt, *'nḫ*, 'Amarna Akkadian *balāṭu*), which he retained exclusively and gracefully conceded. 'Life' in political terms meant the right of reigning as a vassal. But according to Egyptian ideology, it was something more concrete and precise, it was the 'breath of life' coming from Pharaoh's mouth (and with his breath, his words) to the benefit of those who were allowed into his presence, or to whom his messages were addressed. Perhaps the king of Tyre exaggerates when he wishes to express his joy for having received a manifestation, though indirect (through a messenger), of Pharaoh's 'breath of life':

> My lord is the Sun who comes forth over all lands day by day, according to the way (of being) of the Sun, his gracious father, who gives life by his sweet breath that returns as a north wind; who established the entire land in peace, by the power of his arm; who gives forth his cry in the sky like Baal, and all the land is frightened at his cry. The servant herewith writes to his lord that he heard the gracious messenger of the king who came to his servant, and the sweet breath that came forth from the mouth of the king, my lord, to his servant – his breath came back! Before the arrival of the messenger of the king, my lord, breath had not come back; my nose was blocked. Now that the breath of the king has come forth to me, I have great joy and I am very happy day by day (*LA* 117 = *EA* 147).

For Egyptian subjects, 'life' was also admission to a redistributive system through which the Pharaoh gave the food necessary for life and, most of all, a possibility of survival after death. The latter at first was a prerogative exclusive to the Pharaoh, but then he conceded it also to his subjects. Foreign subjects were of course excluded from the last two benefits, though they made some clumsy attempts to get some 'life' in terms of food, and not merely words:

> For two years I have been short of my grain; we have no grain to eat. What can I say to my peasantry?... May the king, my lord, heed the words of his loyal servant, and may he send grain in ships in order to keep his servant and his city alive (*LA* 154 = *EA* 85, from Byblos).

Pharaoh was in fact a distant god, and Palestinian kings tended to consider him rather inert and silent, and thus hard to understand and not particularly reliable. Palestinian kings were used to a system of political relations based on reciprocity, which had no equivalent in Egyptian ideology. They were used to being faithful servants of their lord, but expected to receive from him protection (i.e. to see their throne defended from external attacks and internal uprisings). They were used to offering tribute, but also expected to be helped in case of need. They were used to answering the messages of their lord, but they also expected an answer to their own messages. But none of those things happened: the Pharaoh even showed irritation at the insistence of their approaches, and in any event did not give an answer. Most of all, he appeared absolutely indifferent to their personal fate.

This 'being silent' or 'keeping still/inert' is expressed in the 'Amarna letters by a verb (*qâlu*) which corresponds in its semantic field to Hebrew *dāmam*. It is used in several passages, all expressing perplexity and dismay for a passive attitude, a lack of reaction that risked compromising the entire system:

> Behold, Turbazu was slain in the city gate of Sile, and the king kept silent/inert. Behold, Zimrida (king) of Lachish was smitten by servants who became *ḫabiru*! and Yaptikh-Hadda was slain in the city gate of Sile, and the king kept silent/inert! (*LA* 41 = *EA* 288, from Jerusalem).

> May the king, my lord, know that Gubla, the loyal maidservant of the king, is safe and sound. The hostility, however, of the enemy forces (*ḫabiru*) against me is extremely severe. So may the king, my lord, not keep silent/inert towards Sumur, lest everyone be joined to the enemy (*ḫabiru*) forces (*LA* 132 = *EA* 68, from Byblos).

> It is not as it was once, for the lands of the king: every year Egyptian troops went out to watch the lands, while now the land of the king and (even) Sumur, your garrison, has passed to the side of the enemy ('it became *ḫabiru*'), yet you keep silent/inert! Send Egyptian troops in large quantities, to send away the enemy of the king from his land, and then all the lands will pass to the king. You are a great king, you cannot keep silent/inert about this! (*LA* 151 = *EA* 76, from Byblos).

In fact, Pharaoh's only interest was in controlling the whole system, since he knew that the possible usurper of a local throne would be faithful to him just like the dethroned king, who was not worth defending. Action was only taken when Egyptian control of the land was really threatened.

Every year a small Egyptian regiment made a tour of Palestinian kingdoms to collect tributes and other requested goods. The regiment (a few hundred soldiers) was preceded by a messenger who announced the imminent arrival and called for preparation of everything for welcoming the soldiers and making ready what was to be handed over. The Pharaonic message also exhorted the petty king to 'protect' the place that had been entrusted to him (meaning: to preserve order and efficiency). These messages provoked replies that are quite indicative of the feelings of local kings, who proclaim the impossibility of protecting their towns and solicit the protection of their lord; or they limited their protection just up to the arrival of Egyptian soldiers, which they considered as a sort of solution to their problems. Finally, they wish the troops to use their authority to deter the enemies of the petty kings, all depicted as enemies of the Pharaoh himself.

But it was all useless: the expectations of local kings, to get from the 'distant god' any help against the threats of the enemies, a solution to their problems, deliverance from the dangers, were left unanswered and nothing happened. Their loyalty was not enough to win protection – and this fact caused the petty kings to have painful doubts about the correctness of their actions, the presence of malicious detractors, and the possibility of shortcomings they were unaware of.

6. *The Palace and its Central Role*

Palestinian Late Bronze towns usually maintained the town plan and city walls constructed during the Middle Bronze, the age of maximum development of the region. The capital, surrounded by walls, was centred on the royal palace, where the king lived with his family, but it was also the seat of administration, of the archives, of the stores and of the shops of specialized craftsmen. The palace of Megiddo has been excavated (VII B), which is not very big: 1,650 m²; while the palace of Ugarit – which was thought to be the biggest and the richest in all Syria (*LA* 144 = *EA* 89), but may be taken as a model – was 5,000 m². The palace, in short, was not only the house of the king but also the management centre of the whole kingdom, which was also in a sense the property of the king.

More concretely, the dependence of the kingdom upon the king assumes two distinct forms, and the population is divided into two major categories. We have the 'king's men', who do not usually own a personal means of production, but work for the king and from him receive in return the necessities for their sustenance. Then there is the 'free' population (the 'sons/children' of the country), who have their own means of production and give the king a portion from their income in the form of taxes. The 'king's men' are prevalent in the capital and live around the palace, while the free population prevails in the villages (including the 'residual village' in the capital, beyond the palace complex).

These two categories differ in their judicial, political and functional aspects, but they are not economically homogeneous. The free population belongs typically to a middle class, families who own a little land and some cattle, enough to live and reproduce; but these may find themselves, when the crops fail, obliged to borrow, unable to repay loans with interest and falling into debt-slavery. On the contrary, among the 'king's men' there are strong socioeconomic disparities, from the military aristocracy of charioteers (*maryannu*), clergy, scribes and officers, to groups of craftsmen, traders, guards, down to slaves in the palace or in royal farms, working on land they do not own. All of these are legally servants of the king, but the form and the amount of their reward varies and comprises a range of different situations. Charioteers, scribes and traders can accumulate great wealth, especially in the form of lands given them by the king. Such lands are not formally their property, but are given in use and as such are conditional upon a service. But normally this service is inherited, and with it are the lands: and some people may be in a position to pay for exemption from the service. At this point, there is no difference (apart from the memory of the origin and of the process of acquisition) between a farm given in concession and a family property.

Around the royal palace flourished a 'high' class of people who administered the economic power, were related to the king and were much involved in military activity (especially in view of the endemic local conflicts that were encouraged by Pharaonic indifference). These cultivated heroic ideals of courage and boldness (as is clear from the poems recited at the Ugaritic court) and enjoyed luxury products (weapons and chariots, jewels and clothes), whether manufactured locally or imported from distant lands through a tight network of commercial exchanges and ceremonial gifts between courts.

The transmission of royal power followed the normal rules for inheritance. It was no longer a time when succession was fixed from birth and did not generate any conflict; now (in the mid-second millennium) the norms were different: 'there is (no difference between) firstborn and younger son' and the succession goes to the one who has 'honoured the parents' – that is to say, who has deserved it. The kingdom is an indivisible unit and can pass to only one of the sons of the reigning king, who will chose his successor at the due time, but without preventing that after his own death the other sons could ask for a different solution. The texts from this period are full of disputes between brothers, usurpations (sometimes depicted as heroic deeds), and even instances of fratricide and parricide.

Finally, something has to be said about the role of the temple. From archaeology we know several architectural types of thirteenth-century temples: the three-axial-room type, like that in Hazor (H XIII) with its rich stone decorations (the stelae called *maṣṣēbôt* in the Bible), the 'tower' type (*migdāl*), like those in Megiddo and Shechem, and others. But in the political setup just described, the temple had a marginal role, unlike what happened in Egypt and Babylon, or even in Anatolia. The priests are classified as 'king's men'; temples are buildings of modest dimensions, dedicated to the cult in a strict sense as houses of the god (ceremonies with the participation of the people took place outside), not involved in economic or commercial activities, but sometimes used for storing treasure. Certainly the rituals that were celebrated mainly by the king (together with the queen, in the case of fertility rites) contributed to increasing his prestige in the eyes of his people, as proof of a correct relationship with the world of the gods, as well as giving him a certain connotation of sacredness. But the political world seems to be the most 'secular' ever seen in the whole Near East up to that period.

7. Economic Prosperity and Commercial Exchange

Within the country's limited resources, palace cities of the fourteenth-thirteenth century are economically flourishing and culturally productive. In the palaces there are scribal schools of the Babylonian type, required for the training of the scribes-administrators who use cuneiform writing and the Babylonian language, not only for external correspondence but also for internal administration and judicial texts. These schools are less important than those in Syria, and their level was clearly different between central and more marginal centres, to judge also from the quality of the Babylonian language used in the 'Amarna letters, which are often crammed with 'Canaanite' glosses and anacolutha (syntactical irregularities). Scribal schools were also the locus of transmission of literary texts, and an effective means for the diffusion of a court wisdom 'style', which left a few traces in Palestine, unlike Ugarit where we have a rich heritage.

Luxury craftsmanship in jewellery and precious metals is documented from archaeology and textual data. Egypt exerted a strong stylistic and iconographic influence but itself often imported luxury goods from the vassal kingdoms of Palestine. Woollen clothes, dyed with purple or with coloured embroideries and applications, strongly contrasted with Egyptian clothes of white linen. Bronze weapons, bows, chariots and horses were produced in Palestine (as well as in Syria and Upper Mesopotamia) and were valued in Egypt. In particular, there was a great demand for glass, which Egyptians would buy in the coastal towns of Palestine (*LA 2 = EA* 314 from Yursa, 11 [= 323] from Ashkelon, 23 [= 331] from Lachish area, 100 [= 235, 327] from Akko, 122 [= 148] from Tyre), and that circulated as a partly-finished product in the form of small blocks that could be turned into coloured juglets and other objects.

Within the so-called 'regional system' trade was intense, between Egypt and Anatolia, the Mediterranean Sea and Babylon, within areas having urban centers and state polities, where writing was in use, and where trade and political-diplomatic regulations could be drafted, so that the inevitable financial and legal disputes could be solved according to agreed principles. Outside the system, on the Mediterranean routes (where Canaanite shipping was apparently barred between the Egyptian Delta and Cyprus or Crete) and on the caravan routes of the desert (which could not be fully exploited for the lack of technical means) such links were scarce (especially if compared with the different scenery of the end of the Iron Age).

Figure 5. *Commercial exchanges: above, Syrian merchants in Egypt;*
below Asiatic tribute to the Pharaoh

Palestine was at the centre of these exchanges, crossed by caravans
partly of local origin and partly travelling between Egypt and the 'great
kingdoms' of Asia – Mitanni, Babylon and Assyria. Relations took place
between one court and another, sometimes according to the rules of diplomatic and ceremonial 'gifts', but mostly according to normal trading conventions. Most trade was in metals and clothing, which are subject to
deterioration and recycling, so are seldom archaeologically attested. But
from the recovery of wrecked ships, from iconographic data and from preserved texts, we know there existed an extensive trade in copper (from
Cyprus) and tin (probably from Iran) in which Palestinian palaces were
also involved. Archaeological documentation is more extensive on the

importation of pottery. The abundantly produced Cypriot and Mycenaean pottery was partly imported for domestic use, as luxury tableware and as containers for aromatic oils, resins and even opium. On the other hand, the presence of large Canaanite jars in Egypt provides evidence of plentiful exports of olive oil.

If we bear in mind that luxury goods were acquired, hoarded and exchanged mainly in palaces, while at the same time agricultural land was being reduced and probably declining in population and in production, we can deduce that the advanced Canaanite culture of the fourteenth and thirteenth centuries was the result of growing socioeconomic pressure exercised from ruling elites on the agrarian and pastoral population. In other words, the 'centrality' of the palace, though quite normal in this kind of socio-economic formation, did not maintain a balanced relationship with its territorial base, but rather introduced a deep instability that could not last for long.

8. *Villages and Collective Bodies*

While the political and cultural centrality of the palace is beyond doubt, the majority of the population (about 80 percent, as stated earlier) lived in villages, relying on its own means of production: family-owned lands and flocks of sheep and goats. We have quite scanty and limited archaeological and textual data on Palestinian villages of the Late Bronze Age; but for the same period, the Syrian archives of Alalakh and Ugarit can be used (with some caution) as a useful basis of comparison.

The village was a settlement unit of modest dimension, but also a kinship unit and a decision-making body. As for dimensions, we may consider the Alalakh lists, where 'villages' (from an administrative point of view) were groups of houses – from a minimum of 2-3 to a maximum of 80, with an average of 25 houses (and 100 people). For Palestine, those numbers should be realistically reduced by a third. The population is divided between a majority of 'houses' of 'free' farmers (*ḫupšu*) and shepherds (Khaneans), and a minority of 'king's servants' (who are not defined as 'son of X', but as 'belonging to X'), with the presence of *maryannu* only in larger villages.

But let us try to describe means and instruments of local interaction. As for family relations, it is obvious that the mechanism of marriages and hereditary subdivision created a situation where everybody in a village – consisting, for example, of some 25 nuclear families – had family ties with all the others. This explains the tendency to consider the settlement unit (the village) as equivalent to a kinship unit (the 'clan', see §3.4) and to call the village by the name of an eponym (or, *vice versa*, to deduce the name of a presumed eponym from the name of a village).

As for the bodies of self-government, the village had collegial (if not fully representative) bodies to deal with two kinds of events. In the first place, there were quarrels or arguments within the village, and the necessity of managing all the social and judicial litigation: marriages and divorces, legacies and adoptions, sales of land and slaves, loans and guarantees, and so on. In the second place, the village was considered as an administrative unit by the palace, and as such had to answer to demands coming from the palace: quotas of goods to give as taxes, people to send in fulfillment of corvée service, additional soldiers whenever needed, searches for fugitives or fleeing slaves, killing and robbing traders who crossed the territory of the village.

In contrast with the 'bureaucratic' management of the palace, the village had a two-tiered management structure. The more select body was a council of 'elders' (*šibūti*) or 'fathers' (*abbū*), the most authoritative and firmly-established heads of families. Late Bronze texts attest some cases of councils of five elders, which was perhaps the minimum number for the legal validity of the decisions, more than the total number of the members. A judicial text from Ugarit (*Ug.*, V, 141-143) exceptionally lists the name of the 'elders' of the village of Rabka, who were warrants for a transaction: 'Babiyanu son of Yadudanu; Abdu and his son; Addunu his son-in-law; and the 'chief-of-the-thousand': this is not an example of democracy, but an affirmation by the strongest clans who controlled the village. Then, besides this select body, there is the popular assembly, which Akkadian texts call 'the meeting' or simply 'the city', in which all free male adults probably took part, and which had to take extraordinary decisions. Finally, exclusively for dealings with the palace, there was an individual officer, the 'mayor' (*ḫazānu*), who was probably nominated, or at least approved, by the king, but lived in the village and was subject to all kinds of pressure, both from above and below.

Within the village the governing principles were family ties, collegiality, solidarity (we see it from the lists of warrants and from the procedures for loans) and collective responsibility (arising, for example, from tacit complicity in the case of unpunished murders). Even if they were small, the villages were real systems, which the palace saw as administrative units and local cells of judicial responsibility, but which were in fact seen by those who lived there as large family groups owning and organizing the exploitation of an agro-pastoral domain.

The capital city, if we ignore the royal palace and the complex of the 'king's men', was itself a village (though larger than others) and therefore had its own council of elders and popular assembly, which in cases of crisis expressed its own opinions and made its contribution in taking difficult decisions, even in explicit contrast to the king's will. The case of the expulsion from Byblos of the old king Rib-Adda is particularly dramatic, but gives a good example of the role that the 'free' population of the town could assume in critical moments:

> When Aziru took Sumura – it is Rib-Adda who informs Pharaoh – the people of Gubla saw this, and said: 'How long shall we contain the son of Abdi-Ashirta? Our money is completely gone for the war.' So they broke with me, but I killed them. They said, 'How long can you go on killing us? Where will you get (other) people to populate the city?' So I wrote to the (Egyptian) palace for troops, but no troops were given to me. Then the city said, 'Abandon him. Let us join Aziru!' I said, 'How could I join him and abandon the king, my lord (the Pharaoh)?' Then my brother spoke and swore to the city. They had a discussion and the lords of the city joined with the sons of Abdi-Ashirta (*LA* 138 = *EA* 78).

Occasionally the assembly assumed political powers, but this happened only when the royal function was vacant, and only temporarily, while waiting for a new authority (see *LA* 194-95, 199, 273 [= *EA* 139-40, 100, 59]).

We have already seen how, in normal villages, pastoral groups were part of the community, in order to manage the sheep-rearing using the method of the transhumance, which brought typical situations (called 'dimorphic' by anthropologists) where the same group lives either together or scattered over the territory, depending on the seasons. After the drastic distinction of the nineteenth century, with its evolutionary quality, between nomads and sedentary groups, a perhaps too unified vision nowadays prevails, implying almost that the same families were at the same time devoted to agricultural and pastoral activities. This agro-pastoral unity exists if we consider the village as a whole; but within it, the Alalakh lists show that the 'houses' of shepherds were clearly distinguished from those (more numerous) of the ordinary farmers – and indeed each kind of activity (transhumant or permanent) required specialization. Shepherds and farmers lived seasonally together and probably frequented together the 'sacred' sites, usually connected with ancient tombs of ancestors and ancient oaks, as places where the gods could appear and sacrifices could be offered to them on open-air altars. This typology is well-known from the patriarchal stories: the oak of Mamre (Gen. 13.18, 14.13, 18.1, 25.9-10) with the tombs of Abraham and Sarah, then of Isaac (35.27) and

Jacob (50.13); the oak of Moreh (12.6) where Yahweh appeared to Abraham, and others. These texts have been edited in much more recent times; but two texts from Ugarit (*PRU*, III, 109 and 131) mention already in the thirteenth century a place called the 'oak of Sherdanu' in the territory of the village of Ili-ishtama and Mati-Ilu, the only theophoric place names in the area: the first, in particular, 'God has listened' (as in the Biblical place name Eshtemoa), was probably a place of oracular consultation or of some other divine manifestation.

9. 'External' Nomads

But Late Bronze texts also mention real 'external' nomads, not given geographical names but rather collective, perhaps tribal, ones: these are the Suteans of Akkadian texts and the Shasu of Egyptian texts. Their main area of activity was the southern and eastern steppes, on the margins of the desert; but some can be found also in the central highlands. Their presence was considered dangerous by who had to cross those territories: the palace had no authority over the external tribes – even if occasionally some were paid as guides or escorts. This is the picture painted by an Egyptian messenger (in the Anastasi I Papyrus, from the Ramesside period):

> (On the Maghara road) the sky is darkened by day and it is overgrown with cypresses and oaks and cedars which reach to the heavens. Lions are more numerous than leopards or bears, and it is surrounded by Shasu on every side of it... (Near the Megiddo pass) the narrow valley is dangerous with Shasu, hidden under the bushes. Some of them are four or five cubits from their noses to the heel, and fierce of face. Their hearts are not mild, and they do not listen to wheedling (*ANET*, 477).

Egyptians met the Shasu not only in crossing the mountains of Syria-Palestine, but also when the Shasu sought for refuge in Egypt in times of famine. Sometimes they did so following the normal procedures in use at the time and were accepted according to the ideology of the Pharaoh as dispenser of life, as we read in the report of a border officer:

> We completed the crossing of the Shasu from Edom, through the fortress of Merenptah-hotep-her-Ma'at in Soko, toward the pools of Per-Amun of Merenptah-hotep-her-Ma'at in Soko, in order to let them live and to let their herds live in the land of His Majesty the good Sun of every country (*ANET*, 259, c. 1230).

Sometimes the nomads try to enter in a hostile and unordered way, and in this case they are certainly killed:

Some foreigners, who did not know how to survive, came in flight from their lands, hungry, compelled to live as the game in the desert' (*ANET*, 251, c. 1300).

The available texts (from contemporary archives or Egyptian celebrative inscriptions) all portray the palace's point of view, considering nomads as external and indistinguishable entities: thus, they use collective terms and very seldom mention specific tribes by name. None of the names of the Israelite tribes recorded in biblical texts is attested in Palestine during the Late Bronze Age: the documentation is too scant, but perhaps those tribes did not yet exist as self-identifying units. We have, in fact, a mention of only two tribal groups, both connected with biblical terminology but not to the 'classical' names of the tribes. A stela by Seti I from Beth-Shean (c. 1289; *ANET*, 255) mentions conflicts between local groups, taking place in the area around Beth-Shean, and depicted as symptomatic of the inevitable anarchy of the local population. The text mentions, besides the '*ḫabiru* from Mount Yarmuti', also a tribe of Raham. We may suppose that the members of this tribe called themselves 'sons of Raham' (*Banu-Raham) and that their eponymous ancestor was a 'father of Raham' (*Abu-Raham), that is, the name of the patriarch Abraham.

Some decades later (c. 1230; *LPAE*, 292-95) a stela from Merenptah celebrates the triumph of the Pharaoh in one of his campaigns in Palestine, mentioning among vanquished enemies towns like Ashkelon and Gezer and regions like Canaan and Kharu: all these names are classified with the determinative sign for 'land'. But one of them, Israel, is marked with the determinative for 'people' (and thus a tribal, non-sedentary group). This is the first mention of the name, which is probably to be placed in the area of the central highlands. In fact the sequence of three place names Ashkelon-Gezer-Yenoam seems to be inserted in a sort of frame created by the two (broader) terms Canaan and Israel: and if Canaan is appropriately at the very beginning of the sequence, in the costal southern plan, the most probable setting for Israel is in the central highlands.

'Abrahamites' and 'Israelites' in the twelfth century were, then, pastoral groups active in the gaps within the Palestinian geopolitical system and, if not too turbulent, they were easily controlled by Egyptian military action.

Finally, to Late Bronze Age nomads (most probably 'external' ones) have been attributed two sacred places sharing a similar square plan, both dated to the end of the thirteenth century: one near Amman (the airport area) and one in Deir 'Alla. They are both placed outside the city and are marginal or completely outside the area where the new horizon of 'proto-

Israelite' villages (see §3.1) would develop. Their extra-urban collocation suggests that those sanctuaries could be places of meeting of nomadic groups; the hypothesis is plausible, but it should also be noted that the sites were abandoned at the beginning of Iron I, around 1150, and after that remained disused (as in the case of Amman) or were replaced by normal villages, with no sacred places (as in the case of Deir 'Alla).

10. *Socioeconomic Tensions*

The Late Bronze Age is a period of strong socioeconomic tensions, caused in particular by a process of indebtedness in the rural population and by the quite harsh attitude on this matter of the king and of palace aristocracy. Serious economic difficulties led 'free' farmers (the word *ḫupšu* in the Babylonian language of Alalakh and Amarna corresponds to Hebrew *hofšî*, 'free') to acquire wheat in exchange for material pledges, especially lands, and then personal ones: wives and sons became slaves of the creditor, in a form of slavery that was supposed to be temporary (and as such did not change the free status of the subjects involved) but in fact became permanent because of the impossibility of paying the debt. The last stage, when the debtor himself had to become a slave, closed the cycle, because recovery of the debt was now impossible: in many cases the desperate debtor chose to escape.

In previous times (Middle Bronze Age, c. 1900–1600) throughout the Syro-Mesopotamian area social and political solutions existed for this serious problem. The king assumed a 'paternalistic' attitude, issuing edicts for the remission of debts and liberation of enslaved debtors. Socio-juridical norms also tended to maintain property in the family, so that the alienation of lands to strangers was forbidden. In the mid-second millennium, those correctives ceased to be valid. The king issued no more edicts of remission – and these, in any case, had already been made useless in the sixteenth and fifteenth centuries by clauses such as: 'even in the event of an edict of remission this person cannot be redeemed'. The selling of land became normal, though it was necessary to use the expedient of 'false adoptions', in which the adoptee gave to the adopter a sum of money to acquire his possessions after his death, in place of natural heirs. More generally, the model of kingship lost its paternalistic features and assumed an entrepreneurial flavour, the king and the court trying to defend their role as major creditors and beneficiaries of the system of debt slavery.

Indebted farmers had no choice but to flee, at first in bordering states, but then (after the introduction of treaties for the capture and restitution of fugitives between bordering states: see *ANET*, 531-32) towards places where the control was more difficult, such as forested mountains and fringe desert steppes. There, groups of refugees could organize themselves and somehow coexist with local clans of shepherds. Such persons, uprooted from their own social context and resettled elsewhere, are called *ḥabiru* (we have already encountered several texts where this term is attested): the word has clearly an etymological and semantic connection with most ancient attestations of the term 'Hebrew' (*'ibrî*), before it assumed an ethnic connotation. The 'Amarna letters contain many denunciations of the turbulent activities of the *ḥabiru* by local kings, and the term soon lost its technical meaning of 'fugitive' to become a synonym of 'enemy', in the sense of 'outlaw', 'rebel against legitimate authority'. In some cases, even kings and members of the ruling class were called *ḥabiru* if they were forced to leave their position and run away: this proves the depreciation in the value of the term:

> The king of Hazor has abandoned his house and has aligned himself with the *ḥabiru*. May the king know, about these fellows, these traitors, who will turn the land of the king into *ḥabiru* land (*LA* 122 = *EA* 148, from Tyre).

> The *ḥabiru* have raided Khazi, a city of the king, my lord, but we did battle against them, and we defeated them. Then 40 *ḥabiru* went to Aman-khatpi (the king of a city nearby), and Aman-khatpi welcomed whoever had escaped. And they were gathered together in the city. (In so doing,) Aman-khatpi himself became a *ḥabiru*! We heard that the *ḥabiru* were with Aman-khatpi, so my brothers and my sons, your servants, drove by chariot to Aman-khatpi. My brothers said to Aman-khatpi, 'Hand over the *ḥabiru*, traitors of the king, our lord, so we can ask them whether they have captured the cities of the king, my lord, and burnt them down.' He agreed to hand over the *ḥabiru*, but then, during the night, he took them with him, and he fled himself to the *ḥabiru* (*LA* 228 = *EA* 185, from the Lebanese Beq'a).

But most of the *ḥabiru* were of modest social origins, fleeing more for economic than political reasons. They found refuge in bordering states (Nuzi texts, fifteenth century) or in marginal areas, where they often acted in association with nomads (Suteans), serving as mercenary troops or practising banditry (see *LA* 210 and 271 [= *EA* 195 and 318]). Those 'interface' activities with the palace sector imply that a symbiosis between *ḥabiru* and nomads was operating even (and maybe more so) in everyday life.

The most alarmed among the Cananean kings feared that indebted farmers (*ḥupšu*) still living in their towns could also make an alliance with the *ḥabiru* and that bloody rebellions could occur as a result:

> If farmers desert, *ḫabiru* will take the town (*LA* 135 = *EA* 74, from Byblos).

> What am I, who live among *ḫabiru*, to do? If now are no provisions from the king for me, my peasantry is going to rebel (*LA* 187 = *EA* 130, from Byblos).

Some cases were recalled in fear, where kings had been killed during such uprisings:

> The *ḫabiru* killed Aduna, the king of Irqata...and just now the men of Ammiya have killed their lord. I am afraid (LA 136 = EA 75).

> I am afraid the peasantry will strike me down (LA 137 = EA 77).

> As for the mayors, their own cities kill them. They are like dogs, and there is no one who pursues them (i.e. the rebels) (LA 187 = EA 130, all from Byblos).

It may be mentioned, in particular, the attempt made by the chief (of tribal origin) of Amurru, Abdi-Ashirta. He wanted to use this milieu of exasperated farmers, refugees and disbanded people to create an ambitious political project of a 'revolutionary' flavour that would completely overthrow the system based on Egyptian presence and royal authority:

> All my villages – Rib-Adda king of Byblos is speaking – that are in the mountains or along the sea have become *ḫabiru*. Left to me are Byblos and two towns. After taking Shiqata for himself, Abdi-Ashirta said to the men of Ammiya, 'Kill your leaders and then you will be like us and at peace'. They acted according to his words, and became like *ḫabiru*. So now Abdi-Ashirta has written to the troops: 'Assemble in the temple of Anat, and then let us fall upon Byblos. Look, there is no one that will save it from us. Then let us drive out the kings from the country, and let the entire country become *ḫabiru*. Let an oath be made to the entire country. Then will (our) sons and daughters be at peace forever. Should even the king come out, the entire country will be against him and what will he do to us?' Accordingly, they have made an alliance among themselves and, accordingly, I am very, very afraid that there is no one who can save me from them (*LA* 135 = *EA* 74).

The severe attitude of Canaanite kings towards economic matters caused a general disaffection for the palace by the population of the agro-pastoral base. If we add to this diffused tendency the damages caused by the indifference of the Pharaoh about local conflicts and quite explicit signals about recurrent famines, demographic crises and the restriction of inhabited and exploited agricultural areas, we have a picture of serious difficulty for Syro-Palestinian (but especially Palestinian) society towards the end of Late Bronze Age. These elements of crisis are warning signals of the final crisis of the Bronze Age, a large-scale phenomenon that will involve in different forms most of the eastern Mediterranean and the Near East. A crisis of these proportions could not be solved without a reorganization that would create an equal impact.

Part I
A Normal History

Chapter 2

THE TRANSITION (TWELFTH CENTURY)

1. *A Multifactor Crisis*

Whether positively or negatively influenced by the biblical narrative, modern scholars (archaeologists as well as biblical scholars) have suggested unequivocal yet strongly contrasting theories about Israel's origins. Even when properly understood as merely one feature in the huge epochal crisis of transition from Bronze Age to Iron Age, the case of Israel continued to receive special attention and more detailed explanation. The historical process has been reconstructed several times, and here it will be sufficient to recall the main theories suggested over the years. (1) The theory of a 'military' conquest, concentrated and destructive, inspired by the biblical account, is still asserted in some traditional circles (especially in United States and Israel), but today is considered marginal in scholarly discussion. (2) The idea of a progressive occupation, currently widespread in two variants that are more complementary than mutually exclusive: the settlement of pastoral groups already present in the area and infiltration from desert fringe zones. (3) Finally, the so-called 'sociological' theory of a revolt of farmers, which totally prioritizes a process of internal development without external influence; after initial consent during the 70s and 80s this has been less widely accepted, sometimes for overt political reasons. The different theories are usually set one against the other, yet all of them should be considered in creating a multifactored explanation, as required by a complex historical phenomenon.

If we compare Late Bronze Age Palestinian society with that of the early Iron Age, some factors are particularly striking: (1) notable innovations in technology and living conditions, which mark a distinct cultural break and are diffused throughout the whole Near Eastern and Mediterranean area; (2) elements of continuity, especially in material culture, that make it impossible to conclude that this new situation was mostly brought about by newcomers arriving from elsewhere (while real immigrants, the Philistines, display cultural features perfectly coherent with their foreign origin);

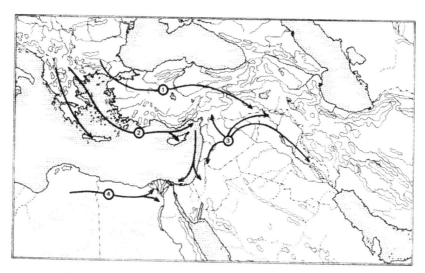

Figure 6. *The invasions of the twelfth century: (1 = Phrygians; 2 = Sea Peoples; 3 = Arameans; 4 = Libyans)*

(3) complementary features in land occupation and use, between a new agro-pastoral horizon of villages and the pre-existing agro-urban system. The resulting competition for the control of economic resources renders plausible some sense of conflict between the two milieus (not necessarily to be read, rather anachronistically, as 'revolution').

If these factors converged at a precise 'moment' (let us say, within a century), that is probably due (as historians of the *Annales* school would say) to the convergence of chronological processes of different duration. There is the *longue durée* that reveals a recurrence of general settlement patterns, especially in semi-arid zones, caused by changes in the relationship between pastoral groups and urban communities, the ultimate cause being found in climatic changes. Then there are (more rapid) fluctuations in social history, made concrete in technological innovation (in this case evidently crucial), socioeconomic tensions and the evolution of political organization. And finally, the faster rhythm of events, that brings together the complex of factors in a specific moment: and here migrations and political and military events come into play.

The socioeconomic crisis of the end of the Bronze Age stretches back over three centuries (c. 1500–1200). The search for a new order took just as long (c. 1200–900). But between those two sociopolitical and socio-economic processes of moderate duration falls a brief period of convulsive events, which brings about the final collapse of the already tottering Late

Bronze Age society and opens the way for a new order. This violent crisis is concentrated in the first half of the twelfth century, while the transition towards the new order, though quite rapid, takes at least another century.

2. *Climatic Factors and Migrations*

Following the enthusiastic, positivist historiography of a century ago the idealistic phase has introduced caution in accepting climatic factors as decisive in historical change, since these are beyond human control and thus seen as a mechanical and artificial *deus ex machina*. The same is true of migration, considered a methodologically obsolete explanation, pointing to the role of ethnic groups, if not races. Today we tend to emphasize socioeconomic processes in accounting for internal evolution and seek to explain the changes in a systemic way, as the working out of variables already in play from the outset.

Though the final crisis of the Late Bronze Age, as we have seen, had all the characteristics of an internal process, we need to recognize that the crucial impulse for the collapse came from outside: a wave of migration, which in turn can be placed in the context of a process of climatic change. In the arid zones of the Sahara and the Arabian desert an intensifying drought was changing broad savannahs into the present day desert. This process peaked around 3000, around 2000, and finally around 1200. Paleoclimatic data are confirmed by historical data: between the end of the thirteenth century and the beginning of the twelfth, a number of Libyan tribes gathered in the Nile Valley. Beginning in the time of Merenptah (c. 1250), and then in years 5 and 11 of Ramses III (c. 1180–1175) actual invasions took place, which the Pharaohs proudly claim to have stopped in epic battles; and the texts record the names of the Libyan tribes that arrived in the Delta, driven by famine to seek pastures and water.

But a series of exceptionally dry years also occurred on the northern shore of the Mediterranean: in Anatolia dendrochronology reveals a cycle of four or five years (towards the end of the twelfth century) of very little rainfall, probably creating a serious famine. In this case too, the historical sources confirm the paleoclimatic data: Hittite and Ugaritic texts mention famines and the importing of cereals from Syria to Anatolia, while Merenptah says he sent wheat from Egypt 'in order to keep the land of Hatti alive' (*ARE*, III, 580). A similar crisis probably occurred also in the Balkans.

As a result, Egypt had to cope with pressure not only from Libyans from the Sahara, but also from the so-called 'Sea Peoples', who at first, in Merenptah's reign, are identified as mercenaries in the Libyan invasion but later, in the time of Ramses III (year 8, 1178), began a wider movement that involved, in clockwise order, all the eastern Mediterranean coast, finally reaching the Egyptian Delta, where it was stopped by the Egyptians in a battle that the Pharaoh celebrates as a huge single victory, but in fact was probably a combined celebration of a series of minor encounters. In describing the arrival of peoples driven by hunger and disorder in their own lands, the Pharaoh records their itinerary, marked out by the collapse of the Anatolian and North Syrian kingdoms:

> The foreign countries made a conspiracy in their islands. All at once the lands were removed and scattered in the fray. No land could stand before their arms, from Hatti, Kode, Carchemish, Arzawa, and Alashiya onwards, being cut off at one time. A camp was set up in one place in Amurru. They desolated its people, and its land was like that which has never come into being. They were coming forward toward Egypt, while the flame was prepared before them. Their confederation was the Peleset, Zeker, Shekelesh, Denen and Weshesh lands united. They laid their hands upon the lands as far as the circuit of the earth, their hearts confident and trusting... (*ANET*, 262).

The texts from Ugarit confirm this invasion, though they describe rather the periodical arrival of relatively small groups. An exchange of letters between the king of Ugarit and the king of Alashiya (Cyprus) betrays a deep anxiety over the approaching invaders:

> 'About what you have written – says the king of Cyprus to the king of Ugarit – have you seen enemy ships in the sea?' It is true, we have seen some ships, and you should strengthen your defences: where are your troops and chariots? Are they with you? And if not, who has pulled you away to chase the enemies? Build walls for your towns, let troops and chariots enter there and wait resolutely for the enemy to arrive!' 'My father – the king of Ugarit answers – the enemy ships have arrived and set fire to some towns, damaging my country. Does my father ignore that all my troops are in the country of Khatti and all my ships in Lukka? They have not come back and my country is abandoned. Now, seven enemy ships came to inflict serious damage: if you see other enemy ships, let us know!' (*Ug.*, V, 85-89).

Their concern was probably fully justified, and the consequences were terrible, as the archaeological data show: not only Ugarit and Alashiya, but a whole series of kingdoms and towns of the Aegean, Anatolia, Syria, and Palestine were destroyed and not rebuilt: this means that they were completely abandoned after a total annihilation. The whole political system of the Late Bronze Age in the eastern Mediterranean collapsed under the assaults of the invaders.

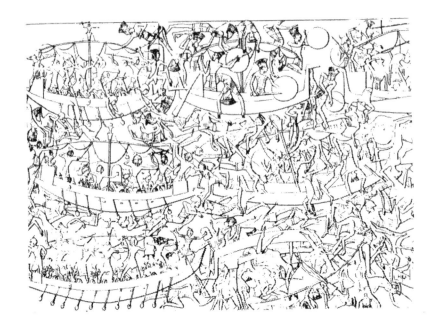

Figure 7. *The 'Sea Peoples' as depicted by the Egyptians: (a) the naval battle with Ramses III; (b) Philistine prisoners*

The protracted socioeconomic crisis, the demographic upheaval, the disdain of the rural population for the fate of the royal palaces, the recent famines, were all certainly factors in the debilitation of Syro-Palestinian society in the face of the invaders. Moreover, these invaders were probably particularly aggressive and determined, with effective weapons (long iron swords) and a strong social cohesion that allowed them to prevail over fortified towns and major political formations. In fact, small groups of 'Sea Peoples' were already active on the Eastern Mediterranean coast well before their large-scale invasion – as pirates, and as mercenary troops (the Sherdana, in particular) serving the petty kings of Syria-Palestine but also Libyans and Egypt itself. Those advance guards probably showed their compatriots the way towards those fertile regions richer and much more advanced than those they came from.

Many of the 'Sea Peoples', having no prospect of reaching the Egyptian Delta, settled on the Palestinian coast. The most important of these were the Philistines, who occupied five towns on the southern Palestinian coast or its immediate hinterland: Gaza, Ashkelon, Ashdod, Gath, and Ekron. On the central Palestinian coast, at Dor, according to Wen-Amun's account, was a settlement of Zeker. It has been suggested (improbably) that the tribe of Dan, settled further north, owes its name (and some of its members) to the Danuna, another of the invading peoples. Once they had occupied or rebuilt the towns, the Philistines established kingdoms on the 'cantonal' model of the previous ones, centred on royal palaces. The evidence of external influence, however, is shown in personal names, in inscriptions of an Aegean type (like the tablets found in Deir 'Alla) and in aspects of the material culture – pottery in particular (first, monochrome Mycenaean III C1, then bichrome, with similar forms but more complex decoration, which is considered typically Philistine), and in distinctive anthropoid clay coffins.

Ashdod, Ashkelon and Ekron have been quite well investigated archaeologically: they all have a phase of initial settlement, exhibiting Mycenaean pottery III C1, and then a fully Philistine phase, with bichrome pottery. Our knowledge of Gaza (probably lying under the modern town) and Gath (probably to be identified with Tell es-Safi) is poor. But the picture is filled out by smaller sites, villages and small towns that replaced the Egyptian garrisons, especially in the northern Negev (see §3.8). At Dor, too, the Iron I settlement is probably to be assigned to the Zeker (the later stratum betrays Phoenician influence). Half a century after the invasion, the towns occupied by the Philistines were again, fully and normally, a part of the Palestinian scenery.

3. *The Collapse of the Regional System*

The invasion of the 'Sea Peoples' had various impacts on the historical fate of Palestine. First of all, it changed the regional political framework of the whole of the Near East bordering the Mediterranean. The two superpowers contending for control of the Syro-Palestinian coastal region, Egypt and Hatti, both collapsed, though in different ways.

The collapse of the Hittite kingdom, which controlled Syria as far as Byblos and Qadesh, was total. The capital, Hattusha, (Boğazköy) was destroyed and abandoned, along with the royal dynasty, and the empire vanished. In Central Anatolia, now occupied by the Phrygians (whose advance forces penetrated during the twelfth century as far as the borders of Assyria), settlements were reduced to tiny villages and pastoral tribes, and a strong cultural regression took place (cuneiform writing and archives disappeared). In the south-east of the former Hittite empire, the kingdoms of Tarkhuntasha (Cilicia) and Carchemish (on the Euphrates) resisted the collapse, and the so-called 'Neo-Hittite' states emerged. Some of these (Carchemish for certain) were in fact the direct heirs of the Late Bronze state formations. Though the collapse of the Hittite Empire did not affect Palestine directly, it brought to an end the conflict between Hatti and Egypt that had influenced Near Eastern politics for the preceding centuries (the older state of affairs is still reflected in the expression 'hire the kings of the Hittites and the kings of the Egyptians' against one's enemies [2 Kgs 7.6]).

Egypt's collapse was less dramatic: the central power absorbed the impact, and victory over invaders from both West and East was solemnly celebrated, as well as newly established peace and internal security. But in fact control over the Libyans was obtained only by ceding them a significant portion of the Delta, where numerous Libyan tribes settled, well beyond the line of fortresses built by the Ramesside Pharaohs. The Sea Peoples, too, could be stopped only by letting them settle *en masse* on the Palestinian coast, in order to preserve some control over Egypt's Asiatic possessions. Thutmoses III's empire in fact came to an end (at least in the terms described in §1.4) after the great battle that Ramses III claims to have won.

Even the powerful Mesopotamian kingdoms of Assyria and Babylonia were reduced to their minimum extent and suffered the invasion of Arameans, who in the ninth and tenth centuries penetrated *en masse* into the 'dimorphic zone' from Northern Syria to the borders of Elam. Thus, Palestine was – for the first time in 500 years – free from foreign occupation and from the menace of external intervention. This situation lasted,

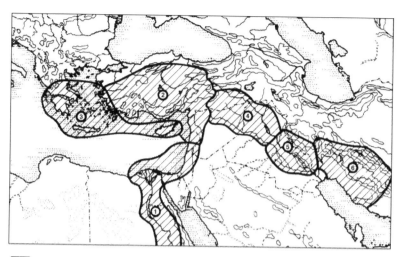

1 = Egypt; 2 = Hittite empire; 3 = Mycenean world; 4 = Middle Assyrian empire; 5 = Babylonia; 6 = Elam

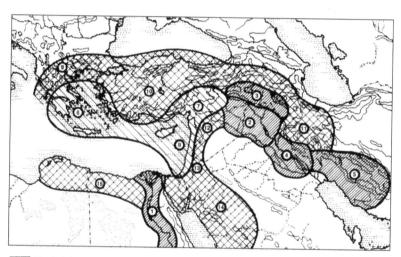

Territorial states (1 = Egypt; 2 = Assyria; 3 = Urartu; 4 = Babylonia; 5 = Elam)

City-states (6 = Greek; 7 = Neo-Hittite; 8 = Phoenicians and Philistines)

Ethnic states (9 = Northern Greeks; 10 = Lydians and Phrygians; 11 = Medes and Mannaeans; 12 = Arameans; 13 = Israelites and Transjordanians; 14 = Northern Arabs ; 15 = Libyans.

Figure 8. *The 'regional system' and the crisis of the twelfth century: (a) the system of the thirteenth century; (b) the system during Iron I*

as we shall see, until the era of Neo-Assyrian imperial expansion, and encouraged the independent development of a dynamic internal political evolution. 'Little' Palestinian kings, accustomed to submission to a foreign lord, were now beholden to no superior authority apart from their gods. So they adapted the phraseology, iconography and ceremony that they had used to show their faithfulness to the Pharaoh, to express their devotion to their city god or national god.

4. The Palace Crisis

Many Late Bronze Palestinian royal palaces and towns were destroyed during or after these invasions: the list is long, since almost all archaeological sites show a picture of destruction dated to the beginning of the twelfth century. Obviously, such evidence is not 'signed' and so leaves room for several different hypotheses: Sea Peoples, 'proto-Israelite' tribes (or perhaps others from the Palestinian interior), Egyptian intervention, local conflicts, peasant rebellions. But the cause of a particular destruction is not as important as the overall picture, which clearly shows the collapse of the palace institution and, more generally, of the type of kingdom based on the palace. The selectivity of the archaeological record may well need to be allowed for, but the general evaluation will hardly be altered by new discoveries: the development of the palaces reached one of its highest peaks during the Late Bronze Age and then fell to its lowest point at the beginning of the Iron Age. Between these successive but very different phases, a real collapse took place.

As well as the palaces, the crisis affected also administrative structures, and the crafts and trades based on them and supporting them. Scribal schools for the study of cuneiform writing and the Babylonian language suddenly disappeared, and only gradually did the alphabet fill the vacuum. Luxury craftsmanship hit a serious crisis, not because the technical ability was lost, but because of the lack of customers (the royal palace and the associated upper classes), as well as a collapse of the system of maintenance and remuneration of craftsmen by the palace itself. Having lost the system of royal 'endowment' on which it was based during the Late Bronze Age, trade had to be reorganized on a different basis (see §2.7). The military specialists, the *maryannu*, who received from the king high rewards in the form of farmland for breeding horses and training themselves as charioteers in battle, suddenly disappear completely from our sources. Presumably something had changed in the conduct of war: not techniques (the horse and chariot remained in use for many centuries), but rather military policy, methods of recruitment and the sociopolitical relationships involved in warfare.

Deprived of their palace nucleus, the towns were reduced in size and in complexity. The process is quite simple: if you take out from a Late Bronze Age town the royal palace, the houses of high officers and of military aristocrats, the craftsmen's shops, the archives and the schools, what is left is a big village like all the others. In the Late Bronze Age, significantly, only the capital city had walls to protect its human and material resources; villages were not walled, because their poverty did not justify such expensive building activity. In the Iron Age, both towns (even small towns) and large villages are walled, and this marks a sort of hierarchical levelling, as well as demonstrating the increased interest of local communities in self-defence.

Obviously, the loss of the palace was neither general nor permanent: some nuclei of urbanization remained, apparently untouched by the crisis. On the Phoenician coast, in the archive of the city of Byblos under Zakar-Baal (c. 1050), one can read documents from when the Egyptian empire still existed. In Syria, the royal dynasty of Carchemish survived the crisis unchanged. Other towns were soon resettled and the rebuilding of royal palaces resumed, along with the restoration of monarchic power. But it was a new process, or at least a new cycle, which needed several centuries to regain the level of the Late Bronze Age.

5. *The Growth of the Tribal Element*

While the invasions from the sea provided the crucial blow in the collapse just described, pastoral groups contributed more than any others to the shape of the new order. We do not, of course, have any texts written by shepherds, but archaeological findings give us the data needed for a historical evaluation. The entire history of Palestine is characterized by processes of nomadization and sedentarization, which result in a smaller or larger number of settlements whose remains can be identified: nomadic-pastoral occupation is thus not only demographically less dense, but also less visible to archaeology.

The process of *nomadization*, which over the long term corresponds to a progressive reduction of permanent settlements from the Early Bronze to Middle Bronze and Late Bronze Ages, is also visible over the medium term in the turbulence and the social disengagement of the *ḫabiru* groups that we have already mentioned (§1.10). Obviously, 'armed troops' and 'pastoral tribes' are different, but they share the same characteristics of mobility and belligerence, as well as an extra-urban location and anti-palace attitudes.

Then, during the twelfth century, begins a process of *sedentarization*, evidenced by the new sites of Iron Age I (as we will see in §3.1). The theory of peasant revolts (briefly described in §2.1) has often been presented in exaggerated and even amateurish ways, but the reinforcement of pastoral groups by marginalized and displaced people with a new self-consciousness is quite a plausible scenario.

The consolidation of the tribe and its kinship ties is the counterweight to the loss of the palace and its hierarchical relationships. In individual villages, formerly no more than cells of a central administrative system, a permanent kinship unit consolidated itself, corresponding to a social unit that occupied and used the same land. Villages close to one another saw themselves as 'brothers' in a broader group (that we may conventionally call a 'tribe'). Within the tribe developed customs of intermarriage, mutual hospitality, joint action in self-defence, and a coordination of the routes and times of transhumance.

The representation of social relations in a genealogical form is typical of the Iron Age. The name of the village was typically (or typically understood) as the name of a common ancestor from whom all the inhabitants descended, while all such village eponyms were considered sons, or perhaps nephews, of the (eponymic) tribal ancestor. Such a genealogical model is clearly artificial: the villages and families involved were certainly related, not through a common origin, but through a long history of intermarriage. Their unity is therefore achieved by a process of *convergence*, not *divergence*. But the genealogical model is obviously more vivid and makes a stronger impact. Agro-pastoral villages ceased to gravitate around the palace – which had collapsed or was at least in serious crisis – and now looked to the tribe. This process, together with the absorption of fugitives (*ḥabiru*) with their anti-palace socioeconomic attitudes, endowed the tribe with a new dimension and a new power.

Understood as a group of villages that decided to regard themselves as related by a common origin, this tribe could present itself to its members as a valid political alternative to the royal palace. In fact, the sense of family ties that is slowly created in a tribe, resulting from a union between villages, is indeed a concrete reality for those tribes consisting of nomad camel drivers (see §2.6), that we find in the Early Iron Age on the borders of Palestine: the Amalekites in the Negev and the Midianites in the northern Hijaz, on the southern borders of Transjordan. For these nomad tribes, the identity of migratory group with family group is real. But even among these tribes can be found a degree of 'artificial' kinship in the construction of broader genealogical ties with other tribes, expressed in stories and anecdotes that define alliance or hostility among them.

This phenomenon is not limited to Palestine, but it is well known amongst the Arameans who created, in Syria, states with names such as Bit Adini, Bit Agushi, Bit Bakhyani, Bit Zamani, where 'Bit' means 'house of' (in the sense of 'household', 'kin group'), and is followed by a tribal eponym. The same phenomenon is found in Palestine, where the state of Judah is called 'house of David' and the state of Israel 'house of Omri'; in Transjordan we find also 'house of Ammon' and 'house of Rehob'.

Finally, even where the palace system survived, the model of kingship had to adapt to the new cultural climate. The role of the city assembly, which during the Late Bronze Age was summoned only in cases of extreme crisis, became a regular practice: we find examples of this in Byblos (at the time of Zakar-Baal: see the Tale of Wen-Amun) and in Shechem under Abimelech (Judges 9). During the Iron Age some 'paternal' and 'pastoral' epithets and attitudes, which had completely disappeared during the Late Bronze Age, recur. The crisis of the twelfth century could be overcome only through patching up that rift between palace and population that had undermined the sociopolitical system of the Late Bronze Age. This was done through a system of kinship solidarity, which could transcend the confines of a village or a pastoral group, and include the town itself.

6. *Technological Change*

The transition from Late Bronze to Iron Age I is marked by important technological and cultural innovations. These are partly caused by external influences and partly by internal developments. The cultural crisis, the emergence of new sociopolitical groups and the new economic opportunities encouraged the adoption of new techniques. And, *vice versa*, the adoption of these new techniques enabled the creation of a new territorial and social order.

The working of iron to make tools and weapons is the innovation that gave the name, in the traditional archaeological terminology of the nineteenth century, to the new cultural phase, the 'Iron Age'. This technique was already known in the Near East in the Late Bronze Age, though limited to small-scale objects, or parts of objects. But the palace preferred weapons and objects made of bronze, exploiting the flourishing trade in copper (especially from Cyprus) and tin (from Iran). The collapse of the palace workshops and of long distance trade encouraged the gradual spread of iron-working. For a few centuries, bronze and iron were both in use: bronze remained the preference for breastplates and vessels, while iron was used mostly for tools and weapons. The consequences of this

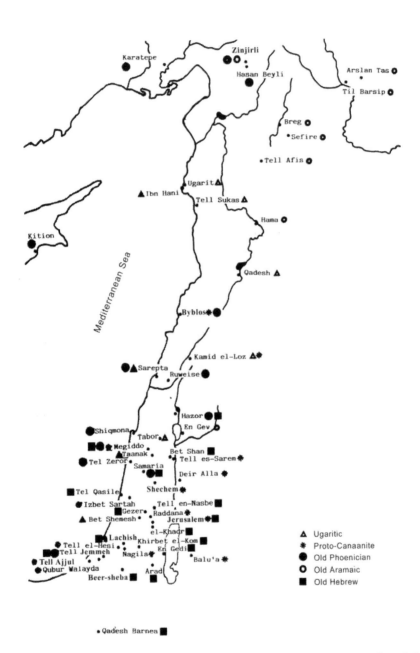

Figure 9. *The spread of the alphabet in Syria-Palestine during the thirteenth–eighth centuries*

innovation were not merely technical (iron is harder and has a wider use than bronze), but socioeconomic. To work iron, simpler tools are needed: it is therefore feasible for village, or itinerant, blacksmiths, without need of a palace workshop. Sources of iron ore were spread over the territory and did not depend on long-distance, organized trade. The result was more local diffusion and wider accessibility, fitting for the requirements of the new age.

A real 'democratizing' effect was produced by the other major innovation, the alphabet. In this case too, the invention had been made during the Late Bronze Age, and in some cases (such as Ugarit) palace administrations had already decided to use this simpler writing system. But most Late Bronze palaces had remained faithful to the complex Babylonian cuneiform system. The prestige and the sociocultural exclusiveness of the scribal craft, using a writing system restricted to a few specialists receiving a long and expensive education, hindered its replacement with an alphabet that is, by contrast, accessible to a broader group of users. Alphabetic writing was not much in evidence at the time of the crisis (a proto-Canaanite ostracon from Beth-Shemesh, a jar handle from Khirbet Raddana, some arrowheads from el-Khadr), but then it spread broadly, along the major trade routes – the Mediterranean sea routes, as well as the caravan routes across the Arabian peninsula.

Mention of trading routes brings us to another important innovation: the domestication and use of the camel (in Iran) and dromedary (in the Arabian desert bordering Palestine) as pack animals. These lived already in the Near East as wild animals, and some attempts at domestication had been made earlier; but their widespread use coincides with the beginning of the Iron Age, and only then spreads from the peripheries to the very heart of the ancient Near East. As is well known, camels and dromedaries can sustain a much heavier burden than donkeys (the traditional pack animals during the Bronze Age) and can last longer between meals and watering places. Their use opened up trade to the broad deserts of Arabia, Central Asia and, later, of the Sahara – areas inaccessible and thus historically marginal during the Bronze Age. The agents of trade were also different: while Late Bronze tribes had been accustomed to interfering with palace-sponsored trade caravans, during the Iron Age tribes of camel breeders acquired a privileged, even exclusive role as traders themselves. This position served as a counterweight to the central function of the palace and created the first 'caravan cities' on the fringes of the desert – this sort of thing did not exist during the Bronze Age.

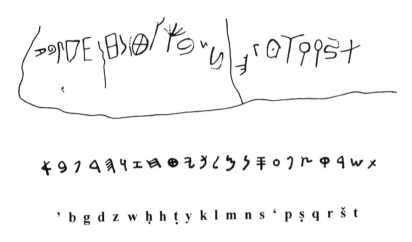

’ b g d z w ḥ h ṭ y k l m n s ‘ p ṣ q r š t

Figure 10. *The alphabet from ʿIzbet Sartah (twelfth century): (a) copy (b) transcription in the 'classical' script of the eighth century (c) equivalents in Roman script*

The camel was not suitable as a draught animal, but could be ridden in warfare. The horse too, which had been used during the Bronze Age for drawing chariots, but only seldom used by mounted messengers, now began to be used mainly for riding. Military strategy changed, and depended more on rapid engagement: pastoral tribes could make quick incursions and raids, and then disappear just as quickly. The palace and city armies still consisted of an elite chariot corps supported by a militia infantry, which was slow to assemble and not very mobile; its superiority was now seriously in doubt.

Some important technical innovations also seem to have taken place in open sea navigation, probably (though this is not yet fully proven) a combination of keel, rudder and sails, to allow sailing with a cross wind. The contrast often drawn between the Canaanites, who cautiously hugged the Eastern Mediterranean coast between the Nile Delta and Crete, and the bold expansion of Mediterranean trade opened up by the 'pre-colonial' Phoenicians and 'Homeric' Greeks, is overdrawn. There is, though, a parallel here between the opening of the desert through the use of camels and the opening of the sea through new sailing techniques, developments occurring more or less at the same period and achieving similar results.

Technical innovations in agriculture and agricultural devices also brought important consequences. The cultivation of upland zones (especially in the highlands of central Palestine), which had been used during the Bronze Age only as forest reserves and as summer pastures, led to deforestation and terracing of the slopes. Deforestation, using fire rather than iron, is explicitly alluded to in a famous Biblical passage:

> Then Joshua said to the house of Joseph, to Ephraim and Manasseh, 'You are indeed a numerous people, and have great power; you shall not have one lot only, but the hill country shall be yours, for though it is a forest, you shall clear it and possess it to its farthest borders; for you shall drive out the Canaanites, though they have chariots of iron, and though they are strong' (Josh. 17.17-18).

Terracing on the slopes, which prevented the rapid erosion of soil no longer held together by tree roots, was not a complete innovation: some instances are known from the Early Bronze Age. But with the beginning of the Iron Age, this technique becomes common and spreads with the establishment of villages in the highlands. The vocabulary of the Bible includes some reference to terracing: *šadmôt* 'terraces' (Deut. 32.32; 2 Kgs 23.4; Isa. 16.8; etc.) and *śĕdê tĕrûmôt* 'upland fields' (2 Sam. 1.21; see *mĕrômê śādeh* in Judg. 5.18).

Irrigation canals were equally important. During the Bronze Age, canal building had been confined to alluvial plains, beginning with those of Lower Mesopotamia. But with the Iron age new techniques for dry farming are tried out, especially on the floors of *wadis*, which are subject to short sudden floods: the beds were dammed, allowing the water to soak into the soil. These dams also retained the soil itself, preventing floods from washing it away. It also became possible to dig deeper wells, and to line cisterns with waterproof plaster. What has been said about terraces also holds for cisterns: we find them in urban environments already in the Middle to Late Bronze Age, but their wider use coincides with the requirements of the Iron Age. In the case of wells, however, we have several Egyptian and Assyrian texts celebrating the digging of particularly deep shafts, all concentrated around the Late Bronze–Iron Age I transition.

Through the use of these techniques, whether new or already available, all of the semi-arid zones like the Negev and the plateaux of southern Transjordan were converted to agriculture. Elsewhere, mainly in distant Yemen, in the same period but on a larger scale, the damming of broad *wadis* that descended from the highlands to peter out in the desert sand represents a major task of hydraulic engineering, involving huge dams, locks and canals.

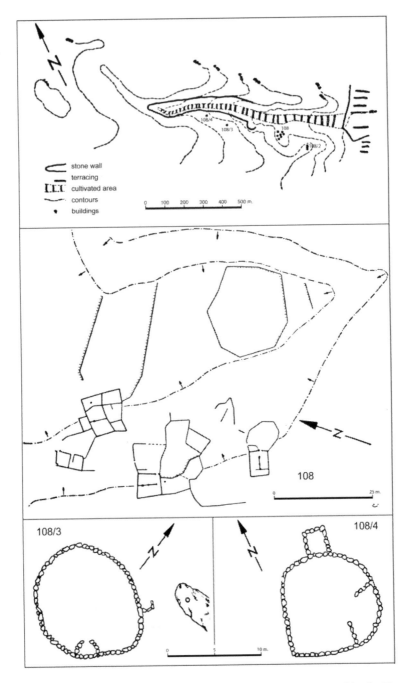

Figure 11. *Wadi dam system used for dry farming in Ramat Matred in the Negev:*
(a) general layout of the area (b) agro-pastoral settlement (c) sheepfolds

Again, a new irrigation technique was applied in the highland zones, one unknown during the Bronze Age. Subterranean canals, provided with air-shafts, began to be dug only in the early Iron Age. This technique was later described in Assyrian texts as being practised in Armenia and Assyria itself, and spreading (though the chronology is still debated) to the whole Iranian highlands (where such canals are called *qanat*) and later still to the Sahara (where their name is *foggara*). Their main advantages were less evaporation and regular gradients, allowing water to flow even across watersheds to valleys or to wider basins that were more suitable for agriculture. In Palestine, where surface water is scarce, we find no trace of such canals. But a similar technology was used to access springs or deep ground water lying under large urban settlements; these 'water systems' characterize Palestine cities of the late Iron Age.

This set of innovations did not develop immediately, nor simultaneously: some techniques spread gradually (iron, alphabet), others were revived (terraces, cisterns), others arrived later (highland water systems), as is normal in the introduction of technical and social change. As a whole, though, these mark the difference between the Iron Age and the Bronze Age and must be recognized if we are to understand the different territorial structure and material culture that arose.

7. *Widened Horizons*

Some of the technical innovations just described produced what we have called a 'democratizing' effect, consistent with the general tendency of the period to empower villages and tribes against the overwhelming supremacy of the palace. But other innovations, too, leading to a wider and more homogeneous use of land, followed the same lines.

We have already mentioned (and we will see in detail in §3.1) how in Palestine a new pattern of territorial occupation was developing: it extended to the highlands and semi-arid steppes, unlike Late Bronze settlement, which had been concentred in the areas easily usable for agriculture. In a single century, deforestation and terracing facilitated the occupation of mountain zones, while techniques of dry-farming, wells and oases, camels and dromedaries, opened up the wide spaces of the steppe and desert. The size of settlements also changed: towns became smaller, but villages became bigger and were fortified. The land was occupied in a more uniform way and the area of settlement became much wider.

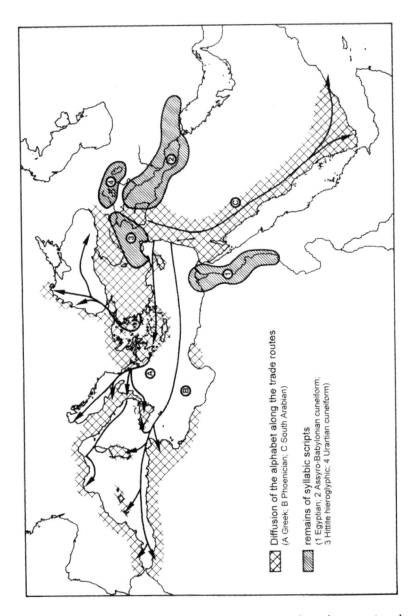

Figure 12. *Trade routes and alphabets during Iron Age I–II*

Diffusion of the alphabet along the trade routes
(A Greek; B Phoenician; C South Arabian)

remains of syllabic scripts
(1 Egyptian; 2 Assyro-Babylonian cuneiform;
3 Hittite hieroglyphic; 4 Urartian cuneiform)

This phenomenon is not limited to Palestine, but characterizes larger areas of the Near East, and it brought about a general widening of horizons. The position of Palestine also changed in this new context. Mediterranean commerce became more intense and far-reaching, opening for the Phoenicians a large horizon for their 'pre-colonial' commerce; important caravan routes along the western belt of the Arabian peninsula established a direct connection between Transjordan and Yemen. After having been marginal for a long time, Palestine apparently now came to be at the centre of a wide network of routes and long distance commerce, with direct access to distant resources.

However, on examining the situation more closely, it becomes clear that this changing of horizons also had a negative effect. During the Late Bronze Age coastal navigation had to utilize Palestinian harbours (even though they were not particularly suitable) while caravans had to cross Cisjordan, the only available corridor between Egypt and Syria. In the Iron Age, while the Palestinian seaboard played some part in the development of sea commerce, and Transjordan of caravan routes, the central highlands (the core of proto-Israelite origins) were cut off from both areas of expansion, constituting a sort of 'hollow centre', avoided by rich caravans that preferred more convenient routes. The involvement of Palestine in the widened horizon was definitely less direct than that of Phoenicia and the states of the Syrian or Jordan desert fringes. The marginality of Palestine changed in character, but essentially it persisted.

Chapter 3

THE NEW SOCIETY
(c. 1150–1050)

1. *Distribution of Settlements*

The most significant phenomenon in terms of settlement, and the most characteristic of the 'new society', is the occupation of the highlands by an agro-pastoral population that built small hilltop villages. Recent intensive surveys by Israeli archaeologists have made possible a reliable, regionally diversified picture of this settlement by identifying more than 250 sites from Iron Age I. The population that occupied these villages was probably a mix of existing tribal elements reinforced demographically and socio-economically by people of an agricultural origin, fleeing the control of the palace, as described in §§1.10 and 2.5. These can be defined 'proto-Israelite'. Strictly speaking, the term 'Israelite' should be reserved for members of the kingdom of Israel, but the name 'Israel' already appears in a text from the end of the thirteenth century (a stele of Merenptah, §1.9), referring precisely to this new ethnic complex already in process of formation and identifiable as such.

The new village society is not entirely homogeneous nor did it emerge all at once. In the areas already partially occupied in the twelfth century (Manasseh and Lower Galilee) we find a greater continuity with the Late Bronze Age 'Canaanite' culture, whereas occupation was radically different in zones where living conditions were harder and therefore had been without permanent settlement for several centuries (Ephraim and Benjamin, Upper Galilee and, later, the Negev). We can also distinguish between denser settlement in areas with higher rainfall (the central highlands and Galilee) and more scattered settlement in drier areas (Judah and, even more, the Negev). In the central highlands settlement is more rapid; in Judah, the Negev and Lower Galilee it occurs later. But as a whole it was substantially one and the same transformation that led to a complete settlement of the highlands, reversing the Late Bronze Age situation. A recent count of the identified sites shows for the central highlands a ninefold increase, from 29 sites in the Late Bronze Age to 254 in Iron Age I. The demographic ratio between the highlands (which saw a rapid increase) and the coastal areas (a slow decrease) changed dramatically: during the Bronze Age it was more or less 1:2, while it becomes 1:1 during the Iron Age. By contrast, the percentage of the so called 'urban' population, living in centres bigger than 5 hectares, was about half of the total during the Bronze Age, and decreased to a third during the Iron Age.

Something similar took place in Northern Transjordan: between the Jabbok and the Yarmuk (a territory later to become Israelite, Gilead) we find many Iron Age I sites, five times more than in the Late Bronze Age. Further south, in Ammon, surveys have not been systematic enough to provide a reliable estimate, but there are many Iron Age sites. In Transjordan as a whole, there is an increase in the number of sites from 32 in the Late Bronze Age to 218 in Iron Age I (an almost sevenfold increase).

Alongside the picture given by surface surveys, more precise information comes from excavated sites: Tell el-Ful and Tell en-Nasbeh in Benjamin territory; Ai and Khirbet Raddana in Ephraim; 'Izbet Sartah, Bet-Sur and Tell Beit Mirsim in Judah; Hazor in Galilee; Tel Masos and Beer-sheba in the Negev. Many sites show one occupational phase only, or are new settlements; in the few cases where they emerge on 'Canaanite' sites (e.g. Hazor), agro-pastoral villages replace urban sites. We can very roughly distinguish between two typologically different phases of the settlement process, which correspond to the stratigraphic sequences revealed in excavation. In the first scenario (twelfth–eleventh century) semi-arid areas are characterized by pastoral camps of seasonal transhumance (Tel Masos III B, with bases of huts and tents; Beer-sheba IX, with partly sunken, circular houses), and in the highlands by 'elliptical' sites where long narrow dwellings are arranged in a circle around an open space, mirroring the pattern of a nomad camp ('Izbet Sartah III, Tel Esdar, and many other sites in the Negev). A second scenario (eleventh–ninth century) contains settlements that are usually oval in shape, but soundly built, with 'pillar-type' houses (described in the next section) built around a central space.

This is a case of colonization 'from below', that is, not arising from state policy, but carried out by little family groups or clans, mostly of pastoral origin. At first (during the 'first generation') the dwellings are flimsy – tents or huts – traceable only by modern archaeological techniques; later (during the 'second and third generation') more permanent, stronger and sustained, dwellings that in their structure and plan still reflect extra-urban origins and the mobility typical of transhumant populations.

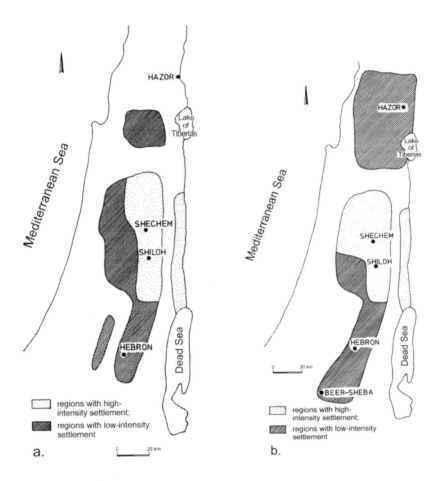

Figure 13. *Areas of 'proto-Israelite' villages: (a) first phase (twelfth century); (b) second phase (end of eleventh century)*

2. Forms of Settlement

The layout of the dwellings in a circle, like tents in nomad camps, tends to create a continuous defensive line (Ai, Be'er-sheba' VII, Tel Masos II, 'Izbet Sartah II-I). It has been noted how the sequence of long rooms in the first phase, or of the back rooms in the 'pillar-houses' in the second phase, created a sort of casemate wall (though used for living as well as defence). Exceptionally (as in Khirbet Dawara) there is a proper city wall, but only in the tenth century. The oval shape of the village is often determined by its position on the top of a hill, but where this is not the case, by cultural habits and by its defensive function, or at least by the desire to enclose an inner space reserved for family activities. The oval plan remains typical even during Iron Age II, when the town has walls and the houses are built in concentric circles, occupying the central space, with a street that separates the central block from that next to the wall.

The typical living unit (though naturally not in every case) of the mature phase of the new settlement is the so-called 'pillar house', with four rooms: one running across the whole width at the rear, probably with an upper floor for bedrooms, and three parallel rooms lengthwise, separated by two sets of pillars and used as working areas (and maybe as a stable). The central room was unroofed. In some cases there are only three rooms, with a single side-room. The typical house occupied 40-80 m^2 and therefore could accommodate five to seven people, that is a typical nuclear family (father, mother, two or three unmarried sons, one or two servants). It has been suggested that even the pillar house derives from the nomadic tent (the back room) with a working space in front.

The village, usually on a hill, unwalled but in a ring formation, corresponds socially to the 'clan' (in genealogical lists clan names are in fact village names). Their size is about half a hectare, one hectare at most, and contained 100-150 people. Archaeologically it is hard to trace the borders between different tribes, but the border separating this tribal world from Canaanite society is marked by the absence of pig bones in the highland villages (showing that the pig was not reared for food) in contrast to their presence in 'Canaanite' centres in the plan – a distinct 'ethnic' marker.

These settlements, established in hilly or mountainous zones rendered cultivable by terracing, reflect a segmented society and an agro-pastoral economy based on cereals and sheep and goats. They had reserves of water supplied by plastered cisterns or nearby springs; grain was stored in pit silos covered with stones, while olives and grapes, or oil and wine, were kept in distinctive storage jars with a raised rim, known as 'collared rim jars'. Olives and vines had been cultivated in Palestine since the Early Bronze Age (if not since Late Chalcolithic), but olives became subject to 'industrial' production only in Iron Age II (the archaeological evidence is obviously the oil-press), while wine production was always kept within the limits of religious acceptability. There is some slight evidence of specialized activities (copper slag) and of writing (some 'proto-Canaanite' signs on a jar handle in Khirbet Raddana, and several arrowheads with personal names from el-Khadr, near Jerusalem); the abecediary of 'Izbet Sartah is from a coastal area, but belongs within the same cultural horizon.

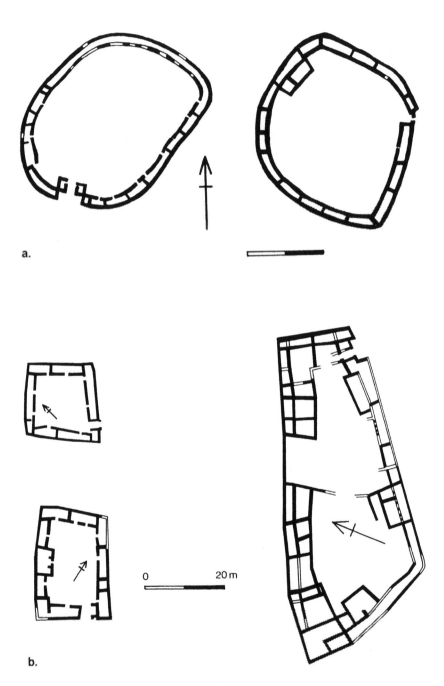

Figure 14. *'Proto-Israelite' villages in the Negev: (a) farmyard villages (b) fortified villages*

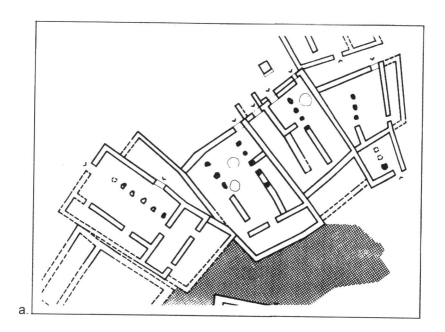

Figure 15. *The structure of living quarters: pillared houses at (a) Tel Masos (b) Tell Beit Mirsim*

Cultic installations in the villages are, of course, modest compared with the contemporary temples of 'Canaanite' cities (such as Temple 1 in She-chem), and quite rare. The complex on the slopes of Mt Ebal near Shechem has been interpreted as an open-air cultic area, but this interpretation is influenced by biblical data on the temple of El-Berith and is debatable; a similar case is the so-called 'bull site' near Dothan (an open enclosure, with a shrine, *maṣṣēbôt* and bull statue). Only one shrine (no more than a 4 m × 5 m room) lies in a village area, in Hazor stratum XI.

Bearing in mind the abandonment of the extra-urban pastoral sanctuaries in Deir 'Alla and 'Amman, which flourished at the end of the thirteenth century, the social ferment at the base of the 'new society' does not seem to exhibit the religious flavour that later historiography attributes to it and which is already foreshadowed in the phase of armed opposition to Canaanite cities – unless it was a religious movement opposed to any large-scale cultic structure.

3. *The Ethnogenesis of the 'Proto-Israelites'*

Archaeology has now provided the settlement picture just described; but we should compare that with the sociopolitical context, as deduced from textual sources, so as to highlight correspondences (or possible divergences) and thus test the reliability and historical value of our data. Undertaken in a rather hasty and prejudicial manner, this method was typical of the obsolete 'biblical archaeology', but done objectively and carefully, investigating ethnic names and attributing them to archaeological horizons that have been previously defined on intrinsic grounds is a normal procedure for any 'proto-historical' context (i.e. with textual data coming from external and/or later sources). The processes of ethnogenesis (the origin of peoples) are always complex and therefore difficult to trace back: we cannot determine simply whether a people existed or not, whether its members were conscious of their identity, whether the forms of material culture were exclusive or not. We need to understand historically the various factors and processes that lead to the emergence of an ethnic group and determine its coordinates in time and space and its characteristics. A too hasty identification is as unacceptable as a too hasty denial.

In defining the horizon of Iron Age I highland villages as 'proto-Israelite', we mean to indicate an ongoing process, not one fully crystallized in a full ethnic consciousness, providing a basis for what will happen later, as reflected in the written sources – and here we mean contemporary sources for the 'historical' kingdoms of Israel and Judah in Iron Age II, rather than traditional sources about the origins, which have undergone considerable ideological revision.

Concerning the new society of Iron Age I villages, our written sources (the books of Joshua and Judges) come from a historiographical tradition of many centuries later, and thus their reliability is highly dubious (see Chapters 14 and 15). In particular, the lists or descriptions of the 'Twelve Tribes of Israel' are scattered over a chronological range from the eighth century (the 'Blessings of Jacob', Genesis 49 and 'Blessings of Moses', Deuteronomy 33) to the fourth century for the clearly post-exilic 'censuses' of Numbers 2 and 26. Given this state of affairs, scholars have taken diametrically opposing positions. Some use the Bible as a historical document, seemingly without questioning its reliability, and suggest that the 'period of the judges' and the 'twelve tribe league' were without any doubt historical. Others, facing the enormity of the problems posed by textual tradition and late revisions, prefer to renounce the use of such data and effectively write off the Early Iron Age as a 'prehistoric' period.

Nevertheless, the distortions and even inventions we find in texts with such a long historiographical tradition have motives more consistent with certain elements of tradition than others (i.e. less relevant to the redactors' own problems). Indeed, the typology of distortion and invention is sometimes revealing: a story can be invented using literary or fairy-tale characters and motives (we have several clear examples), while it is difficult to make up a social setting that never existed. We can retroject laws that deal with controversial political decisions or property rights by attributing them to authoritative characters of past history or of myth (again, examples are available), but there is no reason to invent these where neutral or politically irrelevant matters are concerned. Finally, since editorial modification of older texts is difficult and imperfect, it always leaves 'fingerprints'. Thus, through a critical analysis of later legal and historiographical material, we can manage to salvage some elements of a more ancient historical context. Let us consider the various problems of tribal structure, the dislocation of single tribes, the existence of a pan-tribal unit and customary norms.

First of all, it is usually believed that in the Early Iron Age 'tribes' existed and that society was organized in units of decreasing size: 'tribe' (*šēbet/ maṭṭeh*), 'clan' or 'lineage' (*mišpāḥāh*), 'large family' (*bêt 'āb*), 'nuclear family' (*geber*). We have seen how the nuclear family, the basic unit of production, corresponds archaeologically to the house (whether pillared house or another kind), and that the clan, the residence unit, corresponds to the village (*pĕrāzôt, ḥăṣērôt* 'precincts', indicating the circular formation). The large family is archeologically traceable only when isolated (as at

Khirbet Raddana), otherwise it is concealed within the village, a structure for controlling the inheritance of a patrimony (*nāḥălāh*), a plot of agricultural land in the open country. It has already been seen how difficult (or impossible) it is to define the territory of single tribes, without information from written texts as a guide.

Such information, especially if transmitted in form of 'founding' genealogies, can of course be easily manipulated: but alterations will tend to affect individual cases rather than the overall structure. A whole tribe may be added or subtracted, a fake affiliation inserted to annex a clan to a tribe or a house to a clan. It is well known that genealogies are flexible and creative in this regard. But the invention of a whole social structure is much more difficult and requires an infinite number of 'corrections' throughout the history of the text. It has been observed that the tribal terminology is quite late (exilic and post-exilic), at least in the case of the terms *šēbet* and *maṭṭeh*. Personally, I think that there was no reason to falsify the detailed structure from 'clan'/village down to the household; that the 'tribe' level was built up gradually over time, often in connection with political events (partly identifiable), and finally that the systematization of the tribes and the idea of a large tribal federation depends heavily on the grand nomadic model that developed especially in the sixth century (see §12.7).

4. *The Dislocation of 'Tribes'*

Our second problem consists in the geographical dislocation of the tribes. Since we know (though from later biblical texts) the location of the main Israelite (and non-Israelite) tribes, it is reasonable to try and connect those names with the main concentrations of new Iron Age I villages. We will at least acquire some useful labels, perhaps not without some degree of historical plausibility.

A tribe of Judah clearly existed (or, better, was formed) in the area between Jerusalem and Hebron (Joshua 15). This tribe formed the basis for the kingdom of David in the mid-tenth century (see §4.4), so it is quite reasonable to think that it existed a century earlier. But the opposite process is also possible: the tribe of Judah might have achieved full self-conscious identity only after the foundation of David's kingdom. The other southern tribes of the biblical list (Simeon and Levi) are, by contrast, very suspect: the first because of its early disappearance (in Josh. 19.9 its territory corresponds to part of Judah's); the second because of its non-territorial character and its very late development (see §17.6). Other tribal groups demoted to clans – in particular Calebites (Josh. 14.6-15, 1.13-20;

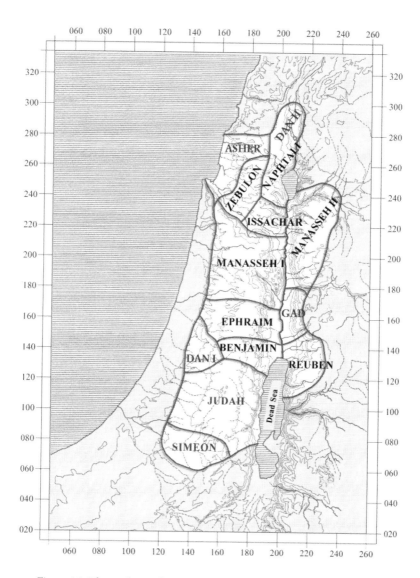

Figure 16. *The traditional arrangement of the 'twelve tribes'*

see also the story of Othniel in Judg. 3.7-11) and Kenites (see Judg. 1.1-21 on the entire complex), complicate the picture of the occupation of Hebron and Beer-sheba area in relation to the Amalekites who apparently occupied it up to the time of Saul and David, and suggest several displacements at different times.

The existence of Benjamin to the immediate north of Jerusalem (Joshua 18) should be considered ancient, as well as that of Ephraim and Manasseh in the central highlands (Joshua 16–17), areas of early and dense settlement. In these cases too, self-identification may be linked with the founding of the kingdom of Saul in the mid-tenth century. The question also arises, whether the territorial boundaries of Saul's kingdom were based on those of existing tribes or, on the contrary, its extent determined the tribal territories themselves. The Benjamin-Ephraim pairing (required by the meaning of Benjaminites as 'southerners') and Ephraim-Manasseh (found in genealogies on the basis of common descent from Joseph) can also be attributed to historical events that can be partly reconstructed (see §§4.4-5, 5.1).

The dislocation of the typically pastoral tribes of Gad/Gilead, Reuben and half of Manasseh to east of the Jordan (Joshua 13) is connected to historical events, again partly amenable to reconstruction – beginning in the time of Saul and related to the struggle for territory against the Arameans and Ammonites: if this not an 'original' dislocation ('original' is in fact an ambiguous concept), it is nevertheless authentic, that is, it is not a late falsification.

Finally, at least the two main Galilee tribes must have originally settled in the area: Zebulon (Josh. 19.10-16) corresponds to the villages of Upper Galilee, and Naphtali (Josh. 19.32-39) to those of Lower Galilee beside the upper Jordan valley. The case of Issachar (Josh. 19.17-23) is different; judging from its name (from *'iš-śākār* 'hired man'; see *'corvée* servant' in Gen. 49.15) its members migrate, as seasonal agricultural labourers, to the (royal) domain of the Jezreel plain. The case of Dan is different again: according to the tradition, the tribe migrated to the north (Judges 18) only after first settling in the Shephelah (Josh. 19.40-48) and, together with Asher, gravitated towards the Phoenician coastal cities between Acco and Tyre (Josh. 19.14-31, see also Judg. 5.17). It is not impossible that Dan's migration to the north is a later invention, aiming to justify claims over the Shephelah in the time of Josiah or after the exile. In fact, the territory of Dan remained almost permanently under non-Israelite control: at first Phoenician, then Aramaic and finally Assyrian.

The picture is therefore variegated. It is no coincidence that the locations of the main tribes correspond quite well to the distribution of 'proto-Israelite' villages and this provides a sort of positive check, confirming the information. Other tribes, later gathered in the 'canonical' list, are nevertheless clearly functional, without any genuine genealogical affiliation, such as Levi (but also Issachar, or the Kenites). Others are of very doubtful origin and relevance (Dan) or have disappeared so early that their very existence is questionable (Simeon).

5. Intertribal Solidarity

Let us now consider the third question, namely the existence of a 'league' of twelve tribes, arriving in the land as a socio-political unit (the conquest theory, based on the book of Joshua), or at least active as formal organization in a later period (the tribal league theory, based on the book of Judges). Since they are clearly later constructions, we will discuss them below, in connection with the political motives that gave rise to them. It is highly improbable that in the twelfth century the groups of people who founded new villages already had a common ethnic self-perception (i.e. that they were properly 'Israelites'). The forms of material culture differed ('collared rim' jars in central highlands, but a different type in Galilee; villages on hilltops in the highlands, but pastoral camps in the Negev, and so on). Moreover, the first mention of the name 'Israel' is apparently much more circumscribed than it is in later use, and perhaps indicated only the complex of tribes settled in the central highlands (Manasseh, Ephraim and Benjamin). It is nevertheless true that these ethnic groups developed on a common basis, from an ecological and cultural point of view: in this sense, even if it cannot be considered a sign of an implausible ethnic consciousness, the material culture of the new villages is still a fairly strong starting point for later developments towards a collective ethnic self-identity. As for common military action, this is still possible even if we reject the idea of a formal league, since the earliest episodes, such as that related in the *Song of Deborah* (Judges 5), already show the tribes firmly settled in their own territories not before the end of the eleventh century. They are therefore contemporary with, or slightly earlier than, other unifying processes, such as what occurred at Shechem, or the kingdom of Saul and the kingdom of David (we will discuss these below).

It is more difficult to imagine an invention of the basic elements of family rights, because such an invention would have been much more complicated, as well as without a motive. Nuptial procedures and strategies, and the protection of widows and orphans within the clan of the 'larger family' are customs geared to the needs of a rural society with a kinship structure: preserving the unity of the family patrimony and ensuring its inheritance, guaranteeing the survival of the whole group over generations and providing a basic standard of living for all its members.

We may assume that some elements, though described in later books or passages, reflect very ancient traditions: the 'levirate' custom obliging the brother of a man who dies without sons to marry his widow in order to secure a line of descent in the name of the deceased (Deut. 25.5-10; the story of Judah and Tamar in Genesis 38 and the story of the book of Ruth); or laws about the redemption (*gĕ'ullāh*) of family properties sold in cases of necessity or enslaved relatives (Lev. 25.47-49; the one exercising the right/duty of redemption is the *gô'ēl*). Internal cohesion is also the outcome of excluding 'outsiders', defined at different hierarchical levels: the non-acceptability of different tribal groups in marriage or commerce; the customs of revenge, blood price and tribal feuding, are all elements that may have been distorted in specific cases (see the story of Dinah in Shechem, Genesis 34), but can be accepted overall as authentic descriptions of customs that persistent over a long time.

The balance between isolation and collaboration is typical of this 'Chinese box'-like tribal society. On the one hand is the total exclusion of groups felt as alien for their different economic organization, language, customs, religious beliefs, with whom competition for territory is unavoidable. On the other hand is the total economic self-sufficiency of the family and, through intermarriage, the clan. Between these extreme opposites, the tribe and intertribal relationships provide an ambiguous intermediate ground that remains substantially 'external' in normal daily life, but may become 'internal' in situations of movement and crisis, such as a famine, requiring access to new pastures, or a war demanding joint action.

The normal management of the 'intermediate' area relies on hospitality procedures and the (mainly judicial) role of the 'elders' (*zĕqēnîm*, see Judg. 8.14; Deut. 19.11-12, 21.1-8 and 18-21, 22.16-19, 25.8; 1 Sam. 30.26-31; etc.). Cases of extreme danger may call for a 'charismatic' leader, but in the hope that at the end of the crisis he will be ready to 'return to the ranks' (like Gideon, in exemplary fashion: Judg. 8.22-27), without using the newly-acquired prestige to permanently change the internal balance of a segmentary society.

6. *Judicial Norms*

According to Biblical narrative, the Twelve Tribes took possession of the 'promised land' after acquiring a 'law' transmitted by Yahweh to Moses on Mt Sinai. We will see later (§18.3) how the complex of legislative texts ascribed to Moses is not only chronologically stratified, but substantially a late creation, related to Deuteronomic or post-exilic priestly ideology. But we should take a different view of the very concise formulation of law directly connected to the story of Moses and the theophany on Sinai. This 'law' (*tôrāh*, Deut. 4.44; comprising *'ēdôt* 'admonitions', *ḥuqqîm* 'duties', *mišpaṭîm* 'sentences', 4.45), is imagined as being inscribed on two tablets and forming, in fact, a synthetic list of 'ten commandments', that are given in two versions (Deut. 5.6-21; Exod. 20.1-17), with slight but significant differences. They are framed in a clearly Deuteronomistic style, with expressions and concepts typical of that school (such as love of God and the observance of commandments). But the nucleus of the ten commandments has a basically moral inspiration, not specifically judicial and certainly not cultic – as is most of the later legislation. The content is hard to locate historically, to connect to specific cultural elements (in either an ethnic or chronological sense) and therefore to date. We know these precepts by heart from childhood, so they seem to us obvious and universal: you shall not kill, you shall not steal, you shall not bear false witness, and so on. How could we 'date' the Decalogue? It appears impossible. We can only say that the first commandment, on the 'monotheistic' exclusivity of the cult of Yahweh, could not be written before Josiah (see §8.5), and this ingredient, in the view of current scholarship, lowers the date of the whole set.

But the fifth (or fourth in the Roman tradition) commandment could have existed in much more ancient times, even as early as the second millennium, and thus during the pre-monarchic 'tribal' age: this early date could actually be extended to the whole Decalogue, leaving aside only the first, monotheistic precept. 'Honour your father and your mother', looks again like a timeless moral imperative. But the text goes on to make a connection between respect for parents and possession of the land:

> Honour your father and your mother, so that your days may be long in the land that Yahweh your God is giving you (Exod. 20.12).

Now, in the Late Bronze Age (fifteenth–thirteenth centuries), 'honour your father and mother' becomes a principle of inheritance (usually of lands and houses). In earlier times heirs were appointed in a quite rigid way, at birth, starting with the privileged role of the firstborn, and so on according to a family 'hierarchy' determined by birth and not behaviour. During the Late Bronze Age the principle 'there is no firstborn and no younger brother' is introduced: the parents' inheritance now goes to the one who 'has honoured them'. Note that in Syrian texts the word used is usually 'honour' (*kabādu*), while in Mesopotamia it is more commonly 'fear' (*palāḫu*), and these different words are both reflected in biblical texts:

while both versions of the Decalogue, evidently originating in a Palestinian context, use 'honour' (*kābēd*), a reference in the Priestly legislation (Lev. 19.3), probably under Babylonian influence, has 'fear' (*yārē'*). Both verbs allude to the duty of sons to respect their parents and to support and maintain them in old age. Only in this way they will earn their inheritance:

> In the presence of Sin-Abu and the elders of the city of Emar, Arnabu (a woman) said: Sin-rabu and Ili-akhi, my two sons, must fear me. If they will do so, after that I will have gone to my fate, they will share between them my house and all my properties. There is no firstborn and no younger (*Emar*, VI, no. 93).

In fact the verb 'maintain' (*wabālu*, Gtn form) is also attested, which clarifies more prosaically the nature of the required 'honour'. Indeed, in the case of adoption especially, the texts insist on this: the person (usually an adult) is adopted precisely for the purpose of supporting aged parents, which he does in anticipation of receiving a part of the patrimony. The problem is particularly acute in the case of widows, who may be mistreated or cut out of the family patrimony by the adult sons. Not only is the duty of 'honouring' them stressed, but they also receive the epithet of 'father-mother', to indicate that the function of both parents is now concentrated in one person:

> Starting from today, Ukal-Dagan made his sons sit down and decided the destiny of his house and of his sons. He said: I have three sons, Ir'ip-Dagan is the oldest, Rashap-Ili is the second daughter and Abi-kapi is the youngest. The big house is for Ir'ip-Dagan; the small house is for Rashap-Ili; and the ruined house is for Abi-kapi. But Ir'ip-Dagan and Rashap-Ili must repair the ruined house. All of them must maintain Arnabu (my wife) as their own father and mother. Any of my sons who does not maintain his own father-mother will leave his clothes on the chair and go (naked) wherever he likes (*Emar*, VI, no. 181).

In judicial texts of Late Bronze Age, the fifth/fourth commandment would read something like: 'honour your father-mother, if you want to inherit the land'.

Our analysis of this commandment shows that the Decalogue contains material from very ancient times (middle of the second millennium) and could have been already compiled in the 'Mosaic' age, then transmitted and inserted – with minor variations in the more banal commandments – into the main legislative corpora of Israel. It has also been suggested that the transmission of the law was effected in the pre-exilic period by regular public reading at festivals. It should also be noted that the basically apodictic formulation of the Decalogue strongly contrasts with the more common casuistic formulation of most ancient Near Eastern laws. The latter derives from judicial procedures, from the resolution of a dispute: if someone commits a certain offence, the punishment, or the compensation, will be such-and-such. The apodictic form is typical of the moral or customary realm, of the stage of moral principle which precedes judicial process (or which is independent of it). This is another reason to consider the Decalogue as potentially very ancient, and not related to a judicial system that would imply precise historical connections.

7. Social Demands

Among the various legislative texts, all probably or certainly late, the only one that might preserve information relating to pre-monarchic Israelite society is the so-called 'Covenant Code' (Exod. 21.1–23.19). Obviously this text is also attributed to Moses, and even put immediately after the Decalogue as a sort of direct development of it. Source criticism regards this as an 'Elohistic' redaction (i.e. northern, eighth century), with some obvious Deuteronomistic reworking. Its origin in the northern kingdom in the pre-exilic period is also indicated by the presence of multiple altars, later banned in Josiah's reform and censured by the Deuteronomistic movement, and is confirmed by the allusion in Amos 2.8 to the custom of returning borrowed clothes before sunset (Exod. 22.25-26). The civil and penal norms described in the Covenant Code are well suited to a village society and an agro-pastoral economy lacking any form of superior authority (king, palace or temple). The cult is here conducted at an individual level and in 'any place', with an earthen altar and a prohibition against using statues made of precious metals.

Some of the norms expressed here have parallels in Mesopotamian law codes of the second millennium, with correspondences so specific that coincidence can be excluded. An example is the case (Exod. 21.28-32) of the bull that gores another bull or a free man or a slave, which is resolved by killing the 'murderer', but with responsibility laid on the owner of the bull only if the animal had already been denounced as dangerous. Such a case is described in the laws of Eshnunna and in the code of Hammurabi. Even if it is true that socio-judicial norms are quite stable over a long period, the concentration of parallels between Mesopotamian laws of the second millennium and the 'Covenant Code' (much more than with later biblical legal texts) is nevertheless noteworthy. The Code emerges as a collection of laws very precisely related to the judicial tradition of the

Bronze Age and may well be attributed to the earliest stages of emerging Israelite society.

But there is an even more relevant topic from the socioeconomic point of view. It is the norm prescribing that a 'Hebrew slave' is to be let free in the seventh year:

> When you buy a male Hebrew slave, he shall serve six years, but in the seventh he shall go out a free person, without debt. If he comes in single, he shall go out single; if he comes in married, then his wife shall go out with him. If his master gives him a wife and she bears him sons or daughters, the wife and her children shall be her master's and he shall go out alone. But if the slave declares, 'I love my master, my wife, and my children; I will not go out a free person,' then his master shall bring him before God. He shall be brought to the door or the doorpost; and his master shall pierce his ear with an awl; and he shall serve him for life (Exod. 21.2-6).

In this passage, the word 'Hebrew' does not have the ethnic meaning it assumes later, but it is used in the same sense as *ḫabiru* in Late Bronze Age texts: a free man who, because of economic difficulties (unpayable debts) is forced to become a slave in order to survive. In this case recognition of the original status of the person, and therefore of the fact that his condition of slave is temporary, is not lost. During the Middle Bronze Age, the release of enslaved debtors was decided by royal edict, usually on the occasion of the accession of a new king, as a sort of amnesty. In a non-monarchic society, one apparently not even organized as a state, the release conventionally follows a seven-year rhythm.

Some other norms are also related to the issue of debt-slavery. It is established that between members of the same community loans should carry no interest (Exod. 22.24), so that the problem can be avoided from the beginning. But the text then turns specifically to the problems of workers, both slaves and free, and a weekly rest (*šabbāt*) is instituted. Similar concerns are present in other legislative corpora too, including the duty of helping a fugitive slave (Deut. 23.16-17) and a remission (*šĕmiṭṭāh*) of debt every seven years, culminating every 50 years (i.e. after $7 \times 7 = 49$ years) in the great remission of the 'jubilee' (*yôbēl*, Lev. 25.8-32). As with the question of ancient Near Eastern parallels, it is the amount that matters. While in the Deuteronomistic code and later Priestly codes 'social' norms occur relatively infrequently, and scattered among other laws with very different aims and motivation, in the 'Covenant Code' these are the main point of interest. This nucleus of 'social' norms has, formally speaking, a strongly utopian flavour, underlined by the expression 'for six years...but in the seventh year...' reflecting more a 'manifesto' of ideals rather than actual practice. But in content this set of norms is radically opposed at every point to the praxis of Late Bronze society, where loans with interests, permanent enslavement of debtors, capture and restitution of fugitive slaves were entirely normal. Israelite 'social' norms aim to stop these practices, going back to laws in use up to a few centuries earlier, when the freedom of debtors was protected and social tensions were sometimes released by the king through edicts of remission (cancelling debts arising from by loans with interest, liberating of enslaved debtors: see §1.10).

These social polemics are taken up again in the later Deuteronomic and Priestly codes with new ethnic and religious connotations and addressing a new situation (the ethnic fragmentation of the post-exilic age). But in the Covenant Code they are most plausibly explained as an original response to the socioeconomic conditions of the Late Bronze Age. If such principles and such utopian proposals circulated in emerging Israelite society, that is probably due to the presence among that society of a *ḫabiru* element: groups of fugitives, subjected to unmerciful treatment by the socio-political elite of Canaanite towns and forced into exile, into a marginalized existence, who tried to introduce in this new society rules protecting debtors and preserving their freedom.

8. *Urban Continuity and Canaanite-Philistine Symbiosis*

The 'new society' we have so far described occupied the northern (Galilean), central (Manasseh-Ephraim-Benjamin), and southern (Judah) highlands, part of the Transjordanian plateax (Gile'ad) and semi-desert zones in the south (Negev). The fertile and densely urbanized coastal region (from Gaza in the south to the bay of Acco in the north), the hills near the coast (Shephelah), the Jezreel plain (from Megiddo to Beth-Shean) and the central Jordan valley remained beyond, and even later historical tradition substantially agrees in regarding them as 'unconquered' (Josh. 13.2-6 and Judg. 3.1-6 for the coast; Josh. 17.12-13, 17 for the Jezreel plain). In all these areas the socioeconomic and political structure of the Late Bronze Age survived. They form roughly half of the territory of Palestine and also comprise the most densely populated zones, where at least two thirds of the total population lived. The persistence of that culture cannot therefore be considered a marginal state of affairs, rather, it is a primary component of the overall picture.

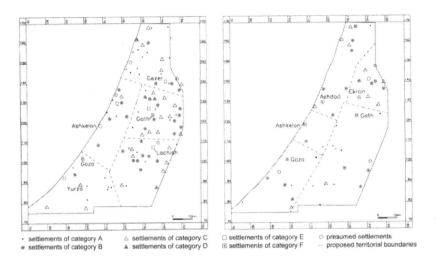

Figure 17. *The Philistine Pentapolis settlement pattern: (a) Late Bronze (fourteenth–thirteenth century); (b) Iron I (twelfth-eleventh century)*

The Philistine pentapolis (described in §2.2) developed strongly during both the twelfth and eleventh centuries and did not suffer the restriction and subordination depicted by later Israelite historiography to make room for the great 'united monarchy' of David. Archaeological evidence is limited to three of the five Philistine cities, all showing a similar development. In Ashdod the first Philistine settlement (stratum XII, between the late thirteenth and the first half of the twelfth century) covers eight hectares, with no city walls and with abundant imports and local imitations of Mycenaean pottery (III C1). In strata XII-XI (second half of the twelfth and eleventh century) the city reaches 40 hectares, has city walls and exhibits the presence of bichrome 'Philistine' pottery. The same occurs in Ekron (Tel Miqne/Khirbet el-Muqanna), a large site of about 20 hectares: stratum VII (first half of twelfth century) is unwalled and contains Mycenaean pottery, while strata VI-IV (from mid-twelfth to the beginning of the tenth century) have walls, public buildings and Philistine pottery. The same is true in Ashkelon (a phase with Mycenaean pottery, III C1, and next a phase with bichrome Philistine pottery), which grew to 60 hectares, with a city wall protecting the semicircular site lying close to the shore. Smaller sites conform to this pattern too: at Tel Qasile (a harbour on the mouth of the Wadi Yarqon, near Tel Aviv), strata XII-X (mid-twelfth to the beginning of the tenth century), is a small centre (2 hectares) but densely populated, with an interesting temple; Gezer XIII-XI, Tel Batash (the Timna of the Samson's stories?) and Bet-Shemesh (III) also show the same compact settlement and typical Philistine pottery. In the second half of the twelfth century, Philistines replaced Egyptians in the garrisons previously maintained by Egypt (§3.9) on the coast (from Deir el-Balah 3 to Tel Mor 4-3) and in the southern Shephelah (Tel Sera' VII, Tel Haror), the western Negev (Tell Jemme JK, Tell el-Far'a south) and reached an advanced position in the Beer-sheba valley (Tel Masos III-II).

Far from being menaced by Israelite tribes, Philistine towns sought, on the contrary, to impose their hegemony on the emerging highland states (see §§4.4-5) and most of all to expand their control of the northern coast to Carmel and then along the Jezreel plain to Beth-Shean and the central Jordan valley (§4.3). Such expansion is indicated, apart from the biblical data, by the diffusion of Philistine pottery. The Philistines, arriving in very determined armed groups, though quite few in number, certainly needed to assimilate to the 'Canaanite' milieu that predominated in the coastal region. As immigrants (and strikingly 'alien', because of their different language and remote origins) they probably represented at first an innovative element, but finally became the major preservers of the fundamental character of local urban culture, preserving a much stronger continuity (compared with the 'new society' of the highlands) with the settlement patterns and cultural traditions of the Late Bronze Age.

To the north of the Philistine zone, the Phoenician centres – probably dependencies of Tyre and Acco – are less well known archaeologically, but probably developed in the same way: a series of destructions at the beginning of the twelfth century, probably related to the invasion of the 'Sea Peoples', was followed by prompt rebuilding, with a culture characterized by continuity with the Late Bronze Age, by some 'Philistine' imports and by the emergence of 'proto-Phoenician' elements. The most significant archaeological sites are in the bay of Acco: Tell Abu Hawam on the coast and Tell Keisan on the inland plain. Phoenician influence, judging from the available archaeological indications, progressively spread along the coast south of Carmel to Dor, and also into the hinterland, to Galilee and the upper Jordan valley (see the story of the scouts in Judg. 18.7, who found it peaceful in Laish/Dan because the area was under Sidonian control). But in the story of Wen-Amun (c. 1050; *ANET*, 25-29) we find a very vivid picture of the lively commercial life of the Phoenician centres (Byblos, Tyre, Sidon), whose harbours were frequented by groups of Zeker, by 'private' commercial companies and by Egyptians, still looking for wood from Lebanon and paying for it with papyrus scrolls.

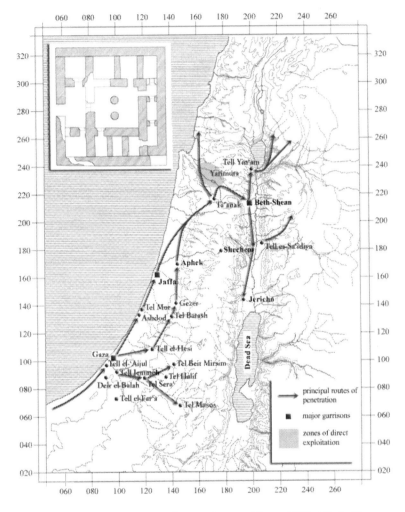

Figure 18. *The 'Egyptian' residencies. Inset: residency 1500 at Beth-Shean*

9. The Permanence of Egyptian Presence

After the invasion of the 'Sea Peoples' in the eighth year of Ramses III, the Egyptian empire in Asia was drastically reduced: all the territory beyond the coastal strip was abandoned and even on the coast, as we have just seen, control was delegated to Philistines, Zeker and Sherdana. The petty kings of the highland regions, subjected to stronger fiscal pressures, could only be bitterly aware (as they had been in the Amarna age, §1.5) of the passivity/silence of the Pharaoh. It is even possible that an echo of this *topos*, in a new tribal key, is found in the core of the story about the battle of Gibeon, the only military episode in the book of Joshua that has any authentic elements within that collection of late aetiological and ideological narratives (see §§13.3-5):

Sun, stand still (*dôm*) at Gibe'on,
and Moon, in the valley of Aijalon (Josh. 10.12).

What the cities feared was what the tribes hoped for: if the 'Sun' (the current epithet of the Pharaoh) 'stops' (*dāmam/dāmāh*, meaning, like *qâlu*, 'be silent/stop/do not intervene'), we can defeat the armies of the Canaanite cities, abandoned to their destiny by their inactive king.

Egypt, though, was not completely out of the game, but as usual showed no interest in defending what was not convenient, concentrating instead on what it considered essential. This meant the coast, and access to the copper of the Arabah and wood of Lebanon. During the entire late Ramesside age, from Ramses III to Ramses VI at least, Egyptians probably considered the 'Canaanite-Philistine' territory of the coast and the Jezreel plain as their own property. After the destruction at the beginning of the twelfth century (caused by the invaders), most of the sites where Egyptian presence is well-attested in the material culture were quickly rebuilt, in clear continuity with the previous phase. This is true for Megiddo VII a (which was also the seat of a local king), with its palace, Egyptian-style ivories (with an inscription of Ramses III) and a statue of Ramses VI. It is also true for the sites of Egyptian garrisons, like Beth-Shean VI, with its temple and the Egyptian residence, papyrus-shape capitals, anthropoid sarcophagi and inscription of Ramses III; like Lachish VI, with the temple and papyrus capital, an inscription of Ramses III and ostraca in hieratic script; like Tell Sera' IX (near Gerar) with Egyptian palace and hieratic ostraca; like Tel Mor 6-5 (on the coast, near Ashdod), with a square Egyptian fortress; and Tell el-Far'a (south), with scarabs of Ramses III, IV and VIII in its necropolis. The same Egyptian presence persists in the mines of Timna (in the southern Arabah, 30 km from the Gulf of Aqabah), exploited by the Egyptians at least until the reign of Ramses V (about 1150) and then abandoned for good; and in the casemate fortress of Ain Ghadian 10 km to the north, one of the few oases in the Arabah, obviously built to control and protect access to the mines of Timna.

In addition we should note that the Philistine settlement on the southern coast (and presumably the Zeker in Dor, too) was endorsed by the Pharaoh, in an attempt to use them as agents to exercise a control that could no longer be maintained through Egyptian 'residencies' and garrisons. In the story of Wen-Amun, mentioned earlier, Egyptian presence is still well established, as seen from the dispute between the Egyptian officer, whose 'theology' regards the supply of cedar-wood as a tribute to Amun, and the pragmatic king of

Figure 19. *The 'way of Horus', as depicted on the temple of Seti I at Karnak. The route connects Sile (B), on the eastern branch of the Nile delta, with Rafia (U), at the*

Byblos, who wants to be paid properly and in advance. The Egyptian interest here is based not only on prestige, but also on a strong commercial presence, which has now replaced the former military deterrence:

> 'Aren't there twenty ships here in my harbor [Byblos], which are in commercial relations with Ne-su-Ba-tneb-Ded? [regent of the Delta]? As to this Sidon, the other place which you have passed, aren't there fifty more ships there which are in commercial relations with Werket-El, and whch are drawn up to his house?' (*ANET*, 27).

We will see later how in the time of Sheshonq (925) Egyptian military activity still takes place mainly on the coastal plain, avoiding if possible the 'tribal' areas of the highlands. Such notional Egyptian sovereignty did not end with the close of the second millennium: throughout the Iron Age, Egypt retained its interest on Palestine and Palestinian states considered Egypt as a place of refuge from recurrent famine, a haven for 'political' refugees, and a potential defender against military threats from the north.

10. *Ethnic States and City-States: Two Cultures*

The difference between the zone of tribal settlement on the highlands and inland tablelands, and the zone of continuous urban settlement on the coast and in the major valleys is matched by a difference between two kinds of co-existing political systems that we can call the 'ethnic' state and the city-state, as we shall now explain. Given the lack of contemporary written sources and the distortion of the information in later historiography, our reconstruction will necessarily remain schematic, aiming to trace lines of development and conventional 'types' – and assuming that their most characteristic profile belongs to the beginning of the Iron Age, immediately after the cultural transition, and that these features gradually disappeared over the course of historical events.

entrance to Canaan, via a series of fortresses (D,E,G,I-J,K,P-Q) and pools (F,H,L,M,N,O,S), of which the names are provided.

City-states are the direct heirs of the 'small kingdoms' of the Late Bronze Age: they maintain the same size, institutional structure and relationship with the rural hinterland. In the Philistine pentapolis, the average size of the coastal city-state (Ashkelon, Gaza and Ashdod) is about 400/800 km² and the inland state (Ekron and Gath) 600/1,200. But the population density, higher in the north and on the coast, partly compensates for differences in size, and total populations may be estimated at about 30,000 people (ranging from 4,000/5,000 in Gath and Gaza to 6,000 in Ashkelon and 8,000 in Ekron and Ashdod). These populations represent a slight decrease from Late Bronze Age levels, but they are differently distributed: fewer villages and more urban centres. A similar density may be calculated for the Jezreel plain.

These states are all centred on a capital city, which stands out clearly from the other settlements: around it are smaller towns and rural villages, but the range of influence of the capital does not require any intermediate administrative district. The capital obviously had a royal palace (to judge from the case of Megiddo: we still await the discovery of the palaces of the Philistine *sĕranîm*), following Late Bronze tradition, and most probably had a formal administration employing literary records – though writing is rarely attested in the twelfth and eleventh centuries – which managed a taxation system that brought goods from the countryside to the city and the palace. Temples were also built here, even if rather modest in size. A tradition of craftsmanship is also preserved, following that of the Late Bronze (the ivories at Megiddo are an example) and specialists in cultic and related activities (singers, diviners) would also be found. Kingship was certainly hereditary, but probably overseen by a collegial body (such as the *mô'ēd* of Byblos in the story of Wen-Amun).

The so-called 'ethnic states', which based their identity on kinship rather than territory, had a quite different structure. Their extent is much larger (though less clearly definable): the nuclei of Judah and Ephraim-Manasseh are about 1,000 km² each and Mo'ab and 'Ammon were similar.

Fully developed, the kingdom of Judah covers about 3,000 km^2 and the kingdom of Israel about 4,500 (not to mention Aram-Damascus). But the population is smaller and less dense than in the city-state. Most important of all, there are almost no cities: these will develop only later on, to meet the needs of a more complex state administration.

In its original, ideal type, the ethnic state requires no urban administrative support, since its internal cohesion is maintained through the family and tribal structure of the society, with its peculiar egalitarian and non-hierarchical configuration. If some kind of leadership exists – as it must – this is more spontaneous (prompted by war) than stable, more charismatic than hereditary, and operates through kinship rather than by administration. In its most typical form, the tribal state does not have a system of taxes to sustain a permanent ruling class. Moreover, while the city-state does not encourage solidarity or a strong sense of community beyond the administrative organization of the territory, the ethnic state develops in its members a strong feeling of belonging, based on the awareness (or rather on the theory) of a common origin, on the cult of a 'national' god, and on the mechanisms of inclusion/exclusion that regulate the norms of hospitality and marriage. The 'sons of Ammon' or the 'sons of Israel' quickly become Ammonites and Israelites, while the subjects of the king of Tyre or Ashdod remain individuals – and ethnic definitions such as 'Phoenicians' and 'Philistines' are imposed from outside and embrace a plurality of different states independent of each other.

In later times, the two types of state tend to converge, and the 'ethnic' type especially is forced to adopt structures more and more similar to those of the city-states with their long history. But the sense of 'ethnicity', of belonging to a human group defined by a common descent, survives and develops 'national' states – a term here confined strictly to the structure of Iron Age Palestine, without any of its modern connotations.

As for the identification of a 'national' god, it has to be emphasized that this is a long process. The adoption of Yahweh as the god of the Israelite tribes from their origin is clearly an interpretation of later historiography. Even the role of Yahweh (with the title of Yahweh Sebaoth) in crucial episodes such as the battle of Taanach (see §4.3) looks suspicious. It is a fact that none of the patriarchs, tribal eponyms, 'Judges' or earliest monarchs has a Yahwistic name. Such names existed (e.g. Joshua, Jonathan the son of Saul), but in a very low percentage, even lower than other names with theophoric elements of Ba'al, El, 'Anat, Zedek, Shalom, and others. We have reason to believe that the cult of Yahweh became a 'national' cult in the kingdom of Judah only between 900–850 (see §6.5) and in the kingdom of Israel between 850–800 (see §5.7).

Chapter 4

THE FORMATIVE PROCESS
(c. 1050–930)

1. *The Palestinian Mosaic in a Widened Horizon*

The processes that formed those political entities we can properly define as 'Israelite' can be explained in the light of several major factors. The collapse of the Late Bronze regional system left the entire Near East autonomous, with freedom of action unrestrained by any external influence. The crisis that befell the central palace institution gave the agro-pastoral component a more relevant political-institutional and socio-economic role (as compared with the recent past). Technological innovation and tribal settlement together brought about a demographic surge and opened up new cognitive, economic and political horizons, in a spatial as well as a social sense.

Israelite tribes were not the only ones to enter this scenario. They were in contact with other groups with whom they felt more or less related, and were economically more or less complementary or competitive in the use of resources. It is interesting to note how independence and complementarity characterize relationships with the old (and new) city-states, but affinity and competition with other peoples of tribal origin and with a similar 'national' political feeling. Conflict with the former could be radical, even violent, and led to serious crises, but in the long run it gave rise to complex and substantially stable solutions. The conflict with the latter tended rather to remain permanent, having roots in common feelings, and in a similar approach to land use.

The phase we call 'formative' lasted almost a century and a half (between the eleventh and tenth centuries). It began with a broad fragmentation into city-states and smaller tribal entities, and resulted in six more or less stable political entities of medium size. It arose from the powerful contrast between the two cultures we have described in the previous chapter: the agro-urban culture in the plains and the agro-pastoral one on the highlands, with the addition of a third, the full pastoralism of the inner deserts, which because of its mobility intervened quite often on the Palestinian scene. At the end of the 'formative process' those different cultures (or at least the first two) are combined into one complex and economically interactive society.

The city-states of the southern coast found a basis for unification in their ethnicity, which generally brought all the Philistines together in dealing with the other emerging ethnic groups on their borders. Their solution to the problem of interaction with different social groups was to penetrate the inland parts of the country: into the Shephelah, the steppes of the Negev and the interior plains of the north.

The highland tribes united into city-tribal units, beginning with the existing 'dimorphic' states of Jerusalem and Shechem and then, more positively, annexing agro-urban areas in the Jezreel plain and on the coast. Such processes of political aggregation, similar to those in Israelite territory, are found in Transjordan, roughly in the same manner and at the same time: other tribal groups, for whatever reasons (origins, religion), decided to distinguish themselves very strongly from 'proto-Israelites', and also from each other. The first such aggregation, chronologically, seems to be the Ammonites in central-eastern Jordan, followed by the Moabites, east of the Dead Sea, and finally by the Edomites, east of the Arabah. To the north, several Aramean tribal groups came together, first forming a little state east of the Sea of Galilee called Geshur (well represented archaeologically at Tel Hadar II and Bet-Saida) and then a larger one, Soba, extending from the Jordan headwaters to the Beq'a in Lebanon. The Aramean impact on the Palestinian scene is rather limited in this 'formative' phase – nothing like what will happen in the Iron Age II (see §5.5).

The dimensions of these state formations are similar to the Israelites in Cisjordan: the kingdoms of Ammon and Moab are as large as those of David or Solomon. They have a similar tribal basis, an aggregation of clans recognizing themselves as related through more or less fictional genealogies: we know (from Genesis 36) that Edomites were divided into twelve clans and claimed descent from Esau by three different wives, while Amalekites were descendents of one of Esau's concubines. Some pre-existing towns, especially near the Jordan valley, are integrated in the same way. Here we see that the processes of ethnic aggregation can be motivated by non-geographical factors: the area of Gilead, between the Arameans and Ammonites, chose to privilege at a symbolic (tribal genealogies) and operative level (trade and marriage, common militia) relations with Cisjordanian tribes rather than with its closer neighbours, with whom it actually had recurring hostilities. Later on, this anomaly allowed the

Cisjordanian states to participate fully in the struggle for control of the important caravan route passing right through Transjordan from south to north. This major route was already open by the mid-tenth century as far north as Khindanu on the Middle Euphrates:

> '(with regard to) the people of of Teima and Sheba, whose own country is far away, (whose) messenger(s) had never come to me, and (who) had never travelled to (meet) me, their caravan came near to the water of the well Martu and the well Khalatum, but passed by and then entered into the city Khindanu. I heard a report about them at midday, (while I was) in the town Kar-Apla-Adad and (immediately) harnessed (the horses of) my chariot. I crossed the river during the night and reached the town Azlanu before noon the next day. I waited in the town Azlanu for three days and on the third day they approached. I captured one hundred of them alive. I captured their two hundred camels, together with their loads – blue-purple wool...wool, iron, pappardilû-stones (alabaster), every kind of merchandise. I took abundant booty from them and brought it into the land of Sukhu' (*RIMB*, II, 300).

This picture, sketched by a ruler of Sukhu around 750 BCE, can be projected a couple of centuries earlier, thanks to the analysis of imports from north and south Arabia mentioned in Assyrian inscriptions that concentrate on the area of Khindanu more or less from 950.

Despite the clear interest of the new ethnic states in the goods transported along the caravan route, that route was firmly under the control of the tribes of camel drivers of the inner desert: Ishmaelites, Midianites and Amalekites. Their centre lay not in Transjordan, but in the Hijaz; and beyond them were other tribes, as far as the extreme south of the Arabian Peninsula. These tribes were considered both closely related and hostile, with whom there was no prospect of agreement or peaceful coexistence. Israelite genealogies reflect a perceived (though remote) genetic affinity with these, especially through stories of separation (Hagar and Ishmael sent into the desert by Abraham, Gen. 21.9-20; the expulsion of Keturah and her sons, including Midian, 'to the east country', Gen. 25.1-6), aiming to fix their homeland well inside the desert, beyond Palestinian agro-pastoral territory proper.

Ishmaelites occupied a large part of the central Hijaz, but especially the Wadi Sirhan, that wide, long depression connecting central Arabia (Dumat al-Jandal) with the hinterland of Amman. The list of Ishmael's 'descendants' (Gen. 25.12-14) includes not only Duma and Teima, whose location is certain, but also two groups closely connected to the Wadi Sirhan: Nebayot and Qedar. Those groups will acquire great power and fame in the

Table 2. Chronology of the 'formative period'

Egypt	Archaeological phases		Historical events	
	coastal plain	highlands	Biblical traditions	External sources
1200 Merenptah 1224–1204			Exodus c. 1260	c. 1210 'Israel' stela of Merenptah
4 brief reigns 1204–1186		c. 1180 invasion of the 'Sea Peoples'	Arrived in Canaan c. 1220	Great Inscription of Ramses III
Ramses III 1184–1153				stelae of Ramses III at Lachish, Megiddo and Beth-Shean
1150 Ramses IV 1153–1146	c. 1150–1100 monochrome ware (Myc. III C)	c. 1200–1050 small villages	c. 1150 Ehud	c. 1150 Egypt abandons Timna
Ramses V 1146–1142				c. 1140 Statue of Ramses VI at Megiddo
Ramses VI 1142–1135				
Ramses VII 1135–1129				
Ramses VIII 1129–1127			c. 1110 Deborah/Barak	c. 1110 Arameans in Syria Tiglath-Pileser in Phoenicia
Ramses IX 1127–1109				
1100 Ramses XI 1099–1069	c. 1100–960 bichrome ware ('Philistine')		c. 1060 Gideon	c. 1060 Ashur-bel-kala in Phoenicia
Smendes 1069–1043				c. 1050 Wen-Amun
1050 Amenemnisu 1043–1039		c. 1050–960 large villages	c. 1040 Abimelech	
Psusennes I 1039–991				
1000 Amenemope 991–984			Saul 1020–1010	
Osorkon 994–978			David 1010–970	
Siamon 978–959				
950 Psusennes II 959–945	c. 960–925 Iron I/Iron II transition		Solomon 970–930	c. 950 Beginning of the south Arabian caravan route as far as Khindanu
Sheshonq 945–924				c. 950 Yehimilk
			925 Invasion of Sheshonq	Stelae of Sheshonq at Megiddo

Neo-Assyrian period, especially the seventh century, while Teima will reach its climax during the reign of Nabonidus, towards the middle of the sixth century. Seen from Palestine, the Ishmaelites are a very large complex of important tribes, located at the crossing point of caravan routes coming from southern Arabia.

Midianites occupied the Northern part of the Hijaz, the al-Hisma plateau, stretching from the Red Sea to the West and the present border of Jordan to the North. The typical 'Midianite' painted pottery is found in large quantities in the major north-Arabian urban sites of Quranya and Teima, and other smaller sites in the same area, but also (as imports) in the Edomite area of Timna and Tell el-Kheleifeh, and in the Negev (Tel Masos) and beyond. This occurrence in stratified contexts ensures a dating in the thirteenth–twelfth century (not ruling out an extension into the early centuries of the first millennium). From their centre in the northern Hijaz, the Midianites turned towards Palestine on frequent occasions, since their main occupation, apart from the caravan trade, consisted in extensive livestock stealing, enabled by their mobility and speed (through the use of dromedaries). In this way, they could easily operate well inside Cisjordan and then escape safely. As the beginning of Gideon's story runs:

> Because of Midian the Israelites provided for themselves hiding places in the mountains, caves and strongholds. For whenever the Israelites put in seed, the Midianites and the Amalekites and the people of the East would come up against them. They would encamp against them and destroy the produce of the land, as far as the neighborhood of Gaza, and leave no sustenance in Israel, and no sheep or ox or donkey. For they and their livestock would come up, and they would even bring their tents, as thick as locusts; neither they nor their camels could be counted; so they wasted the land as they came in (Judg. 6.2-5).

Finally, the Amalekites settled more permanently in southern Cisjordan, occupying the Negev: the first phase of Iron Age I sites in the valley of Beer-sheba (Tel Masos IIIB and Beer-sheba IX) is probably to be assigned to them. They controlled the transverse caravan route from Edom to Gaza, the short and final, but strategically crucial, stage of the 'Mediterranean' branch of the major caravan route from southern Arabia; they also made raids in the central highlands to steal cattle and crops, activity that led to sharp conflicts with Israelite tribes (see §4.4-5).

Information on the Ishmaelites and Midianites is given in biblical texts of quite late redaction, coinciding with their peak in the seventh to sixth centuries – a development documented in both Assyrian and Babylonian texts and from the scanty information obtained from archaeology in Saudi

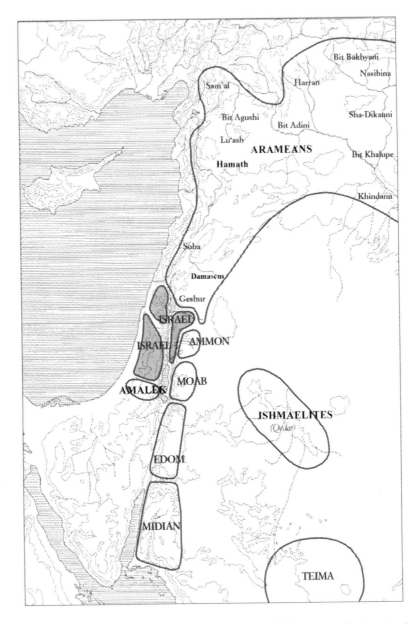

Figure 20. *Palestine in a larger context: distribution of 'ethnic states' in Iron Age I*

Arabia, an area still inaccessible to scientific research. But the archaeological data on the emergence of North-Arabian tribes in the early Iron Age (Midianites and Amalekites) confirms the basic accuracy of this picture.

The opening of caravan routes and the use of camels widened – a great deal – the horizon of exploitation of new territories during the Iron Age, in comparison with the restricted world of the Late Bronze Age. But, on the other hand, the network of diplomatic relations – exchanges of gifts, dynastic marriages, messengers and traders, soldiers and administrators – that had brought Palestine to the centre of the intensive exchange between the big powers of the time (Egypt, Hatti, Mitanni, Assyria, Babylon) had collapsed. In the new age, Egypt maintained some formal claims to control, but without being able to translate them into concrete action. In the North, once the Hittite rule collapsed, we must wait until the emergence of the Assyrian empire before we have again another external power able to assume the control of this part of the Near East. Already around 1100 Tiglath-Pileser I showed the Assyrian interest in the Levant, but it was limited to the Phoenician costal towns, without any consequences for the kingdoms of the hinterland. The picture remains the same in the time of Ashurnasirpal II, in the middle of the ninth century.

This state of affairs means that from 1150 to 850 all of the Levant had the opportunity to develop its internal political dynamics with no outside interference. This development spread progressively and consistently throughout the entire Syro-Palestinian strip; but the capacity for consolidation seems to have been greater in the north than in the south, and on the coast than inland. The area occupied by the Israelite tribes, located as it was inland and in the far South, could not attain to any miraculous priority.

2. The Central Highlands and the Role of Jerusalem and Shechem

We have already seen (§§1.3, 3.1) how the central highlands, because of their geographical configuration, did not contain a large number of city-states, but were clustered around only two palace cities: Shechem to the north, and Jerusalem to the south. In the territory of those two cities occurred the earliest and most intense settlement by the new tribal elements of the beginning of the Iron Age. In this formative phase, corresponding to the archaeological picture of final phase of Iron Age I (with its oval shaped villages and pillared houses), the modest size of the two cities, compared with a powerful increase in the tribal element, must have given rise to the special relationship that has been labelled a 'dimorphic state' (i.e. combining urban and tribal features).

The control of the two royal palaces over their relatively wide territory cannot be comparable to that exercised by the city-states in the plains. Under the pressure of the tribal element, the situation gradually changed from a more or less effective control of the whole territory by the royal palace, through a phase of uncertain control and a growing political autonomy of the tribal element, to a predominance of the tribal groups over the old palaces, finally absorbed into a new political formation. It is a process of internal evolution, quite different from the one that took place on the plains, where small but compact city-states clashed with substantially extraneous tribal elements.

Already in the fourteenth century, at the time of the Amarna archives, Shechem and Jerusalem – as compared with the 'normal' and relatively small city-states of the plains – had demonstrated a clear tendency to enlargement, and a privileged connection with *ḫabiru* elements:

> Moreover, Lab'ayu (king of Shechem), who used to take our towns, is dead, but now another Lab'ayu is Abdi-Heba (king of Jerusalem), and he seizes our towns (*LA* 27 = *EA* 280.30-35, from the king of Gath).

> Are we to act like Lab'ayu when he was giving the land of Shechem to the enemy (*ḫabiru*)? (*LA* 37 = *EA* 289.23-24, from Abdi-Heba).

> The two sons of Lab'ayu have indeed given their money to the *ḫabiru* and to the Suteans in order to wage war against me (*LA* 94 = *EA* 246.rev 5-10, from Megiddo).

The transitional phase is the most interesting, though very difficult to reconstruct. There are two contemporaneous but different points of view (and, eventually, historical traditions) about it. From the point of view of the city-states, there was the increasing turbulence of the pastoral element and a growing difficulty in controlling the territory. From the point of view of pastoral groups, there was the sense of a deeper political consciousness, of the development of autonomous power structures, with the palace city fading into the background, until completely absorbed into the new reality. It should also be noted that the stories of Shechem and Jerusalem were probably different: Jerusalem developed through opposition and violent annexation, while in Shechem a gradual assimilation took place.

We know the point of view of Jerusalem only from the Amarna archives, when the town controlled in theory a quite broad territory, but was already having to cope with the turbulence of the *ḫabiru* and pastoral groups. By the eleventh–tenth centuries the city had to concede the formation of Saul's kingdom in the northern part of its territory (§4.4) and of David's at Hebron, in the southern part (§4.5). On the other side, the tribal point of view, as it emerges in biblical traditions, apparently narrates the story of the two new Israelite kingdoms (of Saul and David), completely ignoring the fact that they insisted on the very territory of Jerusalem. At the end of the process, Jerusalem controlled only a very small section of that territory – between Bethlehem (already part of Judah) and Gibeah (already in Benjamin), no more than 10 km. The extraneousness of Jerusalem from the new tribal formations is marked by the ethnonym 'Jebusite' referring to its inhabitants, while the final annexation is narrated as a conquest – sudden and violent – by David, who turned it into his own capital.

The case of Shechem is different: tradition presents it as a process of gradual assimilation – confirmed archaeologically by the continuity between the flourishing fourteenth century (stratum XIII) and the more modest thirteenth century (stratum XII) city, to the 'proto-Israelite' settlement of Iron Age I (stratum XI). The story of the Shechem and Jacob group oath (Genesis 34) already sets it in the 'patriarchal' age, that is, in a remote and founding past, beyond historical time. The narrative, however, focuses clearly on problems of religious and racial assimilation, which are completely anachronistic before the post-exilic period. The seizure of power by the Ephraimite clan, under the leadership of Abimelech, is located in the age of the 'Judges'. Abimelech proposes (or imposes) a change from the protection of the pastoral group over the city to his formal recognition as king (Judg. 9.1-6). This narrative, as we have it, is strongly influenced by pro- and anti-monarchic polemics (expressed by Jotham's fable, Judg. 9.7-15; see §16.2) and above all by a violent anti-assimilation and anti-Samaritan ideology that betrays the exilic age (see §13.6), in the form of the tragic and cruel destiny reserved for Shechemites both in Jacob's and in Abimelech's time. The truth is probably that the city evolved during the eleventh–tenth centuries: it changed its *status* from a Canaanite-type palace town to the centre of a tribal formation.

It is impossible to suggest a precise chronological date of the Abimelech episode: we could follow the traditional eleventh century one, but just as well imagine that his kingdom was more or less contemporary with those of Saul and David, since the three had almost no geopolitical overlap. The memory of an intertribal role played by Shechem, placed as it was between a central-southern formation (Ephraim-Benjamin and the kingdom of Saul, Judah and the kingdom of David) and the central-northern tribes (Manasseh and the Galilee tribes) could have survived in the tradition of a pan-Israelite assembly (ascribed to Joshua at the end of the 'conquest', Joshua 24): but certainly the details of such assembly, its pan-Israelite character, and the contents of the oath stipulated there are clearly late.

3. *The North: The Plain of Megiddo and Galilee*

In the north, the situation is initially complex, lacking the clear distinction between coastal plain and central highlands characteristic of the central southern region. The plains, occupied by a dense network of Canaanite city-states (with an Egyptian, and later a Philistine presence), spread from the coast inwards, along the Jezreel plain (with Megiddo as the main centre), the central Jordan valley and the basin of the lake of Galilee (dominated by the city of Hazor). Phoenician presence (indicated by the typical bichrome pottery) is firmly embedded on the coast south of Tyre and in the bay of Acco (Tell Abu Hawam, Akzib, Tell Keisan), but also penetrates into the hinterland of Galilee.

Different pastoral tribes gravitate around these urban centres: Manasseh to the south of the Megiddo plain, and the Galilean tribes of Asher, Zebulon and Naphtali to its north. Manasseh, cut off by Shechem from the nucleus of political developments in Ephraim-Benjamin, turned northwards and established relations with the Galilean tribes, in a series of episodes that the Biblical chronology dates to the age of the conquest and the Judges.

The first episode is the clash in Merom between the city of Hazor ('the head of all those kingdoms', Josh. 11.10) and other towns in the area, against the tribal league led by Joshua (Josh. 11.1-14). The pan-Israelite character of the clash and the rigid application of the rules of holy war (the killing of all enemies) point to a late redaction of the account. Moreover, the chief characters, Joshua and Jabin king of Hazor (protagonist in the following episode) are artificially duplicated, with the aim of giving Joshua the credit for completing the conquest in the north.

The second battle is historically more plausible. It is located in Ta'anak near Megiddo, where the tribal forces of Galilee (Zebulon, Issachar and Naphtali) and of the central region (Machir/Manasseh, Ephraim and Benjamin), led by Barak and incited by the prophetess Deborah, come down from the mountains to face the fearsome chariots of the Canaanite cities, under the leadership of Jabin king of Hazor and commanded by his general Sisera. The 'Song of Deborah', unanimously considered one of the most ancient texts of the Bible, is the nucleus from which the entire surrounding narrative was built. The text is important, in depicting a tribal coalition that included in theory ten tribes, only six of which take part in the battle, while the other four do not participate (and are mocked because of this): Asher and Dan because of working on the Phoenician fleet, Reuben and Gilead because of their occupation with the summer pastures in Transjordan.

The coalition of tribes is significantly called 'Israel' (corresponding to the name of the future Northern Kingdom) or 'people of Yahweh'; but the collective name 'peasants' (*pĕrāzôn*) is also used, meaning people living in open villages (*pĕrāzôt*) as distinct from the Canaanite cities with walls and gates. Also mentioned are the 'fugitives', descending from the mountains (where they had found refuge) to fight against the 'nobles', with a clear allusion to socioeconomic conflicts and the situation of the *ḥabiru*, one that endowed the victory with the sense of an 'act of justice':

> There they celebrate the acts of justice (*sidqôt*) of Yahweh
> the justice of his peasants (*pĕrāzōnô* Masoretic *pirzōnô*) in Israel,
> Then the people of Israel went down against the city gates...
>
> when the fugitive (*šārîd*) came down against the nobles;
> the people of Yahweh came down against the mighty ones. (Judg. 5.11-13: author's translation).

The battle, which can be dated around the eleventh century, was probably critical to the collapse of the Canaanite city-state system in the north. Indeed, the situation later appears radically different: on the one side, incursions of nomadic camel drivers; on the other side, the consolidation of the Philistine occupation.

The incursions of nomad camel drivers (Midianites) are consistent with a context of sociopolitical collapse, causing people to live in caves. The response comes from a coalition (similar to the previous one, but smaller) of Galilean tribes (Asher, Zebulon, Naphtali) together with Manasseh. From this last tribe comes the leader, Gideon, whose clan gravitates around Shechem. We are now at the beginning of the tenth century. The topography is quite precise and reliable (from the clash in the Jezreel plain to the chase in Gilead), circumscribed by the late involvement of Ephraim and the hostility of the towns beyond the Jordan (Sukkot and Penuel), and later (clumsily) widened so as to become pan-Israelite, through small textual alterations, like the addition of Amalekites and some totalizing glosses.

On the other side, the power vacuum left by the collapse of Hazor, the Midianite incursions and the inability of the Galilean tribes to create a more compact structure (in some cases because of their subordination to Phoenician and Cananean cities, see §3.1) created the conditions for Philistine penetration all along the Jezreel plain to Beth-Shean. Immediately afterwards, at the time of Saul, they play the same role of opposition to political consolidation of the tribes played earlier by Hazor and the other Canaanite city-states. The agro-urban 'corridor' of the Jezreel plain, not strong enough to form a political entity like the Philistine cities, was nevertheless a sufficient obstacle (throughout the tenth century, but perhaps even later) to a union between Manasseh and Galilee, thus preventing a coalition of northern tribes similar to that of the central and southern ones.

4. *The Centre: The 'Charismatic' Kingdom of Saul*

In the border area between the old city-states of Jerusalem and Shechem, the first kingdom that the biblical tradition considers properly 'Israelite' takes shape: the kingdom of Saul and of his short line. According to the indirect chronological connections between Saul and other characters and events relating to him, we are around the year 1000; and we are in the central highlands, in the territory of Ephraim and Benjamin. Here we find the highest concentration of 'proto-Israelite' villages of the mature phase, and we can identify some reliable information, though presented in the book of Samuel in a clearly late and artificial pan-Israelite context, with negative political and moral judgements emanating from various later periods that are not easy to pin down precisely. These later embellishments are not too difficult to remove, so as to extract some factual information about the kingdom of Saul: and the result is in fact entirely compatible with the character of the 'formative' phase.

First of all – once we have removed all the late generalizations such as 'all Israel', 'from Dan to Beer-sheba' and such – the geographical horizon of the kingdom appears limited to the territory of Ephraim and Benjamin, where all the places with an institutional role or any other relevance in the story of Saul are to be found. The ceremonial centres are all in the territory of Ephraim, where the 'prophet' Samuel also comes from: Shiloh (where the ark of Yahweh Sebaoth is located), Bethel (the major sanctuary of the region), Gilgal (where Saul is acclaimed king). The political centres are in Benjamin, from where the king originates: Mizpah (where the popular assembly gathers), Gibeah (Saul's home town), Ramah (where Samuel lives), and Michmash (the battlefield). The two tribes of Ephraim and Benjamin form a small political unit, bipartite and complementary: Ephraim is in the north, the cultic centre; Benjamin in the south (as its name indicates: 'son of the right hand', i.e. of the south) and the political-military centre. Because of semantic polarity, the Benjaminites, 'sons of the right hand', are described in the biblical narrative as left-handed (the famous left-handed archers) and 'sinister': fierce and arrogant, rebel and hostile, disrespectful of cultic rules.

What we know of the administration of the kingdom of Saul corresponds to this geographically limited horizon and to a charismatic leadership. The army (1 Sam. 13.1-2) comprises 2,000 men from Ephraim and 1,000 from Benjamin. The court has a family quality (cousin Abner, son Jonathan) and serves a military function; the king himself is handsome and tall, strong and proud, and crowned to lead the people in war. There is no trace of any fiscal or administrative system. It is more a chiefdom than a kingdom; and in fact Saul is called 'chief' (*nāgîd*) more often than 'king' (*melek*). The archaeological picture is consistent with this. Shiloh and Mizpah are in fact occupied at this time, but quite modest in size: Shiloh is little more than a hectare, well built and yielding typical 'collared-rim' ware; Mizpah (Tell en-Nasbeh 4) is more than two hectares, but still lacks the imposing walls it has in Iron Age II. Gibeah (Tell el-Ful II) has a square fortress, perhaps part of a fortified complex covering almost all of the tell: but it is still doubtful whether this was built by Saul or rather by the Philistines (see below, on the *nĕṣîb*).

To the north of this little kingdom of Saul, beyond the city-state of Shechem, lies the tribe of Manasseh; to the south, beyond the city-state of Jerusalem, the tribe of Judah. With both these neighbours the kingdom of Saul has a quite ambiguous relationship. There is trace of some family relationship and intertribal collaboration in the shape of interventions by Saul in the Negev, against Amalekite nomads, and in the valley of Bet-Shean against Philistine penetration. But there are also tensions and violent contrasts, connected with the 'sinister' character of the Benjaminites. The saga of the war between Benjamin and the other tribes (Judges 19) may be related to the story of the kingdom of Saul, since the scenery is the same, and the role of Jabesh-Gilead in both is especially indicative.

The eastern and western neighbours are, by contrast, clearly 'other': strangers with whom conflict is perennial and bitter. To the east, beyond the Jordan, lies the ethnic-tribal state of the Ammonites, probably undergoing a process of political consolidation similar to that of Ephraim-Benjamin. Clashes with the Ammonites do not take place on the immediate border, but slightly to the north, at the river crossing of Jabesh-Gilead, a place at the centre of Saul's interests: the king wants to established privileged relations (of protection), so as to secure a bridgehead to the pastures of Gilead and the Transjordanian caravan routes.

The western neighbours, the Philistines, are a major obstacle to the political consolidation of the new little state in the central highlands. Heirs of the politics of Canaanite city-states (since Jerusalem and Shechem are unable to play this role), the Philistines aimed at political and fiscal control over the country and the tribal territories. This control was already in effect when Saul assumed the leadership of the two tribes. As long as these

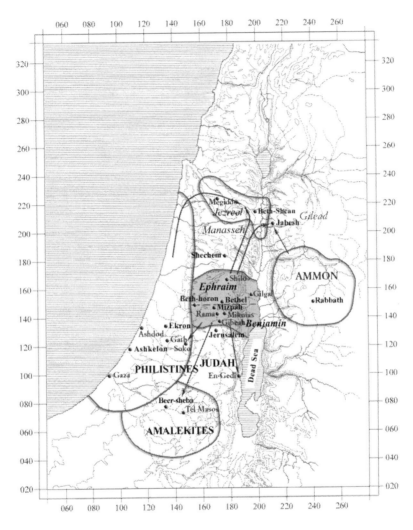

Figure 21. *The kingdom of Saul*

tribes fought the Ammonites or Amalekites, the Philistines probably preferred not to intervene. But the 'bringing down' of the Philistine *něṣîb* in
Gibeah (Saul's residence) was a signal of rebellion: if this term refers to a
stela, the rebellion was a symbolic act of insubordination; if it indicates
a governor, it was a concrete political act (1 Sam. 1.3-4 calls the rebels
'Hebrews' in the sense of *ḥabiru*). The first clashes against the Philistines
took place on the border (from Beth-Horon to Beth-Shemesh), and Saul
won some unexpected victories. Then the scene moves north: after the

power vacuum that followed the collapse of Megiddo and Hazor under pressure from Galilean tribes, the Philistines had the opportunity to take control of the Jezreel plain with its agricultural resources and its strategic position between the coast and the Jordan valley. Saul tried to oppose them, maybe concerned for his bridgehead at Jabesh, but was defeated in the battle of Gilboa, where he died.

His son Ishbaal (a Baalistic name, like Saul's nephew Meribbaal) succeeded him for a few years, under the guidance of Abner, and he reigned not only over Ephraim and Benjamin, but also Gilead (according to 2 Sam. 2.8-10), in a climate of uncertain alliances and open treachery. After the (violent) death of both Abner (2 Sam. 3.26-32) and Ishbaal (2 Sam. 4.5-8), the 'elders of Israel' – and here we can only take it to mean 'of the kingdom of Saul and Ishbaal', that is, only Ephraim and Benjamin! – decided to join the new state formation that had been established (parallel with the kingdom of Saul) to the south, in the territory of the tribe of Judah, through the activities of David. Here ends the short but significant political adventure of the two central tribes.

The story will be used in different times and ways. First of all, it will be given an exaggerated, pan-Israelite, horizon and put into a chronological sequence with the kingdom of David (which was rather contemporaneous), so as to form the first two steps of a unitary history of the people of Israel. This revision is limited to a few generalizing additions. Secondly, a debate about merits and faults of kingship, clearly post-exilic (as we will see in §16.2), will be added. Thirdly, the difficult relations (both institutional and personal) with David and the rising kingdom of Judah created a general anti-Benjaminite attitude, maybe already widespread but exacerbated when the little tribe of Benjamin assumed a central role, and Saul was specifically 'criminalized', changed from a charismatic leader into an impious madman. Saul celebrates sacrifices personally instead of through the priest Samuel (1 Sam. 13.7-15), does not punish the breaking of vows (1 Sam. 14.24-35), and consults a necromancer (1 Samuel 28). This denigration may have begun already in the time immediately following the events, in order to give more prestige to David. It should be noted that Saul's court was unable to transmit any propagandistic or historiographical version of events to rival that of David. But later on his denigration was reread in the light of the relationship between monarchy and priesthood (the only legitimate interpreter of God's will), in a period when this relationship was the subject of violent disagreement.

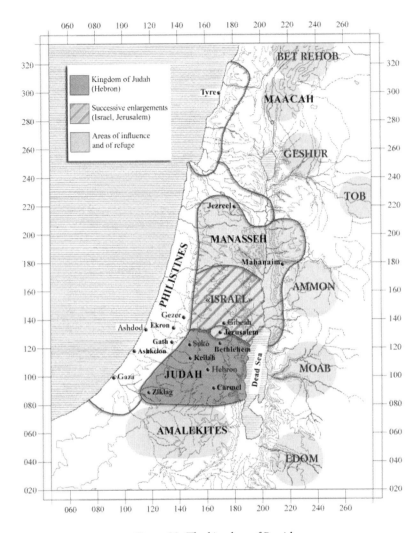

Figure 22. *The kingdom of David*

5. *The South: The Kingdom of David between Reality and Utopia*

While in the territory of Ephraim-Benjamin a new kingdom was rising, a similar process was taking place in Judah, south of the city-state of Jerusalem. This process is tied to the character of David. Just a little larger than Saul's kingdom, the kingdom of David eventually acquired much greater relevance. Consequently, the material on it underwent a long process of much deeper revision and integration, that exceeds by a long way the sparse reliable information.

The story of the gradual ascent of David also takes place in a restricted area, within Judah: he comes from Bethlehem, where the 'house of his father' is (1 Samuel 16); he goes to Socho to fight against Philistines on behalf of Saul (1 Samuel 17); then to Keilah, where he orchestrates a rebellion against the Philistine presence (1 Samuel 23); finally in Ziklag he wins his first possession, granted him by the Philistines so as to separate it from the hegemony of Saul (1 Sam. 27.1-7; Ziklag is identified with Tel Sera'; stratum VIII, with its Philistine pottery and pillared houses, corresponds to the time of David). Throughout this phase, David behaves as the leader of an armed band, including all the members of his own clan and several stragglers ('Hebrews' in the sense of *ḫabiru*):

> David left there and escaped to the cave of Adullam; when his brothers and all his father's house heard of it, they went down there to him. Everyone who was in distress, and everyone who was in debt, and everyone who was discontented gathered to him; and he became captain over them. Those who were with him numbered about four hundred (1 Sam. 22.1-2).

The 'ringleader' David had an ambiguous relationship with the Philistines, who nominally ruled the area: this was partly one of subordination and collaboration (he could have taken part in the battle of Gilboa on the Philistine side, if they had fully trusted him, 1 Samuel 29), but partly hostile, later culminating in open rebellion. With the 'tribal' population of Judah, David applies the typical policy of a brigand chief: he demands money in return for protection (1 Sam. 25.4-8) and then distributes part of the booty from robberies committed against the 'foreign' Amalekites (1 Sam. 30.26-31).

David's activities, confined to the territory of Judah, culminate (after the defeat and death of Saul in Gilboa) in his election as 'king of Judah' in Hebron, which was then the main centre of the area (2 Sam. 2.1-4). His reign in Hebron is marked by clashes with the adjoining 'kingdom of Israel', that is, the kingdom of Ishbaal, successor of Saul. These are in fact inter-tribal clashes (between tribes knowing each other and somehow related), conducted more through duels and ceremonial challenges (2 Sam. 2.14-16) than pitched battles, and interspersed with personal plots aiming, most of all, to separate Ishbaal from the powerful Abner (2 Sam. 3.12-21).

Then follows a period when David becomes 'king of Judah and Israel', beginning with two episodes. The first takes place on the death of Ishbaal, when the elders of Israel invite David to rule their territory as well (2 Sam. 5.1-3). Despite the late 'pan-Israelite' disguise, these are most probably the elders of Saul's kingdom, so that the united kingdom could only comprise the three tribes of Judah, Ephraim and Benjamin. The second episode is the conquest (through a clever action of courage, 2 Sam. 5.6-10) of Jerusalem, a city already surrounded by tribal territory, and considered 'Canaanite', or more specifically 'Jebusite'.

We have no significant archaeological remains of the Jerusalem of the time of David; the so-called 'terraced building' on the eastern slopes of the Ophel may well be dated to the tenth century. David 'imported' from Hebron to Jerusalem the cult of Yahweh, which was added to the cults of local deities: it is noteworthy that his sons born in Hebron have Yahwistic names, while those born in Jerusalem bear names formed with the divine name Shalom (Absalom and Shelomo/Solomon), an element in the name of the city also. Another characteristic divine name is Zedek, which appears already in the names Melchizedek in the Abraham story (Gen. 14.18) and Adonizedek, in the story of Joshua (Josh. 10.3). Of the two priests of David, Zadok is clearly connected with local cults, while Abiathar, who survived the slaughter at Nob committed by Saul (1 Sam. 22.20), is evidently Yahwistic.

Among the settlements in the Judean highlands, Khirbet Dawara represents the fortified type of the period. In line with the biblical narrative, it is common to attribute to David destructions such as Megiddo VI A, the annexation of sites beyond the territory of Judah, and in particular, an expansion towards the sea, along the Wadi Yarkon, to Tel Qasile IX (X is Philistine), Jarisha, Aphek (X 8), Tel Batash (IV), Bet-Shemesh (II a); or even settlements (much larger than the Amalekite) in the Negev (Beersheba V and VII, Tel Masos II). Those attributions, typical of 'biblical' archaeology, must be carefully evaluated, but it cannot be ruled out that the picture we get in the Yarkon and the Negev is in fact related to the creation of David's kingdom.

This Davidic kingdom now covers all the central and southern highlands, but it remains nevertheless a small political entity under Philistine hegemony. The inclusion of Jerusalem (with its royal palace and its modest 'Canaanite' bureaucracy) indicates the earliest administrative organization, previously absent in both the kingdom of Hebron and that of Saul: there is a mention (2 Sam. 8.15-18) of a chief of the army and a chief of the personal royal guard, a herald and a secretary (his personal name is the Egyptian word for 'scribe': a similar misunderstanding is already evident in *LA* 4 = *EA* 316), and two palace priests. There is also a list (2 Sam. 23.8-39) of 30 members of the king's personal guard, which appears a reliable one, since it is not a pan-Israelite unit, but formed by Judeans and foreign mercenaries.

On the international level, David inherited the previous situation, with the two 'hot' fronts to the east and west. On the eastern front, in addition to the traditional enemies (Ammonites) there were the Arameans of Soba (2 Samuel 8), the third contestant for the control of the land of Gilead, a strategically crucial segment of the Transjordanian caravan route. The late and triumphal reinterpretations of those wars ('everywhere he went...') do not override the impression of conflicts with alternating results, without any real conclusion, probably reshaped in the light of Aramean wars of two centuries later. The same is true for the wars against the Philistines, who remained the hegemonic power over Palestine as a whole. If we cannot accept that the kingdom of David expanded firmly in Gilead (Mahanaim is more a foreign place of refuge for Ishbaal and then for Absalom, 2 Samuel 17–18), we have even less reason to believe that it ever included the central and northern highlands and Galilee. That David takes wives from Jezreel and Geshur is easily explained by the normal procedure of marriage exchanges between neighbouring kingdoms. To the extreme south, it is probable that Negev remained outside (with a sort of chiefdom centred on Tel Masos II) as well as hostile (as demonstrated by the conflicts with Amalekites).

Even within the territory that David controlled, there is plenty of rebellion and outbursts of tribal autonomy, especially from the Benjaminites ('every man to his tents, O Israel!' 2 Sam. 20.1), sometimes in connection with personal ambition and court feuding over the succession. Large parts of the biblical narrative about David deal with his rise and then the struggle for the succession, both described with a novelistic flavour. We must admit that the stories about the succession appear less reliable than those related to the rise, because of the different genre of the narrative and its possible sources.

As for David's rise, clues about its origin can be found in a type of monumental autobiography (the best example is the statue of Idrimi, fifteenth century Syria [*ANET*, 557-558]), in which the new king tells his own story in a fairy-tale manner: being the youngest of seven brothers, persecuted, fleeing into the desert, recruiting *ḫabiru*, spending 'seven years' in Hebron and then 'forty years' of total reign, popular acclamation and divine protection – these are all typical elements of this literary genre. We can therefore suggest that the data derive (via a series of processes that we cannot reconstruct) from an apologetic inscription of David himself and contain authentic information, even if propagandistically formulated and enriched with fairy-tale motifs.

The long and detailed description of David's succession to the throne (2 Samuel 9–20; 1 Kings 1–2) is, in contrast, very suspect; in its long and developed form it cannot be dated to the tenth century and there are no sources from that time of a genre that could readily record information of that kind. It is conceivable that David managed to hand over power to one of his own sons (the last born, Solomon), so creating a real dynasty. Two centuries later, an Aramaic royal inscription found in Tel Dan (about 840) shows that the kingdom of Judah, as distinct from the northern kingdom, was still called the 'house of David' (*byt dwd*).

In general, it is very hard to accept that the kingdom of David ever included an area much further north than Shechem. It is late pan-Israelite theories that try to add the fictional conquests of Ammon (2 Sam. 12.26-31) and Aram (2 Sam. 8, 10.15-19), to create the image (or rather the utopian model) of a 'united kingdom', including all of Transjordan and Central Syria, but whose dimensions are incompatible with the still fragmented political landscape of the tenth century. The reasons why the kingdom of David – the founder of the dynasty that built and administered Jerusalem temple – came to be considered as the utopian model of a perfect and united Israelite realm are perfectly clear, as we will see later on (§16.3). But we have to recognize that the reality was very different from such a utopia, though quite consistent with the historical conditions of the time.

6. *The Kingdom of Solomon, between Administration and Legend*

The figure of Solomon (who succeeded David after a bloody power struggle) is even more concealed under later rewriting that endows him with considerable political and religious significance, ascribing to him a kingdom even greater than 'pan-Israelite' and the construction of the temple. While an uncritical acceptance of these attributions is nowadays out of the question, two different scenarios remain possible. The first one is of a kingdom no larger than David's, possibly entering a power crisis. The alternative is a still expanding kingdom that includes all the tribal territory from the Negev to Upper Galilee.

The extent indicated by late textual interventions stretches from the Euphrates to the 'border of Egypt' (1 Kings 5.1) and corresponds to the Persian satrapy of Transeuphratene. Such an extent was never reached by any local kingdom, but reflects a real imperial project: not simply a model for a national unification, but rather a dream of being able to match the great powers. By contrast, the merely pan-Israelite territory is based on a

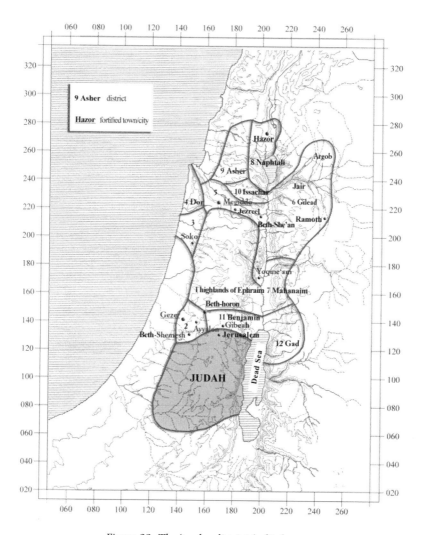

Figure 23. *The 'twelve districts' of Solomon*

list of the 'twelve districts of Solomon' (1 Kgs 4.7-19). In this list, which excludes the territory of Judah, we find the region north of Jerusalem as far as Hazor, including three Transjordanian districts. The number twelve is inspired by the monthly rota for sustaining the needs of the royal palace. The exclusion of Judah is motivated by its exemption from taxation, an arrangement that makes sense (anachronistically) in the context of the separation of Judah and Israel, but is not consistent with the formative process we are considering here. There are no clues as to when (whether under David or Solomon) the Jerusalem dynasty extended its political and administrative control to the north, doubling the extent of its territory. It appears much more reasonable that a later project was attributed to Solomon. Such a project would have been formulated at a time when the kingdom of Judah, in a hegemonic position and exonerated from the payment of taxes, planned to extend its control to the northern territories: this could happen only in Josiah's time (seventh century).

In the choice between the two scenarios, the factual information in the biblical text points toward a reduction in power (no military victories are mentioned) and a reduction of territory in comparison with the kingdom of David (see 1 Kgs 11.14-25 on the loss of Edom and Aram), rather than an expansion. The daughter of the Pharaoh as a wife (1 Kgs 3.1), is not so implausible, but the dowry consisting of the city of Gezer (1 Kgs 9.16, with an aetiological flavour) implies a really modest extent to the kingdom of Solomon (Gezer is only 30 km from Jerusalem!). The 'non-factual' information, couched in a celebratory and generalized tone, is clearly late and remains unsupported by any concrete data.

Archaeology enables to focus on a problem, but does not offer – at the present stage of research – a solution accepted by all scholars. Once again we have two different scenarios. Traditional chronology attributes to Solomon the palaces of Megiddo V A- IV B and Hazor X: this view assumes a pan-Israelite kingdom and implies the Solomonic origin of the 'twelve districts', accepting the reliability of the data on the construction of 'stables' and palaces that we shall examine again later. But it is not easy to accept that a small, poor city, lying in an area of scarce settlement, could rule over a kingdom that in the north included important centres such as Hazor and Megiddo, characterized by remains of monumental architecture and indications of conspicuous wealth. If we adopt instead (as we do here) the low chronology suggested by I. Finkelstein, who attributes to the Omrides (885–853) the public buildings of Megiddo VA-IVB and Hazor X, nothing monumental is left to be dated to the age of Solomon, whose kingdom would appear modest and quite irrelevant, placed in the transition between Iron Age I and II and consistent with the reduced scenario of his reign.

In the capital, Jerusalem, Solomon inherited an administrative structure that under David had been noted without any emphasis. For Solomon we have a list of functionaries (1 Kgs 4.1-6) whose titles partly correspond to those of David (head of the army, head of the royal guard, priest, herald, secretary) and are partly connected with new administrative structures and building initiatives (head of the prefects of the twelve districts, head of corvée, prefect of the palace). This administrative structure is not impossible at the time, but the mechanical correspondence between David's and Solomon's functionaries, where the second list is usually made up of the sons of the first, invites some doubt. It is possible that the list of David's functionaries was derived from an authentic list of the time of Solomon. It is also possible that after a military kingdom (David's) came an administrative one (Solomon's), with an emphasis on the corvée (1 Kgs 5.27-28, 9.22) and taxation (1 Kgs 5.2-8).

The typical qualities of kingship are concentrated in Solomon on the doublet 'justice' (*sedāqāh*, also *mišpāṭ* 'judgement') and 'wisdom' (*ḥokmāh*, also *bînāh* 'intelligence'), which he projects even further backwards to David (1 Kgs 3.6 'truth, righteousness and uprightness of heart'). This profile corresponds well with what we know of Syro-Palestinian kingship of the time: Yehimilk of Byblos, probably mid-tenth century, defines himself as 'a just king and a righteous king' (*mlk.ṣdq.wmlk.yšr*: *SSI*, III, 6), Bar-Rakib of Sam'al towards the middle of the eighth century indicates as his major qualities wisdom and justice (*ḥkmt* and *ṣdq*: *SSI*, II, 14 and 15) and a little later Azatiwata of Karatepe mentions justice, wisdom and goodness of heart (*ṣdq, ḥkmt, n'm.lb*: *SSI*, III, 15). It is not impossible that Solomon had used this same terminology in one of his inscriptions, saying: 'For my wisdom and for my justice, and for that of my father, Yahweh made me reign', or something similar. The inscription, perhaps visible in the temple or in the palace for centuries, could give rise to traditions, later enriched by anachronistic rewriting and fairy-tale embellishment. Such rewriting is clearly part of a late narrative genre: 'Solomon's judgement' in the famous story of the two mothers (1 Kgs 3.16-28) and 'Solomon's wisdom' which included encyclopaedic knowledge (of Babylonian origin, 1 Kgs 5.13 [EV 4.33]) and composing riddles (1 Kgs 10.1-13, again with many parallels in ancient near Eastern narratives) can only be late.

Solomon is chiefly famous, however, for the construction of the temple of Yahweh and the royal palace (1 Kings 6–9). Those buildings, whose dimensions are described in the biblical text, are certainly too large for the space available in the tiny Jerusalem that archaeology reveals to us in the tenth century (i.e. only the 'city of David'). As we will see (§17.2), these are projects of the Persian age, retrojected to the time of Solomon to endow them with the glory of an ancient foundation. But there must have been a reason to attribute the construction of the temple and of the palace to Solomon, rather than, as would perhaps have been more obvious, to David, the founder of the dynasty. Here again, Syrian royal inscriptions of the ninth century (in this case, Kilamuwa of Sam'al, *SSI*, III, 13, and most of all Bar-Rakib, *SSI*, III, 15) can help us, suggesting the existence of an inscription by Solomon proclaiming: 'my father did not have a palace/ temple, but I built a palace/temple', conveying pride emphasized by contrast with a previous lack. On this basis the theological explanation might have developed according to which David had been punished for his faults (for having organized the 'census' or rather the military con-scription, for having shed innocent blood) by being deemed unworthy to build the temple of Yahweh. This theological condemnation, incidentally, is used by 'biblical archaeology' to justify the fact that (in Jerusalem and elsewhere) there are no remains of large building works that can be attrib-uted to him. But this reasoning makes even less sense of the invisibility of the building activity ascribed to Solomon who, according to the Bible, was a great builder.

Solomon's building activity, of which the construction of the temple of Yahweh is the most famous, includes also the construction of fortifications and stables in some cities (1 Kgs 9.15-19), both in the immediate vicinity of Jerusalem, to guard the Philistine border (Gezer and Beth-Horon), or much further north (Megiddo and Hazor), thus fitting the image of a pan-Israelite kingdom. These biblical data were formerly used to interpret the archaeological remains of city gates and 'stables', in Megiddo (V B), Gezer and Hazor. Now, however, the chronology of the monumental city gates has been lowered to the ninth century, the age of the Omride dynasty of Samaria, and it remains uncertain whether the monumental buildings of Megiddo V A–IV B, slightly older, can really be ascribed to Solomon. Solomon's reign remains, then, lacking in monumental buildings.

His commercial enterprises are also quite suspect. The maritime ven-tures (1 Kgs 9.26-28, 10.11, 22) involving the king of Tyre, who is said to have contributed his own experienced sailors, exhibit the literary form of a fairy-tale and are quite implausible for a kingdom centred in the highlands. The first settlement in Tell el-Kheleifeh (the presumed 'Solomonic' har-bour of Ezion-Geber) can be dated archaeologically to the eighth century.

The commercial exploits on land (albeit of a passive nature: 1 Kgs 10.1-13), along the caravan route connecting the Yemen to Transjordan, are all woven of fairy-tale elements (the arrival of the queen of Sheba, attracted by the fame of Solomon's wisdom) and historically quite implausible. This major caravan route was in fact opened in the tenth century (see §4.1), but the story of the visit of the queen of Sheba remains a literary construction, incredible on a sociopolitical level (caravan routes are for traders, not for queens) and also on the geoeconomical level: the kingdom of Solomon was cut off from tenth-century traffic and unable to exercise any control on the commercial route that ran from the Yemen and the Hijaz, passed through Transjordan and went on to Damascus, the oasis of Palmyra and the centres of the middle Euphrates. This was rather a role that Israel tried to assume in the time of the Omrides, with the wars against Damascus.

7. Sheshonq's Campaign

The 'formative' period of the kingdoms of Judah and Israel ends with a traumatic event: the military campaign of the Pharaoh Sheshonq [biblical Shishak] through the whole of Palestine (about 925 BCE). This episode is known from the inscription of the Pharaoh himself in the temple of Karnak (see *ANET*, 242-43, 263-64), including a long list of the places traversed and conquered, or possibly destroyed, and from a short paragraph in the book of Kings (1 Kgs 14.35-38; see 2 Chron. 12.1-12) on the tribute paid by Rehoboam of Judah. The campaign appears there to have taken place after the death of Solomon, with the two kingdoms of Judah and Israel already divided. The synchronism between Egyptian and biblical chronology, however, presents problems and some scholars suggest dating the campaign to the final years of Solomon's reign. The invasion is useful for reconstructing the Palestinian context of the transition from the presumed large and united kingdom of Solomon to the divided kingdoms of Judah (Rehoboam) and Israel (Jeroboam).

The list of place names mentioned by Sheshonq is quite long (about 180 in total) and divided into two sequences: one relates to the expedition from Gaza to the north, through most of Cisjordan; the other one to the expedition from Gaza to the east, through the Negev. This second list is very detailed (85 names: no other ancient document gives so many toponyms in the Negev), but quite difficult to reconstruct: we have too few points of reference (from Yursa and Sharuhen to Arad). But it is interesting from a typological point of view: many place names are built with the word *ḥqr*, probably Hebrew *ḥāqôr* 'ring', in the sense of '(fortified) circuit' and allude to the typical Iron Age I settlements in the Negev, characterized by a ring plan. The place name *ḥqr 'rd rbt* refers to 'the large' Arad (providing a useful chronological correspondence between text and archaeology). Other place names contain the name 'Negev' (and are therefore internal subdivisions), plus a local or tribal name that has some equivalent in biblical references. It is possible that the Egyptian expedition reached the gulf of Aqaba (if *šbrt n gbr* is the biblical 'Ezion-Geber). At any rate, Sheshonq's strong interest in controlling the Negev makes no sense unless we bear in mind the east-west communication routes between Edom and Gaza.

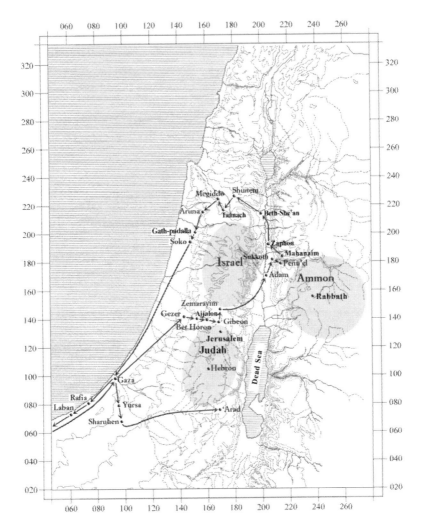

Figure 24. *The campaign of Sheshonq*

The main list (if read alternately left-right and right-left) seems to provide an itinerary from Gaza to Gezer (through territory probably still considered 'Egyptian'), and from there towards Jerusalem, but without reaching
it, and then to the central Jordan valley (Penu'el, Mahanaim, Sukkot,
Zaphon) and to Beth-Shean, Megiddo, and, through the pass of Aruna,
south again. A final section of the list, mostly lost, was probably devoted to
the section of the return march along the 'Philistine' coast.

If we draw the itinerary on a map, we see that it forms a kind of large
sideways S, systematically avoiding the territories of Judah and Israel, but

passing close to their borders. The main interest seems to be focused on the plains (central Jordan, Jezreel, coastal plain), areas where Egypt had a traditional control that had become quite weak, and that Sheshonq tried to revitalize by his expedition. If this interpretation is correct, it appears clear that the kingdoms of Judah and Israel were not only separate (already divided, according to biblical text, or never united earlier, as is also possible) but also quite small. In particular, the kingdom of Israel was still separated from the Galilean tribes, allowing a 'Canaanite' corridor to remain between the bay of Akko and central Jordan. A fragment of a stele of Sheshonq in Megiddo, clearly left when his army passed through, shows how Egyptian claims on the area were still realistically pursued towards the end of the tenth century. A fragment of a statue of Sheshonq from Byblos and a statuette of a '(Pharaonic) messenger in Canaan and Palestine' of the same period (both coming from the antiquarian market: *ANET*, 263-64) also reveal official diplomatic contacts.

Sheshonq's campaign has been used (and still is), even too systematically, to date all the destructions of Palestinian sites ascribed, more or less, to that period. This procedure is questionable, but it is not unlikely that the crisis that befell the settlements in the Negev (the so-called chiefdom of Tel Masos) was a result of the Egyptian expedition. It is also certain that the campaign of this Libyan Pharaoh marks a strong rupture and may be used in archaeological periodization to separate Iron Age I from Iron Age II, as well as in historical periodization to mark the conclusion of the formative age, the last burst of Egyptian presence, and a definitive coalescence of the Palestinian mosaic into a limited number of states, together with the absorption of the opposition between the 'two cultures' that had characterized the previous age.

Chapter 5

THE KINGDOM OF ISRAEL
(c. 930–740)

1. Uncertain Beginnings and Consolidation

After Solomon's death, the biblical account places a 'schism' of the tribes of Israel from the 'house of David' that took place in an assembly in Shechem. Here, as a result of excess taxation, the rule of Solomon's heir, Rehoboam was rejected, and Jeroboam (formerly the official in Jerusalem in charge of the corvée) was elected king. This story serves to link the presumed Davidic-Solomonic 'United Kingdom' to the later reality of the permanent separation of two centres of political power in Jerusalem and Shechem. It is narrated in a colourful way, with the dialogue between king and population underscoring the opposition between tribal allegiance and royal oppression:

> 'My father made your yoke heavy, but I will add to your yoke; my father disciplined you with whips, but I will discipline you with scorpions'...
>
> "What share do we have in David? We have no inheritance in the son of Jesse. To your tents, O Israel! Look now to your own house, O David' (1 Kgs 12.14, 16).

What probably happened is that the tribe of Benjamin strengthened its ties with Jerusalem, a city on its borders, and with Judah; on the other side Ephraim joined together Manasseh, forming a privileged relationship that was expressed and emphasized in the tribal genealogies by providing them with a common offspring from Joseph. The new political entity was named Israel (that is, Jeroboam will have called himself 'king of Israel'), using a name linked with the central highlands since the time of Merenptah (§1.9), and adopting the 'patriarchal' sagas of the Jacob cycle (about a legendary figure whose other name was just 'Israel', Gen. 32.29) that centred on the Shechem and Bethel region and were linked to the tradition about the entry of the tribes into the land from the east.

Jeroboam's kingdom (c. 930–910) does not seem to have spread – at least at first – beyond the 'house of Joseph', with a small addition in Gilead: he himself came from Ephraim, his capital was Tirzah (Tell el-Far'a north, whose stratum VIIb, with a new urban complex and three-roomed pillared houses, is to be dated to this time); the kingdom's most important cult place was Bethel (1 Kgs 12.29, to which a gloss adds Dan so as to provide a pan-Israelite dimension), the meeting place of the popular assembly was Shechem. Jeroboam's building activities concern Shechem and Penu'el (which also figures in the Jacob sagas), the prophets with whom the king deals gravitate around Shiloh, military operations take place along the southern border (Benjamin) against Judah, and the western (Gibbethon) against the Philistines.

However, Sheshonq's military expedition in the fourth year of Jeroboam, if intended to strengthen the Egyptian presence as far as the Jezreel plain and the central Jordan valley, failed: his devastations led to the political collapse of those areas, rendering them at the mercy of the new political configuration of Israel and finally allowing that union between the 'house of Joseph' and the Galilean tribes, that intermittently extended back to the times of Deborah and Barak.

We do not know much about Jeroboam's successors, who succeeded by coups and with military support: Nadab, Jeroboam's son, reigned a couple of years before being killed by Baasha (1 Kgs 15.25-31). Baasha reigned 24 years, but his son Elah was killed after a couple of years by Zimri (1 Kgs 15.33–16.14). Zimri and Tibni reigned only few days, before Omri succeeded them (1 Kgs 16.15-22). Baasha came from Issachar, and with him the Galilean tribes for the first time participated in the political control of the northern kingdom. It is very likely that after Sheshonq's expedition the Galilean tribes recognized in the polity centred on Shechem and Tirzah, an effective aggregation point against external threats, and an opportunity for taking possession of the intervening and neighbouring plains. If the tribe of Manasseh extended north to Megiddo, Taanach and Beth-Shean, and west to Dor and thus access to the sea (Josh. 17.11), Issachar absorbed the city of Jezreel (Josh. 19.18), Asher Achshaph in the plain of Acco (Josh. 19.25), and Naphtali Hazor (Josh. 19.36). The combination of the 'two societies' in the north was thus achieved totally in favour of the tribal element.

After Sheshonq's violent but short-lived intervention, the external threat was no longer represented by Philistines and Ammonites, but now by the Arameans, who, simultaneously with Israel, strengthened and consolidated in the great kingdom of Damascus that embraced previous Aramean formations such as the modest Geshur and the temporary Zobah, and extended as far as the Israelite territories in Galilee and Gilead. During

Table 3. Chronology of the Kingdom of Israel 950–720

	Assyria	Israel	Tyre	Damascus	Hamath
950	Ashur-dan II 934–912 Adad-nirari II 911–891	Jeroboam I 930–910 Nadab 910–908 Baasha 908–886	Hiram I 973–930 Ba'al-'ezer I 930–914 'Abd-'Ashtart 914–906	Hadad-'ezer (Soba) 960 Rezon 940 (Hezyon) (Tab-Rimmon)	
900	Tukulkti-Ninurta I 890–884 Ashurnasirpal II 883–824	Elah 886–885 Tibni, Zimri 885 Omri 885–874 Ahab 874–853 Ahaziah 853–852	Mit-'Ashtart 906–895 'Ashtar-rum 895–887 Itto-Ba'al I 887–856 Ba'al-'ezer II 856–851	Bar-Hadad I 900–875 Bar-Hadad II (Hadad-'ezer) 875–845	Urkhilina 870–840
850	Shalmaneser III 858–824 Shamshi-Adad V 823–811	Joram 852–841 Jehu 841–814 Jehoahaz 814–798	Mattan I 851–823	Haza'el 845–800	Uratami 840–807
800	Adad-nirari III 810–783 Shalmaneser IV 782–773 Ashur-dan III 772–755	Joash 798–783 Jeroboam II 783–743	Pygmalion 823–777 Itto-Ba'al II 760–746	Bar-Hadad III 800–780 Khadyanu 780–750	Zakir 807–780
750	Ashur-nirari V 754–745 Tiglath-pileser III 744–727 Shalmaneser V 726–722 Sargon II 721–705	Zechariah, Shallum 743 Menahem 743–738 Pekahiah 738–737 Pekah 737–732 Hoshea 732–724	Hiram II 740–730 Mattan II 730–729 Luli/Elulaios 729–694	Rezin 750–732	Azriyau 730–738 Eni-llu 738–730 Yaubi'di 730–720

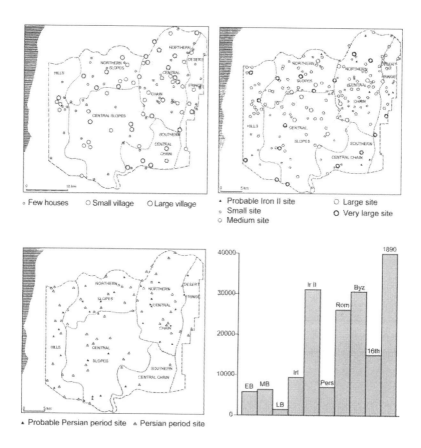

Figure 25. *Settlement in the highlands of Ephraim and population estimates over time: (a) Iron I (b) Iron II (c) Persian period (d) demographic chart*

Baasha's time, Ben-Hadad (Bar-Hadad in Aramaic, and probably a dynastic epithet) took advantage of internecine wars between Israel and Judah, being summoned for help by Judah (1 Kgs 15.18-20), and invaded the far north (Dan and Naphtali). The king of Israel suddenly had to change his battle front to face a danger that was becoming very serious and could dismantle the northern enlargement of Israel kingdom achieved after so many difficulties.

The entire 50 years between Solomon and Omri (c. 925–885) was thus characterized by the extension of the kingdom of Israel from a core corresponding to the old city-state of Shechem and the 'house of Joseph', up to and including the plain of Megiddo, Gilead and the Galilee. However, there was no adequate institutional consolidation to match the geographical expansion. Sociopolitical fluidity, an obvious outcome of the clear superiority of the tribal element over the city element, is indicated by violent royal succession, prophetic intervention, the role of assemblies, modest building activity, rejection of fiscal and administrative structures, and recurring tribal loyalty ('every man to his city!', still echoing in 1 Kgs 22.36). The layout of Tirzah, capital of Jeroboam and Baasha, was no more impressive and its administration no more sophisticated than Saul's old city of Gibeah: villages taking on a role that remained to be filled. Right at the end of this period, we have evidence in Tirzah of reconstruction on a more consistent basis (Tell el-Far'a North, VIIc), but we do not know if this is due to Baasha or already to Omri. However, the project was interrupted, evidently by Omri's decision to move the capital to Samaria. The modest Megiddo VB, the citadel of 'En Gev 4 (with its casemate wall), and Beth-Shemesh IIb can also be assigned to the pre-Omride period.

2. *Samaria and the 'House of Omri'*

Omri's coming to power marks a decisive change in the political-institutional and economic development of the kingdom of Israel. Omri reigned about ten years (885–874) and his son Ahab about 20 (974–853). This solid dynasty then came to be known by the name 'Omri's house', which the Assyrians used to designate Israel. The 30 years of Israelite stability and growth was not an isolated achievement, but is consistent with the Levantine area as a whole. Over the same period the Aramean kingdoms of Damascus and Hamath also consolidated and their size and power increased; an united kingdom of Tyre and Sidon was formed, and the kingdom of Moab was formed east of the Dead Sea. The entire Syro-Palestinian 'mosaic' was thus completed, replacing the instability of the 'formative' period and achieving its definitive shape and size in the form of larger political units.

The main achievement of Omri was the building of the new capital Samaria, which the biblical text (with an obvious anti-Samaritan prejudice) disposes of in a single verse (1 Kgs 16.24). A completely new location was chosen for the new capital (compensating the landowner is a *topos* that we find in Assyria too), north-west of Shechem, in a dominating position along the road leading to the plain of Jezreel and the coastal plain of Sharon, as a result of the enlargement of the kingdom. For the first time its capital was not merely a simple (and temporary) royal residence, but a real administrative centre, a seat of an administration, created by a specific and ambitious building programme that the extensive archaeological excavations have largely restored (see further on §5.7). In the stratigraphy of the

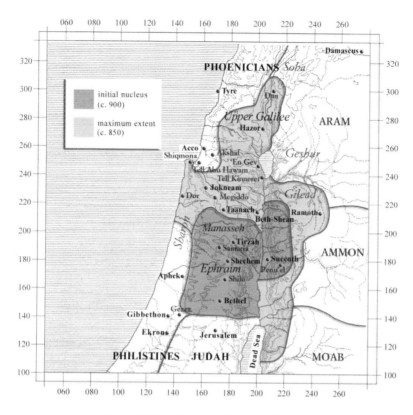

Figure 26. *The kingdom of Israel c. 925–800*

new capital, it seems clear that after a pre-Omride phase (0) stratum I is to be ascribed to Omri and stratum II to Ahab.

Ahab was also responsible for the enlargement of Israel's political perspectives, which we will discuss below. The network of matrimonial and commercial alliances and wars on a regional scale gave rise to (or at any rate sharply escalated) social and religious tensions; moreover, the antimonarchic attitude of some of the prophets resulted in the painting of a dark picture of a dynasty that in fact promoted the economic and cultural evolution of the kingdom. Almost accidentally the Elijah cycle mentions Ahab's sensational victory over Ben-Hadad at Aphek, his subsequent policy of far-sighted alliances, diplomatic initiatives and exchange of trading outposts:

> [The servants of Ben-Hadad] tied sackcloth around their waists, put ropes on their heads, went to the king of Israel, and said, 'Your servant Ben-hadad says, "Please let me live".' And he said, 'Is he still alive? He is my brother.'

Now the men were watching for an omen; they quickly took it up from him and said, 'Yes, Ben-hadad is your brother.' Then he said, 'Go and bring him.' So Ben-hadad came out to him; and he had him come up into the chariot. Ben-hadad said to him, 'I will restore the towns that my father took from your father; and you may establish bazaars for yourself in Damascus, as my father did in Samaria.' The king of Israel responded, 'I will let you go on those terms.' So he made a treaty with him and let him go (1Kgs 20.31-34).

Ahab's policy, after his death in the battle at Ramoth-Gilead (1 Kgs 22.22-38), was pursued by his sons Ahaziah (853–825; 1 Kgs 22.52-54) and Joram (852–841; 2 Kgs 3.1-3), who are almost totally ignored by the author of Kings. Joram was particularly engaged in wars in Transjordan – Moab in the south and Gilead in the north (see §5.4) – that brought him to ruin.

3. *The Dynasty of Jehu*

The Omride dynasty was bloodily wiped out by Jehu, the general who operated on behalf of, and with the support of, the king of Damascus. Jehu personally killed Joram and ordered the death of Ahaziah of Judah, his ally in a new war over Ramoth-Gilead (2 Kgs 9.22-29). Jehu was a military man and led an integralist and nationalist revival against the compromises that had characterized the religious and international policies of the Omrides. His support for the cult of Yahweh (involving the massacre of priests of Baal) should be linked with the support of Elisha for Damascus, and thus to an anti-Omride and anti-Phoenician position. Like many integralists, Jehu seems to have been driven by an implacable hatred, inducing a level of cruelty that exceeded the normal strategies of dynastic change in the ancient Orient: Joram was shot in the back and his body dropped in a field; his mother, the Phoenician Jezebel, was thrown out of the window and left to the wild dogs, and finally the whole royal family (70 'sons' of Joram) was eliminated on his orders, the heads piled up in front of the palace door with a public claim of partnership in crime that implicated all the officials, leaving them no time to reconsider:

> 'You are innocent. It was I who conspired against my master and killed him; but who struck down all these?' (2 Kgs 10.9).

Apart from religious reasons (Yahwism against Baalism, see §5.7) there were also different political strategies: alliance with, or rather subjection to, the Arameans of Damascus replaced alliance with the Phoenicians of Tyre – hence a return in the pastoral background of the ethnic states with their tribal origins replaced the attempt at a Mediterranean orientation (this in the period when Tyre began its substantial colonization in the central Mediterranean).

However Jehu's dynasty (841–814), carried on by his son Yehoahaz (814–798; 2 Kgs 13.1-9), his grandson Joash (798–783; 2 Kgs 13.10-13) and his great-grandson Jeroboam II (783–743; 2 Kgs 14.23-29), also ensured the stability and economic development of the country, and did not depart from the previous policy on the regional level: alternating alliances and wars in the north (against Damascus) and east (against Moab), hegemony over Judah, mobilization against the first Assyrian incursions. Under Jeroboam II Israel escaped the yoke of Damascus and regained its prestigious position. Building activity also continued, and it is reasonable to assign stratum III of Samaria to Jehu and IV to Jeroboam, plus a good deal of building work in other cities (see below, §5.7).

This prosperous century for Israel and the whole Levant experienced a crisis in 745, when Tiglath-Pileser III ascended the Assyrian throne and a phase of powerful Assyrian incursions began. These strongly affected local strategies. In Israel the change is suddenly marked (purely by coincidence) by the two short reigns of Zachariah and Shallum (743, each for few months only; 2 Kgs 15.8-15), who seem to bring the country back to the pre-Omride scene of spasmodic usurpations and coups.

4. *Wars and Alliances within the Regional System*

During the two dynasties of Omri and Jehu, nearly a century and half, Israel became a relevant part of the system of alliances and wars within the Syro-Palestinian region. The previous situation, with small states in the central plateaux confronting Ammonites on one side and Philistines on the other, seems over. The wars against the Philistines in the Gibbethon region, already regarded during the pre-Omride period (in the reigns of Nadab and Zimri; 1 Kgs 15.27, 16.15-17) as being of little concern, ceased. The borders stabilized and the respective spheres of influence shared no more areas of friction: Israel had access to the sea from Dor as far as Carmel, the Philistines were continuing their penetration into the interior by going round Judah to the south rather than Israel to the north, since the wide plain between Megiddo and Beth-Shean was now denied them.

In Transjordan the scenery was also different now: south of the Ammonites the kingdom of Moab had consolidated, and further south still the kingdom of Edom. While Edom seems to have been a satellite first of Judah (late detached: 2 Kgs 8.20) and then of Israel, Moab quickly became the largest element in that mosaic. The wars between Israel and Moab are well known, thanks to two sources: the book of Kings (2 Kgs 3.4-27) tells of the achievements and represents the point of view of Israel (and Judah), while those of Moab are recorded in the large inscription of king Mesha (*SSI*, I, 16), which stamps the authority of a contemporary epigraphic source on the events in question.

Nevertheless the scenery, as already noted, has widened. Ahab married a daughter of Ittobaal (Ethbaal), king of Tyre, the famous Jezebel (1 Kgs 16.31), forming an alliance that must have provided useful access to trade and to crafts. The Phoenician presence was firmly established in the bay of Acco, and is documented in sites like Tell Abu Hawam and Tell Keisan, as well as the fortress (and commercial store) of Horvat Rosh Zayit in Lower Galilee. Surprisingly, the technical support of Tyre is not mentioned in Ahaziah's offer to join Jehoshaphat in Judah's business ventures in the Red Sea (1 Kgs 22.48-50): the stories of Hiram and Solomon would fit more plausibly here, but their removal to the 'united kingdom' scenario has probably helped to confuse our information about the ninth century.

Ahab enjoyed a fluctuating relationship with his northern neighbour, Damascus: military battles sometimes favourable to one side, sometimes to the other, then treaties for the mutual opening of markets in Damascus and Samaria (1 Kings 20). The battles focused on Ramoth-Gilead, which lay in a key position for ensuring crucial access for Israel as well to the important Transjordan caravan route exclusively controlled by Moab in the south and by the Arameans in the north. Ahab and Joram fought in Ramoth where, directly or indirectly, they met their deaths. The reports that in Jehu's time Hazael, king of Damascus, totally excluded Israel from Transjordan (2 Kgs 10.32-33), and then that in Jeroboam's time those territories were all regained (2 Kgs 14.25), sketch the general picture. However, much of the information about these wars – reported in the prophetic sagas of Elijah and Elisha – displays a novelistic quality with a 'king of Israel' and a 'king of Damascus' as anonymous characters, the miraculous intervention of the prophets, and sieges and famines against whose historicity there are strong objections.

Also on the broader scale, in the face of the first threats of the Assyrian incursion, Samaria and Damascus changed their policy several times. First they thought it was advantageous to set aside their rivalry so as to join forces in the battle of Qarqar (853) – which Shalmaneser III claims he won (*RIMA*, III, 23), but where Ahab and Hadadezer could have (rightly) claimed they were not defeated. This military engagement shows the ratios between the forces of Damascus, Hamath and Israel: for Damascus 20,000 infantry, 1,200 chariots and 1,200 cavalrymen; for Hamath 10,000, 700 and 700 respectively; and for Israel 10,000 infantry and 2,000 chariots. Ten years later Jehu is represented as submitting and being laid under tribute

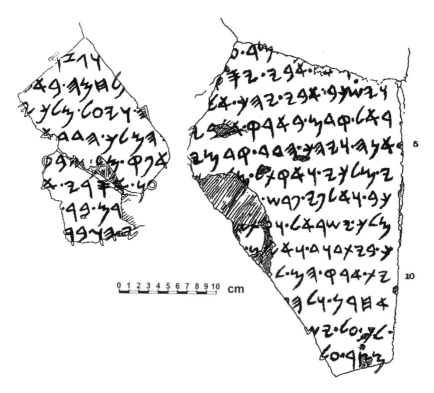

Figure 27. *The Tel Dan inscription*

on the so-called 'Black Obelisk' of Shalmaneser III. When Assyria retreated, Damascus took the upper hand in relations with Israel. In 796, when Assyria suddenly reappeared under Adad-Nirari III, Joash of Israel was ready to pay him tribute (*RIMA*, III, 211).

In this outline of regional hegemonies, while Israel could aspire to a prominent role, it is clear that the tiny kingdom of Judah was nothing but a sort of Israelite vassal. In the expedition to conquer Ramoth-Gilead, Ahab was accompanied by the king of Judah, Jehoshaphat; again, during Jehu's insurrection, Joram was fighting at Ramot together with Ahaziah, king of Judah; and in the expedition against Mesha of Moab, Joram was accompanied by the kings both of Judah and Edom, clearly as his vassals.

5. *The Aramean Hegemony*

Among the major recent archaeological discoveries directly concerning the history of Israel must be mentioned three fragments of an Aramaic royal inscription dated to the mid-ninth century, and reused in a later construction (at the beginning of the eighth century), in Tel Dan. It is worth quoting here the central part, which is the easiest to restore (ll. 3-10):

> (When) my father fell ill and went to his [ancestors], the king of Israel entered in front of my father's land. But Hadad made me king, and Hadad went in front of me, and I departed from the seven [...]s of my kingdom, and I slew [seve]nty kin[gs], who harnessed thou[sands of cha]riots and thousands of horses. [I killed Jeho]ram son of [Ahab] king of Israel, and I killed [Ahaz]iahu son of [Jehoram kin]g of the House of David. And I made [their towns into ruins and turned] their land into [desolation...].

The inscription is closely related to the account in 2 Kgs 8.28-29 (which helps in completing the partially broken names), but it introduces new elements. It is clear that the author of the Tel Dan inscription is Hazael of Damascus, who after his victory would occupy the city of Dan for long enough to erect his commemorative stele. It is also clear that Jehu's revolt against Joram/Jehoram was part of the Damascus offensive, inasmuch as Hazael boasts of having killed the kings of Israel and Judah who, according to the books of Kings, were killed by Jehu. Jehu, put on the throne by Hazael, or at least as a result of Hazael's victory, began his reign as a vassal of the king of Damascus.

Hazael's victory was neither an isolated event nor without consequences. From 2 Kgs 10.32-33 we know that at the time of Jehu Haza'el occupied all Israelite territory in Transjordan (Gilead and Bashan); and from 2 Kgs 12.18 we know that he had also conquered Gath and subdued Judah. In Shalmaneser III's Assyrian inscriptions, starting with his eighteenth year (*RIMA*, III, 54, 60, 67), Hazael is named as the major Syrian opponent, inheriting his father Hadadezer's role (from the sixth to the eleventh year) and holding out against repeated campaigns. His son Bar-Hadad (III) in turn led the coalition that besieged Hadrach in northern Syria (*SSI*, II, 5). A Bar-Hadad appears on a stele dedicated to Melqart, god of Tyre (*SSI*, II, 1), and the ivories discovered among Assyrian booty at Arslan Tash are dedicated to Hazael (*SSI*, II, 2). It is clear that for 60 years (c. 845–785) Damascus was the dominant power in much of Syria-Palestine, and Israel (as well as Judah) had to submit to the role of vassal kings, which the biblical account minimizes and, moreover, attributes to divine punishment.

Given this scenario, we can link Hazael's intervention with archaeological contexts both of destruction and rebuilding, documented in the northern cities of Israel in the second half of the ninth century. Of course, the flourishing of the Aramaic state is attested in the area (formerly Geshur) around the lake of Galilee: Bet-Saida, Hadar II-I, and the fortress of En Gev 3-2 show clear signs of prosperity. But it is also possible that Hazael

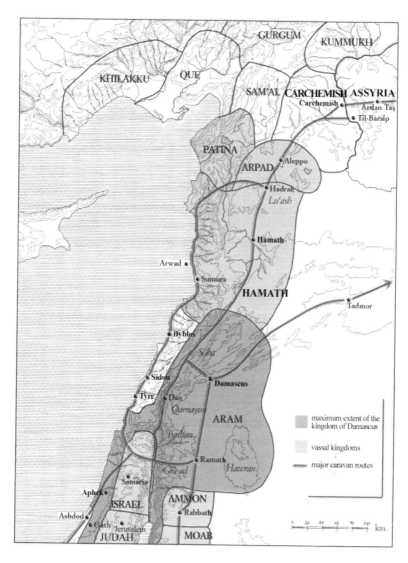

Figure 28. *Maximum extent of kingdom of Damascus under Hazael*

has also left traces of building activity in the cities of northern Israel that he held for nearly 50 years. In addition to Dan, where occupation by Damascus is confirmed by the commemorative stele, the Aramaic occupation may have left imposing architectural traces at Megiddo (IV a), Hazor (VI), Jezreel, and in the reoccupation of Deir 'Alla (stratum IX) after a century of abandonment. After the Israel of the dynasty of Omri, condemned as Baalist by the prophets and later historiographers, but politically strong and culturally flourishing, came the Israel of Jehu's dynasty, celebrated as Yahwist but politically subdued and territorially brought to its lowest point.

6. *Policy-making and Prophecy*

As in all ancient Near Eastern kingdoms, the political decision process, which centred on the royal court and the personal responsibility of the king, used two parallel methods to ascertain the facts, evaluate them and plan strategy: human information and consultation, and divine information and consultation. For the human way, the king consulted the court officials, as experts in administration and war, for technical advice, and the assembly as an expression of the will of the whole community. There were two collective bodies, differentiated in the texts by age ('elders' and 'young men'): however parallels with ancient Near Eastern evidence suggest that these were bodies of a different size. The council of elders was restricted to few people (representing the tribal clans), while the assembly of all free men (both young and old) was a plenary body that met at Shechem (1 Kgs 12, 20.7). If the opinion of the elders was too cautious, the king could appeal to the general assembly which seems as if it was more easily persuaded. The event of 1 Kings 12 is related in detail: Rehoboam, considering his attitude towards the northern tribes, intolerant to the taxes, is advised by the select council of 'elders' to be cautious, while the plenary assembly of the 'people' approves a hard line.

However, the biblical evidence is more extensive regarding the process of divine consultation. Each king's decision (military and civil) had to be approved in advance by God. The scanty biblical pattern:

> David inquired of Yahweh, 'Shall I go up against the Philistines? Will you give them into my hand?' Yahweh said to David, 'Go up; for I will certainly give the Philistines into your hand' (2 Sam. 5.19).

is no more than a simplified echo of the Assyrian procedures for consulting the god Shamash:

> Should Esarhaddon, king of Assyria, propose and send his officials, with men, horses, and an army, as many as they wish, to go against Kashtaritu of Karkashi and the troops allied with him, to wage war on the city of Kasasu? If, having proposed and sent them, will the officials and the army of Esarhaddon, king of Assyria, conquer that city?... Will the troops of the Medes escape?... Will they emerge safe and sound from the district of Karkashi? Will they attain their objective? Will they return alive to Assyria? (*SAA*, IV, 62).

If Shamash's response was favourable, the action commenced. Probably due to later religious censorship, the mantic consultation (the most usual in Assyria and in the ancient Orient) was omitted from the biblical texts, or negatively described; on the contrary, great importance was attached to the consultation of 'prophets' (who had a secondary role in Assyria, and a position outside the court) as able to convey divine messages. They are called *nābî'* 'prophet' (etymologically probably 'the one who proclaims'), as the technical term for a positive and legitimate function; or *hōzeh* ('diviner'), which can also be used in a pejorative sense, 'visionary'.

We see prophets both as lone individuals, tending to be located in fringe or distant places (1 Kgs 13.11; 19.3-8), and as groups organically linked to the court (1 Kgs 18.20-40) or to sanctuaries (Shiloh: 1 Kgs 14.1). The divine message could be transmitted both by the spontaneous initiative of the prophet (particularly the lone prophets: 1 Kgs 11.31-39; 13.1-2, 21-22; 16.1-4; 19.9-18; 20.42; 21.17-19; 2 Kgs 1.3 etc.), and at the express command of the king (1 Kgs 14.5; 2 Kgs 1.29). The public and political function of the prophets is an emerging role; their activities were also directed to everyday and personal matters. The prophet operated as a kind of hermit or shaman, about whom more or less credible accounts would circulate: multiplying bread and oil (1 Kgs 17.7-15; 2 Kgs 4.1-17, 42-44), curing the sick (2 Kings 5), raising the dead (1 Kgs 17.17-24; 2 Kgs 4.18-37), bringing rain and ending famines (1 Kings 18). They acted in the name of, and by order of, a god: in the accounts of the kingdom of Israel this was by order of Yahweh or Baal, with the obvious conflict between these that later tradition wishes to emphasize.

Prophets were consulted by the king on important matters of the moment: stopping a drought, finding water during an expedition (2 Kgs 3.17-18), and whether and how to initiate a war (1 Kgs 20.22-28). Through these persons the deity was asked about even the smallest details of military operations: no move was carried out except with prior divine approval. (1 Kgs 22.5-28). For greater assurance, the king could simultaneously consult different prophets or groups of prophets: this was a procedure well attested in contemporary Assyria, and the book of the Kings focuses on opposition between prophets of Yahweh and Baal (as in the grand scene on Carmel, 1 Kgs 18.20-40). In fact the king could be wary of obtaining invalid assurances, especially given the tendency of those prophets dependent on the court to offer the most positive and encouraging messages possible, omitting risky or negative aspects.

It is clear that the activity of prophets carried a strong political influence: in the name of the god they could encourage the king (or else retain him) in his military activities, but they also could freely reprimand him for improper behaviour (whether public or private), intensify religious and social conflict, and even influence the choice of successor to the throne or incite a *coup d'état* (as in the case of Jehu).

There is scant mention of prophets before the beginning of the period in question: the tale of the anonymous prophet who curses the altar of Bethel is an obvious creation of the post-Josianic period (1 Kgs 13.2) since it is entirely motivated by the centralization of the cult in Jerusalem (cf. §8.5). However Ahijah of Shiloh, who operates in Jeroboam I's time (1 Kgs 14.1-18), and Jehu ben Hanani, under Baasha (1 Kgs 16.1), though filtered through Deuteronomist ideology, seem historically reliable; the same holds good for the Judean prophet Micaiah (bearing the same name as the more famous prophet of Hezekiah's day) whom Jehoshaphat involved in the wars against Ahab at Ramoth (1 Kgs 22.8-28). These are all Yahwistic prophets, and it is striking when a sick king turns to a 'lay' doctor, or to Baal-zebul, god of the Philistine city of Ekron, instead of Yahweh:

> 'Is it because there is no God in Israel that you are going to inquire of Baal-zebub, the god of Ekron? Now therefore thus says Yahweh, "You shall not leave the bed to which you have gone, but you shall surely die" ' (2 Kgs 1.3-4).

However, it is difficult to determine how much this scandal in the eyes of the author of the Elijah cycle, or of the Deuteronomist, was seen as such at the time.

But then we have a wealth of stories about 'life, death and miracles' of two prophets whose activity is placed at the time of the Omrides, in the context of the wars against Damascus: Elijah, who originally came from Tishbe in Gilead (see esp. 1 Kings 17–19), and Elisha his successor at the head of a 'brotherhood' of 50 prophets (2 Kings 2–8). Their stories are filled with miracles and healings, culminating in Elijah's ascent to heaven (2 Kgs 2.1-13), bearing the hallmarks of a popular genre that is difficult to date with any precision, and which will re-emerge (even down to details) around the figure of Jesus many centuries later.

The Elisha cycle also raises the question of prophetic legitimization of the Aramean domain – a legitimization that obviously will eventually be censored. It is a fact that Jehu, whom we know was Hazael's agent, was inspired by Elisha's prophecies to usurp the throne (2 Kgs 9.1-10), while we also know that the prophet shared responsibility for the long and difficult siege of Samaria by Ben Hadad (2 Kgs 6.31), had close contacts with Damascus (2 Kings 5) and prompted Hazael's own usurpation (2 Kgs 8.7-15). Another possible indication of prophetic legitimization of the events in Damascus are the texts from Deir 'Alla (stratum IX) relating to Balaam, the ambivalent Aramean prophet (he originally came from Pitru on the river Euphrates) whom the king of Moab wanted to force to prophesy against Israel, but whom Yahweh forced to prophesy in favour (Numbers 22–24). But it is not easy to explain through which channels and for what reasons these prophecies (perhaps composed in the context of the wars between Aram and Israel for control of Moab) came to be inscribed on plaster at Deir 'Alla during the Aramean occupation.

Finally, we have the first prophetic book, that of Amos, who was Judean (originally from Tekoa, south of Bethlehem) but who prophesied at Bethel in the time of Jeroboam II. Amos prophesied Israel's decline, following what was already occurring to the Syrian kingdoms subjected to Assyrian aggression, and he probably added revisions *ex eventu* after the violent campaigns of Tiglath-Pileser III. Amos identifies two reasons for the imminent decline: on one hand, the non-Yahwistic cults prevailing in Samaria, but on the other hand, and above all, the excessive luxury at the court and cruel exploitation of the common people – and thus, strictly speaking, social factors. We should now pay specific attention to these two aspects, the religious and the social.

7. *Religion: Baalism and Yahwism*

In Samaria and throughout Israel reigned a religious pluralism that was later to be represented as a struggle between the popular, national god Yahweh and the foreign deity Baal who predominated at court. However, Baal did not need to be 'imported' by the Phoenician Jezebel, wife of Ahab: Baal was the traditional god (or better the god-*type*) of the countryside, along with the goddesses Astarte and Asherah. This does not mean to deny that dynastic marriages and international relationships may have helped in diffusing the cult of prestigious foreign deities. Around 860, Bar-Hadad of Damascus also dedicated a statue to a typical deity of Tyre, Melqart (*SSI*, II, 1). There were also many other deities who appear occasionally even in a text such as the Bible, where deuteronomistic and post-exilic editors wished to reduce the situation to an alternative between Yahweh and Baal.

At court there were undoubtedly prophets of both deities, rivals because they were questioned by the king in turn and each consulted by the typical procedures. At Samaria there were official temples of both deities: Ahab built a temple of Baal (1 Kgs 16.32). In the whole country there were, nevertheless, well-known sanctuaries of Yahweh, at Bethel and Dan (rebuilt by Jeroboam II), but also at Shiloh and in other places. The sanctuary of Dan has been revealed by archaeology, with a sacred area enclosed by a rectan-

gular fence, a large, high podium in the middle, and elongated buildings
for associated cult activities. The biblical text (1 Kgs 12.26-33) points to
the political role of the Bethel sanctuary as a centre of religious unification
of the kingdom, as an alternative to the Jerusalem temple in Judah; the
report of its development by Jeroboam II, after its pervasive Josianic motivation has been purged (1 Kings 13), is entirely plausible. There were also
modest cult places serving the immediate locality and situated outside the
towns: these are the so-called 'high places' (*bāmôt*) containing steles and
altars. The Yahwistic prophets rail at such places, and later the representatives of the Deuteronomistic party, partly of northern origin, will do the
same (cf. §§8.5-6). The Yahwistic polemics focus on 'immoral' elements in
the cult of Baal and Astarte, connected with the issue of fertility (of land,
cattle, and humans) and performed since the Bronze age, through ceremonies with a sexual connotation and with intoxicating drinks. As a result of
these polemics, one may come to think that the cult of Yahweh opposed
such practices, and thus was typologically different. However, the difference has rather to be assigned to the reinterpretation of the post-exilic era,
while during the period we are analysing the rural population will have so
absorbed the fertility cults that the Yahwistic religion could not have excluded them without risking total rejection.

The only period in which the 'Yahweh-alone' party or movement (to use
the term coined by Morton Smith) seems to prevail comes between 850–
800, a period marked by the Yahwistic names of Joram (due to intermarriage with Judah), Jehoahaz, Joash and particularly by the anti-Baalist
measures of Jehu; however such a position never took firm hold in Israel,
unlike in Judah.

As for the elite, one can utilize the onomastic data. In the limited but
authentic data given by the Samarian ostraca (first half of the eighth century, cf. §5.8) there are six Baalist names as opposed to nine Yahwist ones.
The names of the kings of Israel seem to change about halfway through the
ninth century: none of the previous kings has a Yahwistic name; after this
point they increase. Paradoxically, the sons of Ahab and of the fanatical
Baalist Jezebel are the first kings of Israel to bear Yahwistic names! And it
is clear that the Moabite king Mesha, in the time of the Omrides, recognizes Yahweh as the god of Israel, counterpart of the Moabite Chemosh
(*SSI*, I, v a, l. 18).

It is therefore possible that Yahweh was the 'national' god already by the
ninth century, but that his cult tolerated, even officially accepted, the existence of other deities, following a policy that the later rigor considered
scandalous, and its conflict with the cult and priesthood (including the

prophets) of Baal was much emphasized by later editing. It is significant how the prophecies of the Yahwist Amos concerning the imminent fall of Israel insist above all on socioeconomic failings, while religious and cultural faults (the materialistic cult with its feasts, sacrifices, music and idols: Amos 5.21-27) are given a very modest weight. The sanctuaries of Bethel and Gilgal are mentioned only rarely (3.14, 4.4), while the role reserved for Yahweh in restoring the lost prosperity is evidently a later addition.

8. *City-building, Architecture, Crafts*

From the end of the tenth to the end of the eighth centuries, the population of Israel steadily increased. A conservative estimate suggests 250,000 inhabitants at the end of this period; but rather than the total in itself – which may be too conservative or based on factors that could be calculated in several different ways – the comparison with the contemporary kingdom of Judah (110,000, half of them in the Shephelah) and with Philistia (50,000) is significant and reliable.

The foundation of Samaria by Omri is the central event that really launches the state of Israel. This event is not exceptional: in the ninth–eighth centuries the whole of the Near East was concerned to increase new foundations, both as symbols of a growing royal ideology that wished to express itself in impressive projects, and also as the result of the growth of revenue and resources, putting labour (general and specialized) and the necessary financial resources at the disposal of the king.

The construction of Samaria followed the plan of an explicit palace project: the hill on which it rose was transformed into a huge platform (90 × 180 m, nearly 2 hectares) by levelling the top and building a casemate wall to contain the backfill. The platform supported rows of storerooms along the northern and western walls, and the royal palace in the large central esplanade, built with square ashlar stones perfectly joined, decorated with proto-Aeolic capitals, and decorated with furniture inlaid with ivory (cf. the ivory and ebony houses condemned by Amos 3.15) of which some splendid pieces (about 500 fragments) of Egyptian-Phoenician style and iconography have been preserved. Temples and storerooms were probably located outside the terrace, and have not been located. The Phoenician influence is well attested in the elegant fine table pottery (usually called 'Samaria Ware'), red-burnished and typical of Phoenicia in ninth–seventh centuries (replacing the bichrome ware of the eleventh–tenth centuries). The successive phases of the citadel are hypothetically, but plausibly, attributed as follows: I to Omri, II to Ahab, III to Jehu, and IV to Jeroboam II.

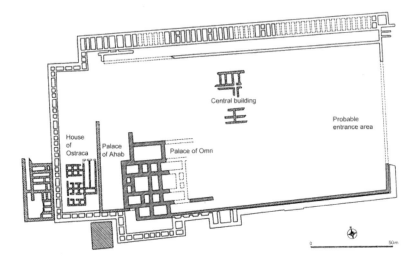

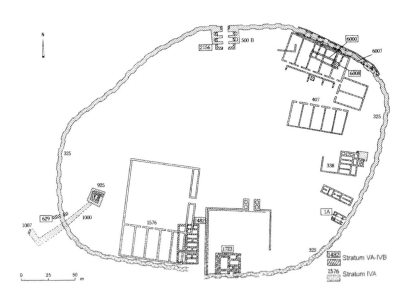

Figure 29. *The town-planning of the Omride dynasty: (a) Samaria; (b) Megiddo*

Another royal palace (a winter palace?, cf. again Amos 3.15) was built at Jezreel, and recent excavations have brought to light architectural structures dating to the ninth century, very close in time to those at Samaria.

Important building activities were then undertaken in other urban and administrative centres. Omride Megiddo acquired an important fortification system with characteristic four-roomed gate, storerooms with large pillars (the 'Solomon's stables' of earlier biblical archaeology), and two palaces displaying a building technique (and proto-Aeolic capitals) similar to that at Samaria and Jezreel. Following the 'low' chronology adopted here, Megiddo V A-IV b (including palaces 6000, 1723 and 1482) belongs to Omri/Ahab, Megiddo IVA (including the enclosure wall with its recesses and projections, double gate, inner and outer, with six rooms, stables, and waterworks) belongs to the time of Jehu and the Aramean hegemony (though the stratigraphy is still debated).

Table 4. *Demographic chart of Palestine in the eighth century*

Region	Number of Sites	Inhabited Area (attested)	Inhabited Area (estimated)	Estimated Population	Percentage of Total
1. Upper Galilee	84	96	100	25,000	6.2
2. Lower Galilee	54	65	90	22,500	5.6
3. Huleh basin	23	63	75	18,750	4.6
4. Jordan valley	66	40	55	13,750	3.4
5. Jezreel plain	55	95	110	27,500	6.8
6. Carmel and Gilboa	24	13	17	4,250	1.1
7. City of Samaria	1	60	60	15,000	3.7
8. Northern Samaria	163	200	200	50,000	12.4
9. Southern Samaria	190	120	120	33,000	8.2
10. Northern Judah	100	90	90	22,500	5.6
11. Jerusalem	1	30	30	7,500	1.9
12. Judean highlands	65	105	120	30,000	7.4
13. Shephelah	100	170	200	50,000	12.4
14. Northern coast	22	73	88	22,000	5.5
15. Central coast	49	47	50	12,5000	3.1
16. Philistia	85	150	185	47,250	11.7
17. Beer-sheba valley	3	5	6	1,500	0.4
Total	1,087	1,422	1,608	403,000	100

NB The kingdom of Israel, at its maximum extent, includes the areas 1-9; the kingdom of Judah at its maximum extent included areas 10-13, 15, 17; while area 14 belonged to the Pheonician cities, and area 16 to the Philistine cities.

Similar gates with four or six rooms have been excavated at Dan, Hazor, and Gezer: and similar pillared rooms have been unearthed at Hazor, in each case belonging to the same period. At Megiddo and Hazor special attention has been paid to the imposing underground structures for reaching the water table – an essential resource for fortified cities that have to withstand siege. The several functional and stylistic junctions actively show coherent urban projects, the first presumably Omride, the second Aramean, the third by Jeroboam II.

The Omride Hazor (phase X, once considered Solomonic, and IX) doubles the size of the inhabited area and is provided with defensive walls; it has an inner citadel with an entrance decorated by proto-Aeolic capitals and beautiful four-roomed houses. The subsequent 'Aramean' Hazor (VIII-VII) has the characteristic stables/storerooms. Less imposing are the Hazor of Jeroboam II's time (VI), and the city destroyed by the Assyrians (V).

Among the other cities we should mention Dan (IV, with the sanctuary re-founded by Jeroboam I, and then restored by Ahab, III-II), well designed with public buildings, imposing fortifications and paved streets; Tirzah (VIId) rebuilt and fortified by Ahab; Shechem (IX, already fortified by Jeroboam I; and then VIII-VII in the eighth century); Beth-Shean (V upper); Dothan (4 Omride; 3 from the Jehu/Aramean period; 2 from Jeroboam II, until the Assyrian destruction); 'En Gev (3 Omride; 2 Hazael/Bar-Hadad III, 1 Joash/Jeroboam II) and Tel Kinneret beside the lake of Galilee; the harbour-city of Shiqmonah below the cape of Carmel.

As always, the villages are relatively less excavated; however one may consider Tel Zeror in the Sharon, and Tel Qedesh near Megiddo. Some groups of villages gravitating around cities show that the opposition between urban and tribal culture had been left behind: as in Tel Qashish (III) and Tel Qiri (VI) around Jokneam, or Tel 'Amal and Tel Rehob around Beth-Shean.

Enclosure walls and the six-roomed gates witness to the defensive organization of the kingdom, as do a number of isolated fortresses: some of these are conspicuous in the vicinity of Samaria, while a line of fortresses running along the eastern border and controlling the Jordan valley (Khirbet esh-Shaqq, Khirbet el-Makhruq, Khirbet Marjama, Rujm Abu Mukhair), could date back to this period (to be later partly reused by Hezekiah of Judah, cf. §7.4).

Clearly, then, the kingdom of Israel had a political construction programme, begun by Omri and subsequently extended until the time of Jeroboam II. The technical level of the work is very high, comparable to that of the major centres in the Levant in the same period. The craftsmanship too, as the fine ware and inlaid ivories demonstrate, is of a refined quality. The solid cultural, commercial and political-military links with Tyre and Damascus had introduced Israel fully into the community of major Iron age II Levantine kingdoms. Indeed, on the eve of Assyrian intervention all the Syro-Palestinian states reached the peak of their development, from Carchemish to Aleppo, Hamath to Damascus, and Ashdod to Gaza.

9. *Administration and Economy*

The book of Kings is not greatly interested in the administration and economy of the kingdom of Israel. However a collection of a hundred ostraca (*SSI*, I, 2), discovered in 1910 in an annexe of the royal palace of Samaria, provides us with first-hand information. These are 'delivery notes' for provisions of wine and oil from the royal farms (called *kerem* or *gat*) to the palace. The notes are dated to the regnal years of the king, but his name is not mentioned. Since the highest figure year is 17, the notes could date to the longer reigns of Ahab (unlikely), Jehoahaz or Jeroboam II. The royal farms were distributed around the territory within a 20-kilometre radius of the capital. The consumption of wine and oil, when set alongside the discovery in ninth-century Samaria of a large amount of fine Phoenician tableware, contributes to a portrait of a royal court enjoying high levels of luxury. Such a lifestyle, it has been suggested, provoked the denunciation of the Samarian aristocracy by Amos in the time of Jeroboam II.

The populist polemic of Amos against the ruling class of Samaria dwells on their unbridled luxury (ivory houses and ivory beds, excess consumption of wine and oil, music), their oppressive taxation of the poor, debt-slavery, the lack of justice ('at the gate': this was the area designated for legal hearings), commercial fraud (false weights and scales, rates of interest set to a timetable favourable to the creditor):

> Hear this, you that trample on the needy,
> and bring to ruin the poor of the land,
> saying, 'When will the new moon be over
> so that we may sell grain;
> and the sabbath,
> so that we may offer wheat for sale?
> We will make the ephah small and the shekel great,
> and practice deceit with false balances,
> buying the poor for silver
> and the needy for a pair of sandals,
> and selling the sweepings of the wheat' (Amos 8.4-6).

The portrait is evidently selective, fiercely polemical, and springs from the impact of a palace economy and heavy taxation upon a society of small landowners, farmers and shepherds who were not geared to maintaining a large royal palace, and were unprepared in the face of the new ruthless commercialism – which constituted a serious and genuine opposition to the traditional solidarity of lineage and village.

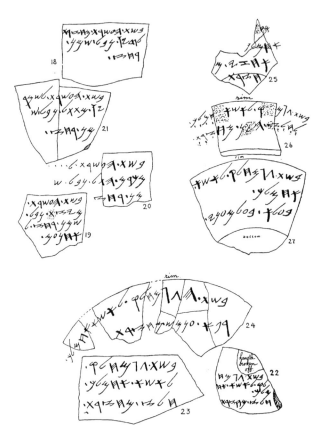

Figure 30. *The 'Samaria ostraca'*

The spread of such socioeconomical practices, which was common in the ancient Orient, can also be detected in the Elijah and Elisha cycles, which indeed represent a precious source of information. One can read of the royal acquisition of the possessions of extinct families (Naboth's vineyard, 1 Kings 21), the enslavement of debtor's sons (the widow in 2 Kings 4), the sale of the sons (denounced as cannibalism) during a siege (2 Kgs 6.24-31):

'This woman said to me, "Give up your son; we will eat him today, and we will eat my son tomorrow." So we cooked my son and ate him. The next day I said to her, "Give up your son and we will eat him." But she has hidden her son' (2 Kgs 6.28-29).

This anecdote dramatizes as real physical cannibalism what in the besieged cities was a quite usual practice of 'legal cannibalism' (well attested in the Babylonian legal texts), with parents forced to sell their sons in order to be able to eat and to live. Examples of this come from the siege of Nippur at the end of the seventh century, when 'the city was besieged, it was not possible to leave by the gates, the equivalent (of a silver shekel) was a litre of barley, and the people sold their sons for money' – drawing up a contract as follows:

> Nergal-akh-usur, son of Iqîsha, said to Ninurta-uballit, son of Bêl-usât, as follows: 'Take my small daughter Sullêa-tashmê and keep (her) alive, she shall be your small daughter! Give me 6 shekels (of silver) so that I may eat' (*Iraq* 17 [1955], 87).

Strong social tensions dramatically mark a period that the archaeological data reveal to have witnessed considerable economic and demographic development, that reached its peak in the long and prosperous reign of Jeroboam II, on which, not without reason, the strongest populist polemics focus. The overall growth of available resources did not produce a general, equally distributed profit, but contributed to a change in the traditional balance, allowing a wealthy class to emerge at the expense of a *de facto* enslavement of the families of small, dispossessed owners. The prophets thunder against this 'injustice', pointing at the earthquake (Amos 8.8) and drought (1 Kings 17) as the first samples of the final punishment that Yahweh will not fail to cause.

Chapter 6

THE KINGDOM OF JUDAH
(c. 930–720)

1. *The 'House of David'*

On the death of Solomon, the kingdom of Judah lost the support of Ephraim, and was restricted to the territories of Judah and Benjamin, the latter being the object of border disputes with Israel. The list of fortresses (or fortified cities) said to have been built by Rehoboam (2 Chron. 11.5-12; Kings does not mention them) is probably to be dated to Hezekiah's time (cf. §7.4). Rehoboam (931–913) also had to suffer the consequences of the campaign of the Egyptian army of Sheshonq directed at the north: he paid tribute, taking money from the treasures of the temple. (Since such a necessity recurred, it should be made clear that the 'Solomonic' temple was actually an annexe of the royal palace, having no independence: economically, it functioned as the treasury of the royal palace.)

The wars against Israel continued during the reigns of Abijam (913–911) and Asa (911–870), and Asa had to press for military intervention by Ben-Hadad, king of Damascus, to avoid submission to Israel:

> 'Let there be an alliance between me and you, like that between my father and your father: I am sending you a present of silver and gold; go, break your alliance with King Baasha of Israel, so that he may withdraw from me' (1 Kgs 15.19).

Ben-Hadad required a substantial payment (*šōḥad*, the equivalent of the *kadrû* in the Assyrian texts, where the practice is well attested), and entered Israel from the north, destroying the territory of Dan and Naphtali, but without preventing that unequal relationship, a kind of vassalage, forming between Israel and Judah.

Thus Jehoshaphat (870–848) gave help to Ahab in the war over Ramoth-Gilead (1 Kgs 22.2-4), and attempted, without any success, some kind of commercial activity in the Red Sea (1 Kgs 22.48-49). Then Joram gave help to his namesake the king of Israel in the war against Moab, together with the other vassal, the new king of Edom (2 Kings 3), and married Athaliah,

Table 5. *Chronology of the Kingdom of Judah, 930–640*

	Egypt	Judah	Transjordanian states			Philistine cities			
			Edom	Moab	Ammon	Gaza	Ashkelon	Ashdod	Ekron
950	XXII DYNASTY Sheshonq I 945–924 Osorkon I 924–889	Rehoboam 931–913 Abijam 913–911 Asa 911–870							
900	Sheshonq II 890 Takelot I 889–874 Osorkon II 874–850	Jehoshaphat 870–848							
850	Takelot II 850–825 Sheshonq III 825–773	Joram 848–841 Ahaziah 841 Athaliah 841–835 Jehoash 835–796		Mesha c. 850					
800	Pimay 773–767	Amaziah 796–781 Azariah 781–740							
750	Sheshonq V 767–730 Osorkon IV 730–715 XXV DYNASTY Piankhi 747–716 Shabako 716–702	Jotham 740–736 Ahaz 736–716 Hezekiah 716–687	Quas-malaka c. 735	Salamanu c. 735	Sanipu c. 735	Hanon c. 735	Mitinti, then Rukibti c. 735		
700	Shabiktu 702–690 Taharqa 690–664 Tanutamon 664–656	Manasseh 687–642	Ava-ramu c. 700 Quas-gabri c. 675–660	Kamosh-nadbi c. 700 Musuri c. 675–660 Kamosh-halta c. 650	Pudu-Ilu c. 700–675 Ammi-nadbi c. 660	Sili-Bel c. 700 Sili-Bel c. 600	Sidqa, then Shar-lu-dari c. 700 Mitinti c. 675–660	Mitini c. 700 Ahi-Milk c. 675–660	Padi c. 700 Ikausu c. 675–660

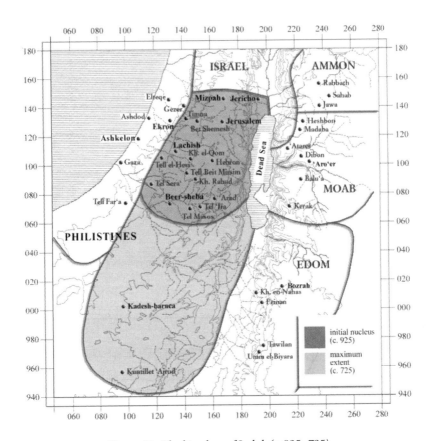

Figure 31. *The kingdom of Judah (c. 925–725)*

daughter of Omri (2 Kgs 8.18, 26). Finally Ahaziah (841) gave a helping hand to Joram in the renewed war over Ramoth-Gilead – he is the king of the 'House of David' mentioned in the Tel Dan inscription – and ran into Jehu's revolt, during which he was killed with all his guards (2 Kgs 9.27-29). Athaliah, after hearing all this, crowned it all by slaughtering every one of Ahaziah's heirs (so extinguishing the 'House of David') and taking power herself. As a result, while the northern reign fell again under the hegemony of Hazael of Damascus, the southern kingdom entered a period of acute instability.

The 'House of David', to which later traditions assigned great glory and centuries of dynastic continuity, in reality survived, somehow, for just a century, always subordinate – first to Egypt, then to Israel, and occasionally to Damascus – squandering its modest wealth and ending in a bloodbath.

2. Dynastic Changes

Athaliah's interregnum (841–835) ended in another usurpation, by Jehoash, whose inscription probably provided the source of the account in Kings; the inscription was lost but has left its traces in the traditional text. This inscription, following the typical folkloristic sequence of damage → hiding → revenge, utilized by many ancient Near Eastern usurpers, relates how a newborn son of Ahaziah escaped by chance, was hidden in the temple 'for seven years', and was then recognized as the legitimate heir by the guards, regained the throne thanks to a coup, and reigned 'for forty years' (2 Kgs 11.1–12.2). Obviously the newborn child cannot have been recognized by anyone, and a seven-year-old cannot have operated by himself, but only as an instrument of fictitious legality in the hands of the priest Jehoiada, the real instigator and beneficiary of the coup. Athaliah was regarded as a foreigner and killed by the rebels, while the 'people of the land' (*'am hā'āreṣ*) were summoned to acclaim the new king. There followed reforms of the management and use by the priests of contributions and donations to the temple. According to 2 Chron. 24.5-14 the new king also effected major restorations to the temple itself; the Solomonic prototype probably did not remain unchanged, as implied by later historiography. The role of the 'people of the land' is significant: it is the common population (outside the court circle of 'servants of the king') that for the sake of political legitimacy takes part only in the case of new kings, while it is absent in the event of regular succession. It should be noted that the numbers of the two reigns in question (seven for Athaliah, forty for Jehoash) are clearly artificial, so that the chronology of the kings of Judah needs to be revised.

However, Jehoash reigned for a certain period; we know only that he suffered an incursion by Hazael, the powerful king of Damascus, against the Philistine city of Gath. Jerusalem again maintained its independence by paying a tribute to the Aramean king (2 Kgs 12.18-19). Jehoash was then killed by his officials, but his son Amaziah (796–781) succeeded him, being adult enough to be recognized as the legitimate heir by all. Amaziah defeated the Edomites and felt able to challenge Israel over its hegemony. The haughty reply of the king of Israel gives us a picture of the power-relations between the two kingdoms:

> King Jehoash of Israel sent word to King Amaziah of Judah, 'A thorn bush on Lebanon sent to a cedar on Lebanon, saying, "Give your daughter to my son for a wife"; but a wild animal of Lebanon passed by and trampled down the thorn bush' (2 Kgs 14.9).

However, they met in battle and the Judean army was soundly defeated at Beth-Shemesh; Jerusalem was captured and despoiled (the Temple treasury, as usual). Amaziah continued to reign until he was killed in a new internal uprising.

In the appointment of the new king the 'people of the land' again take part – a sure mark of a problematic succession – and choose a young son (still not appointed as successor) of the murdered king, named Uzziah (781–740; 2 Kgs 14.20, 15.1-6). The new king is also given the name Azariah, and in the past he had been identified as the 'Azriyau' mentioned in the inscriptions of Tiglath-Pileser III, which give the impression of a large and warlike kingdom. On the contrary, this character comes from the area of Hamath, having no connection with Judah. Uzziah contracted leprosy and was confined to a 'private house' (*bêt hofšît*: the expression is often misunderstood) while his son Jotham reigned *de facto* (740–736, Jotham *de facto* 752–736). During Jotham's reign Israel's influence over Judah recovered. To this time (mid-eighth century) can be dated a number of inscriptions from Kuntillet 'Ajrud, a fortress and caravan station in the southern Negev that yielded pottery, not only from Judah and the Philistine coast, but also from the north (Israel and Phoenicia), but especially some inscriptions on plaster that cite a 'Yahweh of Teman' (Teman is the ancient name of Kuntillet 'Ajrud) parallel with a 'Yahweh of Samaria'. This seems to point to a garrison or troops coming from the north, operating either on behalf of the kingdom of Israel or even of the kingdom of Judah but in a clearly subordinate role. Late in Jotham's reign, Rezin of Damascus and Pekah of Israel invaded Judah, and under his successor Ahaz (736–716) they besieged Jerusalem. Yet again, a king of Judah sought to escape the danger by paying a heavy tribute (always called *šōḥad*), taken again from the Temple treasury – but this time to the Assyrian Tiglath-Pileser III, requesting his intervention in exchange for submission:

> Ahaz sent messengers to King Tiglath-pileser of Assyria, saying, 'I am your servant and your son. Come up, and rescue me from the hand of the king of Aram and from the hand of the king of Israel, who are attacking me' (2 Kgs 16.7).

This appeal threw the doors open to Assyrian military intervention and marked a drastic change on the Palestinian scene (to which we shall return in the next chapter); several prophets acted as spokesmen for the widespread disapproval of such an appeal to outside intervention that would bring a yoke heavier than the one it replaced.

3. The Formation of Transjordanian States

The slow growth of Judah during the tenth–eighth centuries was not an anomalous development, but became part of a larger panorama of new state formation in the hinterland of Palestine and in Transjordan. This panorama does not include the Philistine city-states along the southern coast, nor the Phoenician cities along the northern coast, where the persistence of the cultural and political traditions of the Late Bronze Age assured the continuation of high levels of state organization.

The region populated by the Ammonites was doubtless the most stable in Transjordan: with a better climate than area to the south, it benefited from a healthy continuity of settlement. In the historical sources, the Ammonites appear already from Iron age I as very competitive and even aggressive at the time of Saul and David – and they remain the most active much later, in the post-exilic period. To Iron Age I we can date the settlement (25 hectares) of Tell Sahab. In Iron Age II an Ammonite kingdom undoubtedly exists, having distinct tribal features: note that it is always called *bĕnê 'Ammôn*, the name conveying a personal and not a geographical identity (unlike Edom and Moab). The kingdom was rather small, gathered around the capital Rabbath Ammon (the modern Amman), and by this time refrains from any intervention in Cisjordan, keeping itself away from the Jordan valley. Besides the capital were smaller, secondary towns within a 10/20 km radius (Jawa, Sahab, 'Umayri); and numerous settlements, with characteristic 'towers' (fortified farms) scattered over the agricultural lands (specially in the Beq'a, 15 km north-west of Amman). Findings (more or less accidental) on the citadel of Amman have included royal statuary pieces of the eighth century, one bearing an inscription; and thanks to the mention of Ammonite kings in Assyrian inscriptions it is possible to reconstruct the outlines of the dynastic succession.

The region of Moab has also been the object of repeated surveys and excavations (specially in the site of Heshbon), so that its territorial history is now relatively well known. Considerable sociopolitical development occurred at the end of the ninth century, and the Mesha stele (*SSI*, I, 16) supplies useful information that can be correlated with the archaeological data. We must presume that during Iron Age I Moab had a rather loose tribal structure, well suited to an agro-pastoral economy in the most favourable areas. The presence of Midianites in Moab (which the sources, though late, frequently suggest: Num. 22.3-4.7, etc.) might be part of this framework. However, by the time of Mesha the process of unification was completed, prompted by the need to compete with the stronger and more organized states that had formed to the north and west. The fact remains that the kingdom of Mesha meant political unification around the capital Dibon (a unification that does not imply the loss of tribal identity), with the existence of regional administrative centres like Madaba, 'Atarot, Yahash, the construction of the fortified citadels of Aroer (IV), Balu'a, Khirbet el-Mudayna el-Muraygha (with a small temple dated to the eighth century) and Khirbet el-Mudayna el-'Aliya, the royal control of the road system and the construction of water cisterns, the creation of monumental royal inscriptions (besides Mesha's there are fragments of a second stele from Kerak, *SSI*, I, 17), and the deployment of a defensive border policy, with territorial acquisition and new settlements populated by deportees (as in the case of 'Atarot).

The wars between Moab and Israel in the ninth century probably give rise to the story of Sihon, the 'Amorite' king of Heshbon, who was eliminated by the Israelites during their exodus, despite their oath to not invade Moab (Deut. 2.26-36). The story shows us the territory of Heshbon as being 'Amorite' and so it could legitimately be claimed by the Israelite tribe of Gilead (Gad) without infringing the 'oaths' to not invade either Moab or Ammon – oaths retrojected to the founding Exodus event, but probably in fact the result of the wars of the ninth century. From the scattered information in Kings, we can trace the essential stability of the kingdom of Moab for a couple of centuries, until the Assyrian intervention, as analyzed below (§§7.1-2).

Edom, the most southerly Transjordanian state, was formed later, and the biblical allusions in the period between Saul and Solomon are clearly anachronistic. The territory, arid and marginal, gave hospitality to a poor agro-pastoral population with no political structures beyond the tribal, until its geographic position became significant for control of important commercial routes: a stretch of the caravan-route to South Arabia, the transversal route linking it to the Mediterranean Sea (at Gaza, which, according to Amos 1.6 sold slaves to Edom, evidently to introduce them into the caravan-routes of the interior), and the convergence of the Palestinian roads to the Red Sea, at the gulf of Aqaba. The archaeological surveys have revealed a rather modest settlement until about 800, followed by a development during the eighth–seventh centuries (with fortified hilltop villages and fortresses along the border, typical features of a semi-arid area), and a crisis following in the sixth century (but this concerned the whole Levant). The book of Kings says that at in the mid-ninth century 'Edom had no king, and King Jehoshaphat built ships of Tarshish to go to Ophir for gold' (1 Kgs 22.48-49). In the following decades an Edomite king participates, in a subordinate capacity, in an expedition by Israel and Judah against Moab (2 Kgs 3.4-27); while in about 845 an Edomite rebellion against Judah gives rise to an independent royal dynasty (2 Kgs 8.20-21).

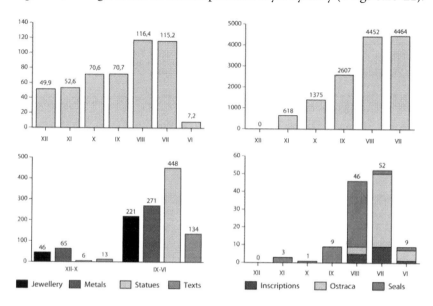

Figure 32. *The growth of the kingdom of Judah in the eighth–seventh centuries (a) demography (hectares excavated); (b) public buildings (square metres); luxury goods (numbers of objects); (d) written material*

The Edomite kingdom was in good shape for a couple of centuries, continually competing with Judah for control of the access to the Red Sea. Tell el-Kheleife, probably ancient Elat, flourished from the eighth to the sixth centuries, as did the other centres of Umm el-Biyara near Petra (single phase, with a seal impression of the Edomite king Qaus-gabri) and Tawilan at the same time. The Edomite 'national' god was Qaus, and two of the three names of Edomite kings (as recorded in the Assyrian texts) are composed from the name Qaus. Assyria then intervened in internal disputes (as we will see later), and it is interesting to notice how Assyria took a great interest in Edom because of its strategic and commercial position, and how Edom reached its climax especially during the period of subjection to Assyria (seventh century), benefiting from its position as an independent kingdom at the outskirts of a large empire, and relying on its caravan business and its resources of ore (the mining sites of the Arabah, such as Feinan and Khirbet en-Nahas, take off from the eighth century).

4. Economy and Material Culture

Between the tenth century (see §4.2), with a tiny Jerusalem in a sparsely populated Judah, and the vigorous development that occurred in the second half of the eighth century (as we will see below, §7.4), a very modest development took place from the mid-ninth to mid-eighth centuries, substantially more like stagnation than real growth. The entire population of Judah in the eighth century has been estimated at about 110,000, half of them in the Shephelah.

Jerusalem was still confined to the 'city of David' (with the nearby temple), about 4 or 5 hectares in size, and enclosed by walls. Some discoveries (such as proto-Aeolic capitals) lead us to think that in the ninth–eighth centuries there were public buildings, later destroyed. Building developments in the capital (the little we can understand of them) and eventually in other 'royal' sites could have been driven by the influence of Israel, as well as of Aram, and in this way could have absorbed Syrian elements (like the *bit hilāni*).

The sites south of Jerusalem increase from about ten in the Late Bronze Age to about 20 in Iron Age I, to 36 in the ninth–eighth centuries, but this region is still the least populated of the plateaux. The most populated area is the Shephelah where the key site of Lachish was reoccupied in the ninth century and is quite flourishing, and clearly a royal possession in the eighth century (it develops even more in the time of Hezekiah, see §7.4); also Tel Batash III, Bet-Shemesh II B-C, Tel Halif VI B in the Shephelah, as well as Tell Beit Mirsim A2 and Tell en-Nasbeh 3 in the highlands, show signs of a slight development. Tell en-Nasbeh, with its imposing walls (featuring 12 towers and a city gate), and with the typical urban ring-shape, may provide the 'type' of the Judean city of the eighth century.

Some sites, like Khirbet Rabud (B III-II), are fortresses; however, the frontier of the western Negev (Tell el-Hesi VII D-C, Tel Sera' VII-VI, Tel Nagila IV, Far'a South) was more probably under Philistine rather than Judean control. In the far south of the Beer-sheba valley, where a former Amalekite settlement had been under Judean control since David's time, there are administrative centres clearly dependent on the capital: Arad XI-VIII (with its citadel and temple), Kadesh-barnea (lower and middle fortresses), Beer-sheba V-III, 'Ira VIII and Tel Malhata C.

The settlements are still based on the type of four-roomed 'pillared house' (well attested in this period at the Judean sites of Tell Beit Mirsim and Tel Masos, at the Benjaminite site of Tell en-Nasbeh, and farther north at Tell el-Far'a North, in the territory of Israel), that, as has been

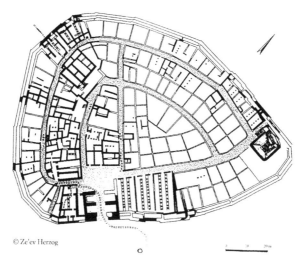

© Ze'ev Herzog

© Ze'ev Herzog

Figure 33. *Town planning in the kingdom of Judah: (a) plan of Beer-sheba; (b) plan of Tell en-Nasbeh (Mizpah)*

shown, corresponds to the traditional family structure. This traditionalism corresponds to an agro-pastoral economy in the semi-arid environment of the Negev and a Mediterranean one in the Shephela and on the plateau, whose rhythms are ruled as listed in the Gezer calendar (which may be dated to the ninth century; *SSI*, I, 1):

> Two months of vintage and olive harvest;
> two months of sowing;
> two months of spring pasture;
> one month of flax pulling;
> one month of barley harvest;
> one month of wheat harvest and measuring;
> two months of pruning;
> one month of summer fruit.

The evolution towards an exchange economy passed round Judah rather than through it: it went through Transjordan (still out of reach for Jerusalem), the southern Negev (along the road between Edom and Gaza), and the coast that was firmly under Philistine control. The imports archaeologically attested (for example, Phoenician pottery) are much more modest than in the north. The urban and architectural projects, that in Israel attest the exceptional achievements of the Omride dynasty, the Aramean interlude, and the reign of Jeroboam II, seem to reach the south rather laboriously, except perhaps in Jerusalem, where they are unfortunately irrecoverable.

5. *Yahwism and Prophetic Activity in the South*

For the northern kingdom of the ninth–eighth centuries the scanty reports in the book of Kings are usefully augmented by the Elijah and Elisha cycles, plus the book of Amos; but for the kingdom of Judah, by contrast, such information does not exist at all. The similar 'historical' notices of Kings concerning Judah are very modest and – if we note carefully – tell us practically nothing unless they interact with events in Israel. Certainly, 2 Chronicles adds many details and reports that are totally different, nearly all of religious interest; however, the extremely late date of the book and its very obvious apologetic aims, which colour almost every verse, do not encourage us (despite some recent reassessment on this question) to use the Chronicler as a reliable historical source. It is obviously safer to follow the fewer data of the Deuteronomist historiography.

The period in which the 'Yahweh alone' movement took shape is the first half of the ninth century, during the prophetic activity of Elijah, in the reigns of Asa and Jehoshaphat (who are in fact positively evaluated by the Deuteronomistic historiography for their attempts to eliminate the worship of idols); Jehoshaphat is the first Judean king to bear a Yahwistic name, a generation before this occurred in Israel. In Judah, from Jehoshaphat onwards the use of Yahwistic names is almost always the practice within the royal dynasty. There is no doubt that Yahweh had a temple of great prestige and influence in Jerusalem, which the later tradition dates back (probably based on inscriptions that could still be seen) to Solomon. The Yahwism of the ruling dynasty does not imply a monopolistic state religion: a large part of the population seems to have been devoted to fertility cults, with *bāmôt* (sanctuaries in the open, on hilltops), *maṣṣēbôt* (stone steles) and *'ăšērot/'ăšērîm* (decorated tree trunks?). In mentioning so often the destruction of these places of worship by the kings of Judah, the compilers (both the Deuteronomist of Kings and the later Chronicler) actually confirm the inefficacy of such efforts in erasing a deep-seated religious loyalty.

It is possible, however, that in public matters Yahweh alone was invoked. Doubtless, the few prophets mentioned as being active in Judah (Ahijah of shilo, and Shemaiah in the time of Rehoboam, Azariah under Asa, Micaiah under Jehoshaphat) even before the great surge of Yahwistic prophetism that took place under Assyrian pressure, were already all Yahwists and helped in putting a stop to the 'fratricidal' struggles between Judah and Israel:

> Thus says Yahweh, 'You shall not go up or fight against your kindred the people of Israel. Let everyone go home, for this thing is from me.' So they heeded the word of Yahweh and went home again, according to the word of Yahweh (1 Kgs 12.24 = 1 Chron. 11.4).

However the socio-political development of this prophetism, leaving aside the personal vocations and their 'shamanic' use in everyday life, took place in the court environment, where discussions took place, strategies were elaborated and different options considered (§5.6). This factor explains how the prophetism of the ninth–eighth centuries is much livelier in the north than in the south, where it seems to be at the level of personal intervention (whether approval or censure) rather than systematic consultation (for political decision-making), an informal stage probably already reached during the formative period of David and Solomon.

Conversely, Yahwism is more solid (and earlier) in the south than in the north, probably for two reasons. The first lies precisely in the marginality of Judah, less exposed to different influences, and centralized on the capital where the temple of Yahweh enjoyed a virtually monopolistic attraction. The second reason lies in the probable southern origin of Yahweh, a view that may be supported by several indications: his first theophany is set in the region of Midian (Exodus 3), the pilgrimage to Sinai (no matter where the holy mountain should be placed exactly) also points to the far south (Exodus 19), the very ancient allusion in the Song of Deborah states that he comes from Se'ir/Edom (Judg. 5.4); and it is not at all improbable that we find the first mention of him by the Shasu already in the thirteenth century. According to later historiography, Yahweh was raised to the status of leading deity in the tribal conflicts, not only in the south but also in the central plateau. Possibly his first configuration was as *Yahweh sĕbā'ôt*, 'god of armies' in the usual translations (later 'god of the celestial hosts' in the exilic age), carried into battle inside a portable ark (1 Sam. 4.4). An original link with *Ršp ṣb'* 'Reshef the warrior', endowed with bow and arrows with which (like the Homeric Apollo) he spreads plague (see 1 Sam. 5.6-12), cannot be ruled out.

In the historical period proper (mid-eighth century) important extra-biblical evidence is provided by the inscriptions from Kuntillet 'Ajrud, a fortress deep inside the Sinai desert. Some of these plaster inscriptions include invocations like 'I bless you for Yahweh of Samaria (/of Teman) and his Asherah'. Also, from Khirbet el-Qom comes a text with the invocation 'may Uriyahu be blessed by Yahweh and his Asherah, he saved him from his enemies'. What clearly emerges from these is a cult that combines Yahweh and his consort Asherah, a cult that may be defined as 'syncretistic' only if one thinks that the original worship of Yahweh was opposed to this kind of relationship (which would then be carefully banned in the Deuteronomist reform of Josiah; see §8.5).

6. The Common Ideology of the Ninth–Eighth Centuries

Although different in their power and their international role, Israel and Judah are, between the beginning of the ninth and the end of the eighth centuries, two kingdoms that share many aspects of religious and political ideology – one, moreover, common not only to them, but also to all the states of the Levant. The basic principles of this ideology (national god, holy war, punishment of disloyalty), that the biblical text presents as already fully established at the time of the conquest, and that over-critical scholarship dates very late, can be dated to the ninth–eighth centuries, as shown by external inscriptions that can be firmly dated. The most important are the steles of Mesha and Zakir.

In the stele of Mesha, king of Moab (c. 850; *SSI*, I, 16) the national Moabite god Chemosh exercises a role similar to the Judean/Israelite Yahweh. It is the national god that (obviously after oracular and prophetic consultation) incites the king to war:

> And Chemosh said to me, 'Go, take Nebo from Israel!' So I went by night, and fought against it from the break of dawn till noon, taking it and slaying all, seven thousand men boys, women, girls and maidservants, for I had devoted them to destruction for (the god) Ashtar-Chemosh (*ANET*, 320).

We find in this passage the typical 'holy war' principle (we will return to this in §14.7), that entails the total, ritual destruction of the defeated enemy, a procedure that the Israelites called *ḥērem*. Another passage in the Mesha stele also refers to it:

> '...and [I] slew all the people of the town, as satiation (intoxication) for Chemosh and Moab.

A highly significant aspect here is that the defeats and the foreign oppression are attributed to the will of the national god, because of sin committed by his people:

> ...Omri, king of Israel, he humbled Moab many years, for Chemosh was angry at his land.

However, liberation from oppression can also only come with the help of the national god himself, as Zakir, king of Hamath (c. 780; *SSI*, II, 5; *ANET*, 501-502) knew well. Besieged inside Hadrach by a coalition of 16 kings led by Bar-Hadad of Damascus, he receives from his god (through the usual prophets and diviners) an assurance that 'he must not be afraid' (a typical formula of a holy war oracle in both in Assyria and the Levant) and he must trust in a deliverance that by human reckoning seems miraculous:

> All these kings laid siege to Hattarikka [Hadrach]. They made a wall higher than the wall of Hatarikka. They made a moat deeper than its moat. But I lifted up my hands to Be'elshamayn, and Be'elshamayn heard me. Be'el-shamayn [spoke] to me through seers and through diviners. Be'elshamayn [said to me]: 'Do not fear, for I made you king, and I shall stand by you and deliver you from all [these kings who] set up a siege against you (*ANET*, 501).

During the wars of Iron Age II, therefore, and before the Assyrian intervention, an ideology takes shape that recognizes the existence of different deities, but gives the national or dynastic deity ('I am the one who made you king') a privileged role, crediting victories to his support and explaining defeats as due to his revenge.

The best known national deities are Yahweh in Judah and Israel, Chemosh in Moab, Qaus in Edom, Milcom in Ammon, Hadad in Damascus and Baal/Melqart in Tyre, all active in the ninth–eighth centuries, even before the figure of the national god Assur looms domineeringly from beyond. Of course it is legitimate to look for the ultimate origins of each of these gods, and particularly Yahweh, but the 'national' role cannot have come into being until the identification of god with the ethnic state was fully effective on a political and military level.

Chapter 7

THE IMPACT OF THE ASSYRIAN EMPIRE
(c. 740–640)

1. *The Conquest of the North*

The lengthy independence of the states in the Levant that had begun around 1150 (when the 'Sea Peoples' had broken Hittite domination in the north and Egyptian control in the south) was about to be ended in the mid-eighth century by the Assyrians. The first phase of Assyrian intervention had already occurred in the second half of the ninth century. After Ashurnasirpal II (883–859) had united Assyria within its traditional borders, as far as the Middle Euphrates, the first phase of expansion was undertaken by Shalmaneser III (858–824) who conducted several campaigns against Damascus, Hamath and other Syro-Palestinian states, among them Israel, including the famous event of the battle of Qarqar (853) in which Ahab took part with a vast army (*RIMA*, III, 23). In 841 Jehu paid a tribute to Shalmaneser III (*RIMA*, III, 48), and again around 800 Jehoash paid a tribute to Adad-Nirari III (*RIMA*, III, 211). During this whole phase, Assyria did not move to any direct annexation, but imposed a payment of tribute to many Syrian states. Actual territorial expansion slowed down, postponed by a 'feudal' change in the structure of the empire, in which some high officials undertook virtually autonomous control over large areas. In the first half of the eighth century Assyrian intervention beyond the Euphrates became quite rare.

It was Tiglath-Pileser III (744–727) who contained the fragmentation process and resumed a policy of inner consolidation and external expansion. Victory in the battle of Kishtan (743) over Urartu and its north-Syrian allies immediately gave him a free hand to expand throughout Syria and as far as Palestine. Thanks to his efficient war-machine, he captured Aleppo, Patina, Hadrach, and finally Damascus (732), which had become the strongest state in Syria (§5.4). After these annexations, Assyria now found itself confronting Israel directly.

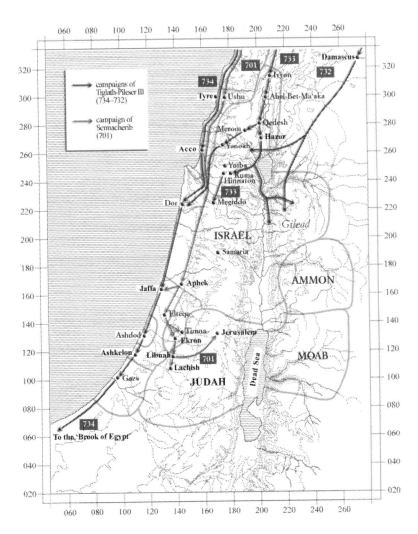

Figure 34. *The Assyrian conquest: campaigns of Tiglath-Pileser III and Sennacherib*

In Israel, Menahem (743–738) had usurped the throne, during the crisis of 747, and he hastened to pay the tribute to Tiglath-Pileser III in exchange for acknowledgement as vassal (2 Kgs 15.19-20; *ITP*, 68-69). His son Pekahiah (738–737) was very soon killed by another usurper, Pekah (737–732), under whom the first act of the tragedy took place. Together with the last king of Damascus, Rezin, Pekah threatened Judah's independence and besieged Jerusalem. The king of Judah, Ahaz (736–716), appealed to Tiglath-Pileser for help, declaring himself his servant (see §6.2). The

Figure 35. *Submission of Jehu, as depicted on the 'Black Obelisk' of Shalmaneser III*

Assyrian king, happy at a pretext to intervene, invaded the northern part of Israel, easily conquering the whole of Galilee and Gilead (734–733). The destructions archeologically attested at Tel Kinneret, 'En Gev and Tel Hadar on the shores of Lake Galilee, at Tell el-Far'a North, Beth-Shean (V b) and elsewhere are generally attributed to this campaign.

Tiglath-Pileser did not conquer Samaria, but had Pekah eliminated in another *coup d'état*, organized by Hoshea, who reigned from 732–724 as an Assyrian vassal over a territory now limited to Ephraim and Manasseh. In the remainder of the territory the Assyrian provinces of Dor (on the coast up to Mount Carmel), Megiddo (Galilee), and Gilead (east of the Jordan) were created. Just previously, the Assyrians had also created the provinces of Damascus, Qarnaim, Hauran, and even the province of Gaza at the southern end, and some years later, the province of Ashdod in northern Philistia. A number of Israelites were deported to Assyria: the passage in the annals of Tiglath-Pileser (*ITP*, 82-83; *ANET*, 282-84) providing a detailed list is partly broken, but the total of 13,520 deportees seems certain.

Hoshea reigned for some years, paying tribute until he decided to suspend it, relying on promises of support from the Egyptian Pharaoh (named So in 2 Kgs 17.4; the Assyrian annals mention a general called Sib'e operating in Gaza at the beginning of the reign of Sargon II). First, Shalmaneser V moved against the cities of the central-southern Phoenicia (Sidon, Ushu, Acco: cf. *Ant.* 9.283-287), then proceeded against Israel: he imprisoned Hoshea and besieged Samaria, which capitulated in 721. Soon afterwards Shalmaneser died, and hence the conquest of Samaria is described (and claimed) by his successor, the great Sargon II, as if it occurred in his first year of reign:

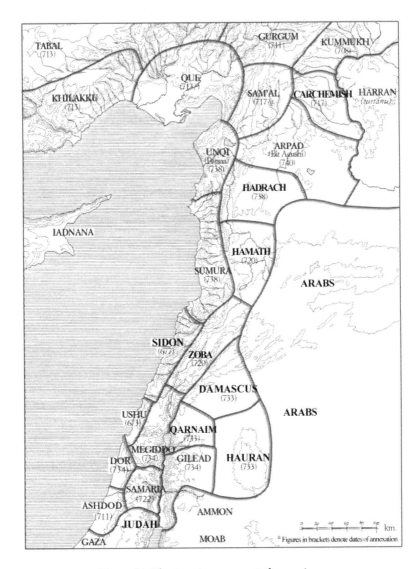

Figure 36. *The Assyrian conquest: the provinces*

With the support of Ashur, who always allows me to achieve my aim, I fought against them... 27,290 of their inhabitants I deported, 50 chariots I took for my royal troops... I changed Samaria and made it larger than before. There I let dwell people of the lands I conquered, I installed one of my eunuchs as a governor over them, and I forced them to pay a tribute and tax as the Assyrians (*ISK*, 313-314; cf. *ANET*, 284-85).

Thus, 27,290 Samaritans were deported, and substituted with deportees from elsewhere. The Assyrian destruction is archeologically demonstrated by Samaria VI; the Assyrian city corresponds to stratum VII. A new province called Samaria was added to the others. Thus, a kingdom that had been mighty (in Levantine terms) and warlike collapsed in the space of a few years: however, this happened to all the states of the region, and the speed of the conquest is simply a clear indication of the large difference of scale between the Assyrian empire and the small Levantine states.

2. *Pressure on the South*

While Israel collapsed, the kingdom of Judah (which had been responsible for the initial intervention) remained unscathed, although it must have been forced to take account of the drastically changed situation. Ahaz went to Damascus to pay Tiglath-Pileser his respects and the tribute (*ITP*, 170-71); on his return he introduced some changes in the layout of the Jerusalem temple (2 Kgs 16.10-18), in particular abolishing the symbols of royalty to adapt the cult to the new political subservience and its ideological implications.

The Assyrian expansion drive, at its height during the 40 years (744–705) of the two great conquerors Tiglath-Pileser III and Sargon II, did not stop but definitely relented in the first half of the seventh century. The new king of Judah, Hezekiah son of Ahaz (716–687), believed he could withhold payment of the tribute, and even began some political initiatives, attacking Gaza, forming relations with Egypt, and later also with the Chaldean Marduk-apal-iddina (the Merodach-baladan of 2 Kgs 20.12-13), in a manifestly anti-Assyrian policy. More concretely, he provided Jerusalem with fortifications and waterworks capable of resisting a siege, and also built the satellite citadel of Ramat Rahel (VB) and several other fortresses to defend the country (see further, §7.4).

Obviously, his neighbours, feeling threatened, asked the Assyrian emperor for help, which led Sennacherib (704–681) to intervene with an army in 701. This campaign is described, with differing perspectives and details, in the book of Kings (2 Kings 18–19) and in the annals of the Assyrian king (*AS*, 31-34; *ANET*, 287-88). It seems clear that Hezekiah, supported by an Egyptian army, had expanded his influence over Ekron and Ashkelon, encouraging revolts against the local pro-Assyrian kings, who were replaced by anti-Assyrian kings. Sennacherib's intervention was successful but not decisive: the Egyptians were defeated in a pitched battle at Elteqe (near Timna), the pro-Assyrian kings were restored in the Philistine cities, and the Judean plain, in the Shephelah, was devastated and handed over to the pro-Assyrian Philistine cities (Ashdod, Ekron and Gaza). The conquest of Lachish is well known from the Assyrian relief that depicts it, which is faithful to the actual topography of Lachish III and the remains of the Assyrian ramp. From the conquered regions the Assyrians claim to have deported 200,150 people. Jerusalem itself was besieged, but did not capitulate, and escaped with paying a tribute, though a very heavy one. The Assyrian version is triumphal:

> As for Hezekiah, the Judean, who did not submit to my joke...himself, like a caged bird I shut up in Jerusalem his royal city. Earthworks I threw up against him, the one coming out of the city-gate, I turned back to his misery...as for Hezekiah, the terrifying splendor of my majesty overcame him, and...his mercenary troops which he had brought in to strengthen Jerusalem, his royal city, deserted him. In addition to the 30 talents of gold and 800 talents of silver, (there were) gems, antimony, jewels, large *sandu*-stones, couches of ivory, house-chairs of ivory, elephant hide, ivory, ebony, boxwood, all kinds of valuable (heavy) treasures, as well as his daughters, his harem, his male and female musicians, (which) he had (them) bring after me to Nineveh, my royal city (*AS*, 32, 33-34).

In reality, this is what happened: the city defences were efficient enough to hold out until the Assyrians (as usually happens in such circumstances) had to move away. The relief that followed this narrow escape – which was helped by the onset of an epidemic among the besiegers and the imminent return of an Egyptian army – was so strong that the rescue was attributed to divine intervention (2 Kgs 19.35; echoed in Herodotus 2.141).

During the rest of Hezekiah's reign, and the long reign of his son Manasseh (687–642), Judah was tributary to the Assyrians. The vast empire abstained, apparently, from transforming into provinces the last independent small states (namely Judah, plus Ammon, Moab and Edom in Transjordan, Gaza and Ashkelon in Philistia), being satisfied with their loyalty and tribute, and assuring a half century of *pax assyriaca*. Assyria did not exactly renounce expansion; rather it had decided to aim higher. Manasseh watched the armies of Esarhaddon (in 673 and 669) and Ashurbanipal (in 663) passing along the roads of Judah on their way to conquer Egypt: in fact he had to supply them with assistance and financial contribution, and he is thus cited in the annals of the former (*IAKA*, 60) and the latter king (*BIA*, 212) as a loyal vassal. However, towards the middle of the century the expansionary impulse had totally vanished, and the aging Ashurbanipal, now inactive, allowed the periphery to pause for breath.

3. *Patterns of Deportation and Provincialization*

According to the evidence of Assyrian royal inscriptions, the conquest of a region involved great damage: destruction of cities, burning of villages, plundering of cattle and crops, cutting down of fruit trees and vineyards, and the deportation of the 'remnant'. The insistence, and the glee, of the accounts can be part of a 'propaganda of terror', but there is no doubt that these war operations (with their direct and collateral consequences), the presence of an enemy army, conquest, and the booty, inflicted great damage on the local population and economy. The totals of more than 40,000 deportees from Israel, and about 200,000 from Judah, given in the Assyrian annals, seem to be realistic (for more populated areas the numbers are much greater) and constitute a significant percentage of the population. It is important to notice that the deportations are not confined to the royal family and palace, that if necessary are dealt with separately, but also include the common agro-pastoral population of the villages and small cities ('male and female, old and young'), although special attention was paid to record any specialized skills and crafts.

In Assyrian ideology this destructive activity makes sense in itself, as a punishment of previous treachery or sacrilegious opposition to the god Asshur and the king, his military agent. But it acquired a fuller sense when combined with the work of reconstruction that the Assyrian kings themselves claim to support – behaviour consistent with the idea that conquest means enlarging order at the expense of sedition, justice at the expense of iniquity. The destructive moment is succeeded by constructive action; the destroyed royal palace and local elite are replaced by a provincial Assyrian palace to house a group of Assyrian officials; the deportation of the local people to Assyria or other Assyrian provinces is compensated by deportation from other provinces to the newly conquered one. The final aim is linguistic, cultural and political assimilation, as complete as possible, aimed at turning the defeated into Assyrians. Assimilation completes the conquest, turning a rebel kingdom into a new province of the cosmos directly dependent on the king and the god Ashur. This is how Sargon II expresses himself:

> By order of Ashur, my lord, and the power of my sceptre, I deported the people of the four parts of the world, speaking a foreign and incomprehensible language, dwellers of mountains and plains, all subjects of the light of the gods and lord of everything. I turned them into a sole language and put them there. I assigned them some Assyrians as scribes and overseers, who were able to teach them the fear of god and king (*ISK*, 296).

Of course, from the imperial point of view this is a process of assimilation, while from the local point of view it is the severe destruction of a culture. The capital cities (Samaria, Damascus, Hamath and many others), already lively centres of political decision and diplomatic relations, handicraft and trade, religious worship, literary production, and all kinds of local and distinct culture, became simply the administrative satellites of the imperial capital, with the sole function of directing human and material resources to the centre. However, the restoration was carried on, aiming to destroy cultural individuality but without causing the economic and demographic collapse.

Archaeology well demonstrates the persistence of settlement in the areas conquered by the Assyrians. At Samaria (VII) a fragment of a stele of Sargon II and two administrative Assyrian tablets have been found; in 690 a governor of Samaria acted as the eponym (*SAA*, Suppl. II, 50). Megiddo (III) was rebuilt to a different (orthogonal) urban layout and two large houses on the 'Assyrian' plan, with a central court were built. At Gezer two Assyrian tablets (indicating the existence of an administrative centre) have been found; at Hazor two 'public' buildings; at Tel Kinneret a fort with a small Assyrian 'residency'. Beth-Shean (IV), Tel Dan, Shechem (VI), Tirzah (Tell Far'a North VII E), Lachish (II) and Dothan (1) were reconstructed, though modestly; at Bethel the temple was rebuilt. Other provincial 'small palaces', showing the typical Assyrian plan and containing fine Assyrian palace ware, are concentrated in the extreme south, between the hinterland of Gaza and the Beer-sheba valley: at Tell Jemme (EF), Tell Abu Salima (G), Tel Haror, Tel Sera' (V-VI). These give a clear indication of Assyrian interest in controlling access to the Egyptian Delta and the transverse caravan route through the Negev. Coastal centres also flourish, from Dor to Ekron (Tel Miqne I C-B, with large oil production facilities).

In this context of demographic and territorial reshaping, all in the interests of Assyria, and under the watchful control of garrisons and Assyrian officials, the custom of 'cross deportation', involving about 4.5 million people over three centuries, played an essential role. The biblical account of the conquest of Samaria tells first of the deportations of the Israelites:

> In the ninth year of Hoshea the king of Assyria captured Samaria; he carried the Israelites away to Assyria. He placed them in Halah, on the Habor, the river of Gozan, and in the cities of the Medes (2 Kgs 17.6).

and shortly afterwards describes the arrival of foreign deportees:

> The king of Assyria brought people from Babylon, Cuthah, Avva, Hamath, and Sepharvaim, and placed them in the cities of Samaria in place of the people of Israel; they took possession of Samaria, and settled in its cities (2 Kgs 17.24).

From the texts of Sargon II we know that he deported some Arabs to Samaria also:

> I crushed the tribes of Tamud, Ibadid, Marsimanu, and Haiapa, the Arabs who live, far away, in the desert (and) who know neither overseers nor official(s) and who had not (yet) brought their tribute to any king. I deported their survivors and settled (them) in Samaria (*ANET*, 286).

The new society had to be mixed, not between dominant and dominated (the dominant were few and important) but between dominated people of different origin.

The results were predictable. Political resistance, deprived of a context in which to develop, was totally crushed, while the local economy was saved. At the beginning the demographic balance was negative, since many deportees died on the way, and those who arrived at their destination had many problems in starting a new life in a totally unknown context (for the Samaritan deportees see *SAA*, I, 220, 255; XV, 280). Demographic difficulties occurred throughout the empire; the Assyrians for their part, however, did not want to turn conquered areas into desert, on the contrary, they did everything possible to make them productive and populated. Whole families were deported, homogeneous communities, just to sustain high morale and the will to live and work.

Linguistic assimilation was totally to the advantage of Aramaic, the most diffused language in the empire and in particular in the regions (Babylonia, Syria) where the majority of the deportees came from. But even in Assyria during the eighth–seventh centuries Aramaic was used alongside Assyrian as the language of administration, and even as the spoken language. Religious assimilation did not result in the imposition of Assyrian religion, except in some state ceremonies or as a statement of basic principle. On the contrary, it resulted in a widespread and variegated syncretism among the several cults imported by the new arrivals: the persistence of the 'Canaanite' cults, and a modification of the Yahwism that some considered as the strongest element of self-identity and also of a link with the surviving sibling kingdom of Judah. However, this outcome was bound to appear unacceptable to the 'orthodox' Yahwists of the south (see the Deuteronomistic condemnation in 2 Kgs 17.29-34, with its account of the deities of the immigrants), who particularly at that moment, and in reaction to the events and the consequent situation in the north, took their religion in a more and more precise and exclusive direction.

4. *Growth and Prosperity in the Kingdom of Judah*

In the south, Hezekiah's goal of resisting Assyrian power depended on having a kingdom rapidly growing in material resources and ideological consciousness. It is probable that after the conquest of Samaria some groups of Israelites from the north found refuge in Judah, assisting demographic growth, administrative efficiency and religious development. However, the major factors of growth can be seen in the political stability (the two long reigns of Hezekiah and Manasseh cover a total of 85 years) and in the proximity to an Assyrian empire that firstly (in its aggressive phase) mobilized the human and moral resources of the peoples it attacked, and then (in the co-existence phase) allowed the inclusion of the neighbouring vassals in a wider economic system.

The initial mobilization translated into the grand urban projects of Hezekiah in Jerusalem and elsewhere. In the capital a new enclosure wall (involving the destruction of private houses, deplored by Isa. 22.10) was built to protect the new quarters that were rapidly being formed on the western hill. The city grew from 5 hectares (mainly occupied by the temple and palace) to 60 hectares, and the estimated population increased from 1,000 to 15,000 in the space of a single generation. The new quarters are called *Mishneh*, 'doubling' (Zeph. 1.10-11) in the north-west quarter, and *Maktesh*, 'pestle' (representing a depression), the valley between the old 'city of David' and the new city. The other great project was the construction of a large catchment pool (Siloam, just at the bottom of Maktesh) fed by a tunnel that carried the water of the Gihon spring to a place inside the walls. This remarkable work of hydraulic engineering is not only attested in the Bible (2 Kgs 20.20; 2 Chron. 32.30) but also by an inscription that celebrates the completing of the work, vividly describing the moment when the two teams of excavators, which had worked from opposite ends, finally met:

> [... when] (the tunnel) was driven through. And this was the way in which it was cut through: – While [...] (were) still [...] axe(s), each man toward his fellow, and while there were still three cubits to be cut through, [there was heard] the voice of a man calling to his fellow, for there was an overlap in the rock on the right [and on the left]. And when the tunnel was driven through, the quarrymen hewed (the rock), each man toward his fellow, axe against axe; and the water flowed from the spring toward the reservoir for 1,200 cubits, and the height of the rock above the head(s) of the quarryment was 100 cubits (*ANET*, 321).

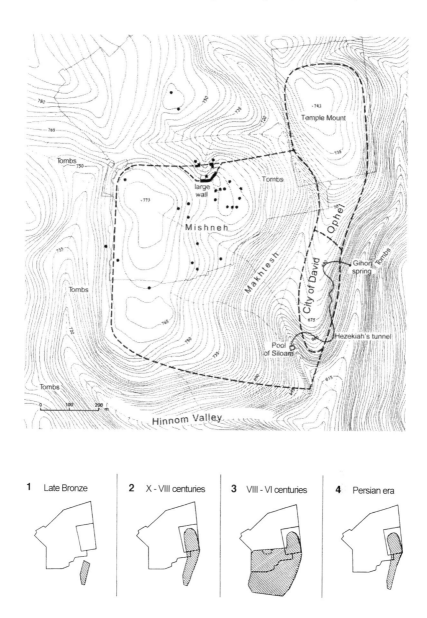

Figure 37. *The growth of Jerusalem: (a) the 'City of David' and the expansion under Hezekiah; (b) the size of the city at different periods*

But the building and settling development continued, both in time and in extent, after and beyond the work needed for the imminent siege, and also in the period of the 'Assyrian peace'. Jerusalem clearly dominated the hierarchy of cities, with its 60 hectares, compared to the 10 hectares of Lachish and the 3-4 hectares of other small cities. Lachish, the major centre in the Shephelah, suddenly grew at the end of the eighth century (strata IV-III), and was enclosed by an imposing wall, with a double city gate: an inner one with six rooms, and an outer one with an hairpin ramp. The gate led into a square from which one entered the palace complex through a second six-roomed gate. Thus, it was an important and well-provided administrative centre at the time of Sennacherib's siege. In addition, the royal residence of Ramat Rahel (V B), halfway between Jerusalem and Bethlehem, was probably built by Hezekiah. The list of Judean fortresses, that 2 Chron. 11.5-12, 23 attributes to Rehoboam, is in all probability Hezekiah's work, and the same is true of a series of fortresses that have been uncovered: Khirbet Marjama and Rujm Abu Mukhayr, in strategic position on the roads toward the Jordan valley; Tell el-Hesi, Tell Judeideh and Tell Zakariya (Azekah) in the region around Lachish, on the border with the Assyrian province of Ashdod; and finally, Khirbet Rabud (B), guarding the southern border.

The agricultural villages, in both the lowlands and highlands, grew in number and size, and the major crisis caused by Sennacherib's destruction seems to have been rapidly overcome. The production of wine is evident at Gibeon in particular by the stamps on the amphorae (*SSI*, I, 14); and a significant development of olive oil production is indicated by the extraordinary number of oil presses found in the excavations of Tel Miqne (Ekron), dated to his period. We also have '1100 (measures/jars) of oil; of the king' written on an ostracon from Tell Qasile (*SSI*, I, 4), in a coastal area but with Yahwistic onomastics. If the resources of the Shephelah were now directed towards the Philistine cities and the Assyrian minor palaces, the resources of the plateaus were obviously directed towards Jerusalem. This is proved by the oil (or perhaps rather wine) amphorae (50-litre capacity) bearing the typical stamp *lmlk*, 'for the king', plus four areas of provenance, Hebron, Soko, Zif, and Memshat (the last of these has not been located). Two kinds of royal seals are found, one with a four-winged scarab, another similar to the winged sun, both showing clear Egyptian influence; also seals of officials, bearing their name and position, among them being Shebna, who is well known from the book of Isaiah. This type of seal seems to cover a limited time span, and the high number of such finds at Lachish III leads us to think of a military defensive set-up, appropriate to the circumstances of Hezekiah's reign. It is possible that the emergency of the Assyrian threat led to a change in the centralized system of provisions formerly used in normal times. Apart from Lachish, many stamps have been recorded among finds at Ramat Rahel VB, Jerusalem, Gezer V, Hebron, Bet-Sur, Beth-Shemesh, Tel Batash (Timna), and in many of the fortresses listed above: the diffusion area, as has been noted, corresponds almost exactly to the list of fortresses in 2 Chronicles 11.

In the eighth century the Judean countryside reached its maximum population density, at the limit of its capacity; and at the same time we see an expansion into neighboring semi-arid areas, which continued up to the time of Josiah (see §8.3). In the Negev, not only in the Beer-sheba valley but also in properly desert areas, fortresses began protecting the frontier and controlling the caravan routes. It is plausible to assign to Hezekiah Arad VIII, Kadesh-barnea (middle fortress) and Tel 'Ira VII – which is a fortified administrative centre. All these fortresses may have been destroyed during Sennacherib's campaign.

The settlement of the desert fringes implies the use of dry farming techniques, with dams to retain water and soil in the wadis subject to sudden floods; these devices had already been utilized in Iron Age I (see §2.6) but were now applied on a larger scale. The kingdom of Judah could probably take advantage of participation in the rich trade coming from south Arabia, something that also accounts for the settlement, growth and economic fortunes of Edom and other states lying along the so-called 'King's Highway', now secure after centuries of relentless wars among Arameans, Israelites and Moabites, thanks to their shared (whether direct or indirect) submission to the Assyrian empire. It is significant that another of the Tell Qasile ostraca records '30 shekels of gold of Ophir for Beth-Horon' (*SSI*, I, 4): the amount is modest, but the name 'Ophir' alludes to South Arabia and the maritime trade on the Red Sea.

5. *Hezekiah's Reforms and the Prophetic Debate*

Assyrian pressure caused a reaction on the ideological level also, exercising a generally disruptive influence from the intervention of Tiglath-Pileser III to the end of the empire, but concentrated in the time of Hezekiah. The moment of reaction came when Hezekiah initiated religious reforms evidently aimed at mobilizing the moral resources of the country in the face of the new and serious danger. The reform (2 Kgs 18.4; with huge additions in 2 Chronicles 29–31) was of a Yahwistic character, abolishing the shrines belonging to the agricultural religion: the 'high places' (*bāmôt*), the steles (*maṣṣēbôt*), the trees or trunks (*ăšērôt*). It even destroyed a bronze snake attributed to Moses that had become an object of popular worship. Hezekiah is the first king of Judah to whom the Deuteronomistic historian attributes the destruction of the *bāmôt*; under all his predecessors, this writer had always said 'however, the *bāmôt* did not disappear, and the people went on in offering sacrifices and incense on the *bāmôt*'. Thus, Hezekiah's action was novel, presumably followed by a rearrangement of the temple (involving not only the furniture but also the structure itself) to make it suitable for the cultic innovations; the reforms marked a first move in transforming Yahweh from the national god to an exclusive one. One can well imagine how the reform will have been received painfully, and resisted, by a population used to its fertility cults. In fact, Hezekiah's successor, Manasseh (687-642), reintroduced religious pluralism, rebuilding the *bāmôt* and other symbols of the fertility cults.

Hezekiah's reform did not take place suddenly, but was the climax of a process triggered by a natural internal evolution, perhaps by the influx of priests and levites from the northern kingdom, and certainly by confrontation with the ideology of the large empire of which Judah was a small peripheral part. The inner evolution is shown by the rise, at the end of the eighth century (and thus some decades later than the North) of prophetic activity originating in the traditional activity of the court diviners, but endowed with a fuller ideological, and now also literary, dignity. Its exponents are Hosea, Micah, and Isaiah: these are all witness to the ideological ferment and debate that followed the terrible events of the Assyrian invasion, the destruction of Samaria, and the threat to Jerusalem itself: events that undermined the trust between people, ruling class, and deity – relationship that apparently was not working properly.

Hosea (c. 760–720) lived in Israel until the destruction of Samaria, but then probably took shelter in Judah, bringing with him his experience of the national disaster in the north. Israel, according to Hosea, was destroyed because of the corruption of the ruling class, but especially because it betrayed its allegiance to Yahweh – an act that the prophet, out of his personal experience, depicts by the metaphor of conjugal infidelity. If now Judah wants to avoid a similar fate, it will have to affirm its loyalty to Yahweh. The prospect of relying on human support (Egypt: Hos. 7.11, 12.2) had emerged as illusory for Israel, and would be the same for Judah.

The text of Micah (c. 750–710) has been extensively rewritten and updated by post-exilic interventions (particularly concerning the final destiny of Jerusalem), but the overall meaning seems to go back to the moment after the collapse of Samaria. In a fictitious 'trial' the deity rebuts the implied accusation of not having protected his people, recalling all the previous benefits that Israel always repaid with serious and persistent unfaithfulness. However, coming from a peasant village in Judah, Micah seems particularly sensitive to the theme of the corruption and injustice of the rulers as the ultimate cause of the downfall:

> They covet fields, and seize them;
> houses, and take them away;
> they oppress householder and house,
> people and their inheritance (Mic. 2.2).

> The women of my people you drive out
> from their pleasant houses;
> from their young children you take away
> my glory forever.
> Arise and go;
> for this is no place to rest,
> because of uncleanness that destroys
> with a grievous destruction (Mic. 2.9-10).

> Its rulers give judgment for a bribe,
> its priests teach for a price,
> its prophets give oracles for money (Mic. 3.11).

It is clearly too late to invoke divine help when the whole people has already been ruined by those who should have been taking care of it.

However, the fundamental exponent of the Yahwistic movement is undoubtedly Isaiah ('First' Isaiah, or 'Isaiah of Jerusalem', author of much of chapters 1–39 of the book that bears his name), who was active roughly between 740–700 and served as a protagonist (an adviser of the king) during the siege of 701. His first predictions, although they support the elimination of the worship of idols, are more concerned with socio-economical problems, as in this vigorous condemnation of the growing power of the landowners:

> Ah, you who join house to house,
> who add field to field,
> until there is room for no one but you,
> and you are left to live alone
> in the midst of the land! (Isa. 5.8).

The *latifundium* (large rural estate) carries its own curse, that will doubtless be fulfilled, because without the care of small landowners agricultural profits will fall off:

> Surely many houses shall be desolate,
> large and beautiful houses, without inhabitant.
> For ten acres of vineyard shall yield but one bath,
> and a homer of seed shall yield a mere ephah (Isa. 5.9-10).

However, with subsequent oracles the concept of loyalty to Yahweh as the only hope of salvation becomes more and more crucial. This concept is introduced into specific political issues, offering glimpses of the current debates. Parallel to the disaster of the north emerges the role of Jerusalem as a focal point for survivors of Israel, the 'remnant' on whom the hope of a forthcoming renewal must be based (Isa. 2.1-5). Criticism emerges of the main court officials. Shebna, secretary of the king, and Eliakim, prefect of the palace (the funerary inscription of the former has been perhaps preserved, *SSI*, I, 8; see Isa. 22.15-18) are responsible for basing Jerusalem's defence entirely on human resources (22.8-11). Criticism is also directed against the building policy of Hezekiah ('You collected the waters of the lower pool. You surveyed the houses of Jerusalem and pulled houses down to strengthen the wall', 22.9-10). We find polemics against the inefficacy of Egypt – which cannot, of course be regarded as a substitute for the saving role of Yahweh (30.1-5; 31.1-3). The prophet rails also against Assyria, firstly portrayed as a divine instrument of destruction against the impious northern kingdom, but then condemned because it displayed too much relish and cruelty in its destructive action (10.5-11; 31.4-9). Finally, he turns against the other states of the Levant, all ready to profit from the misfortunes of others.

With Isaiah the so-called 'oracles against the nations' (Isaiah 14–21 and 23) take on a more powerful form than with Amos (1–2) at the time of the Aramean wars. Such oracles are laments and curses hurled at states and neighbouring peoples guilty of profiting at each other's expense, and in particular at the expense of Israel and Judah, as a result of the imperial intervention, and accusing each king of crimes committed to secure advantages that will later turn out to be illusory, as they incur divine vengeance. The oracles of Amos had been particularly blunt, in the context of the Syro-Palestinian wars in which Assyrian intervention represented divine retribution:

Thus says Yahweh:
For three transgressions of the Ammonites,
and for four, I will not revoke the punishment;
because they have ripped open pregnant women in Gilead
in order to enlarge their territory.
will kindle a fire against the wall of Rabbah,
fire that shall devour its strongholds,
with shouting on the day of battle,
with a storm on the day of the whirlwind;
then their king shall go into exile,
he and his officials together, says Yahweh (Amos 1.13-15).

The oracles of Isaiah are much more sophisticated, issuing from within the framework of a political debate over a wider range that also includes kingdoms against which Judah did not bear a grudge. Here, for example, is a lament over Sidon, conquered by Sennacherib in 701 (with the king fleeing to Cyprus):

> Wail, O ships of Tarshish,
> for your fortress is destroyed.
> When they came in from Cyprus
> they learned of it.
> Be still, O inhabitants of the coast,
> O merchants of Sidon,
> your messengers crossed over the sea
> and were on the mighty waters;
> your revenue was the grain of Shihor,
> the harvest of the Nile;
> you were the merchant of the nations.
> Be ashamed, O Sidon, for the sea has spoken,
> the fortress of the sea, saying:
> I have neither laboured nor given birth,
> I have neither reared young men
> nor brought up young women."
> ...
> You will exult no longer,
> O oppressed virgin daughter Sidon;
> rise, cross over to Cyprus –
> even there you will have no rest (Isa. 23.1-4, 12).

It becomes clear how the status of an area politically divided, when subjected to imperial pressure, accentuates the tendency to self-identification of each unit, especially by means of asserting contrasts with other units. In this movement towards ethno-political identity, religion plays a very central part.

This is the context of the Yahwistic reforms (or more simply, anti-idolatry measures) of Hezekiah, which make sense when set against the debate within a city under threat of imminent siege, where a totally religious solution of complete submission to the one god Yahweh, advocated by the prophets, encounters the human politics of alliances and military and economical measures adopted by the king and his officials.

6. Imperial Ideology and Local Strategies

During the siege of Jerusalem in 701, several exchanges took place between the general of the Assyrian army (the *rab-šāqēh* 'chief cup-bearer') and the chiefs of the besieged Judeans (Eliakim prefect of the palace, Shebna secretary of the king, Joah herald), narrated in 2 Kgs 18.17–19.19 and Isaiah 37, and which represent, as best one can, the conflict of ideologies in play during the course of the military engagement. The Assyrian officials intervene twice orally, then deliver a letter from Sennacherib; after this, all that is left is military action. In a text of Esarhaddon (of the 'letter to the god' genre) the siege of the rebel city of Shubria is also marked by interchanges between the besiegers and besieged, with the Assyrian king finally losing his patience after repeating his order to surrender 'three times':

> Have you ever heard the order of a mighty king twice? And I am a very powerful king, and have spoken to you three times, but you have not listened to the words of my mouth. You did not fear of [...] of my person, you did not worry. You are the one who forced me to cause a war; you are the one who aroused the fierce weapons of Assur from their place! (*IAKA*, 103-104).

It is interesting to notice that below the walls of Jerusalem the Assyrian negotiators address the besieged in Hebrew (and not Aramaic as demanded by the spokesmen of the besieged), with the explicit aim of being heard by all the people on the walls witnessing the negotiation, whose interests did not correspond to those of the ruling class.

The Assyrian arguments are as follows: the trust of the Judeans in their walls and in Egyptian help is in vain; all the Syrian cities have had to capitulate, and yet they had their own gods; Hezekiah's argument that he can count on his very special god Yahweh is invalid, because Sennacherib has been sent by Yahweh himself, who has abandoned his people; and finally (directly addressed to the people), anyone who will submit is given the promise of being deported to a fertile land where he will resume a normal life.

The arguments echo precisely the fundamental principles of Assyrian imperial ideology: in particular, that Assyrian power is based not only on great military strength, but also on proper trust in the god Ashur, while the enemies are forced to capitulate because they foolishly trust in human elements (material defences, and the aid of allies) or in deities that have already recognized the Assyrian supremacy and have abandoned their faithful. Also typically Assyrian is the distinction between 'guilty' rulers and the population, who are unaware, and can be redeemed.

However, the speeches of the Assyrian officials also show a good knowledge of the arguments circulating in Jerusalem during the siege. Apart from the temptation to surrender (which could circulate among the common people), two parties face each other: one (technical/political) that advocated resistance through relying on Egyptian intervention, and the other (prophetic/populist) that advocated trust in Yahweh alone. The oracle of Isaiah, expressing this complete (and humanly irrational) faith, seeks to mobilize the resistance of the besieged:

> Therefore thus says Yahweh concerning the king of Assyria: He shall not come into this city, shoot an arrow there, come before it with a shield, or cast up a siege-ramp against it. By the way that he came, by the same he shall return; he shall not come into this city, says Yahweh (2 Kgs 19.32-33 = Isa. 37.33-34).

Isaiah, supporter of the 'religious' strategy, occupies, after the conclusion of the siege, a favorable stance in asserting that Egyptian help was totally ineffective, while it was Yahweh who saved the city. The definition of Egypt as a 'broken reed', that wounds the hand of the one who leans on it (Isa. 36.6) becomes proverbial (and is reused by Ezek. 29.6-7).

Thus, the Assyrian and local ideologies agree in considering that the military outcome can only be the consequence of decisions already taken at a divine level. The Assyrians thought they were carrying out a commission of the god Asshur: every report of their campaigns starts with 'by order' (*ina qibit*) or 'by reliance (*ina tukulti*) on the god Ashur and the mighty gods'. The Assyrian action also met with the consent of the enemy gods themselves (as the *rab-šāqēh* says concerning Yahweh), disgusted by the disloyalty of their people. It is worth quoting the passage in which Esarhaddon explains the destruction of Babylon by his father Sennacherib, despite some embarrassment, and the total omission of the name and action of his father. The connivance of the Babylonian god is even more necessary since this is a deity worshipped by the Assyrians themselves:

> Formerly, at the time of a previous king, there were unfavourable signs in Sumer and Akkad. The inhabitants of Babylon split into two factions ('they answered each other yes/no'), and hatched a rebellion. They got their hands on the treasure of Esagila, the temple of the gods, and looted it of gold, silver and precious gems to give them to Elam as payment (for the troops). Marduk, lord of the gods, flew into a rage, and took the unfavorable decisions of devastating the land and destroying his people. The canal Arakhtu, a river in flood, furious current, reproduction of the deluge, was deflected and its water flowed over the city of his residence, and over his own sanctuary, turning everything into a ruin. The gods and goddesses who dwelt there fled away as birds and ascended into heaven. The people who dwelt there passed under the yoke and whip, and became slaves. Seventy years, as measure of the desolation, he wrote (in the destiny); but then the merciful Marduk, whose rage lasts a moment, changed it and considered restoration after eleven years (*IAKA*, 12-15, D).

The idea that the invaders were agents of the offended gods, who wanted to punish their people, had a long history throughout the Near East, going back to the times of the fall of Akkad at the end of the third millennium. However, there is of course a difference between involving the gods of the defeated to explain one's own success, and imputing to one's own god the responsibility of one's own defeat. The possible reactions to this syndrome of abandonment and punishment could, of course, be either of two: in the event of defeat, acknowledgement of the superior power and trustworthiness of the god Asshur, and thus adherence to the Assyrian religion; or, conversely, in the event of an ambiguous outcome, or an averted danger, more probably a strengthening of trust in the local god and an increased commitment to eliminate the reasons for the guilt and treason that were in the final analysis the primary causes of the threat.

7. *Loyalty and Protection: The Emperor and the God*

The concept of 'reliance, trust' (*tukultu*), in both Assyrian and local ideology, coincided with principle of 'loyalty' (*kittu*). At this point, in the whole Levantine periphery of the Assyrian empire, re-emerge reminiscences of a remote past (the Late Bronze Age), when each city-state had no choice but to be 'servant' (we would say 'vassal', using feudal terminology) of one of the 'great kings' who dominated the area: either of Egypt or the Hittites. In local expectations, the 'small king' had to preserve his loyalty (*kittu*) and should then be rewarded by the protection (verb *naṣāru*) of his lord. If two lords faced each other, the battle would decide (as in an ordeal) to which of them the local king had to submit and be loyal.

Egypt, to tell the truth, had not once convincingly adhered to this ideology of protection as a reward for loyalty, maintaining that submission was due unconditionally. After the twelfth century, its role had been reduced until it was only nominal. Thus, the local kings became accustomed to being no-one's vassals, only the servants of their god, and placing in him all those expectations of protection that formerly rested in the earthly lord. The 'oath of vassalage' to the earthly lord was replaced by an oath of total trust in the divine lord. Already in the prophets of the eighth century (as we will see further in §14.4) we find the theme of the 'exodus from Egypt', namely liberation from Egyptian sovereignty, set in the foundation period, and ascribed to Yahweh, who had therefore imposed his own oath of unconditional loyalty.

When Assyria appeared on the Palestinian scene, in the mid-eighth century, the ancient paradigm was partly re-established. As a result, the local kingdoms could develop their two alternative strategies. The political strategy depended on trusting in the Egyptian protection in an anti-Assyrian stance. However, the forces on the field were rather ill-matched: against the deadly Assyrian war-machine and ideology stood an Egypt that was militarily weak (the Assyrian officials below the walls of Jerusalem call it a 'broken reed', 2 Kgs 18.21) and ideologically untrustworthy. Hence the recourse to a theological strategy: trust in divine protection in opposing the threat of the Assyrian emperor. And under the influence of Assyrian political-legal conventions, the ideology of the oath takes shape.

In all the royal Assyrian inscriptions, from Tiglath-Pileser's time onwards, Assyrian intervention is always motivated by violation of the oath. A minor king is not guilty of refusing submission, or withholding tribute, or dealing with third parties: but he is always guilty of having violated the oath that obliged him to submission and to the payment of tribute, and to not recognizing other lords but Asshur. In practice, there was a two-stage strategy: first, Assyria imposed a vassalage oath, next it used any violation of that oath as an excuse to punish the rebel, who was thus guilty more of a theological breach than a political one, since the oath was taken before 'Asshur and the other (Assyrian) mighty gods'. The punishment was inflicted by the god, the Assyrian king being the agent and enforcer of the curses written at the end of the text of the oath. As an example, it is sufficient to cite the following text from Asshurbanipal:

> The rest of the Arabs, who escaped my weapons, the warrior-god Erra (= the pest) defeated them. Famine broke out among them. To satisfy their hunger, they ate the flesh of their children. All the curses written in the oath that they stipulated, in my name and in the name of the great gods, you, Ashur, quickly applied them as a terrible fate. The offspring of the camels, donkeys, cows and sheep, sucked seven times without being filled with milk. And the Arabs were asking each other: 'Why did all these misfortunes happen to Arabia?' And they answered: 'This happened because we did not follow the conditions we swore before Ashur!' (*BIA*, 248).

The Assyrians of the eighth and seventh centuries knew two kinds of oath. One was called *adû* (there is also an Aramaic example on the stele of Sefire, *SSI*, II, 7-9, dated to the first half of the seventh century): it was the appropriate oath sworn by the lesser king as an obligation of loyalty to the emperor and of payment of tribute (*biltu* or *madattu*). The second kind was called *kitru* and was an ill-advised attempt of securing human protection through payment, not of a tribute, but of a disqualifying 'bribe' (*ta'tu* or *kadrû*). In spite of recourse to the *kitru* (= support of human allies), the rebel would, sooner or later, directly or indirectly, be punished through the fulfillment of the curses of the *adû* and the power of the guarantor deity. The Judeans did not take over the term *adû* (they used *běrît*), but they did adopt the ideology of the oath: they decided to transfer their trust to Yahweh, and to retroject to a remote and foundational past (the period of David, Joshua, or even of Moses) the making of an oath that could guarantee its security, in exchange – obviously! – for absolute and exclusive loyalty. The biblical expressions of the oath (starting from the first commandment: 'I am the Lord; you will not have other gods before me') clearly replicate the Assyrian expressions of the loyalty oath:

> We will love Ashurbanipal, king of Assyria, and hate his enemy. From this day on for as long as we live, Ashurbanipal, king of Assyria, shall be our king and lord. We will not install nor seek another king or another lord for ourselves (*SAA*, II, 66).

Chapter 8

PAUSE BETWEEN TWO EMPIRES
(c. 640–610)

1. The Collapse of the Assyrian Empire

The Assyrian empire reached its peak under the reign of Ashurbanipal (668–631), who sent his generals to subdue the two rival kingdoms that were still independent: Elam in the far East, and Egypt in the far West. The magnificence of the enormous metropolis of Nineveh, enriched by palaces and works of art, and the famous library where all the Babylonian literary works were collected (included the canonical series of omens and the lexical lists) show a power that had now reached its final maturity. By the mid-century, however, complacency and stagnation and inactivity mark the beginning of the decline of an empire that could only maintain its strength through continued expansion. Assyria lost *de facto* control of the most distant provinces (from Egypt to Anatolia), the inflow of booty and tribute noticeably decreased, and the administrative and ceremonial apparatus had expanded too much, becoming a burden that could no longer be met. The last years of Ashurbanipal, moreover, witnessed the beginning of a war of succession that would last for 20 years and take its toll of the ruling class, the state finances and the army.

In 625 a Chaldaean chief, Nabopolassar, became king of Babylon and, with renewed energy, took charge of the armed opposition that had always caused problems to Assyrian control over Lower Mesopotamia. Year by year, the scene altered as the Assyrians were progressively expelled from the cities of Lower Mesopotamia, and the Babylonians began to move up the Tigris and Euphrates, taking the conflict to the middle of the empire itself. During this phase the Medes people proved a useful ally of the Babylonians: they were important horse-breeders, and occupied the central Zagros mountains and the commercial route that led from Babylonia to central Asia (the so-called Khorasan road). The Medes had for many centuries suffered Assyrian raids and plundering, but they had also benefited from their contiguity with the empire, developed more advanced state structures, with their tribal chiefs installed inside fortified, ceremonial citadels. They became rich selling horses to the Assyrians and controlling the Khorasan road, they equipped the Assyrians with auxiliary troops, and even provided the guards for the king and crown prince.

When the conflict between the Chaldaeans and Assyrians finally turned in favour of the former, the Medes entered the fray, probably motivated not only by the long-standing grudges and desire for revenge of mountain dwellers continually oppressed by the empire, but also by the new Zoroastrian religion that, at that very moment, was taking root on the Iranian plateau (according to tradition, the Zoroaster flourished around 630): the Zoroastrian religion was an ideology based on the fight between the forces of good and truth against those of evil and falsehood, and it could readily identify Assyria as the main representation of the domain of evil. Be that as it may, Median intervention was characterized by destructive violence: Ashur was conquered and sacked in 614, Nineveh in 612, and several other cities followed the same fate. The region that for three centuries had been the centre of the world, and had determined the fates of all the people of the Near East, was turned into a desert and wasteland (and would remain so for many centuries):

And he [God] will stretch out his hand against the north,
and destroy Assyria;
and he will make Nineveh a desolation,
a dry waste like the desert.
Herds shall lie down in it,
every wild animal;
the desert owl and the screech owl
shall lodge on its capitals;
the owl shall hoot at the window,
the raven croak on the threshold;
for its cedar work will be laid bare.
Is this the exultant city
that lived secure,
that said to itself,
'I am, and there is no one else'?
What a desolation it has become,
a lair for wild animals!
Everyone who passes by it
hisses and shakes the fist (Zeph. 2.13-15).

While the intervention of the Medes was decisive in the offensive action, it was the Chaldaeans who profited politically and territorially from the war, replacing the Assyrians in the control of much of the empire. The Medes, returning to their mountains in Iran, did not form

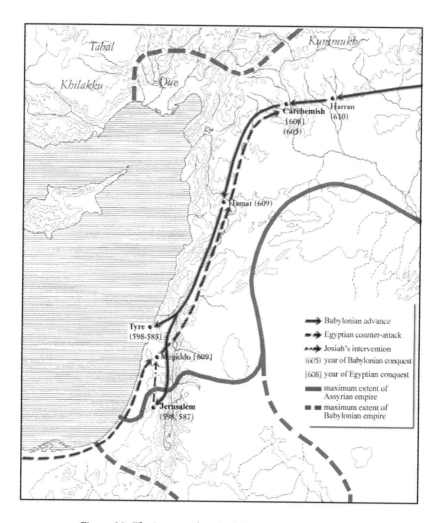

Figure 38. *The Levant after the fall of the Assyrian empire*

any empire (as the classical tradition maintains), but on the contrary reverted to forms of tribalism without cohesion or formal administration. The ceremonial citadels that flourished when the Assyrian empire was still working, were also abandoned: the periphery declined along with the centre. In Neo-Babylonian inscriptions the distinction of the roles is clear: the Medes performed the 'shabby' task of destroying the Assyrian cities, while the Chaldaeans were responsible for imperial reconstruction and continuity:

He (i.e. Marduk) provided him (i.e. [Nabopolassar], the king of Babylon) with helpers, let him acquire a friend and cause the king of the Manda-hordes [=Medes] who has no rival, to bow to his orders in submission and to come to his assistance. (And) he (the king of the Manda-hordes) swept on like a flood storm, above and below, right and left, avenging Babylon in retaliation. The king of the Manda-hordes, without (religious) fear, demolished the sanctuaries of all the gods of Subartu (Assyria). He also demolished the towns within the territory of Akkad [= Babylonia] which had been hostile against the king of Akkad and had not come to his assistance (in his fight against Subartu). None of their cult(-centers) he omitted, laying waste their (sacred) towns worse than a flood storm. The king of Babylon, however, for whom this sacrilegious action of Marduk was horrible, did not raise his hand against the cult(-places) of any of the great gods, but let his hair unkempt, slept on the floor (to express his pious desperation) (*ANET*, 309).

At this moment of Assyrian decline, soon after 612, Egypt itself tried to join in, and the Pharaoh Necho again marched up the Syro-Palestinian corridor to the far North, not to support what remained of Assyria, but rather to confront the Chaldaeans on the Euphrates and regain control of Syria-Palestine, which Egypt had never ceased to regard as its permanent property. However, the Egyptians failed in this, and the Chaldaean armies (Nebuchadrezzar II succeeded Nabopolassar) progressively conquered what had been the Assyrian territory west of the Euphrates (see further on, §§8.7, 9.1).

2. *An Interval of Freedom*

The 50 years (c. 640–590) spanning the Assyrian collapse were, then, for the populations subjugated to the empire and the neighbouring vassal states, an interval of freedom, or at least a period of renewed possibilities for initiative. The imperial armies were no more in a position to suppress potential revolts. The slackening (or loosing) of taxation and tribute led to an increase in the resources locally available.

It is understandable that the collapse of the Assyrian empire was greeted with joy by the subdued and threatened populations. The song of the prophet Nahum on the news of the destruction of Nineveh is an example of this reaction:

Ah! City of bloodshed,
utterly deceitful, full of booty –
no end to the plunder!
The crack of whip and rumble of wheel,

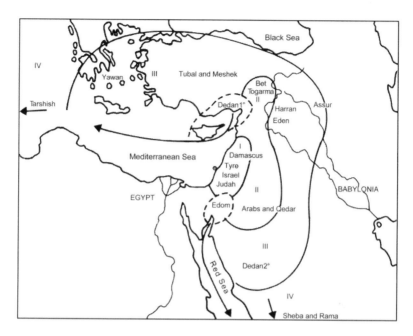

Figure 39. *Tyrian trade in Ezekiel 27 (I agricultural products; II livestock products; III handicrafts and slaves; IV luxury goods, metals)*

galloping horse and bounding chariot!
Horsemen charging,
flashing sword and glittering spear,
piles of dead,
heaps of corpses,
dead bodies without end –
they stumble over the bodies!
...
Then all who see you will shrink from you and say,
'Nineveh is devastated; who will bemoan her?'
Where shall I seek comforters for you?
...
There is no assuaging your hurt,
your wound is mortal.
All who hear the news about you
clap their hands over you.
For who has ever escaped
your endless cruelty? (Nah. 3.1-3, 7, 19).

In the theological reading of this event, it was recognized that Assyria had operated by divine order, as an instrument of punishment for the guilt and infidelity of the defeated; however, in its punitive action it had exercised too much gusto, and had taken advantage of the divine order to enlarge its own power (see in particular Isa. 10.5-19).

However, just before the final collapse, the local autonomy left by the Assyrian crisis between 640–610 had been exploited for some important initiatives in the Syro-Palestinian region. The areas that had been turned into provinces and lacking a strong culture could not express any reaction. However, the kingdoms that had kept their autonomy at the margins of the empire profited from the end of vassalage to Assyria to assert their own independence. We will shortly see what happened in the kingdom of Judah. A somewhat parallel situation occurred in Tyre, a Phoenician city that retained its autonomy. A long passage in Ezekiel (Ezekiel 27), precisely dated to the years 610–585, describes the trade network of Tyre in its whole extent, both in the Mediterranean and, especially, on land. The network significantly spread in the interstices between Egyptian and Babylonian territory, occupying all the zones from Anatolia to Arabia that during the period in question had regained a substantial independence from these empires. Thus, it seems that – just like the kingdom of Judah under Josiah – Tyre also pursued, during the Assyrian eclipse, a strategy of disengagement and expansion that, given its own circumstances, could only be commercial.

Judah and Tyre were not the only instances. In Transjordan a remarkable resurgence in the kingdom of Ammon is attested in the late- and post-Assyrian age by royal statues and the royal inscription of the citadel of Amman, by the Assyrian-inspired palace in the lower town, and the enlargement of the kingdom as far as Heshbon in the south (stratum 16, with Ammonite ostraca), Deir 'Alla VI and Tell es-Sa'idiya IV on the Jordan, and Gilead in the north. The important (if authentic) inscription on a bronze bottle, from Tell Sihan, is also to be dated to the seventh century.

In Anatolia, the old Assyrian provinces of Khilakku and Que formed what then became the kingdom of Cilicia, and, further north, Melid and Tabal became the kingdom of Cappadocia. During the same period the Persians replaced Elam (already destroyed by Ashurbanipal) as the emerging state in the region (ancient Anshan) that came to be called Fars. Thus, the 50 years 640–590 were a period of renewed freedom of action throughout the imperial periphery, and probably also a period of ideological ferment, notably of religious activity (from Iranian Zoroastrianism to Hebrew prophecy) of great importance and enduring consequences.

3. *Josiah and the Unification Project*

The period of Assyrian loss of control over its most distant provinces falls within the long reign of Josiah in Judah (640–609). Ascending to the throne when very young, with the support of the 'people of the land' (2 Kgs 21.24) to face a coup against the short-lived Amon, Josiah was able to profit from the favourable situation to give new life to the kingdom of Judah: the main aspects of his initiative were religious and ideological, but their material and political basis is also noteworthy.

Josiah inherited a kingdom that had experienced a long, favourable period under Manasseh, and this situation continued under him. It is archaeologically difficult to distinguish (given the lack of clear distinctive markers) the respective contributions of each king. However, the royal citadel of Ramat Rahel, already established by Hezekiah (V B), was enlarged (V A) by the construction of a palace with a central court, storerooms on the four sides and two administrative buildings in the middle, of a high quality of architecture, with ashlar masonry, proto-Aeolic capitals and balustrades with small twisted columns. The defence works at Debir (Tell Beit Mirsim A 2) and Timna (Tel Batash II) were also put into service again. It was probably the independent Josiah, rather than the vassal Manasseh to whom we should attribute the fortresses of Khirbet Abu et-Twein and Khirbet Rabud (A) west of Hebron, the fortress of Horvat Eres west of Jerusalem, and those of Tell el-Ful (III) and Horvat Shilha guarding the northern border.

The establishment of outposts in desert areas, both in the east and south, is of particular interest. In the east, where the Judean desert had been uninhabited since Chalcolithic times, began a process of reoccupation and control of key places, probably already begun by Manasseh (if not by Hezekiah): in particular we can point to the excavated sites of En-Gedi (Tel Goran V), the three fortresses of the Buqeia (Khirbet Abu Tabaq, Khirbet es-Samra, Khirbet el-Maqari), and Vered Jericho. The arid environment required sophisticated techniques of dry farming in the wadis and water conservation, with fortresses guarding the communication routes. It must be noted that the district known as the 'desert' (*midbār*) in the list of villages of the tribe of Judah (Josh. 15.21-63) leads us to date this document to the time of Josiah, and shows how the colonization of the arid areas was part of a clear administrative programme.

Towards the south, we may note in particular building activity in the Beer-sheba valley: Tel 'Ira (VI) seems to be the administrative centre of the area, but Aroer (IV) also has an imposing citadel of 1 hectare, with a

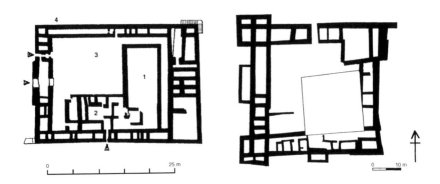

Figure 40. *Judean buildings of the seventh century: (a) the palace at Ramat Rahel; (b) the fortress of Arad VII*

crenellated wall. The citadel of Arad VII (with temple) is probably dated to the time of Josiah, while the citadel of Arad VI (now without a temple) could date from immediately afterwards. However, well beyond the area of Beer-sheba lie other sites of particular importance for the control of the roads (in a desert area this means control of the frontier): the fortresses of Mesad Haseva in the Arabah, Kadesh-barnea (with a casemate wall, Hebrew ostraka with numerals in hieratic) in the southern Negev, and Kuntillet 'Ajrud, really in the Sinai desert. In view of this expansion to the south, one can also assign to Josiah the first (casemate) fortress of Tell el-Kheleifeh that predates the second fortress of the Edomite period.

However, the disappearance of Assyrian control also made possible extension west and especially north, into the territory of those Assyrian provinces that had earlier been taken from the kingdom of Israel: Judah recognized an ethnic and religious bond with the kingdom of Israel, which was emphasized in the situation under Josiah. As for the extension to the west, in the territory of the province of Ashdod, it is certain that Josiah regained control of centres like Lachish and Gezer in the Shephelah. It is more doubtful that he was able to reach the coast: the fortress of Mesad Hashavyahu (near Yavne Yam), with its Hebrew ostraca (including a particularly well-known one, see §8.5) and its abundant Greek ware (a possible indication of the presence of Greek mercenaries) was not strictly managed by the kingdom of Judah but rather by the revived kingdoms of Ekron and Ashdod.

Regarding the extension and consolidation of the expansion to the north, the biblical sources are nevertheless elusive. Having narrated in detail the religious reform in the area of Bethel, 2 Kings briefly mentions

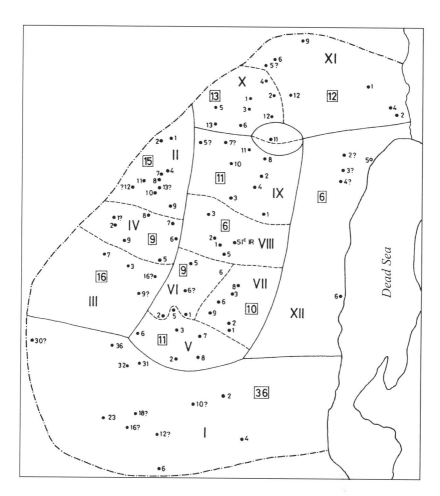

Figure 41. *The twelve districts of Judah and Benjamin (Joshua 15 and 18). The numbers within squares indicate the total of cities per district*

the extension of these reforms to the whole of Samaria, in a passage that looks like a later expansion (2 Kgs 23.19-20). In 2 Chron. 34.6 we also find the reform extended to the central plateau (Ephraim and Manasseh), to Simeon (which was, however, part of the kingdom of Judah), and 'even to Naphtali', as the extreme limit. The archaeological data are ambiguous: Megiddo is an indicative case, where stratum II, immediately after stratum III (when the city was capital of the Assyrian province named after it) has been interpreted as belonging to the kingdom of Josiah by those who attribute to him a large expansion to the north, and to an ephemeral Egyptian presence by those who deny such an expansion. The most common indicators of material culture show the kingdom of Judah consolidated between Bethel and Beer-sheba, but without any spread visible to the north nor to the Mediterranean coast.

Furthermore, there are two biblical documents that place the kingdom of Judah into a particular relationship with the rest of the territory of Israel. The first is the description of the tribal territories in Joshua 15–19, in which two different descriptive schemes are clearly followed. The territories of Judah, Benjamin, Simeon and Dan (still located west of Judah) are described not only by their borders, but also by a systematic list of cities and villages. Judah has a district in the Negev (with 29 cities), three districts in the plain (with 14, 16 and 9 cities respectively), seven in the highlands (11, 9, 10, 6, 11, 2, 6 cities) and one in the desert (6 cities); Benjamin has two districts (12 and 14 cities), while Simeon is said to be located within Judah (in fact many of its cities coincide), and Dan is said to have had to migrate elsewhere. By contrast, the territories of the other tribes are described only by their borders, without any detailed listing. Thus, it seems that underlying this passage is an administrative document from the kingdom of Judah, filled out with a wider scope. The number twelve recurs, because the division of Judah-Benjamin into a total of twelve districts is enlarged to a scheme of twelve tribes. As already mentioned, the presence of a district specifically for the cities of the Judean desert is an important chronological indication.

The case of the twelve districts of the kingdom of Solomon is analogous, in that we have seen how problematic it is to assign these to the 'United Monarchy'. In the description of these districts (1 Kgs 4.7-19), Judah is excluded, as not subject to forms of taxation that are imposed on other districts. In this case too, the difference in treatment between Judah and Israel suggests a process (or at least a project) of enlargement. If one tries to compare the two documents (tribal territories, districts of Solomon), one notices a correspondence in broad outline, but also a divergence in detail. It should be noted that the Solomonic districts 2, 11 and 12 could have been, together with the privileged district of Judah itself, part of the kingdom of Judah, while district 1 corresponds to the Assyrian province of Samaria, 3-4 to Dor, 6-7 to Gilead, and 5, 8-10 to Megiddo.

These textual materials might reflect, if not an effective enlargement of the kingdom of Judah to the whole of the north (which we have said was not achieved), at least the plan of Josiah to enlarge his kingdom to include all the territories inhabited by Israelites worshipping Yahweh, 'from Dan to Beer-sheba'. This plan – whose religious assumptions we will now analyze – came to nothing because of the Egyptian intervention and the death of Josiah that occurred before it was effectively accomplished.

4. The Discovery of the Law

If the biblical text is elusive about the political aspects of the kingdom of Josiah, it is fulsome on the cultural aspects. Thus, it is said (2 Kgs 22.8-10) that in the eighteenth year of Josiah (622) the chief priest Hilkiah consigned to the king's secretary Shaphan, who in turn gave it to Josiah, a manuscript found in the temple of Jerusalem, containing the Law. On reading the text, Josiah was struck by despair in realizing that the Law had not been enforced for such a long time, which on one hand explained why divine support was so often withheld, and on the other hand made it a matter of urgency to apply the Law faithfully and fully, so as to avoid disasters that were otherwise inevitable.

The expedient of the finding of an 'ancient' manuscript serves precisely to lend the sanction of a traditional authority to something that in fact represents an innovative reform. However, it is especially important to observe how this reform takes place at exactly the same time as the weakening of imperial Assyrian authority. In short, Josiah saw the opportunity for formally substituting dependence and loyalty to an earthly lord, the emperor, by dependence and loyalty to a divine lord, Yahweh.

The biblical text does not say which text (or how much of it) was found in the temple, but only records that it was seen as 'the book of the Law' (*sēfer hattôrāh*). However, for a long time (since W. de Wette, 1805) scholars have accepted that it must be connected with the book of Deuteronomy, and with the original core of that editorial stratum known as 'Deuteronomic', which is to be assigned to this period on the basis of a number of features. The question is complex and much-debated, and it is difficult to specify which is the original, properly Josianic, nucleus of Deuteronomy and which are later expansions and redactions, often of obvious exilic and post-exilic origin. A reasonable possibility is that the text Josiah claims to have found in the temple corresponds to Deuteronomy 4–28, the so-called 'Deuteronomic Law-Code' (chs. 12–25) together with its setting as a 'covenant oath', in which Moses acts as mediator between Yahweh and Israel: such an oath implies exclusive loyalty to Yahweh and the Law by the people, in return for blessing and on pain of curses.

The fundamental concepts of deuteronomic ideology are as follows: (1) Yahweh is the sole god; (2) the special relationship between Yahweh and his 'chosen people' is based on the covenant oath, whose core is the 'tables of the Law' of Moses, preserved in the ark of Yahweh, kept in the temple since Solomon's time; (3) Yahweh has brought Israel out of Egypt and given it the land of Canaan; (4) Canaan must be conquered according to the procedures of 'holy war' and the *herem*; (5) the duty of loyalty to Yahweh and his Law is laid upon the people, and the people have therefore to resist any temptation to apostasy and idolatry; (6) the temple of Yahweh has to be unique, in Jerusalem, 'the place where Yahweh's name dwells' and bereft of any cultural manifestations that are too tangible (included imagery), which are seen as foreign and dangerous.

Among these points, the one most immediately 'operative' is the last, but the historically more specific is the second. First, this contains a true memory (even if deformed by the notion of 'migration', as we will see in due course, §14.4), of the liberation from subjugation to Egypt and acquisition of full political control of Canaan. Second, it contains a projection for the immediate future: the same god who allowed us to escape from Egyptian slavery will allow us to escape every enslaving king, both the Egyptian, who looks like becoming of contemporary interest again, and the Assyrian, who is in fact in deep crisis, as well as others in the future. Relying on sole divine support alone, the people of Israel (the reunited ancient kingdoms of Judah and Israel) will remain autonomous if it stays loyal.

5. *A Single God in a Single Temple*

The central, ideologically significant statement of the reform certainly did not lie in the content of the legal stipulations, which on the whole could belong to any kind of religious framework; it resided, rather, in the exclusivity of the people's dependence on the one god Yahweh. In terms of the Decalogue we could say that the fundamental and innovative commandment was the first: 'I am Yahweh your god; you will not have any other god except me'. The other commandments of the Decalogue are routine socio-juridical principles, probably of remote antiquity (see §3.6). The same can be said of the longer and more detailed 'Deuteronomist law-code', that is, the actual text 'found' in the temple by Josiah.

Thus, the main objective of the king was to impose the exclusivity of the god, the cult, and the sanctuary: positively by reinforcing the place of the Jerusalem temple of Jerusalem, and negatively by abolishing other places of worship. On the work on the Jerusalem temple, the occasion for the finding of the Law, the biblical text does not dwell a great deal, but it mentions work on the masonry and interior furnishings, involving many kinds of craftsmen, and the problem of their payment. A reform based on the single temple could not have avoided being concerned with the temple under question. The importance of Josiah's works in the Jerusalem temple has probably been to some extent (perhaps a large extent) obscured by the purpose of the later historiographer in attributing the temple construction and furnishings to the 'foundational' period of Solomon, creating a structure that was miraculously unchanged over centuries, despite occasional sacking and partial destruction. Unfortunately, the temple is archeologically inaccessible, but it is not unreasonable to suggest an important phase of construction in Josiah's time, which may have established within the temple of Yahweh, doubtless already an ancient ('Solomonic') attraction centre on a regional scale, the structure and furnishings that decades later would be remembered by the exiles.

The biblical text particularly dwells on Josiah's Passover celebration (2 Kgs 23.21-22): and here too the statement that 'Passover had not been celebrated since the time of the Judges' (2 Kgs 23.21) serves in a way to disguise an innovation, providing the pretext of an ancient foundation. Passover had to be an old pastoral festival, with a sacrificial meal of lamb and unleavened bread, connected with the return from winter pastures (at the spring full moon). The transformation of Passover into a pilgrimage feast (*ḥag*) is probably an innovation by Josiah intended to enforce the gathering of worshippers from the whole land at the central sanctuary. The idea of connecting it to the founding event of the 'exodus from Egypt' is to be attributed to the Deuteronomist ideology.

However, the main requirement (2 Kgs 23.4-14) is directed at the demolition of the non-Yahwistic shrines – the notorious *bāmôt* (with their *maṣṣēbôt* and *'ăšērôt* attached) – in Jerusalem itself and in all the territory of Judah 'from Geba to Beer-sheba'. We know from this that in the temple of Jerusalem, formally dedicated to Yahweh, there were cultural trappings of Baal and Asherah (the ancient agricultural rites), the sun and the moon and other astral deities (perhaps recently introduced from Assyria); there was a factory where the women weaved cloth for Asherah, and there were (at the entrance of the temple) horses and a chariot of the sun. The presence of these non-Yahwistic cultic elements is partly attributed (by the Deuteronomist historiographer) to the recent 'apostasy' of Manasseh, but is partly dated back to the time of Solomon (and his foreign wives): for that reason it had to be a notoriously ancient practice. Also mentioned – and morally condemned – are practices with a sexual content, and those with sacrifices (*lammōlek* 'in sacrifice', not 'to Moloch'!) of children in the valley of Ben-Hinnom immediately south of the city. The violent fury of these destructions is partly the work of post-exilic rewriting, but it may have been a part of the reforming fury of Josiah himself.

The reform was also extended to the north, at least (and with urgency, 2 Kgs 23.15-20) to the rival sanctuary just beyond the border, because of

Bethel's ancient prestige. Its extension to all of Israel seems to be a later textual addition. The priesthood of the alternative temples abolished in Judah was centralized in Jerusalem but with subordinate functions; the news that the non-Yahwistic priests of the north were all killed (2 Kgs 23.20), and that the reform was extended 'to all the cities of Samaria' (23.19) belongs to a later rereading of the event. We should remember that in fact the co-religionists were invited to join together around the temple of Jerusalem, recognizing that the sole hope of salvation was their submission to Yahweh. In the words of Jeremiah:

> Go, and proclaim these words toward the north, and say:
> Return, faithless Israel, says Yahweh.
> I will not look on you in anger,
> for I am merciful, says Yahweh;
> I will not be angry forever.
> Only acknowledge your guilt,
> that you have rebelled against the LORD your God,
> and scattered your favours among strangers under every green tree,
> and have not obeyed my voice, says Yahweh (Jer. 3.12-13).

This aim of unification and assimilation, essential to the political project of a united 'greater Israel', can also have been encouraged by the presence in Jerusalem of northern refugees (who had already arrived the day after the fall of Samaria), including priests and administrators, with their own ideological agendas. In the Deuteronomist work itself northern elements are in fact recognizable.

Archaeological and epigraphic confirmation of the monotheistic reform of Josiah is not easy to find, due to the difficulty of precise dating (to the decade) of undated ostraca. Different temporal contexts are indicated by various inscriptions found in the Negev. Recall that at Kuntillet 'Ajrud, in about the mid-eighth century, there was a 'syncretistic' situation with Yahweh cultically linked with his consort Asherah. A group of ostraca from Tel Arad from the end of the seventh century, (strata VII-VI, dated to the time of Josiah; *SSI*, I, 13) point to a strongly Yahwistic background: many personal names are Yahwistic: one person greets another in the name of Yahweh, and (Josiah would say *but!*) there is a temple of Yahweh here also. An ostracon from Mesad Hashavyahu near Yavne Yam (*SSI*, I, 9), also dated to the last third of the seventh century, is interesting from the judicial aspect: a harvester protests because his clothing has been seized – a legal pledge that the law (Deut. 24.12-17) permits only until sunset, and that Amos (2.8) had earlier condemned. Finally, an ostracon of unknown provenance (but laboratory analysis confirm its authenticity) records silver furnishing for the temple, ordered by Josiah himself:

So orders (J)osias (*'šyhw*) the king: to give, from the hands of Zakaryahu,
silver of Tarshish for the temple of Yahweh, 3 shekels.

6. The Deuteronomistic History

The backdating of the covenant to previous centuries, throughout the
period from Moses to Josiah, could to some extent attach to past events,
but it especially required a wide re-arrangement of that past from the key
perspective that the reform of Josiah now offered. In the same style and
with the same basic concepts as Deuteronomy, comes the long historiographical work (known as the 'Deuteronomistic history') that encom-
passes the books of Joshua, Judges, 1–2 Samuel and 1–2 Kings. It is not
easy to reconstruct the historiographical undertaking accomplished in
Josiah's time. The historical work of the 'Deuteronomist' has in fact
reached us in a text that (even if one leaves out of consideration the later
additions) cannot be placed before the exilic period, since the final disaster
of the kingdom of Judah occupies an important position. Thus, the work in
question should be attributed to a current (or school) of thought, rather
than a single author, that started with Josiah's reform and then extended
for several generations (we will return to this subject in §11.6).

The essence of this work lies in following, over the centuries, the history
of the relationship between Yahweh and his people, explaining the positive
or negative fortunes of the kingdoms of Judah and Israel in terms of loyalty
or the disloyalty to the covenant. In the initial formulation, dated to Josiah's
time, the historical trajectory had to begin with Moses and finish with
Josiah himself, describing a trajectory with a positive ending, the celebration of Josiah's reign as the final realization of the covenant, which had
been for so long ignored. Josiah set up as founding models the figures of
Moses (who stipulated the covenant), Joshua (who carried out the conquest of Canaan), David (who had accomplished the political unification),
and Solomon (who had built the temple).

On every one of the 'historical' kings, succeeding each other in parallel
in Judah and Israel, from Solomon to Josiah himself, a verdict was given,
based not on their effective political accomplishments but on their will and
ability to apply the fundamental principle of the covenant – in other
words, on their action in favour or against the exclusiveness of Yahweh
worship and its centralization in Jerusalem. In short, all those kings who
did not destroy the *bāmôt* of Baal and Asherah are considered wicked,
while those who did are considered good. The practical result of this
ideological distinction (of 'retroactive monotheism') is that all the kings of

Israel, without exception, are considered guilty of apostasy, because of their tolerance or favour of Baal worship. On the kings of Judah judgement fluctuates: some are good, some evil. The historical validity of these judgements was under everyone's nose: the kingdom of Israel had effectively been overwhelmed by divine punishment, while the kingdom of Judah had taken a different course. The climax was reached in the reform of Josiah that affirmed unambiguous loyalty to the covenant, centralized the whole worship in the single temple of Jerusalem, and attempted to unify politically the entire population of Yahweh worshippers. Thus, the perspective was positive: Yahweh would reward this adherence to the covenant (even if tardy, and preceded by too much hesitation and treachery) with Judah's political survival.

7. Failure and its Aftermath

In 609 an Egyptian army, led by the Pharaoh Necho, marched up the Palestinian coast in a move against the Babylonians who had by now defeated the last residues of the Assyrian empire. At Megiddo, Josiah confronted the Egyptians to stop them, but was routed, wounded, and died soon later. The biblical account is brief and ambiguous (with some disagreement between 2 Kgs 23.29 and 2 Chron. 35.20-24), but it is clear that Josiah tried to oppose Necho militarily. This decision was totally coherent with his ideological view: if Egypt had replaced Assyria, Israel would have returned to 'slavery' that had pertained before the covenant in return for which Yahweh had just 'brought out of Egypt' his chosen people. Exclusive loyalty in Yahweh implied opposition to Necho's action, despite the imbalance of forces on the battlefield. Yahweh had clearly said this – or the Deuteronomist on his behalf, perhaps precisely in the book 'discovered' in the temple:

> When you go out to war against your enemies, and see horses and chariots, an army larger than your own, you shall not be afraid of them; for Yahweh your God is with you, who brought you up from the land of Egypt (Deut. 20.1).

Trusting in the divine word, Josiah 'did not fear' and tried to block the progress of the Egyptian army, more furnished and well-trained than his, but he got the worst of it.

The tragic failure of his action had negative consequences that were immediately evident: Necho deported to Egypt the heir to the throne, Jehoahaz, and put on the throne another of Josiah's sons, Eliakim, or Jehoiakim (609–598), who reigned as his tributary (2 Kgs 23.31-35). However, in a very short time, Necho himself failed in his attempt to control

Syro-Palestine, and he was defeated by the Babylonians, led by Nebuchad-rezzar who in that same year succeeded his father Nabopolassar. The *Babylonian Chronicle* tells us that the Egyptians were first defeated at Carchemish on the Euphrates (*ABC*, 99; see the anti-Egyptian oracles of Jer. 46.2-12) and then were pursued as far as Hamath in central Syria and again defeated. In the space of few years Egypt was thrown out of Palestine, and Judah fleetingly regained its independence.

However, Josiah's death left his project uncompleted: the unification of Israel remained a dream, loyalty to Yahweh was suspect, and the reforming zeal abandoned (Josiah's successors 'did what was evil in Yahweh's eyes'); the political-military emergency prevailed over cultic issues, and what for a short while might have appeared as a culminating reign was reduced to just one more event in an alternative and troublesome outcome. The Yahwistic reforms had certainly been supported by an elite circle centred on the families of not only the king but also Shaphan and Hilkiah; it is otherwise difficult to judge how successfully the reforms had spread among the population.

The destiny of Josiah's reforms, in the years immediately following his death, is confirmed by the deeds and writings of the prophet Jeremiah who, already at the time of the king, had expressed his explicit support for the principles of the reform and his readiness to save the country from the otherwise inevitable fate presaged by the northern kingdom. In some passages the reference to the new Josianic covenant is quite explicit:

> Thus says Yahweh, the God of Israel: Cursed be anyone who does not heed the words of this covenant, which I commanded your ancestors when I brought them out of the land of Egypt, from the iron-smelter, saying, Listen to my voice, and do all that I command you. So shall you be my people, and I will be your God, that I may perform the oath that I swore to your ancestors, to give them a land flowing with milk and honey, as at this day (Jer. 11.3-5).

Jeremiah is also in agreement with the practical accomplishments of the reform (the destruction of the *tōfet* of the valley of Ben-Hinnom: 7.30-33; the abolition of the sanctuary of Shiloh: 7.12-15), and he seems worried about the return of Baalism in the time of Jehoiakim, and the persistence of idol worship:

> For your gods have become as many as your towns, O Judah; and as many as the streets of Jerusalem are the altars you have set up to shame, altars to make offerings to Baal (Jer. 11.13; see 2.28).

However much he is in keeping with the spirit of the reform, he is equally critical of its political management by the priests, who wanted to monopolize the interpretation of the Law, which automatically shifted the prophets from their role as royal advisers. In one passage he is even suspicious of its authenticity:

> How can you say, 'We are wise, and the law of Yahweh is with us,' when, in fact, the false pen of the scribes has made it into a lie? (Jer. 8.8).

Against the 'power' management, against the material application of the Law, Jeremiah supports the purity of the hearth, condemns luxury, and condemns Jehoiakim and the royal house for their injustice and corruption (22.13-19). In his criticism of the royal house his prophetic activity becomes more strictly political: the search for foreign support (Egypt) is considered as a crime of apostasy. Put on trial for being a defeatist, he risks being condemned, but is saved by a group consisting of influential members of the party centred on the family of Shaphan (Jeremiah 26). Two parties evidently confronted each other, expressing through prophetic messages their respective policies of submission or rebellion, between Egypt and Babylonia. The pro-Babylonian and anti-Egyptian party seems to be led by the son of Shaphan who, as secretary of Josiah, had brought the king (if not authored!) the 'Law' found in the temple – and thus a person very close to Josiah in the promulgation of the reform and the anti-Egyptian policy. If, however, the anti-Egyptian position could be justified on a theological basis, when this position became pro-Babylonian, it displayed its human realism. In this political context of feuding and dealing, the substance of the reforms rapidly lost its effect.

The action of the reformist king was not without effect, however. On the contrary, it had decisive results in the long term. Indeed, the subsequent tragic events served to provide the reform with the fundamental values that were necessary for the survival of the people of Israel. Josiah's political project furnished the model of a union (ethnic and political) that had never before been realized – nor even conceived. His vision of a covenant with the divine overlord provided a crucial interpretation of the tragic events that would very soon have befallen Judah. And above all, the historiographical scheme that the 'proto-Deuteronomist' (perhaps Shaphan, the royal 'scribe' of Josiah?) drew up during Josiah's reign supplied the framework for a retrospective reconstruction of the history of Israel that would assert itself over the following centuries.

Chapter 9

THE IMPACT OF THE BABYLONIAN EMPIRE
(c. 610–585)

1. Nebuchadrezzar and the Imperial Reconquest

After defeating the Egyptians in 609 at Carchemish and Hamath, Nebuchadrezzar persevered with annual campaigns to subjugate to the new Neo-Babylonian empire all the territories of Syria Palestine that had previously submitted to Assyria, and even those that until then had been independent. The *Babylonian Chronicle* presents the submission as initially spontaneous and bloodless: 'All the kings of Hatti (= Syria-Palestine) came into his presence and he received their vast tribute' (*ABC*, 100.17). However, a prophetic source describes the terrifying effect that the new 'scourge of God' had on the local population:

> For I am rousing the Chaldeans,
> that fierce and impetuous nation,
> who march through the breadth of the earth
> to seize dwellings not their own.
> Dread and fearsome are they;
> their justice and dignity proceed from themselves.
> Their horses are swifter than leopards,
> more menacing than wolves at dusk;
> their horses charge.
> Their horsemen come from far away;
> they fly like an eagle swift to devour.
> They all come for violence,
> with faces pressing forward;
> they gather captives like sand.
> At kings they scoff,
> and of rulers they make sport.
> They laugh at every fortress,
> and heap up earth to take it (Hab. 1.6-10).

The current depiction of the Babylonians as less 'fierce' than the Assyrians depends on their respective communicative strategies. The Assyrian kings had practised (in their celebrative inscriptions, as well as palace reliefs) a real 'strategy of terror', while the Chaldeans tried to promote an image of benevolence and devotion to the care of the temples, even omitting military deeds from their celebrative inscriptions. When they do mention them, they point to the liberation of the people and the cultic use of their resources, virtually without mention of the cruelties of war:

> (this Lebanon) over which a foreign enemy [= Egypt] was ruling and robbing (it of) its riches – its people were scattered, had fled to a far (away region). (Trusting) in the power of my lords Nabu and Marduk, I organized [my army] for a[n expedition] to the Lebanon. I made that country happy by eradicating its enemy everywhere (lit.: below and above). All its scattered inhabitants I led back to their settlements (lit.: collected and reinstalled)... I made the inhabitants of the Lebanon live in safety together and let nobody disturb them (*ANET*, 307).

Times had changed, and the destruction of the Assyrian empire under the aegis of freedom had left its own signature, at least as far as declarations of principle. However, in the practice of warfare, the levels of cruelty remained unchanged; indeed the Chaldeans were able to combine the effectiveness of the battle and siege warfare (similar to the Assyrians) with the mobility of the raider, a feature of their tribal origins.

Some, however, tried to resist; and the two sieges of Jerusalem and Tyre have become famous: these two kingdoms had tried to profit from the power vacuum by following policies of autonomous development that could not be fulfilled without at least an attempt at resistance.

The siege of Jerusalem was concluded very swiftly. Jehoiakim had been a tributary of Nebuchadrezzar for three years when he decided to try rebellion. However, in the same year (598) he died and his son Jehoiachin, 18 years old, succeeded him. (A seal of Eliakim, an official of Jehoiachin, has been found at Ramat Rahel VA). Jehoiachin, pressed by the Babylonian siege, immediately decided to capitulate. The Babylonians deported him, his family, the ruling class, and the specialized craftsmen. They sacked the temple treasures and the royal palace, included the golden furnishings originally made by Solomon (but how many times they had already been sacked or given for tribute!). They left Zedekiah, Jehoiachin's uncle, as their vassal king (the third of Josiah's sons to reign, after Jehoahaz and Jehoiakim.

Tyre, on the other hand, withstood a 13-years siege (598–585, *C. Ap.* 1.21), thanks to its island status, making the usual siege strategies applied by the Babylonians ineffective. Finally, it capitulated, and the 'rebel' Ittobaal III was replaced by the vassal Baal. The fall of Tyre has been celebrated by Ernest Renan as an example of obstinate and very noble resistance in the name of the values of freedom against imperial oppression:

Table 6. *Chronology of the Near East 650–525*

	Egypt	Judah	Tyre	Assyria	Babylonia	Media
650	XXVI Dynasty			Ashurbanipal		Kashtaritu
	Psammetichus I	Josiah		668–631	Kandalanu	670–625
	664–610	640–609			647–627	
		Jehoahaz 609		Ashur-etil-ilani	'no king': 626	
				630–627		
		Jehoiakim		Sin-shar-ishkun		
		609–598		627–612		
	Necho 610–595			Ashur-uballit	Nabopolassar	Cyaxares
				611–609	625–605	625–585
600	Psammetichus II	Jehoiachin 597	Ittobaal III		Nebuchadrezzar II	Astyages
	595–598		?–585		605–562	585–550
	Apries 589–570	Zedekiah	Baal 585–575		Awil-Marduk 561–560	
		597–586	Judges 574-562		Neriglissar 559–556	
	Amasi 570–526				Labashi-Marduk 556	
550	Psammetichus III		Merbaal 561–559		Nabonidus	
	526–525		Hirom 559–539		555–539	

Tyre was the first city that defended its autonomy against the fearful monarchies that from banks of the Tigris and Euphrates threatened to extinguish the life of the Mediterranean... One hundred, two hundred years before the victories of Greece, 'Persian wars' nearly as glorious of those in the fifth century, took place, and Tyre bore the whole brunt of them.

However, it has to be said that at that time the fall of Tyre was greeted with manifest satisfaction in Judean prophetic circles (as we will shortly see) and presumably also by other Syro-Palestinian people who had followed, with envy and concern, the economic and political growth of the Phoenician city – growth probably marked by extortionate credit and mercantile activities.

2. Local Strategies and the Oracles against the 'Nations'

In the face of the Babylonian pressure the local kings adopted divergent policies, indeed conflicting with each other. The news (2 Kgs 24.2) that Nebuchadrezzar had sent against Jerusalem 'troops of Chaldeans, Arameans, Moabites and Ammonites' confirms his employment of local auxiliary troops, also exploiting ancient grudges among the Palestinian peoples. At first, some asked for Egyptian help, as always happened. A fragment of a letter (written in Aramaic) has survived, in which a king of Ekron (if the reading of the demotic endorsement is correct) presses the Pharaoh to intervene against the Babylonians, referring to the oath of loyalty in return for protection:

> To the lord of the kings, Pharaoh, your servant Adon, king of E[kron. The welfare of lord of the kings, Pharaoh, may...all the gods] of heaven and earth and Baalshamayn, the [great] god, [seek at all times; and may they make the throne of lord of the kings,] Pharaoh, enduring like the days of heaven. What...[the forces] of the king of Babylon have come; they have reached Aphek and (encamped)...they have taken...For lord of the kings, Pharaoh, knows that your servant...to send an army to deliver me. Let him not abandon me...and your servant has kept in mind his kindness (*SSI*, II, 21).

However, the Pharaoh (as 2 Kgs 24.7 reports) 'did not leave his country', and Egypt remained instead the place of refuge for the elites who escaped the destruction.

Our main source of information on these local conflicts aroused by the Babylonian pressure are the so-called 'oracles against the nations (*gôyîm*)' pronounced by the prophets Zephaniah (already in Josiah's day) and then, particularly, by Jeremiah (46–51) and Ezekiel (25–32). This literary genre is not new: we have seen (§7.5) how a first group of 'oracles against the nations' related to the Assyrian invasions; now the main group issues with the Babylonian invasion: after that the genre disappears (except for a sporadic use against the Edomites in the post-exilic period). The connection is evident between the imperial intervention and the beginning, in explicit and violent ways, of local disagreements and of the process of ethnic self-identification within the Palestinian mosaic. Just at the moment of their disappearance as politically autonomous entities, the local states (both city-states and, particularly, ethnic-tribal ones) appear to acquire a high degree of self-identity and mutual antagonism.

The central event of imperial subjugation, and its theological interpretation, obviously provoke oracles against Israel and Judah, punished because of their unfaithfulness; and against the Assyrians and Babylonians, divine agents of the punishment but destined – because of their excess of destructive fury – to suffer divine punishment in turn; and also against the Egyptians as a potential human protector in place of the divine one. However, the majority of the curses or woes are directed against other nations, fellow-victims of the imperial conquest. Behind these oracles lie several motives: at the time of the Assyrian invasions, the ruin of the most northerly states, who had already submitted, was needed as an example to those still struggling. At the time of the Babylonian invasion, however, such a warning effect was now obsolete, and the prophecies give vent in particular to jubilation over the ruin of ancient rivals and resentment over their collaboration with the invaders:

Figure 42. *The letter of Adon, king of Ekron*

Thus says the Lord Yahweh: Because Edom acted revengefully against the house of Judah and has grievously offended in taking vengeance upon them, therefore thus says the Lord Yahweh, I will stretch out my hand against Edom, and cut off from it humans and animals, and I will make it desolate; from Teman even to Dedan they shall fall by the sword. I will lay my vengeance upon Edom by the hand of my people Israel; and they shall act in Edom according to my anger and according to my wrath; and they shall know my vengeance, says the Lord Yahweh (Ezek. 25.12-14).

Exultation over the ruin of close neighbours is easily predictable: on the one hand the Philistine cities and on the other the Transjordanian states had a long history of conflict with Judah over border zones (the Shephelah to the west, and Gilead to the east), conflicts that collaboration with the invaders had exacerbated. However, in Ezekiel the urgency and sophisticated literary elaboration of the oracles against Tyre (26–28) and Egypt (29–32) are remarkable. Tyre is above all 'guilty' of having taken advantage of the power vacuum in 640–600, to expand in competition with Judah, albeit on the commercial and economic level. Egypt is probably guilty of having boasted of a power that turned out to be inadequate against the Babylonians – although the invasion of Egypt by Nebuchadrezzar, prophesied both by Ezekiel (29–30) and Jeremiah (43.8-13;

46.13-26), was not to happen in the way they foresee. On the theological level, finally, both Tyre and Egypt are criticized for a conception of royalty that sets the king too high, on a divine level, with ideological claims that it is easy (for one who does not share them) to expose to sarcasm and ridicule:

> Mortal, say to the prince of Tyre, Thus says the Lord Yahweh:
> Because your heart is proud
> and you have said, 'I am a god;
> I sit in the seat of the gods,
> in the heart of the seas,'
> yet you are but a mortal, and no god,
> though you compare your mind
> with the mind of a god.
> You are indeed wiser than Daniel;
> no secret is hidden from you;
> by your wisdom and your understanding
> you have amassed wealth for yourself,
> and have gathered gold and silver
> into your treasuries.
> By your great wisdom in trade
> you have increased your wealth,
> and your heart has become proud in your wealth.
> Therefore thus says the Lord Yahweh:
> Because you compare your mind
> with the mind of a god,
> therefore, I will bring strangers against you,
> the most terrible of the nations;
> they shall draw their swords against the beauty of your wisdom
> and defile your splendour.
> They shall thrust you down to the Pit,
> and you shall die a violent death
> in the heart of the seas (Ezek. 28.2-8).

3. The Internal Political Debate

In describing Zedekiah's rebellion (see below), the Chronicler criticizes his breach of the sacred oath of vassalage:

> He did what was evil in the sight of Yahweh his God. He did not humble himself before the prophet Jeremiah who spoke from the mouth of Yahweh. He also rebelled against King Nebuchadnezzar, who had made him swear by God; he stiffened his neck and hardened his heart against turning to Yahweh, the God of Israel (2 Chron. 36.12-13).

This criticism might appear unexpected and artificial, but it recurs in Ezekiel too, and thus shows that some people upheld the importance of loyalty to an oath ratified in the name of both Babylonian and local gods as much as Yahweh (the plural *Elohim* may be intentionally ambiguous).

Thus, during the period between the first siege in 598 and the final destruction of the city in 587, an internal debate developed in Jerusalem, one that we can follow in the books of Jeremiah and Ezekiel especially, and that reduced political choices to general theological principles. In this sense, it would be simplistic to speak of a 'pro-Chaldean' and an 'anti-Chaldean' party. There were some who supported the rebellion, trusting that Yahweh would never permit the arrival of the Chaldeans (Jer. 37.19), and the king seems to lean towards this hypothesis. There were some who advocated reliance on the Egyptian assistance that had evidently been asked for and negotiated, and in effect arrived, but was totally ineffective (Ezek. 17.15-18). Questioned on the matter by the king, Jeremiah had expressed doubt about the efficacy of Egyptian intervention (Jer. 37.6-8). There were also, as already seen, some who maintained that the vassalage oath sworn to the Chaldeans should be observed for judicial-theological reasons.

We are familiar most of all with the position of Jeremiah who was by now an established prophet, whom Zedekiah consulted (surely along with other prophets with different opinions) on policy towards the Babylonians. Jeremiah asserted that the Chaldean intervention and the consequent disaster were unavoidable as instruments of divine wrath against the treachery (apostasy, among other things) of Jerusalem:

> I myself will fight against you with outstretched hand and mighty arm, in anger, in fury, and in great wrath. And I will strike down the inhabitants of this city, both human beings and animals; they shall die of a great pestilence. Afterward, says Yahweh, I will give King Zedekiah of Judah, and his servants, and the people in this city – those who survive the pestilence, sword, and famine – into the hands of King Nebuchadrezzar of Babylon, into the hands of their enemies, into the hands of those who seek their lives. He shall strike them down with the edge of the sword; he shall not pity them, or spare them, or have compassion (Jer. 21.5-7).

The prophet was thus opposed to the idea of forming a large anti-Chaldean coalition consisting of Judah, Tyre and Sidon, Moab and Edom (Jer. 27.1-6). To some extent, his position was pro-Chaldean, or could be so understood, with the result that the prophet was imprisoned during the siege, as a collaborationist. In effect, the prediction 'Whoever stays in this city will die by sword, famine, or by plague; but whoever leaves it and surrenders to the besieging Chaldeans will live' (Jer. 21.9 = 38.2) was an invitation, not even veiled, to desertion. Jeremiah's was not an isolated voice: his vicissitudes during the siege show that his person was protected, and his opinions shared, by some of the most influential royal officials belonging to the family of Shaphan. The symbolic act of buying a field at the darkest moment of the crisis (Jer. 32.1-15), affirming a return to normality, can also be read in a political sense. And his 'prediction' of the fate of deserters, which was correct, must have been the result of talks between the besiegers and the 'surrender party'. After the conquest of the city, Nebuchadrezzar in person gave orders to liberate Jeremiah and protect him from possible retaliation (Jer. 39.11-14): in a way that shows he knew Jeremiah's position and considered him as his own man.

The position of Ezekiel (who had already been deported to Babylon with the group of 598, but then returned, or kept in contact with the situation in Jerusalem) is similar to Jeremiah's in theological principles, but different in political application. Ezekiel, too, considers the destiny of Judah as reflecting that of Israel (see in particular Ezekiel 23), and motivated by a long history of unfaithfulness; he also believes that the Babylonians are acting in the name of divine will, and that the outcome is unavoidable. To anyone hoping in Egyptian assistance, the prophet replies that the rupture of the vassalage oath brings about a fate that is certain:

> But he [Zedekiah] rebelled against him by sending ambassadors to Egypt, in order that they might give him horses and a large army. Will he succeed? Can one escape who does such things? Can he break the covenant and yet escape? As I live, says the Lord Yahweh, surely in the place where the king resides who made him king, whose oath he despised, and whose covenant with him he broke – in Babylon he shall die. Pharaoh with his mighty army and great company will not help him in war, when ramps are cast up and siege-walls built to cut off many lives. Because he despised the oath and broke the covenant, because he gave his hand and yet did all these things, he shall not escape (Ezek. 17.15-18).

However, the fact that Yahweh has abandoned his temple (Ezek. 10.18) and his city (Ezek. 11.23) does not permit the people to rely on the Babylonians or to indulge in idolatrous Babylonian customs (for which Ezekiel reproaches the pro-Chaldean party of the house of Shaphan in 8.11): the only salvation lies through Yahweh. Yahweh has already saved his unfaithful people many times, and he will save them again, establishing a new covenant, gathering the dispersed and releasing them from among the nations where they have been displaced, as he once released them from

Egypt (Ezek. 11.14-21; 20.32-34). In this positive outlook, which could well have already been adopted among the first exiles before the conquest of Jerusalem, the prophetic text has doubtless undergone some *post eventum* editing.

4. *From Vassal State to the Final Destruction*

We return now to the political events. Zedekiah, installed as king in Jerusalem after the end of the first siege, reigned for nine years (598–589) as a Babylonian vassal. The houses excavated in the Ophel date from this final phase of pre-exilic Jerusalem: the 'house of the *bullae*' (so named because of the large number of *bullae* with Yahwistic names, among them a Gemaryahu son of Shaphan), the 'house of Ahiel', the 'burned room' and the 'ashlar house': an entire quarter showing the usual prosperity of the city.

Then Zedekiah decided to rebel, after the political debate that, as already stated, had taken place in Jerusalem. Nebuchadrezzar, who was expecting nothing but that, stormed the Judean fortresses in the Shephelah (Lachish and Azekah), besieged Jerusalem, a siege temporarily interrupted by the arrival of an Egyptian army, but quickly resumed (Jer. 37.5-8). It lasted for a long time, in conditions that became harder and harder because of famine. Already before the siege, Zedekiah had proclaimed the liberation of 'Hebrew slaves' (Jer. 34.8-10) to mobilize all the available forces, reviving ancient principles of the utopian social legislation that went back perhaps to the period of ethnic formation, and had been repeated in the Deuteronomist law-code. However, the harsh economic conditions in the besieged city led again to the debt enslavement of the new freemen, provoking an uproar from Jeremiah (and the party represented by him) against the perverted justice of the king and nobility (34.11-22).

In addition to the biblical account, some ostraca found at Lachish (stratum II) go back to the time of the Babylonian siege: the garrison at Lachish communicates with that in Azekah by smoke signals, and the cessation of those signals signifies capture. Two thirds of the names on the ostraca (a good non-biblical sample for the kingdom of Judah at the end of its life) are Yahwhistic, and the writers greet each other in the name of Yahweh: 'Yahweh allows my lord to hear today good news' or such expressions (*SSI*, I, 12).

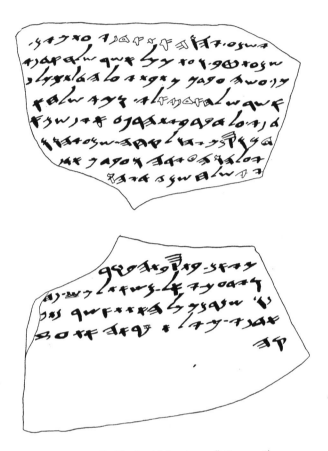

Figure 43. *The Lachish ostraca (letter no. 4)*

After two years of siege, Zedekiah succeeded in escaping, together with his sons and guards, but he was overtaken near Jericho: the troops were dispersed, the king was captured, brought into the presence of Nebuchadrezzar, who killed his sons in front of him, then blinded him, and finally deported him to Babylon (2 Kgs 25.4-7 = Jer. 39.1-7).

The city resisted for another few months (without king or elite troops) until the Chaldeans, under the command of Nabu-zer-iddin and Nergal-usur (known also from the Babylonian texts: see *ANET*, 307-308) entered the walls, burned 'the temple of Yahweh, the royal palace and all the houses of Jerusalem' (2 Kgs 25.9), then demolished the walls to prevent future rebellions. The temple was despoiled, and the bronze furnishings (again attributed to Solomon) were sacked. About 60 nobles (including the chief priest Seraiah) were brought to Nebuchadrezzar, who put them to death. The urban population (both those left in the besieged city, and those who had previously surrendered) was deported. The farmers in the neighbouring countryside were left there (2 Kgs 25.18-22).

The archaeological data confirm the destruction in all the districts of Jerusalem (in particular the 'house of the *bullae*' and the other buildings of the Ophel were destroyed), and also show that the fate of Jerusalem was shared by a large number of Judean cities: Ramat Rahel (V A), Lachish (II) and Azekah, Timna (Tel Batash II) and Bet-Sur (II), Tell Beit Mirsim (A 2) and Gezer (V), Debir (Khirbet Rabud A) and Hebron were all destroyed. The sites in the desert of Judah (En Gedi and the Buqeia) and the Arabah (Mesad Hasheva) disappeared. In the Negev, the destruction of the sites in the area of Beer-sheba (Arad VI, Aroer IV), and of Kadesh-barnea, is attributed to the Edomites who, in some other cases, seem to have supplanted Judeans (Tel Masos, Tel Malhata, Horvat 'Uza, Horvat Qitmit, and further south Tell el-Kheleife).

By contrast, in the territory of Benjamin there is some continuity of settlement: Mizpah is still inhabited (Tell en-Nasbeh 2), although with walls and city gate no longer in use; Gibeon and Bethel are also normally inhabited, and the fortress of Khirbet Abu et-Twein is still in operation, while that of Tell el-Ful is destroyed. At Megiddo II the fortress built by Josiah or by the Egyptians, is now used by the Babylonians; however, the city no longer exists.

The Babylonians left Gedaliah as 'governor' of Judah, or, better, as responsible for what remained of Judah, with a residence in Mizpah (2 Kgs 25.22-23). Gedaliah had been prefect of the palace of Zedekiah (*'šr 'l hbyt*, says his seal, from an impression found at Lachish II), and he was the most powerful member of the family of Shaphan and the pro-Chaldean party at Zedekiah's court. Other members of the elite who had not been deported gathered together him, among them Jeremiah, and swore an oath of collaboration drawn up by Gedaliah declaring submission to the new regime, and pursuing the best means of survival, economic recovery and social cohesion:

> Gedaliah son of Ahikam son of Shaphan swore to them and their troops, saying, 'Do not be afraid to serve the Chaldeans. Stay in the land and serve the king of Babylon, and it shall go well with you. As for me, I am staying at Mizpah to represent you before the Chaldeans who come to us; but as for you, gather wine and summer fruits and oil, and store them in your vessels, and live in the towns that you have taken over' (Jer. 40.9-10; see 2 Kgs 25.24).

Groups of Judeans who took refuge in Transjordan returned to the country, and there was a good harvest. However, the collaborationist party got the worst of it: after few months Gedaliah was killed together with all his court, both Judeans and Chaldeans, by a group of conspirators 'of the royal family' (2 Kgs 25.25; see the fuller account in Jeremiah 41), who had not been deported, since they were fighting in peripheral areas that the Chaldeans had not conquered.

The massacre of Gedaliah caused a popular uprising in fear of Babylonian reprisals. The conspirators fled to Ammon; the nobles and 'the rest of Judah', although they had not taken part in the conspiracy, decided to take shelter in Egypt with many followers among the people (2 Kgs 25.26; a fuller account in Jeremiah 42–43). Jeremiah, questioned about what to do, advised remaining in Judah, under Babylonian sovereignty, since the wrath of Yahweh was now satisfied, and the tide of war and Babylonian destruction was threatening to move precisely towards Egypt:

> If you will only remain in this land, then I will build you up and not pull you down; I will plant you, and not pluck you up; for I am sorry for the disaster that I have brought upon you. Do not be afraid of the king of Babylon, as you have been; do not be afraid of him, says Yahweh, for I am with you, to save you and to rescue you from his hand. I will grant you mercy, and he will have mercy on you and restore you to your native soil. But if you continue to say, 'We will not stay in this land,' thus disobeying the voice of Yahweh your God and saying, 'No, we will go to the land of Egypt, where we shall not see war, or hear the sound of the trumpet, or be hungry for bread, and there we will stay,' then hear the word of Yahweh, O remnant of Judah. Thus says Yahweh of hosts, the God of Israel: If you are determined to enter Egypt and go to settle there, then the sword that you fear shall overtake you there, in the land of Egypt; and the famine that you dread shall follow close after you into Egypt; and there you shall die (Jer. 42.10-16).

However, his advice was not heeded, and the 'remnant' moved to Egypt. Judah was left in a total chaos, without any ruling class, and with the population decimated by the war, plague, famine and emigration.

5. *One-way Deportations and Demographic and Cultural Collapse*

The biblical text gives rather limited numbers for the deportations of Nebuchadrezzar: for 598 it speaks, within two verses (2 Kgs 24.14-16), of 10,000 nobles in addition to an undetermined number of artisans, or of 7,000 notables plus 1,000 artisans. Jeremiah (52.28-30) furnishes even more modest numbers: 3,000 people in 598, 832 in 587, another 745 people five years later, making 4,600 altogether. It is clear that the deportation was confined to the ruling class, while the peasant population was left. Unlike the Assyrian deportations, there were no other places for the deportees but Babylon itself; and there is no mention of foreign groups deported to Palestine.

Thus, the two imperial strategies of Assyria and Babylon had in common the aim of acquiring specialized workers and crushing the ruling class; but they diverged in essential points. While the Assyrians wanted to mix different populations to create a uniform 'Assyrian provincial' culture, and to run the new provinces by providing them with efficient local administrative structures (the Assyrian provincial palaces), the Babylonians indeed seemed to be resigned to abandoning the conquered lands to total socio-political and cultural degradation, but in the meantime allowed the deported elites to keep their own individuality.

In these differences lies one of the causes of the different outcomes of the two deportations, together, of course, with other factors such as the different lapse of time between deportation and return, and the different national consciousness of the deportees of the sixth century compared with those of the seventh century. In short, the Assyrian deportations were tremendously effective in eliminating national identity, so that one knows nothing about the destiny of the Assyrian deportees, and the 'ten tribes' of the north disappear, assimilated into the neighbouring world. By contrast, the Babylonian deportations could not extinguish the deportees' sense of identity, so that they were able, if they wanted, to rebuild their ethnic-political, religious and habitual individuality.

Conditions in Judah after the sack of Jerusalem, deportation of the ruling class, and the other events that followed, caused a severe demographic and cultural crisis. All the archaeological indicators point to a real collapse. On a summary evaluation, from the seventh to the sixth century the number of inhabited sites was reduced by two-thirds (from 116 to 41), and the mean surface area of the surviving sites reduced by two-thirds (from 4.4 to 1.4 hectares), so that one can estimate a population collapse of 85-90 percent. The nature of the settlements is also impoverished because of a lack of enclosing walls and public buildings (no provincial palaces were built by the Babylonians), the production of luxury craft items ceases, the use of writing (no longer necessary for the royal administration) becomes intermittent. It is a vertical collapse: only the central zone of Benjamin (Tell el-Ful, Tell en-Nasbeh, Bethel, Gibeon) survives, where the collaborationist government of Gedaliah was established, as perhaps proved by the jar stamps reading *m(w)sh* that are concentrated in that area and in this period.

It must be borne in mind that the kingdom of Judah had been built on the prominence, even excessively so, of the capital relative to the rest of the country: a quantitative and qualitative prominence, considering the centralization not only of administration, but also of worship in Jerusalem.

The destruction of the capital, together with the few intermediate sites, particularly in the Shephelah (Lachish and Azekah), resulted in a region with poor villages and modest resources, and with a peasant population estimated at between 10,000 and 20,000 people.

The empty spaces were partly occupied by neighbours better equipped to stage a recovery. The case of the Negev is well attested: here groups of Edomites installed themselves, moving from their traditional territory east of the Arabah, at that time in a prosperous phase (its capital Bozrah was furnished with enclosing walls and public buildings). The Edomites progressively penetrated into the Negev, their names compounded with the name of the god Qaus, as ostraca from the following centuries demonstrate. The Edomite small temple of Horvat Qitmit is dated to the seventh century, perhaps prior to the fall of Jerusalem; however, the fortress of Horvat 'Uza (near Arad) with its regular plan, orthogonal arrangement, and Edomite ostraca, well reflects the new situation. The fortresses, formerly Judean, of Tel Masos (I) and Aroer (II) were also occupied by the Edomites. The Judean prophets are particularly bitter against Edom because of the help it gave in the destruction of Jerusalem (Jeremiah 34; also Lam. 4.31): thus it is probable that they offered concrete support (in the form of auxiliary troops) to the Babylonians, who rewarded them with control of the Negev. We know that in the following centuries 'Idumaea' no longer corresponds to the Edom of Iron Age I-II, but to the area that had formerly been southern Judah and Simeon, around Beer-sheba and as far as Hebron.

Similar processes took place in the Shephelah, where the expansion of the former Philistine city-states took over what they had always considered as their natural hinterland. The coastal strip was also invigorated (at least economically) by the growing presence of Phoenician merchants and Greek mercenaries (as shown by pottery imports and epigraphic data), expanding in the sixth century that Mediterranean orientation that had previously always been confined to Phoenicia proper.

We do not have concrete data on the judicial-administrative status of Judah under the Babylonians, but it is possible that the plateaux were annexed to the province of Samaria, the Shephelah to the province of Ashdod, and that southern Gilead was occupied by the Ammonites. This administrative fragmentation did not make easier the maintenance of a local sense of unity, either. More effective than the numerically modest deportations, therefore, was the process of cultural decline resulting from the collapse of sociopolitical relations, without the support of a local ruling class that could have led the way to recovery.

6. The End of an Historical Trajectory

The Babylonian conquest of Palestine marks by all accounts the end of a long historical trajectory, begun six centuries earlier, that the entire Levantine region had shared. Thanks to the archaeological and textual evidence, as far as we can coordinate them, we can reconstruct a meaningful process, explicable from coherent causal and contextual factors, in both its chronological sequence and its regional variations – and thus 'normal' in terms of historical plausibility.

The outlines of such a process can be summarized as follows. After the fall of the political and cultural system of the Bronze Age, strongly centralized in the palace cities – a collapse due to internal decline and external pressure – the whole territory had to re-structure itself in accordance with new perspectives. The twelfth and eleventh centuries witness progressive demographic growth, the introduction of new techniques of controlling territory and exploiting resources, in which the pastoral element has a much greater influence than in the previous phase. Beside major features of continuity, centred on the coast (Philistine and the Phoenician cities) and in northern Syria (the neo-Hittite states), new political entities gradually crystallized, on a tribal basis and with a 'national' character. Among these new entities, Israel (in north central Palestine) and Judah (in the south) are the especial interest of this book.

Only gradually, and one might say laboriously, during the tenth-ninth centuries, did the new political entities provide themselves with solid state structures, appropriate town planning and relevant buildings, and a functioning administration. The process was doubtless more rapid in the north and on the coast (thanks to the cultural continuity mentioned earlier), and later spread towards the south and the interior. During this phase all of the Syro-Palestinian territory benefited from political independence, had at its disposal its own resources, and could develop its own culture.

The high point of this process, in terms of population numbers and quality of culture, occurred in the north in the ninth-eighth centuries and in the south in the eighth-seventh centuries. The neo-Hittite (such as Carchemish and Patina), the Aramean (Aleppo, Hamath and Damascus), Phoenician (e.g. Arwad, Byblos, Tyre, Sidon), Philistine (e.g. Gaza and Ashdod), Israelite (Samaria and Megiddo), Judean (Jerusalem), and the Transjordanian (Rabbath Ammon, Bosra) centres all created a very lively culture, as evidenced by important urban and architectural programmes, artistic and technical accomplishments (metallurgy, ivories), epigraphic and administrative texts (with an increasing use of the alphabet), and literary and religious compositions.

The evidence for all this is uneven: the architectural and technical achievements depend on finding rich, well preserved archaeological contexts, while the literature depends on the transmission of texts (such as the biblical books) that we must otherwise regard as largely lost, and irrecoverable from archaeological excavations except for modest examples in the monumental inscriptions. Despite this imbalance in the evidence, which is of course normal for cultures that are archaeologically recovered, it is nevertheless possible – by patient examination and contextualization – to reconstruct a common trajectory and a fairly homogeneous cultural character for the whole of the Levant, a *koine* that still, of course, allows for important or interesting local variation to emerge.

This world of the Levant, rich and prosperous, lively and original, was put into crisis by the imperial advance: first, the Assyrians (between 750 and 640), then the Babylonians (between 610 and 550) intervened in strength in the area, driven doubtless by their expansionist and totalizing ideologies, but attracted also, more concretely, by the economic and cultural prestige of the region. In a repeated pattern, they first entered into commercial relations, then they submitted the people to tribute, and finally conquered and annexed, destroyed and deported. While imperial intervention in its first phase brought positive effects, introducing local economies to wider regional trade, in the second phase it was absolutely disastrous.

Despite their different strategies of control and exploitation, Assyrians and Babylonians both destroyed *de facto* demographic growth, intensive land exploitation, and, generally, creative and cultural originality. Without local elites commissioning architectural and artistic work, and promoting ideological debate, the residue of the population suffered a deep cultural decline, as is well known from analogous (and historically better documented) instances of imperial conquest and forced ethnic mixing. In the space of few decades (staggered over time, from north to south) all the kingdoms and peoples that initiated the very lively Levantine world of Iron Age II collapsed to their lowest demographic and cultural levels. It was the end of an epoch, the end of a world, something that traditional history books are unable to adequately convey, but was indeed a crucial historical event, since the crisis of identity became in its turn the starting point of a new trajectory.

Table 7. *Chronology of imperial expansion*

SHALMANESER III
    859–856 conquest of Bit-Adini
    854 battle of Qarqar (Ahab of Israel, Hadad-'ezer of Damascus)
    850–840 campaigns against Damascus (Hadad-'ezer; from 845 Hazael)
    842–tribute from Jehu of Israel

ADAD-NIRARI III

805–802 campaign against Damascus (Mari' = Bar-Hadad III); tribute from Joash of Israel

SHALMANESER IV

773–772 campaigns against Damascus (Khadiyanu) and Hadrach

ASHUR-DAN III

765 campaign against Hadrach

755–754 campaigns against Hadrach and Arpad

TIGLATH-PILESER III

743–740 campaign against Arpad

738 tribute from Menahem of Israel and Rezin of Damascus

734 campaign against Philistia

733 campaign against Damascus and Israel (in response to appeal from Ahaz of Judah)

732 Damascus, Megiddo, Dor and Gilead reduced to provinces

SHALMANESER V

722 capture of Samaria

SARGON II

721 Samaria reduced to a province

711 Ashdod reduced to a province

SENNACHERIB

702–701 siege of Jerusalem, tribute from Hezekiah

ESARHADDON

677 Sidon reduced to a province

673 Ushu and Acco reduced to provinces

673–669 campaign against Egypt; tribute from Manasseh of Judah

ASHURBANIPAL

663 campaign against Egypt; tribute from Manasseh of Judah

NEBUCHADREZZAR II

609 march of Necho; death of Josiah

604 conquest of Philistia

598 beginning of siege of Tyre

598-597 first siege of Jerusalem, deportation of Jehoiachin

586 second siege and capture or Jerusalem; deportation of Zedekiah

585 capitulation of Tyre

582 conquest of Ammon and Moab

CYRUS

539 conquest of Babylonia; inherits control of Syro-Palestine

INTERMEZZO

Chapter 10

THE AXIAL AGE

1. *The Individual and the 'Distant Power'*

The sixth century is an important turning-point not only for Israel, but also for a large part of the ancient world. It is the so-called 'axial age', marked by the rising of a series of innovators (personified symbols of general tendencies in their respective communities): in China, Confucius (550–480), in India, Buddha (560–480), in Iran, Zoroaster (end of the seventh century), in Greece the Ionian philosophers and 'scientists', who began philosophy, tragedy and historiography. In Israel we have the major 'ethical' prophets (such as Ezekiel and Second Isaiah) of the exilic period. The protagonists and tendencies of the 'axial age' are different from each other, because of their cultural background and the specific traditions and tendencies of each culture; also different are the innovative directions that they take, ranging from rationality to ethics. Not all historians agree with the concept of the 'axial age', nor of its value as a cognitive tool, that risks becoming something meta-historical if it is not set against the background of precise historical conditions. If it is not merely a coincidence, or a curiosity, the same fruit ought to spring from the same kind of soil, since it produces the same deepening of the role of the individual, signifying a major break with previous ways of life.

I do not believe it is an accident that the axial age coincides with the achievement of the 'universal' imperial formations (from the Assyrian to the Persian in the Near East; but analogous situations occurred also in India and China), representing the highest point and the end result of an entire process of organizational growth over two millennia, and arising from assumptions that have now exhausted their capacities. And, not by accident, it contrasts and exceeds the basic principles of the empires, and develops at the margins, and against them. The rise of intellectual elites is a common feature of the period: they are not organic to power, as had always been the case previously, but they represent its critical spirit, opposing and surpassing it.

The major traditional cultures and their privileged centres are not the protagonists of the new ferment, but rather their antagonists. Babylonia and Egypt did not produce 'axial' characters, since they retreated into a formalistic and archaic re-elaboration of their cultural heritage, leading to esoteric Chaldean astrology and to Egyptian hermeticism. The energizing centres of the new tendencies have a marginal or unconventional location: they are the Greek *poleis* at the margins of the Persian Empire, the groups of deportees inside the Babylonian empire, the new communities of the Iranian highlands, and the political and religious circles outside the traditional power structures of India and China.

The main expressions of the axial age – ethical religion (see further §2) and rational thought (the latter mainly applying to the ancient Greek world) – can be connected with individual identity, the development of the personality, the direct relationship between the human being and his problems, without the mediation of sociopolitical structures that are now over-expanded. The dimensions of the citizen-state, the ceremonial relations between subjects and power, become ineffective when the political community expands and assumes an imperial scale. The slow rise of the individual personality that one can trace (for the entire Late Bronze and Iron Age I–II) in customs and legal norms (see further §4), with the liberation of the individual from the network of 'horizontally' shared responsibilities (whether of group or 'corporation', as it is usually called) and 'vertical' ones (generational), came to a halt and gave way to an improvised reaction in Iron Age III, the age of imperial expansion. The structure created by conquest and administrative unification on a very wide scale left the individual too remote from access to, and even simply knowledge of, the political and religious centres of decision-making. While Near Eastern society was on the way to assume that image of 'generalized slavery' that later struck Greek observers of the fourth century, the ferment, the individualistic and ethical tendencies of the axial age, are signals of a reaction against complete absorption, a reaction necessarily (or at least preferably) placed in the interstices or on the frontiers, outer or inner, geographical or social, of imperial society.

2. *The Question of Monotheism*

The rise of monotheistic religion is considered an essential element of the 'revolution' of the axial age. Thinking mythically (through archetypes) instead of historically (through processes), the Bible presents monotheism as already achieved since the origins of the history of Israel, and then as perpetuated, unchanged, over time. The enigmatic self-presentation of Yahweh to Moses serves as the founding moment for Yahwistic religion:

'If I come to the Israelites and say to them, "The God of your ancestors has sent me to you," and they ask me, "What is his name?" what shall I say to them?' God said to Moses, 'I AM who I am.' He said further, 'Thus you shall say to the Israelites, 'I AM has sent me to you' (Exod. 3.13-14).

The text is doubtless very late, as is its logical, abstract approach, and it has no possible context in a 'Mosaic age'. Scholars have long agreed that the rise of the monotheism is the result of a long process; however, different historical contexts are still proposed. At one time (in particular by Renan) the idea was advanced that monotheism was the result of environmental conditioning, the outcome of the life in the desert with its empty and boundless spaces. Then (and still recently), it was thought of as a reprise of the presumed monotheistic revolution of the 'heretical' Pharaoh Amenophis IV – a way of saving monotheism's Mosaic 'antiquity' (we would find ourselves in the fourteenth century!) and its punctuated, rather than evolutionary, invention. Others have thought of the influence of Zoroastrian concepts, which with their dualism (the principle of evil opposed to the principle of good) are really a form of monotheism: and here we are already in the exilic period and in the sphere of ethical-theological principles typical of the axial age.

It is obviously necessary to separate the two strands (although they are linked at a certain point in their development) of the deity Yahweh and the ethical perspective that generates monotheism. Yahweh had for long time been a deity among many others, in the sense that his believers were conscious of the existence of many other gods, equally all existing and 'real'. The route via henotheism (a single god for 'us', but not universally) runs through at least two courses. The first is the character of the 'national god' (Yahweh for Israel, as Chemosh for Moab, Milcom for the Ammonites, and so on) typical of the Iron Age and of tribal descent. The second is confrontation with the god Assur and the Assyrian emperor that requires unambiguous, exclusive fidelity (see the quotation at the end of §7.7). With the substitution of the 'one emperor' with the 'one god' we are in the age of Josiah and his reforms.

Conditions in the Diaspora doubtless had their effects, leading in different ways toward the same development: not only by reinforcing national henotheism as a powerful way of self-identification, or even in separating the community of believers from its specific cultic points of reference, but also in introducing processes of identity-absorption, already developed in Babylonia in this late period, where all the deities were identified with functions or aspects of Marduk:

Urash is Marduk of the plantation
Lugalidda is Marduk of the abyss
Ninurta is Marduk of the pick
Nergal is Marduk of the battle
Zababa is Marduk of the war
Enlil is Marduk of the rule and consultation
Nabu is Marduk of the book-keeping
Sin is Marduk who lights the night
Shamash is Marduk of the justice
Hadad is Marduk of the rain
Tishpak is Marduk of the troops
The Great Anu is Marduk of the [...]
Shuqamuna is Marduk of the container
[...] is Marduk of everything (*CT*, XXIV, 50).

However, the existence of different cities in Babylonia, each having its own pantheon and city-god, with important sanctuaries (endowed with socioeconomical functions), contributed towards keeping this tendency to the unification at the level of theological speculation. The historical context has its own significance: it is not by chance that the Babylonian theology of 'identification' (or 'reductionism': the entire pantheon becomes facets of Marduk), the rise of Zoroastrian 'cosmic dualism' and of the Judean 'ethical prophecy' all occur within the same timespan (sixth century) and in a rather confined geographical area.

The main issue is not the number of the gods (whether one, two, or more) but their typology, and also the relationship created between believer and deity. We must remind ourselves, just to complete the picture, that polytheism, as structured in a pantheon, develops in parallel with the so-called 'urban revolution', namely with the rise of complex societies through the diversification of specialisms, stronger socioeconomical stratification and the presence of a controlling elite. The pantheon is a hypostasis and a legitimation of these complex societies (and of the elite). Each god is put in charge of a specific sector, and the whole pantheon is maintained by the offerings of the community – which of course also maintains the specialists and the ruling elite. The rise of monotheism does not unify the different divine personalities, but cancels them out: it removes their distinctive characteristics in relying on a global definition of the divine that cannot but have an ethical character. We are confronting a real change.

Instead of being a reflection, and a justification, of social imbalances, of unequal distribution of resources, religion becomes an expression of shared moral values, a point of reference for the distinction between good and evil, justice and injustice, truth and falsehood. Up to that point, religion had been managed by the holders of political power, who represented themselves as intermediaries (the only legitimate ones) between human society and the divine sphere. Now this political and ceremonial mediation can be avoided, and direct means of contact between the individual and the divine are sought. A proof of this different function of the sacred is that in the monotheistic religions the diversification of skills, and the separate divine patronage of various social categories, is catered for by the proliferation of 'demons' and 'saints' (as in Christianity); and, conversely, those societies that placed their ethical values in civil or royal codes, or in philosophical knowledge (as in the Greco-Roman world), were able for many centuries to maintain their traditional religion and their pantheon alongside, for 'ceremonial' purposes.

The religion of Israel already had within it some ethical, non-ceremonial elements, as for example aniconism (Exod. 20.4; Deut. 5.8; Isa. 40.18-20; 44.9-20; Jer. 10.2-10) or a ban on intoxicating food or drink during cultic celebrations, or the prohibition of worship of the dead, or the proscription of oracles (unless through Yahweh; see §5.6). It therefore found its strongest impulse towards the new typology, the new function of the sacred, in the direct link between the Law and God (without the intermediation of the king) – and this went further in the device, substantially political, of substituting the 'oath to the Emperor' with the 'oath to God' (see §7.7).

Of course, an ethical religion aims at becoming universal, since the basic ethical values are (or can be) universally shared. The God who is responsible not only for the fortunes of his worshippers but for the fortunes of all peoples and of the behaviour of all sociopolitical subjects (Emperor included), must become the God of all:

> You are my witnesses, says Yahweh,
> and my servant whom I have chosen,
> so that you may know and believe me
> and understand that I am he.
> Before me no god was formed,
> nor shall there be any after me.
> I, I am Yahweh,
> and besides me there is no saviour.
> I declared and saved and proclaimed,
> when there was no strange god among you;
> and you are my witnesses, says Yahweh.
> I am God, and also henceforth I am He (Isa. 43.10-12).

In this way, already with Second Isaiah and then even more so with Third Isaiah, the perspectives of universal monotheism begin to open up, and its means of fulfillment – that is, proselytizing (§18.8). However, proselytizing entails a serious existential or identity crisis for the 'chosen people', a crisis whose effect is not at all to be taken for granted: it can also cause the phenomena of rejection, fanatical segregation or intensified formalism; and in fact historically different monotheisms have each pursued their own solutions.

3. *From Ceremonial Worship to Ethical Religion*

For the entire monarchic period, the religion of Israel had been a typical 'ceremonial' and state religion: it was based on the relationship between temple and royal palace, king and priesthood, and it found expression in the regular performance of acts of formal worship, both daily and seasonal, all intended to affirm (and demonstrate) the right relationship between deity, king, and people. A ceremonial religion is not conceivable without a political reference point, a temple (or another prescribed place for collective worship), or without the participation of the community in the official cult. With the end of political independence, the destruction of the temple, and deportation to a foreign land, these conditions had ceased. Imperial worship was too distant, and was not shared. The situation called for the rise of a religion at the personal level, practised internally, with less of a public, ceremonial character, and with a quite different basis: ethical values.

This tendency found a precedent in important aspects of pre-exilic religiosity; but it also encountered a contradiction in the strategy of self-identification, a strategy that, as we have seen, was peculiar to the community of exiles, and which aimed at capturing the individual in a network of group relations. Hence, these contrary impulses created a certain conflict.

As for the precedents, it is enough to recall the attacks of Amos (5.21-24) on the feasts, offerings and sacrifices of an official cult that was insincere, contradicted by a lack of justice. However, in the pre-exilic age the critiques of worship were focused almost exclusively on the persistence of non-Yahwistic worship, characterized by immoral practices (sacred prostitution, child sacrifice) and directed at fictitious deities. During the exile, the situation was different, since the exiles lived in an environment of generalized idolatry, and thus the temptation to venerate not the 'true God' but the work of human imagination (Jer. 1.16, 'for all their wickedness in forsaking me; they have made offerings to other gods, and worshipped the works of their own hands') was much stronger.

Certainly, the greatest concentration of anti-idolatrous rhetoric is placed precisely in the exilic age, and the prophecies of Ezekiel and Deutero-Isaiah are full of it; it later culminates in the prophecies of Third Isaiah. The refusal to worship idols, which in the Diaspora did not and could not be opposed to a formal cult of Yahweh as such, was aimed at promoting inner worship. As mentioned at the beginning of this chapter, when those reference points at which mediation was effected disappeared, the individual felt lost in such a large, strange empire, and had to find a direct relationship with the deity in terms of the 'private' issues of justice and happiness, guilt and illness, success and hostility. Among the many relevant passages, any number of excerpts from the Psalms could be quoted:

> If you try my heart, if you visit me by night,
> if you test me, you will find no wickedness in me;
> my mouth does not transgress.
> As for what others do, by the word of your lips
> I have avoided the ways of the violent.
> My steps have held fast to your paths;
> my feet have not slipped.
> I call upon you, for you will answer me, O God;
> incline your ear to me, hear my words.
> Wondrously show your steadfast love,
> O saviour of those who seek refuge
> from their adversaries at your right hand (Ps. 17.3-7).

However, with nothing but interior religion, a community wishing to remain united on the religious as well as the ethnic level could not support itself – and in fact the individual prayer just quoted, was inserted in a cultic collection and employed in collective liturgy. In this we see the counter-tendency to stress the formal (even formalistic) ceremonial character that served as a distinctive sign of membership of the community. The two most evident signs, distinguishing 'us' from 'others', were circumcision and the observance of the sabbath (see §18.6). However, even more significant was attention to purity, to a fear of contamination (see §18.7), leading to ritualistic behaviour that could become obsessive, and to a haughty isolation that contrasts with an otherwise potentially shared piety.

In these and similar contrasts between the tendency of the age towards the ethical conception of religion on the one hand and on the other the need to strengthen group identity in the midst of a foreign world, we find the root of problems that will persist throughout the post-exilic age (and then into Judaism in general) both in the repatriated communities and those remaining in the Diaspora.

4. *Collective and Personal Responsibility*

Alongside personal religiosity lies another theme, central to the concerns of the so-called 'axial age', namely the question of individual responsibility, which assumes a judicial but also, more generally, an ethical perspective. In this case, too, we must bear in mind the changed political scene. The place of the individual in a small state and a compact social network is quite different from his place in a 'universal empire' and a dispersed social fabric. In the first case (which we can define as 'close power'), the individual takes part in the state ceremonial worship, as well as in political decisions and he shares the destiny of the community he belongs to. In the second case, of 'distant power', this identification between personal and corporate fate does not work.

In the ancient Orient, and in Israel in particular, collective (or corporate) responsibility has two spheres of application, one 'horizontal' (in space) and another 'vertical' (in time). The 'horizontal' collective responsibility holds responsible for a crime not only the perpetrators individually, but also their families and local communities (villages, cities). If the person responsible is not identified, his community (which is evidently protecting him) must carry the guilt. The body of legislation in force in the Late Bronze Age requires the elders of the city or village to swear that their community has had no part in the bloodshed:

> If some merchants of the king of Ugarit are killed in the land of Carchemish...and their murderers are not caught, the sons of Carchemish will go to Ugarit and declare under oath: 'We do not know who the murderers are, and the goods of the merchants disappeared' (*PRU*, IV, 154-157).

> The prefect (of Ugarit) appealed to the King: 'The inhabitants of Siyannu cut off our vineyards!' The king replied with the following verdict: 'The inhabitants of Siyannu swear: "We did not cut off the vineyards, and we do not know the men who cut off the vineyards!" ' (*PRU*, IV, 162).

> If (the slave) is not found, the mayor and five elders will declare under oath: 'Your slave does not live among us and we are not hiding him'. If they are unwilling to take the oath, they must return his slave. If they take the oath and later he discovers his slave [among them], they are considered thieves their hands are cut off, and they will pay 6,000 (shekels of) copper to the palace (*ANET*, 531; from Alalakh).

The same procedure of collective responsibility recurs in the Deuteronomic legislation in respect of a crime committed in the open country and imputed to the nearby village:

> If, in the land that Yahweh your God is giving you to possess, a body is found lying in open country, and it is not known who struck the person down, then your elders and your judges shall come out to measure the distances to the towns that are near the body... All the elders of that town nearest the body...shall declare: 'Our hands did not shed this blood, nor were we witnesses to it' (Deut. 21.1-3, 6-7).

However, we should also take into consideration the many stories of reciprocal vengeance, reactions that involve the whole family or city of the culprit, which characterize several episodes during Israel's monarchic period. And these are not residual 'tribal customs', but represent the normal, generalized conception of collective responsibility.

This 'horizontal' responsibility intersects with a 'vertical' one, which is generational: the children are responsible for the parents' guilt 'up to the seventh generation'. The connection with the norms of property inheritance are clear: firstly, automatic (the privilege of the firstborn), then discretionary (as with several patriarchal death-bed 'blessings'; and one should note the wordplay between *běrākāh* 'benediction' and *běkorāh* 'primogeniture') – but always from father to son. Along with the benefit of patrimonial inheritance, the son also assumes the obligation of reparation, not only financial but also penal.

Both kinds of corporate responsibility gradually move toward a crisis through socioeconomical changes over a long period; however, the crisis suddenly accelerates with national disaster and exile. The individual is now no longer embedded in a political structure and a social fabric that protects him, and in which the regular transmission of property guarantees one's livelihood. Thus, the individual aims to create a system of purely personal reference, in which he assumes all his own responsibilities but does not wish to assume those of others, (including his parents):

> In those days they shall no longer say: 'The parents have eaten sour grapes, and the children's teeth are set on edge.' But all shall die for their own sins; the teeth of everyone who eats sour grapes shall be set on edge (Jer. 31.29-30).

The new covenant foreseen also by Second Isaiah (e.g. 59.21) implies a personal punishment or retribution, unlike the old covenant based on the collective responsibility of the whole people.

In addition to recalling the same proverb (18.1-3), Ezekiel, in a clear criticism of 'vertical' joint responsibility, also explores the 'horizontal' relationship between the righteousness of an individual, who will personally be saved, and the injustice of the community in which he lives, or even of one of its own families that will fall even though it includes a just person:

> Mortal, when a land sins against me by acting faithlessly, and I stretch out my hand against it, and break its staff of bread and send famine upon it, and cut off from it human beings and animals, even if Noah, Daniel, and Job, these three, were in it, they would save only their own lives by their righteousness, says the Lord Yahweh. If I send wild animals through the land to ravage it, so that it is made desolate, and no one may pass through because

of the animals; even if these three men were in it, as I live, says the Lord
Yahweh, they would save neither sons nor daughters; they alone would be
saved, but the land would be desolate (Ezek. 14.13-16).

This is the same trajectory as in the 'foundational' stories of the Flood
(where the whole of humanity dies because of its guilt, but Noah's family is
saved), and of Sodom and Gomorrah (destroyed because of their impiety,
except the family of the innocent Lot); however, we are talking in reality
about the destruction of Jerusalem and the desolation of Judah.

In effect, while Jeremiah and Ezekiel deal with the problem of personal
responsibility, they are not so much interested in minor judicial matters,
but in the central problem of guilt and punishment as traditionally conceived and its bearing on the relationship of Yahweh and his people. The
individualist approach questions the whole understanding, in the negative
aspect of punishment (destruction and exile) inflicted by God on his people, and the positive aspect of restoration that the whole people may
expect if they reaffirm their loyalty to God. At the level of high abstraction,
Second Isaiah sublimates collective responsibility, inverting the 'pyramid'.
The 'servant of Yahweh' (a pre-figuration of Christ, according to Chris-
tians) shoulders the whole guilt of the entire people, despite being personally innocent:

> But he was wounded for our transgressions,
> crushed for our iniquities;
> upon him was the punishment that made us whole,
> and by his bruises we are healed...
> through his knowledge.
> The righteous one, my servant, shall make many righteous,
> and he shall bear their iniquities (Isa. 53.4, 11).

It is not likely that such a theological sublimation had a strong effect on
the common people. The individualist approach perceives a real 'injustice'
in the fact that, using the words of Lamentations,

> Our ancestors sinned; they are no more,
> and we bear their iniquities (Lam. 5.7).

It dawns on the people that 'the behaviour of the Lord is not right' (Ezek.
18.29; 33.17), a declaration that by itself provides a dramatic hint of a crisis
of values that the ruling group must have done everything possible to hide.
The prophet can only reply that the basic injustice involves the people of
Israel, not Yahweh; but he ends up with a guarantee that all will be judged
by their own guilt and their own behaviour, shifting *de facto* from the
national to the individual level. He goes even further: not only are the chil-

dren not responsible for their parents' guilt, but each individual has a right to be judged by his final status. If he was evil but he repented, he will be forgiven, but *vice versa*: if he was a just man and then became evil, he will be punished:

> The righteousness of the righteous shall not save them when they transgress; and as for the wickedness of the wicked, it shall not make them stumble when they turn from their wickedness; and the righteous shall not be able to live by their righteousness when they sin (Ezek. 33.12; see 18.21-25).

The debate surely did not finish with this exchange. We can only perceive on one hand an official position (Deuteronomist and Priestly) that continues to affirm the principles of collective and intergenerational responsibility, applying them especially in historiographical retrospect; on the other hand, we can see taking root an individualist position that will find particular expression in the choice of the many who do not want to benefit from the reward of national rebirth, preferring to continue benefitting – whether in Babylonia, Egypt or elsewhere – from the profits of their work and their personal business.

Chapter 11

THE DIASPORA

1. *The Fate of the Political Elite*

While Zedekiah, who had betrayed his sworn oath and tried to resist the siege, suffered a terrible punishment, Jehoiachin, who had surrendered in time, was brought to Babylon as an honoured prisoner. From administrative Babylonian texts (*ANET*, 308), dated between the tenth and thirty-fifth years of Nebuchadrezzar, it is clear that the ex-king not only received food and oil rations (like other foreigners of various origin: Phoenicians, Lydians, and Greeks), together with his five sons, but also retained the title of 'king of Judah'.

When eventually Nebuchadrezzar died in 562 and Awil-Marduk succeeded him, the new king celebrated his enthronement with an amnesty from which both the king of Tyre, Merbalos and Jehoiachin benefited. The former was returned to his city (*C. Ap.* 1.158), while Jehoiachin became a kind of 'guest' (2 Kgs 25.27 = Jer. 52.31-34) who ate at the king's table, with a place even higher than that of the other kings in a similar situation.

Recognized as 'king of Judah' by the Chaldaeans, Jehoiachin was also obviously recognized as such by the Judean exiles in Babylon, who considered him the chief of their community, respected by all. His sons Shealtiel and Sheshbazzar, and then his grandson Zerubbabel, Shealtiel's son, were to play an important role in the events of the exile and the return. Sheshbazzar is called 'prince of Judah' (Ezra 1.8) and 'commissar' (*pehah*) of the Persian king (Ezra 5.14) at the time of the return, while Zerubbabel is clearly the civil leader of the returnees (Ezra 2.2; Hag. 1.1). In truth, the events of the return are chronologically confused (as we will see below), and the dates of the texts of Ezra, though debated, come from later; however, the book of Haggai, which refers to the beginning of the kingdom of Darius is consistent with what we can calculate from the genealogies, which indicate Zerubbabel as Jehoiachin's grandson.

It is clear, however, that the 'house of David' had kept its 'royal' prestige among the community of exiles (*gôlāh*) that placed in it all their hopes of national renewal, which traditionally it could not conceive other than in a monarchic form, and which it now took for granted should unite Judah and Israel. Indeed, even those who began to develop alternative strategies (that is, of a priestly kind, see further, §7.5) could not express themselves other than through royal imagery:

> My servant David shall be king over them; and they shall all have one shepherd. They shall follow my ordinances and be careful to observe my statutes. They shall live in the land that I gave to my servant Jacob, in which your ancestors lived; they and their children and their children's children shall live there forever; and my servant David shall be their prince forever. I will make a covenant of peace with them; it shall be an everlasting covenant with them; and I will bless them and multiply them, and will set my sanctuary among them forevermore. My dwelling place shall be with them; and I will be their God, and they shall be my people (Ezek. 37.24-27).

It should be noticed that this prediction of Ezekiel, substantially temple- and priest-centred, still cannot manage without a royal figure (David), whose title of 'king', however, it replaces by 'shepherd' and 'prince' – and I do not believe this was out of consideration for the Chaldean monarch. More poetically, (First) Isaiah had envisaged a king so perfect that the actual scion of the 'house of David', given past experience, could hardly appear a plausible candidate:

> A shoot shall come out from the stump of Jesse,
> and a branch shall grow out of his roots.
> The spirit of Yahweh shall rest on him,
> the spirit of wisdom and understanding,
> the spirit of counsel and might,
> the spirit of knowledge and the fear of Yahweh.
> His delight shall be in the fear of Yahweh.
> He shall not judge by what his eyes see,
> or decide by what his ears hear;
> but with righteousness he shall judge the poor,
> and decide with equity for the meek of the earth (Isa. 11.1-4).

Next to the king and royal family were collegial bodies and classes: the 'elders of Israel' to whom Jeremiah (29.1) wrote a letter and who regularly consulted the will of Yahweh through Ezekiel (8.1; 14.1; 20.1); 'the priests and the prophets' (again Jer. 29.1); and finally a ruling elite, even though without any state apparatus. There is no palace nor temple, and this consideration, apparently banal, nevertheless carried grave repercussions for the way they conceived their function. In effect, a kind of invisible structure (or even a 'shadow government') comes into being, subject to the very visible government of the Babylonians (and then Persians) – a situation that for a long time will cause the problem (particularly for those with political responsibility) of a dual loyalty arising from the choice between a formal allegiance to the empire (and loyalty towards the emperor) and an essential solidarity with their own people.

Obviously, if formal political structures were inconceivable in the Diaspora, those of worship could easily be reconstructed; however, it was precisely the expectation of return and the symbolic influence of the temple of Jerusalem that prevented this from happening. In fact, there are no reports of 'synagogues' among the exiles in Babylonia motivated by hopes of restoration, while later, in the post-exilic age, those who wanted to remain in the Diaspora and did not entertain dreams of return needed places of assembly to hear and cultivate the Law in a decentralized structure.

2. *Adapting to New Circumstances*

In contrast to the virtual disappearance of the 'ten tribes' of the North, deported by the Assyrians (and scattered mainly in Upper Mesopotamia and Media), a strong cohesiveness persisted among the Babylonian exiles. If, already in the second generation (and for manifest political convenience) the royal family had had to adopt Babylonian names such as Sheshbazzar (Šamaš-ab-usur?) and Zerubbabel (Zēr-Babili), the common population kept its own Judean names as a sign of ethnic consciousness and endogamy. Some Assyrian deportees and voluntary emigrants from previous decades must surely have got in touch with the 'strong' core of Judean exiles of the royal group, and, after all, an ex-Israelite component (i.e. from the North, not Judean) must have been present even in the priestly and scribal groups deported by the Chaldaens. As well as closing ranks against foreigners, the idea of a pan-Israelite unity (inherited from the Josianic project) must have intensified through the vision of a common origin of the two families, founding the myth of the conquest on a concerted effort of twelve tribes, and taking the northern tradition of the 'House of Jacob' as a common foundation.

The Babylonian deportees, apart from the royal family accepted at court, were concentrated in Babylonia itself: around the capital and in the area of Nippur, along the Chebar canal (Ezek. 1.3; 3.15; the Nar-Kabaru of the Babylonian sources), and in general 'along the rivers of Babylonia' (as the famous Psalm 137 begins). They were especially settled in small cities or abandoned villages, to recolonize them, as the names with 'Tel' show (the Babylonian *tīlu* means 'hill or mound of ruins'), such as Tel-abib (Ezek. 2.59) and others (Neh. 7.61). From some Babylonian texts we also learn the existence near Sippar of a small city called Judah, with a population possessing Judean names.

The main aim of deporting the common people was to employ them as agricultural settlers, within the context of a general revival of Babylonian agriculture. After centuries of neglect in the management of the network of canals and the cultivation of the agricultural land (reaching its peak in the seventh century), the archaeological evidence (extensive surveys in the Lower Mesopotamia) and textual records (the temple archives of Uruk and other cities of central-southern Babylonian) agree in dating to the sixth century, under the Chaldaen dynasty, a phase of demographic and agricultural recovery in the lower Mesopotamian countryside that marks a stark contrast to the continued abandonment of peripheral regions. The important policy of leasing temple lands to financial operators, with tax concessions and royal support, can only have been carried out with the arrival of additional labour, preferably slaves or forced immigrants.

The use of Judean deportees as farmers who totally fulfilled the requirements of the Babylonian kingdom provides the obvious setting for the instructions in Jeremiah's letter to the exiles:

> Build houses and live in them; plant gardens and eat what they produce. Take wives and have sons and daughters; take wives for your sons, and give your daughters in marriage, that they may bear sons and daughters; multiply there, and do not decrease. But seek the welfare of the city where I have sent you into exile, and pray to Yahweh on its behalf, for in its welfare you will find your welfare (Jer. 29.5-7).

Here is a passage that well expresses the strategy of the leaders of the exiles: to fight against the natural tendencies to depression and passivity that could lead to rapid assimilation and disappearance – but, on the other hand, to encourage a strong-willed resistance and a hope of recovery.

Alongside the agricultural activity of the deportees of middle-low status, those with the means to do so began to participate in financial and commercial activity. These perhaps included families of wealthy exiles, but in particular voluntary emigrants of previous decades, along with emigrants of other Syro-Palestinian people (Arameans, Phoenicians, Transjordanians). It is a fact that in the archives of the family 'bank' of the Murashu of Nippur, dated to the mid-sixth century – a century after the deportation – we find people (or families) with undoubtedly Judean names such as Yahu-natannu (*Yhwntn* in Aramaic) son of Yadih-Yama and grandson of Bana-Yama; or Yahu-zabaddu and Zabad-Yama and Tub-Yama. Assuming that Yama is a form of Yawa, the Yahwistic form of these family names is evident. However, they are localized cases and to present the entire firm of Murashu as

'Judean' is a mistake. It is even less likely that the 'bank' of the Egibi (active in Babylon between 560–500, agents of the Chaldaean and Persian royal house) was Judean: the founder was probably called 'Aqiba (see the *Bĕnē* *'Aqqûb* among the survivors of Ezra 2.42), but the remaining family names are all Babylonian.

We see, then, how (unlike the royal house) the population remained true to traditional names. But some elements of assimilation were inevitable and particularly important: the Aramaic language and script were adopted instead of the Hebrew, conforming with the general tendency of the whole imperial territory that continued into the Persian period. The names of the Babylonian months (Nisan, Iyyar, Sivan, Tammuz and so on) were also adopted instead of the 'Canaanite' ones (Ziv, Etanim, Bul, etc.).

Despite these important aspects of acculturation, the exiles firmly maintained their ethnic and religious self-consciousness. Paradoxically (though not very much so), while the community in Judah crumbled within its multi-ethnic surroundings, the core of exiles, by contrast, bonded together around the values that consolidated their national, as well as religious, identity. Obviously, as often happens with 'mental' facts, the determination to preserve things unchanged in a confined setting also resulted in elements of genuine innovation. Some practices and customs acquired a significance and efficacy as marks of unity and tradition. The families kept a memory (including written records) of their genealogies, their tribal and clan belongings, their property titles, with lists to be used at the time of return (Ezra 2.59; Neh. 7.61). They continued observing the Sabbath (Isa. 56.2-4; 58.13; Ezekiel 44–46) and practicing circumcision. They continued to listen to messages from Yahweh through the prophets (Ezek. 33.30-33), although this now took place in private or in an assembly, since the political structure within which prophetic messages had previously been sought had vanished. They continued to regard the temple of Jerusalem (even though destroyed) as their reference point, without substituting it with local temples – unlike the groups who emigrated to Egypt – and continued their allegiance to the 'house of David' in the event of a future restoration.

3. Deportees and Emigrants

The Diaspora was not restricted to groups *deported* to Babylonia. Other groups existed alongside, maybe equally numerous, who were in foreign countries from personal or group choice, whether freely or forced by events and political or economical pressures. So there existed several distinct and well-defined groups of *emigrants*: we know in particular of those in Egypt, but we can assume that other areas were also affected by this early Diaspora (i.e. of the Neo-Babylonian period) even if these only come to light in the following centuries.

The origin of the Judean communities in Egypt can be reconstructed on the basis of Jeremiah (42; 43.7) in the aftermath of Gedaliah's assassination (see §9.4): the refugees took shelter in Tahpanhes (in the eastern Delta). It is clear that Egypt was the most obvious place of refuge from Palestine (examples recur throughout the history of Israel). And it is also clear that Egypt willingly gave hospitality to groups that could be used for agricultural labour, and even more willingly to well-trained groups that could be used as mercenaries in warfare and as garrisons. The Letter of Aristeas refers to Judeans who went to Egypt as auxiliary troops of Psammetichus against the Ethiopians. Jeremiah (44.1; 46.14) tries to summon home the Judean garrisons stationed at Migdol (in the eastern Delta), at Memphis, Tahpanhes and in the land of Patros (Upper Egypt); Isaiah (11.11) also desires the return of Jewish groups living in Egypt, in Patros and Kush (Nubia), alongside the deportees to Assyria. It is clear that troops and Judean garrisons were regularly present in Egypt from the seventh century, and particularly in the sixth.

More direct and extensive evidence comes from the well-known archive of Aramaic documents (about 200 papyri and 50 ostraca) found at various times (mostly by clandestine excavators) at Elephantine in Upper Egypt and dated to the fifth century, that is, in the Persian period. Smaller groups of Aramaic papyri also come from Hermopolis (*SSI*, II, 27: letters of an Aramean colony, written from Memphis to Aswan and Thebes, c. 500 BCE) and from Migdol (*SSI*, II, 28: letters written by a Judean to the temple of Yahweh at Elephantine, c. 450 BCE).

The Judeans of Elephantine were self-governing, as was appropriate for a military 'colony', practising their own worship and applying their own laws. First of all, they venerated Yahweh (*Yhw*), observed the Sabbath and celebrated the Passover. However, they also venerated (and swore in the name of) 'syncretistic' deities such as Anath-Bethel, Anath-Yahu, Ashim-Bethel, or completely foreign ones: Aramean, such as Nebo (of Babylonian origin), Bethel, and the 'Lady of Heaven'; and Egyptian, such as the local pair of Khnub and Satet. They contributed to the cults of both Yahweh and the syncretistic deities. Unlike the Babylonian community, which did not use any temple, in deference to the uniqueness of that in Jerusalem, the Judeans of Elephantine had a local temple of Yahweh. Indeed, this temple, which dated back 'to the days of the kingdom of Egypt, and when Cambyses came to Egypt he found it built' (*ANET*, 492), provoked a strong reaction from the Egyptian community: it was destroyed by the priesthood of Khnub, and rebuilt with the permission of the Persian authorities (significantly, by the Persian governor of Judah!). However, apart from this incident, normal relationships of intermarriage and commercial exchange are attested among Judeans, Arameans and Egyptians. The Judean cult apparently abstained from animal sacrifice so as not to offend Egyptian customs.

The existence of this temple of Yahweh (from the mid-sixth century, and continuing after the reconstruction of the 'second' temple of Jerusalem) does not imply, as suggested by some scholars, that the arrival of the Judean settlers was prior to the reforms of Josiah, but rather that such reforms had been accepted only by the Deuteronomist circles, and prophetic groups among the exiles in Babylonia. The community of Samaria – as we will see – also had its own temple, challenging the monopolistic claims of Jerusalem; and the colony of Elephantine seems to have included many northerners.

With the aid of this fifth-century evidence, we can understand more clearly the situation that arose from the letter of Jeremiah (44) to the Judean communities in Egypt, and from the subsequent debate. The Judeans, and particularly their women, opposed a prophet who ordered the cessation of the cult of the 'Lady of Heaven' so as to avoid a terrible divine punishment. They simply refused, and retorted in the same vein: until we venerated (in Judah) the 'Lady of Heaven' everything went well; when we stopped, disaster occurred, and we had to emigrate. In the face of such an attitude the prophet gave up attempts at persuasion and abandoned the Egyptian community to its fate, foreseeing an invasion of the land by the Babylonians that will not in fact happen.

We are dealing, therefore, with very different situations in Egypt and Babylonia, which generated two different responses: while the 'forced' deportees tended to react by consolidating their unity and encouraging the prospect of liberation and restoration, the 'voluntary' emigrants, by contrast, had no such motivation, and were instead inclined to assimilate to the host country – unless they (or part of them) encountered, among the groups of deportees, a call to join in the programme of national recovery. And this is just what happened: some groups of voluntary emigrants, who otherwise would quickly have merged into their surroundings, developed a strong and persistent orientation towards Jerusalem and their country of origin, following the example of the exiles – and of their eventual achievements.

4. *Who Is the 'Remnant'?*

Alongside the creation of opposing strategies (explicit or implicit, in close proximity or at a distance) among the several Diaspora groups, a dispute developed between the groups of exiles (who regarded, or came to regard themselves, as the 'remnant') and the groups of those not exiled by the Chaldeans, who remained in Judah, (whom we shall call 'remainees') about their respective rights to be regarded as the authentic heirs of the Judean-Israelite nation. The question is not abstract, as the 'remnant' would in fact provide the legitimate foundation for national recovery.

The concept of 'remnant' is well attested in Assyrian and Babylonian texts, indicating (with the term *sittu*) the survivors of destruction and massacre, and also those who avoided imperial deportation. The term itself has no technical meaning, but indicates that part of the population whose destiny has not yet been described, and it is only the narrative sequence that usually indicates this 'remnant' as being the survivors. Hence, the 'remnant' can designate those left behind, and also those deported (for example 'their remnant I deported and I settled it in Samaria' says Sargon II about some defeated Arab tribes, see §7.3). From the imperial point of view, the 'remnant' that is left in place can become the basis of a new (obviously subject) political order. Sennacherib speaks as follows about his expedition in 701:

> I drew near to Ekron and slew the governors and nobles who had committed sin (that is, rebelled), and hung their bodies on stakes around the city. The citizens who sinned and treated (Assyria) lightly, I counted as spoil. The rest of them, who were not guilty (carriers) of sin and contempt, for whom there was no punishment, I spoke their pardon. Padi, their (former) king, I brought out of Jerusalem, set him on the royal throne over them and imposed upon him my kingly tribute (*AS*, 32).

Already in the Assyrian period, the concept of 'remnant' (*šĕ'ār*) is employed also in Israel (the term is typical of First Isaiah 10.20-22; 11.11, 16; 28.5; see also 4.2-3; but the concept is already in Amos 9.8-9), not without an echo of the imperial ideology: those guilty of the violation of the covenant are eliminated, while the innocent are spared. However, it is after the Babylonian deportations that the debate between the 'remnant' of those left in Judah and the 'remnant' of the deportees begins: who is the legitimate heir? Those left in Judah obviously think they are the remnant: the deportees have been punished by Yahweh, so they are guilty, indeed their departure purifies the land, prevents the 'rotten figs' turning the 'good figs' bad as well. Jeremiah (24.1-10), however, reverses the metaphor in favour of the Babylonian deportees, in his dispute with the emigrants in Egypt.

As those left behind assert (quoted by Ezekiel so as to refute them), the identification of the legitimate remnant is significantly linked with the right of patrimony (*môrāšāh*). This is not only proved by their obvious settlement in the country in general, but also extends to the more specific possession of individual plots and properties (of previous royal and aristocratic ownership) that had remained abandoned because of the deportations, and were evidently exploited by the 'remainee' farmers, with the consent of the Babylonians:

> The inhabitants of Jerusalem have said, 'They have gone far from Yahweh; to us this land is given for a possession' (Ezek. 11.15).

> The inhabitants of these waste places in the land of Israel keep saying, 'Abraham was only one man, yet he got possession of the land; but we are many; the land is surely given us to possess' (Ezek. 33.24).

There is doubtless a strong polemic in the deportees' reversal of these affirmations, asserting that *they* are the real remnant, and implicitly maintaining that the issue is not material possession of the lands, but comes down to the moral and political level. To possess the land proves nothing, if that is accompanied by idolatry and conformity with the surrounding culture. A valid claim to possession of the land is not established by the mere fact of being there, but by the covenant that was first drawn up by Yahweh for his people, on condition that it was faithful to him. Indeed, in the prophecies of Ezekiel and Deutero-Isaiah the 'remnant' is repeatedly identified as those who kept loyal to Yahweh, wherever they are, those to whom Yahweh assures redemption and homecoming from every country; while the 'remnants' of the other peoples are destined to extinction. The idea of the 'remnant' is also linked to the concept that the survivors have been saved by Yahweh because of their righteousness (one can think of the founding stories of Noah and Lot) and thus for their persistence in their faith amid an unfaithful world destined for divine punishment. The 'moral' and not 'patrimonial' remnant becomes one of the foundations of the ideology of the return.

This ideology forms the basis for the subsequent restricted use of the term 'remnant' in the post-exilic age, to indicate only the homecomers from exile, in contrast with those left behind, who are now considered foreigners. The process reaches its peak in Ezra (9.8) where God is praised for having preserved in exile a pure remnant, unblemished by the abhorrence of idolatry and mixed marriages that has now transformed the 'promised land' in an impure domain needing a thorough reconsecration.

5. *The Prophecy of Return and the 'New Covenant'*

For the Babylonian exiles, the factors of national unity were above all two: the prophetic message, heralding a future return and reconstruction, and the historiographical activity directed to rewriting the past. While this rewriting will have a deep impact only in the long term, the prophetic activity had an immediate effect, thanks to the activity of two quite exceptional figures: Ezekiel (already deported with the first group, together with Jehoiachin), and the so-called Deutero-Isaiah (a generation later, on the eve of Cyrus' arrival). In general, these men endorsed the interpretation already established in the seventh century, and eloquently expressed by Jeremiah on the eve of the national disaster, and adapted it to the new situation of a community in exile. According to this interpretation, the national tragedy does not imply the superiority of the foreign gods (Babylonian in this case) over Yahweh, such as would lead Judeans to desert their national god in favour of imperial ones. On the contrary, Yahweh himself had used the Babylonians to punish the treachery of his people, and thus, to achieve reparation, one must rather strengthen loyalty to Yahweh, the only one who will bring his people back home and assure them a future of prosperity (as well as punish the Babylonians).

In the message of Ezekiel, we find declarations of a general significance: the destruction of the temple, the exile as divine punishment, and a way of understanding divine justice (5.7-17 and other passages, probably formulated earlier with reference to Israel as the northern kingdom, before the fall of Jerusalem). But we also find proposals for a more precise political strategy. Its first point states that the hope of return must embrace both Judeans and Israelites:

> Thus says the Lord Yahweh: I am about to take the stick of Joseph (which is in the hand of Ephraim) and the tribes of Israel associated with it; and I will put the stick of Judah upon it, and make them one stick, in order that they may be one in my hand (Ezek. 37.19).

This pan-Israelite vision, already rooted in the pre-exilic period (we need only think of Isa. 11.13), thanks to the presence of scribes and priests among the refugees from the north, gained strength by building on the Babylonian core expectations of a more general Diaspora, including the Assyrian.

National restoration will be based on the 'house of David' (for example Ezek. 34.23-31), probably not out of sympathy or loyalty to Jehoiachin and his circle, but because of the implication of Jerusalem in the ancient oath on which the 'new alliance' (*běrît hădāšāh*; see §18.3) must be moulded. The new alliance must be different from the first (with its disastrous outcome), a more personal, spiritual one, based on a 'new heart' and a 'new behaviour', without royal mediation, without end, but eternal, and thus with an eschatological rather than political aspect (see especially Jer. 32.37-41; and also Ezekiel 36).

Table 8. *Chronology of the Prophets*

	Israel	
900	Elijah (875-850)	
850	Elisha (850-830)	
800	Amos (780-745)	Judah
750	Hosea (760-720)	Micah (740-700)
700		Isaiah I (740-700)
650		
600		Zephaniah (640-610)
		Nahum (610)
		Jeremiah (625-585)
		Habakkuk (605-595)
550	Babylonian exile Ezekiel (595-570; Isaiah II (590-550)	
500	Judaea Haggai and Zechariah (520-515)	
450	Malachi (500-450)	
400	Isaiah III (450-400) Joel (400)	

The question of the ancient covenant on which the new must be fashioned is inseparable from the issue of the former Jerusalem temple, on whose model the 'new temple' will be built, and which is the very basis of Ezekiel's redeeming expectations. The final vision of the new Jerusalem (Ezekiel 40–48), whose name will be *Yahweh šām* 'Yahweh is there', does not provide a basis for a renewed monarchy but, in his spatial-utopian project, for a temple-city that has the temple in the centre (with a totally idealistic plan) and the twelve tribes all around, following an artificial arrangement that does not correspond to their historical location. Within a few decades, the project of Josiah – a piece of *Realpolitik*, but also a failure – to unify the former Israel with Judah through the expansion of the latter, was transformed into a completely new project: a radically new foundation, a common unification of all the tribes around a single central temple – a vision whose capacity for realization comes precisely from its powerful utopian charge (as subsequent events proved).

The ideas of Deutero-Isaiah (who wrote during the decline of Babylonia) are different, and although expressed in a high poetic language and with penetrating images, they were to have a lesser effect at the political level. Ezekiel, too, was a visionary, but his visions appealed to the rising nationalistic spirit and the religious exclusivism that served as powerful engines of political action. Second Isaiah, by contrast, was inspired by concepts so universalistic that they were ineffective: he emphasized the idea that Yahweh is creator of the whole world, and thus king of all the peoples, and no longer one of a number of existing deities, exclusive for his believers only, but a unique universal god who controls the entire course of history, to whom all must submit:

> The wealth of Egypt and the merchandise of Ethiopia,
> and the Sabeans, tall of stature,
> shall come over to you and be yours,
> they shall follow you;
> they shall come over in chains and bow down to you.
> They will make supplication to you, saying,
> 'God is with you alone, and there is no other;
> there is no god besides him' (Isa. 45.14-15).

In this context it is hardly surprising that the political hopes of Deutero-Isaiah were focused on Cyrus, considered the Messiah of Yahweh (Isa. 45.1) for Israel and all the nations. In effect, the prophet's universalistic vision required a supra-national king-Messiah; and more prosaically, with the approach of the Persian armies the moment had arrived to prophesy the fall of Babylon (Isaiah 47) and its gods (46.1-2). The Chaldean dynasty that a generation earlier (in Jeremiah's time) was invoked as the agent of divine anger, to which one had willingly to submit, now suffered the fate of all divine instruments, to be in its turn condemned and punished.

6. *The New Theologies*

The national crisis thus implied a rather radical new way of conceiving not only the political but also the theological structures. In the late pre-exilic period (as represented especially by First Isaiah) it had been believed that Yahweh was present in the temple of Jerusalem, as a king in his palace, seated on the throne supported by the cherubim (*Yahweh sĕbā'ôt yōšēb hakkĕrūbîm*, 1 Sam. 4.4; 2 Sam. 6.2; Isa. 37.16), physically present yet invisible, as expressed by the verbs *šākan* 'dwell (*piel*)' and *yāšab* 'reside'. This is the so-called 'Zion theology' that we might define somewhat less cryptically as a 'theology of presence', one traditionally shared by all the cultures of the ancient Orient.

Evidently the national disaster, the dispersion of the community, and in particular the destruction of the Jerusalem temple caused several problems: not only the theological-moral issue of explaining the causes of the disaster and the divine abandonment, but also the more technically theological problem of finding a place for Yahweh that could no longer be the temple of Zion. We must bear in mind that in the Mesopotamian world the conqueror 'deported' the statues of the gods from the temples of the conquered city, just so as to symbolize the desertion of the defeated by their gods, and to take possession of their own basis of legitimation. The defeated people could hope one day to recover the statue of their god and re-establish normality. However, in the temple of Zion there was no statue of the worship of Yahweh (because of the aniconic principle), only two empty bases (the ark, the throne) symbolically representing the belief that the true seat of the god was 'the heaven and the earth', that is the whole universe. More than a real seat (*miškān* 'place', from *šākan*; *šebet* 'seat', from *yāšab*) it was a place of 'presence', *šĕkīnāh* (to use a term that will have later a particular development in the post-biblical period).

During the restoration, two new theologies took shape: the theology of the 'name' (*šēm*) typical of the Deuteronomist movement, and the theology of the 'glory' (*kābôd*) typical of Ezekiel and the priestly movement. Both confer on the divine presence in the temple a less material connotation. The theology of the name is linked to the expression 'establish the name' (*šikkēn šēm*) in a certain place: and it derives from existing phraseology, above all Babylonian, describing how the king, after his victorious deeds, establishes his name concretely (by means of a celebrative inscription) and symbolically (as reputation, fame). For example, at the end of the Babylonian 'synchronistic History' it is said:

> Let a later prince, who wishes to achieve fame (*šuma šakānu*) in Akkad, write about the prowess of [his] victories (*ABC*, 21.23-25).

We should note that in the case of Jerusalem the expression is attested as early as the Amarna age (*LA* 38 = *EA* 287.60-61) with reference to the Pharaoh and his celebrative inscription erected there.

An analogous conception is the 'glory' that also has its origin in royal phraseology, and that conceives the materialization as a momentous luminosity (something similar to the Babylonian *melammu* and the Persian *xvarĕnāh*, 'luminous halo that strikes terror' or something similar. In Assyrian texts (*SAA*, IX, 18.21-23) it is stated that the deity, conferring royalty on the king, automatically assures him of his support and thus prowess and victory over the enemy. The same concept was present in Syria from the eighth century (*SSI*, II, 5, quoted at §6.6). In several passages 'strength/might' (*'oz*) and 'glory' are linked with each other, evidently as the prerequisite and the outcome of victory:

> Ascribe to Yahweh, O heavenly beings,
> ascribe to Yahweh glory and strength.
> Ascribe to Yahweh the glory of his name (Ps. 29.1-2).

Thus, name, power, glory, fame are all qualities of the victorious king. In the conditions of exile, this conceptual field, no longer applicable to a king, is directly applied to Yahweh, 'king of glory' (*melek hakkābôd*: Ps. 24.10) and it becomes a kind of hypostasis of him. Among other things, this remedies the lack of a physical place of residence, keeps God in heaven, and regards as important for the human community – though not for God himself – his possible symbolic presence, as Name or Glory, in the earthly sanctuary. One has to remember that the epithet *Yahweh Sebaoth*, originally 'god of the (victorious) troops', also loses its materiality in the exilic period (following military defeat) and comes to mean 'god of the (celestial) ranks', that is, of the universe. And *vice versa*, the theology of Glory allows a 'presence' of God to be established in the midst of the community of exiles, despite the lack of a temple to provide concrete visibility and cultural activity.

There were also significant changes to the cultic calendar, partly linked to what has been observed so far. The pre-exilic calendar, with New Year's Day in autumn, had been centred on the celebration of Yahweh's victory over the forces of chaos, like other religions of the ancient Orient. In the exilic (and post-exilic) calendar, with New Year's Day in spring, the Passover celebration of the exodus becomes the focus, a foundational event to which all the hopes of liberation and national recovery are linked.

7. *The Deuteronomist Historiography and the Babylonian Models*

The historiographical task of rereading the past to undergird political strategies for state reinforcement or national recovery had begun to some extent in the time of Josiah (see §8.6): the 'Deuteronomist' school had then formulated a trajectory, based on alternating sequences covenant → transgression → punishment, and covenant → observance → prosperity, ending in the reign of Josiah himself as the ultimate fulfilment. After the national disaster of 587 the scheme clearly had to be rebalanced and even left 'open' to a future perspective, since the present definitely did not depict a 'happy ending'. This new balance was achieved, however, while keeping stable the role of the monarchy (and of the 'house of David' in particular) and maintaining the Deuteronomistic theological principles.

The result was a narrative of the monarchic period in a shape roughly corresponding to the text we have in the books of Samuel and Kings, as part of a more comprehensive Deuteronomist historical work that already begins with the events of exodus and conquest. We are dealing here with a historiographical enterprise of considerable importance, the first (in the Hebrew language) whose period, background and main thematic components one can reasonably suggest. In addition to these components (already summarized in §8.6), the Deuteronomistic historiography is characterized by recurrent and significant terms, largely inherited from the ancient oriental terminology of the covenant: Yahweh 'loves' (*'āhab*) his people, who must obey 'with the whole heart and soul', must 'observe' (*šāmar*, corresponding to the Akkadian *nasāru*) and 'carry out' (*'āśāh*) the commandments, must 'do what is right (*'āśāh hayyāšār*) in the sight of Yahweh', who will intervene 'with mighty hand/outstretched arm' in the conquest of the country 'that Yahweh gives you'.

It is not difficult to perceive that the historical trajectory here divides into two very different parts: from the conquest up to Solomon we find very detailed and dramatic narratives, of a folkloristic or legendary kind, chronologically vague (40 years for David and 40 for Solomon are obviously fictitious numbers), and historically not very reliable; while the period of the 'divided' kingdoms is dealt with in a scanty yet precise way, chronologically well related in detail, and without using legendary materials (apart from the clearly demarcated prophetic cycles of Elijah and Elisha). The point here is that only from the beginning of the 'divided' kingdoms (i.e. from the end of the tenth century) to 587, did the writers have reliable official documentation at their disposal: palace archives, visible royal inscriptions, chronicles.

The author or authors of the history of the kingdoms of Israel and Judah, active during the exilic period, no longer had access either to royal inscriptions or to the archives of the destroyed palace, even if some official documents had perhaps been taken by Jehoiachin in 598 or by the Chaldeans in 587. However, they had chronicles taken from those official documents, and these are repeatedly quoted as 'the book of the annals of the kings of Israel' (1 Kgs 14.19 for Jeroboam I; 1 Kgs 15.31 for Nadab; 1 Kgs

16.5 for Basha; and so on) and 'the book of the annals of the kings of Judah' (1 Kgs 14.29 for Rehoboam; 1 Kgs 15.7 for Abijam; 1 Kgs 15.23 for Asa; and so on). The 'book of the acts of Solomon' (1 Kgs 11.41) that dealt 'with his deeds and his wisdom' probably had a different nature, of a celebrative and folkloristic kind.

Babylonia was the main centre of a tradition of chronicle-like works that based their information on official records, such as the 'astronomical diaries', which were registered daily. The tradition had probably begun in the mid-eighth century under Nabu-nasir, and was updated for centuries, up to the Persian and even Hellenistic periods. Now, the narrative structure of the events of the divided kingdoms shows traces of the Assyrian and Babylonian patterning that the Judean scribes must have encountered during their stay in Babylonia. The more evident comparisons are as follows.

First of all, the general idea of fitting together the events of the kingdoms of Israel and Judah is analogous to the 'synchronistic history' (*ABC*, n. 21) and 'Chronicle P' (*ABC*, n. 22), which narrate the events in which the kingdoms of Assyria and Babylonia came into contact; and also to the 'synchronistic Chronicle' (*ANET*, 272-74), which compares the dynastic sequences of Assyria and Babylonia, first schematically but then in the final part in quite some detail. The more specific correlations in the books of Kings are provided by the dating system, according to which each new reign in Israel is dated to the years of reign of the contemporary king of Judah, and *vice versa*. This system is analogous to the Babylonian chronicles, which date the enthronement of Elamite and Assyrian kings to the year of reign of the Babylonian king.

Another striking and systematically recurrent piece of information furnished by Kings is the burial-place of the kings of Judah and Israel, in the formula: 'Rehoboam slept with his fathers and was buried in the city of David' (1 Kgs 14.31), or 'Baasha slept with his fathers and was buried at Tirzah' (1 Kgs 16.6), or 'Jeroboam slept with his fathers and was buried at Samaria alongside the kings of Israel' (2 Kgs 14.29). The obvious comparison here is with the Babylonian 'Dynastic Chronicle' (*ABC*, n. 18), based on the pattern: 'Simbar-shikhu...died by the sword; reigned 17 years; he was buried in the palace of Sargon' or 'Eulmash-shakin-shumi, son of Bazi, reigned 14 years; he was buried in the palace of Kar-Marduk', and so on.

The supporting theme – and ideologically more significant – of the book of the Kings consists of the verdict passed on each king, depending on his behaviour, right or wrong, namely the application of the fundamental principles of religious worship. In the case of Israel and Judah, generic formulae are used: '(that king) did what was right (*yāšār*)' or 'what was evil (*ra'*) in the sight of Yahweh', but there often follows a reference to the central problem, the elimination or not of the non-Yahwistic cult places (*bāmôt*). In Babylonia, the central problem was different: the regular performance of the New Year festival (*akītu*) in the appropriate sanctuary outside the city, where the god Marduk went in procession, and met Nabu coming from nearby Borsippa. In particular, Nabonidus is often said to be responsible for having omitted celebrating this festival: 'Nabu did not come to Babylon, Bel (= Marduk) did not go out, the *akītu* did not occur' (*ABC*, n. 7). But an entire chronicle (the 'Chronicle of the *akītu*': *ABC*, n. 16) tells of the omission of the festival from the time of Esarhaddon to Nabopolassar; and the problem is also foremost in the 'Religious Chronicle' (*ABC*, n. 17). The political significance of these remarks becomes evident in view of the explicit polemic of Cyrus against Nabonidus (*ANET*, 313 and 315): the Persian king boasts of having restored the correct celebration of the *akītu* that the last Babylonian king had deliberately and guiltily ignored – thus legitimizing the transfer of power in the eyes of the clergy and population of Babylon, who were devoted to Marduk. This central problem of Babylonian worship, celebration or omission of the *akītu*-festival, corresponds to the central problem of Judean worship, the abolition or maintenance of the *bāmôt*.

On the other hand, the more general link between cultic sin/omission and divine punishment is the guiding principle of the 'Weidner Chronicle' (*ABC*, n. 19), which links dynastic succession to the regular supply of fish at Marduk's sanctuary, or the 'Chronicle of the Ancient Kings' (*ABC*, n. 20) that points to the disgrace of famous rulers like Sargon of Akkad and Shulgi of Ur on account of their sins against Babylon.

If the main lines of the Deuteronomist ideology had been shaped in Jerusalem before the disaster, it is nevertheless clear how the Judean priests and scribes found in Babylon a fertile soil for consolidating their 'philosophy of history', based on the sin-punishment nexus, and above all for expressing their ideology through already proven historiographical forms.

Chapter 12

THE WASTE LAND

1. *The Empty Land*

The sixth century, particularly the first half, from the Assyrian collapse of
614–610 to the formation of the empire of Cyrus the Great in 550–539, is
a period of deep depression for a large part of the Near East, similar to the
great crisis that in the twelfth century had marked the change from the
Bronze to the Iron Age. However, while the crisis of the twelfth century is
now established as a major feature of the history of the Near East and the
eastern Mediterranean in ancient times, the crisis of the sixth century has
not yet been similarly recognized. Its explanatory potential is nevertheless
enormous, though less for the material conditions of existence (as in the
Bronze-Iron Age transition) than for ideological features.

Not all of the Near East experienced the crisis as a quantitative reduction (of population, land use, exploitation of resources); in this respect
huge differences are evident between one region and another. Generally,
one can say that the two vast and enduring empires of Assyria (until 610)
and Persia (from 550) were responsible for a generalized development of
the entire region; while the interlude between 610–550 witnessed two
quite different kinds of scenario: growth in the strong core areas and depression elsewhere.

The two strong, ancient cores of irrigated cultivation and urbanization
were densely inhabited and pursued policies involving building programmes, urban development and political and military activity. Babylonia
under the Chaldean dynasty experienced a period of demographic growth,
as shown by the inventory of settlements (based on the extensive surveys
of Robert Adams), by the resumption in land management (easily detect-
able in administrative documents, see §11.2), and by town planning and
building activity (illustrated by archaeology and royal inscriptions). Likewise, Egypt under the Saitic dynasty managed to regain its initiative, as
demonstrated especially by temple-building activity and by a renewed
presence on the Asiatic scene. Other zones, too, lying in the extreme

periphery of that part of the world, and sheltered from imperial expansion, like Lydia (and neighbouring Greece in the 'Archaic' period) or the south Arabian caravan-cities, flourished during the sixth century.

However, the overall scene presents a different picture. Comparing a distribution map of the main cultures of the Iron Age II (eighth–seventh centuries) with a map of the same regions in the sixth century, one is struck by the impression of a real overall collapse. We have already discussed (§9.5) the collapse of Palestine, and the specific causes for this; but a similar situation, with similar causes, can be observed in a large part of the Levant. In central and eastern Anatolia there is also a period of depression: on the central plateaux the kingdom of Phrygia disappears (this extraordinary, flourishing state is attested by the royal necropolis of Gordion, and its wealth became proverbial in the story of Midas' golden touch), while in the upper Euphrates valley the important neo-Hittite centres (from Melid to Samosata/Kummukh and Carchemish) totally collapse. In Armenia, the kingdom of Urartu, still strong and prosperous at the end of the seventh century, with its network of fortresses and hill-top citadels, now suddenly vanishes. In Iranian Azerbaijan, the culture of the Manneans suffers a similar fate. And even the thriving ceremonial citadels of Media (Godin Tepe, Nush-i-Jan, Baba-Jan), are abandoned in the sixth century, just when one would expect them to develop further after the formation of the phantom 'empire' of the Medes. Assyria (and with it all of Upper Mesopotamia), which in the seventh century was the real centre of the world, with sumptuous imperial palaces and the capital Nineveh, with its 300,000 inhabitants the biggest city of that time, has now become a landscape of ruins (see §§8.1-2). Susiana suffers only a partial collapse after the Assyrian destruction of Susa, but the mountainous territory of Elam (Anshan) witnesses a period of major abandonment. In most of these cases, the sites of former major cities and royal palaces of Iron Age II are occupied by groups of squatters, finding precarious shelter among the ruins. The contrast between the two scenes, at the end of the eighth and the beginning of the sixth century, is quite dramatic.

The collapse occurred in some instances (and representing the earliest stage), in the wake of the Assyrian conquest; in others as a result of the collapse of Assyria itself, which took with it neighbouring regions that had undergone a secondary development alongside the large imperial centre; in still further instances, it was the Chaldaean conquest that caused the destruction of what remained. Thus, there is no single cause for the collapse, but they are all linked to the phenomenon of empire. The number of political and cultural centres drastically decreased over 150 years; the

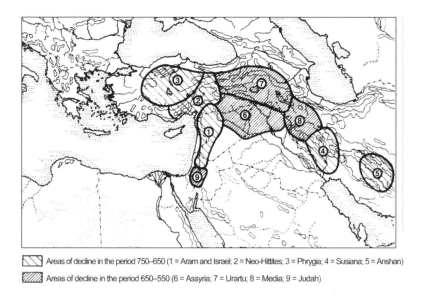

Figure 44. *The collapse in the sixth century*

calculations of de-urbanization and depopulation that we have seen for Judah (§9.5) can be considered as roughly applicable to many other regions. Simultaneously, tribal formations appeared and re-appeared, with their greater flexibility in modes of economic exploitation, dependent not on centralized control but on more dispersed activity based on small, autonomous centres. This revival of nomadism requires a separate discussion (see further, §7).

Turning to Chaldean Babylonia, it is evident how all its human energies and economic resources were invested in the strengthening of the centre, leaving the periphery in a ruined state. The urban and architectural development of Nebuchadrezzar's Babylon, an extraordinary development in which the size of the metropolis overtook Nineveh in its heyday (with an estimated 500,000 inhabitants) contrasts sharply with the dereliction of the provincial centres. A picture of the situation is unintentionally given in a text of Nebuchadrezzar (*ANET*, 307-308) that describes the Neo-Babylonian kingdom in its administrative divisions. The list comprises about 30 governors of Lower Mesopotamian districts that form the core of the kingdom, followed by (vassal) kings of cities of the Mediterranean coast, at the western extremity of the empire: Tyre, Sidon, Arwad, Gaza, Ashdod and a couple of cities whose name is lost. All the intervening territories, of Upper Mesopotamia, Syria, inland Palestine, are absent, evidently assigned to minor officials, thus projecting the negative image of an enormous desert surrounding the few densely inhabited and urbanized areas.

It is thus easy to understand how, seen from Babylon, Palestine seemed to be an 'empty' land, a country of miserable squatters camped in the ruins of ancient cities, infested by nomadic incursions, a country abandoned by God and humans.

2. *The Flood*

In Palestine, such a scene of destruction and degradation of the landscape provided a fitting context for a proliferation of aetiological stories, attached to the landscape of ruins and abandoned settlements, that contributed some basic features to the retrospective vision of Joshua's 'conquest' (as we will see below, §14.5). But in Babylon, too, the exiles found a landscape some features of which were amenable to similar kinds of interpretation: a canal system in disorder and needing huge investment, ancient cities in ruins and in the process of restoration. Some biblical legends, set in Babylon or in some way to be attributed to the Babylonian Diaspora, reflect memories of this desolate world that needs rebuilding. Placed in a mythic, distant past, they have no other historical reference other than the context in which they were conceived or elaborated, inspired by the cultural atmosphere of the time.

The Babylonian origin of the biblical story of the Flood (Genesis 6–10) is well known since George Smith (in 1872) identified the Babylonian narration of the deluge in a tablet from Ashurbanipal's library. In spite of the clumsy and ignorant opposition of more conservative circles who considered that both stories (and others) could be dated back, via a 'memory' stretching over millennia, to a real event of geological times, here we have a clear case of literary transmission. The parallels between the biblical story and Babylonian versions of the myth preserved in the Atrahasis and Gilgamesh epics, are too numerous and precise. The very resting of the ark 'on the mountains of Urartu [Ararat]' (Gen. 8.4) not only reveals the Babylonian origin of the biblical narration, but also places its transmission in the Neo-Babylonian age.

Indeed, the idea of such a rise of waters able to flood the entire earth hardly fits the Palestinian region, with its hills and mountains, but it fits very well with the Babylonian 'mental map', comprising a large alluvial plain (the Tigris-Euphrates valley) surrounded by mountains – a basin whose rim holds in the water. In Babylonia the experience of flooding was recurrent, following a seasonal rhythm. Each year (in April and May), when the Tigris and Euphrates were swollen, their excess water was discharged onto the plain. Earthworks built over centuries, consisting of raised banks, canals, catchment and drainage basins, were intended precisely to control these seasonal floods, transforming them into a means of irrigating the countryside. Sometimes, however, exceptional floods transformed this annual event from a positive to a negative one, exceeding the limits of human control and flooding entire districts. Particularly violent instances would create a change in the course of the Euphrates and of major canals. In the Middle Babylonian and again in the Neo-Babylonian periods, the progressive depopulation of Lower Mesopotamia led to a reduction in available labour for building banks and maintaining canals, and less need for cultivated land. The well-ordered agricultural landscape was damaged everywhere, and in some zones it totally collapsed, turning them into perennial marshland. The drainage programmes undertaken by the Neo-Babylonian kings were aimed exactly at halting this deterioration, at least in areas that were still recoverable.

The story of the Flood is thus a typical 'foundation myth': it aims to transform a natural, seasonal phenomenon into a mythic archetype of extreme proportions. And it seeks to establish that the negative experience of this ordinary event can be resolved positively, here and now in the real world, just as it happened once in the archetypal event. At a more trivial level, the final part of the biblical narrative depicts it as a 'foundation myth' of the meaning of the rainbow as a sign of restoration (but this addition fits Palestine, a land of rainfall agriculture, better than Babylonia, a land of irrigated cultivation).

As a mythic archetype, the Flood cannot, and must not, be 'explained' as a memory of a prehistoric catastrophe: it can, and must, be explained as an elaboration of a recurrent event (annual in this case), and thus part of everyday experience. The archaeological evidence of strata of alluvial deposits, found first at Ur but then also at other sites, dated to different periods, does not point to an archetypical deluge but to recurrent 'historical' flooding.

The biblical narrative (in which a priestly writer, in the post-exilic period, fused two parallel accounts) has been inserted into the genealogical traditions of Israel for its moral lesson, as the first instance of the recurring pattern of divine punishment for human violence (*ḥāmās*, a term favoured by Ezekiel) – a primordial episode, and thus not specifically referring to Israel and its covenant with Yahweh, but capable of being used to prefigure it. The connection with the figure of Noah may be due to etymology and deduction: the name of Noah (*nōaḥ* 'to have rest' from *nwḥ*, not from *nḥm* as in the popular etymology of Gen. 5.29) nicely suits the 'calm after the storm', while his threefold lineage (Shem, Ham, Japheth, founders of all the known peoples), fits a repopulation of the entire earth from which all previous inhabitants had been removed.

3. *The Tower of Babel*

The Babylonian landscape displayed cultivated fields and irrigation canals, but also areas abandoned through salination or swamp; it also offered densely inhabited cities and functioning temples, but also derelict buildings and monumental remains, ruins that signified a past more prosperous than the present. Among these ruins was the 'tower of Babel', or rather, many of them, ruins of *ziqqurats* (high temple buildings) built from the end of the third millennium and then repeatedly restored over the following centuries, but finally turned into huge ruins sticking up from the flat Lower Mesopotamian horizon. The use of mud-brick as building material implies that in Mesopotamia the alternation of dilapidation and restoration is such a regular experience that it prompts the emergence of a kind of philosophy of history that takes periodical ruin as inevitable and structural.

In popular folklore, however, the ruin (really the result of dilapidation following construction) is often interpreted instead as an unfinished building, unlocking the imagination to produce stories of why the building was not finished, but remained condemned forever. The short narrative of the tower of Babel (Gen. 11.1-9) clearly belongs to this type of aetiological story.

The tower was so tall as to touch the heavens, symbolizing impious human arrogance, and was left unfinished after work on it ceased when the deity mixed up human languages to make further progress impossible. Thus, around the enormous ruin a story develops that expresses the values of a popular, commonplace theology about the finite limits of the human realm. One must imagine that the huge *ziqqurat*, standing up like a mountain on the flat horizon of the alluvial plain particularly impressed the Judean deportees, coming from a land that lacking any building as impressive as this, and so inclined to link it to imperial presumption and arrogance.

But the narrative is also influenced by the experience of the deportee workers, each one having a different origin and language (Hebrews, Arameans, Anatolians, Iranians) employed by the Babylonians on building projects, under the control of supervisors who gave orders in yet another language – with all the difficulties deriving from such polyglot activity. Another ancient idea (as old as the Sumerians) found its way here, too: that the plurality of languages and the difficulties of mutual comprehension are part of a historical and ruined world, but that in the perfect

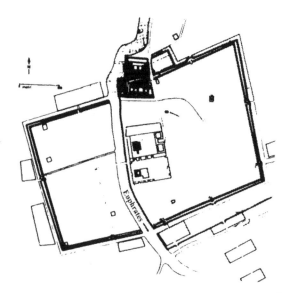

a.

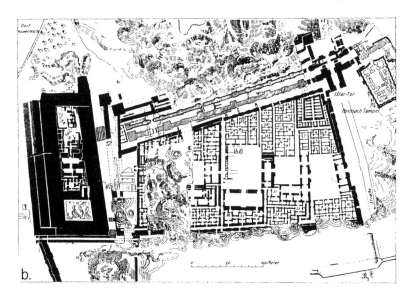

b.

Figure 45. *Babylon in the sixth century: (a) general plan; (b) southern palace and fortress*

world, as originally created by the divine order, all people spoke a single language. The false etymology of the name of Babel in Gen. 11.9 conveys a distinct note of derision: not 'gate of God' (*bāb-ili*), but 'place of confusion' (*bālal*). And this implicit anti-Babylonian pun, together with the disintegration of the tower, leads us to think of the second half of the sixth century as the date of the narrative.

4. The Garden of Eden

In the middle of the barren and wild landscape of Babylonia, some centres of order and productivity were to be found. These were agricultural farms where the garden area (with date-palms, fruit-trees, and plots of onions, lettuce and other vegetables) was carefully nurtured by small irrigation canals, constantly attended by experts, and enclosed for protection against theft and human and animal damage. However, these productive units found a model and an idealized form, in the cause of opulence and ostentation, in royal gardens where trees and ornamental plants, animals and birds came together. These royal gardens are the model for the 'garden of Eden' where the biblical story of Adam and Eve is set (Gen. 2.4–3.24). The word paradise (Heb. *pardēs*, Bab. *pardēsu* 'park') is of Persian origin (*pairidaēza* 'enclosure'), and the Persians were responsible for the spread of this kind of enclosed garden. Thus, the Eden narrative should be assigned to the Babylonia of the Persian age; however, it is better to deal with it now rather than fragment the theme of landscape that actually covers several centuries.

The Persian 'paradise' has a long history behind it. Already in Egypt's New Kingdom, Thutmose III (c. 1450) assembled in a sort of 'botanical garden' all the exotic plants that his armies had collected in expeditions to Syria and Nubia. Later the Assyrian kings, beginning at least with Tiglath-Pileser I (c. 1100), assembled exotic plants and unusual animals in their enclosed gardens, as if they wanted to represent, in a ceremonial way, their control over the whole world, as demanded by their ideology of universal empire. At the climax of the Assyrian empire, under Sargon II and Sennacherib, the royal gardens were linked to the royal palace, and included not only plants and animals, but also buildings characteristic of different parts of the conquered world and exhibited for people to admire. The Persian paradises extended this Assyrian custom. On the one hand, there were 'ceremonial' *paradises* attached to the imperial capitals, and the one in Parsagadae reveals the typical structure of quadripartite irrigation (with a clear cosmic allusion) that is also apparent in the four rivers of the biblical Eden. On the other hand, the Persian administration proliferated the installation of the 'paradise', and so in some way made it rather commonplace: even provincial administrative centres were provided with them, particularly in a practical version, a royal agricultural business combining amusement and exhibition, typical of the garden, with actual food production, as on a horticultural farm.

Figure 46. *An Assyrian royal park*

First of all, the biblical Eden narrative is a further expression of the recurring pattern of transgression and punishment, placed this time at the beginnings of humanity. The garden is, however, also a symbol of an existential condition, marked by the oppositions of inclusion/exclusion, protection/risk, comfort/labour. Inside the 'paradise' everything is easy and spontaneous: irrigating water, fruit-trees, even the inhabitants themselves living in peace and innocence. Outside, everything becomes difficult and tiring: the open spaces become productive only after exhausting work. However, access to the garden is forbidden to common mortals, who have thus to undertake a life of hardship to secure a hard-won existence.

Hence, besides its 'landscape' values, the story of the earthly paradise is also an expression of the vain search for immortality, which recurs in the Babylonian tradition, where it is linked to the mythic figures of Adapa and Gilgamesh. In these episodes too, as in the story of Adam and Eve, the archetypical characters try to obtain eternal life, nearly succeed, to the alarm of the divine world, and finally have to be satisfied – for themselves and their descendants – with normal mortality, obtained as a consolation prize from the gods. The parallels between the biblical story and that of Adapa are especially obvious. Adam, on the advice of the snake, had access to knowledge, and if he had also obtained immortality he would then have become like the gods; but he was prevented by Yahweh. Similarly Adapa, on the advice of Enki, had access to knowledge, but not the immortality that Anu had promised to give him. Gilgamesh, the prototypical king, and Adapa, the prototypical priest, had consolation prizes appropriate to their roles (glory for the king, cultic practice for the priest); Adam, by contrast, the prototype of humanity as a whole, gained (in the form of a curse!) the survival, not of the individual but of the human race, by virtue of sexual reproduction and human labour:

> To the woman he said, 'I will greatly increase your pangs in childbearing; in pain you shall bring forth children, [...] to the man he said: '...Cursed is the ground because of you; in toil you shall eat of it all the days of your life; thorns and thistles it shall bring forth for you; and you shall eat the plants of the field (Gen. 3.16-18).

The story of Adam and Eve is thus set in a Babylonian landscape, but in the Persian period, and it develops reflections on human mortality of a clearly Babylonian type. The compilers of the biblical story must therefore have lived in Babylon in the early Achaemenid era.

5. *The Tripartite World*

As is usual for peoples of tribal origin, accustomed to formalizing political relations in terms of natural or acquired relationships, the Israelites had for a long time created genealogical patterns linking the tribal eponyms, and had evolved a series of legends establishing the hierarchical relations among the tribes and relationships of friendship and rivalry with their neighbours. However, such a pattern, which changed over time as new historical links were formed, had, in the pre-exilic period, remained confined to the Palestinian sphere. It was only the experience of dispersion, following the deportations, that can have suggested and facilitated a 'genealogical tree' of universal scope. Obviously, the geographical width of this framework implies a corresponding generational (chronological) expansion, simply because of the structure of the genealogical tree, which depicts an exponential growth. To contain the whole population of the world, then, it was necessary to go back to the single ancestor.

The 'List of Nations' in Genesis 10 is precisely the product of this global genealogy of all the peoples in the world. The single ancestor must be Noah, sole survivor of the disaster of the Flood; and the lines of descent start with his three sons Shem, Ham and Japheth. The genealogy ends by embracing the entire world as it was known at the time of the list's redaction, obviously with a larger grouping of peoples in the central area (from the point of view of the author), and with a progressive thinning out towards the periphery that shades into the unknown. The date is roughly calculable: at a first estimate the list is later than 690, since it mentions the Ethiopian pharaoh Sabteca (Gen. 10.7), and prior to 550, since the Persians do not play any important role in it. On a closer approximation, it is more

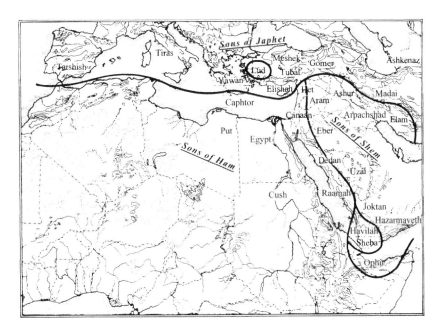

Figure 47. *The tripartite world: geographical distribution of the 'table of nations'* *(Genesis 10)*

probably after 610, since, despite the recent memory of the Assyrian cities, the general picture does not correspond to the Assyrian empire. On the contrary, it is the tripartite world that emerged after the collapse of that empire that is now taking shape. The three main divisions between the 'children of Japheth', 'children of Shem', and 'children of Ham' correspond, in general, to the sphere of Median hegemony, Chaldean hegemony and Egyptian hegemony: just the scenario between 600–550. Moreover, the inclusion in particular of Lydia within the sphere of Shem (Gen. 10.22) instead of Japheth (as would be geographically more obvious) betrays the hostility between Media and Lydia that culminated in the battle of 585. The same is true for the inclusion of Elam in Shem in the same verse, which indicates the exclusion of Persia from the Median confederation that ended in the battle of 553. In addition, the biblical equivalents for the less obvious nations are concentrated in Ezekiel (especially 38.1-6, 13; also 32.22-30) which date to the first half of the sixth century.

There are, however, some inexplicable oddities that lead us to suspect a laborious editorial process. For example, Babylonia is called Shinar (Gen. 10.10, and again in 11.2), which is an Egyptian designation, while Nimrod, important hunter and founder of Mesopotamian cities, is inserted among the 'sons of Cush'. The Chaldeans seem, at first reading, to be surprisingly absent, but they are in reality to be recognized (as *Ant.* 1. 144 does) in Arpachshad (*-kšd*, see *Kašdîm* from **Kaldîm*). In the whole 'list' there is, moreover, a strong preponderance of tribal peoples, especially in the areas settled by Arabs, hinting at a major contribution from genealogical traditions from the desert region and the Arab-Aramean peoples. The 'Hebrews' (*Eber*: 10.25) are inserted into this tribal sphere, within a genealogy that links Arpachshad with Abraham (Gen. 11.10-26) and thus belongs to the same tradition that has Abraham come from Ur-Kašdîm, 'Ur of the Chaldees'. The land of Canaan (from Sidon to Gaza) belongs to the line of Ham, and thus to the Egyptian sphere. The 'List of Nations' is not a document of specifically Israelite origin (Judah and Israel do not even appear), but could derive instead from a north-Arabian source close to Mesopotamia (the Teima of Nabonidus?). It belongs to a time and a background where the need to insert an 'Israel' into the network of genealogical relations of the known world was not felt.

6. Genealogies and Antiquarianism

The 'List of Nations', although exceptional for its breadth of perspective, is not an isolated document. The entire prehistory of Israel, from before the deluge and up to the 'patriarchs', is composed according to a system of 'generations' (*tôlēdôt*) and is crammed with genealogical trees that show the origins of various peoples: Arameans (Nahor: Gen. 22.20-24), Ishmaelites (Gen. 25.12-27), Edomites (Genesis 36, with several lists, perhaps of different origin). These 'generations' link, backwards to Adam, the first man; but they also nearly always connect forwards with the Israelite tribal genealogies. Apart from the function of establishing the relations among the nations (near and far), this genealogical system also serves a chronological purpose, going back from generation to generation and tracing the whole human story back to the deluge and the creation: this is a historiographical function, even if it has a mythical form.

Such a genealogical interest seems to be a peculiarity of the sixth century, and not only in the Near East. In Greece too (probably under Babylonian influence) the first 'historiographical' works date from this time, and assume a genealogical form: the first 'Genealogies' known, those of Acusilaus from Argos were written around 550, and the most famous 'Genealogies', by Hecateus of Miletus, around 490. These works also aimed to link the present (confined to the immediate locality and city) with the mythical origins of the deluge and the heroic and divine worlds.

Not by chance, other embryonic forms of historiography also take the form of a geographical inventory, *periegesis*. Here Hecateus' work should be seen against the contemporary (in fact a little earlier) Near Eastern interest in the geographical classification of nations, visible in the 'mental maps' that can easily be extracted from the description by Ezekiel of the commercial network of Tyre (Ezekiel 27; see §8.2) and from the 'List of Nations', both composed around 600.

The devices of genealogical reconstruction and geographical arrangement were both useful in keeping under control (in a mental, cognitive way) a world that had enlarged considerably following the Mediterranean and Arabian trading networks and the emergence of the Iranian and Trans-Iranian world, yet at the same time had lost the administrative control achieved through the Assyrian 'universal' empire, later to be regained by the Persian empire from Darius onwards. In the intervening world of the sixth century, cognitive schemes were evolved allowing the various ethnic groups to be classified both spatially and chronologically.

Among the surviving 'hard cores' of nationalism, that is, in Chaldean Babylonia and Saitic Egypt, we see a similar interest for the past, but manifest in quite a different way. Doubtless, this interest in the past was long-standing: both countries had kept up-to-date lists of kings for millennia. However, in the sixth century the recovery of the past takes the form of a hoped-for 'national' recovery after centuries of political and cultural crisis and foreign intervention. In Babylonia the crisis had persisted (with ups and downs) from the second dynasty of Isin, through the Aramean infiltrations and then Assyrian dominion, from 1025 to 625. In Egypt it had begun in late-Ramesside times, through the Libyan dynasties and Ethiopian domination, from 1100 to 665. When these two parallel courses turned in a positive direction, the local political elites tried to revive the ancient models. In both cases, an archaizing style (promoted as 'classical') was adopted in the figurative arts as well as architecture, literature and palaeography. In the royal palace of Chaldean Babylon, a 'museum' with monuments of venerable antiquity was set up, and kings devoted themselves to 'archaeological excavations' in search of the foundation inscriptions of the ancient rulers of Akkad. Forgeries (more or less 'pious') were also made to endow the temple patrimonies with 'foundation documents' of an ancient date, such as the so-called 'cruciform monument' that wished to ascribe to the Akkadian king Man-ishtusu certain privileges and donations to the temple of Shamash at Sippar.

This is the broad context, on both tribal and state level, of that sudden and remarkable growth of interest in the past that characterizes the era of the deportation of the priestly and scribal Judean elite to Babylonia. It was in this cultural ferment, that the elite found available most of the ideological and formal resources to undertake a coherent project of research into, and rewriting of, the national past that gave a meaning and a reason for trust in an anticipated re-foundation.

7. *Nomads of the Mountains and Desert*

As already mentioned, the Near Eastern stage in the 50 years following the collapse of the Assyrian empire witnessed a remarkable expansion of the nomadic-tribal element, in two main blocks; the Iranian peoples on the northern highlands and the Arabs of the Syro-Arabian desert. In the Assyrian-Babylonian and biblical historical texts one can follow the details of this expansion, but also the growth of mental images deriving from the pressure (mostly threatening) that these people exerted on the agricultural and urbanized lands.

The nomads of the Iranian highlands had been a perennial threat to Mesopotamia, which had periodically suffered the invasions of Gutians, Lullubites and Kassites. In the Assyrian period, the danger had remained confined to its mountains, its route being blocked by the strong defensive and punitive machinery set up by the empire. However, at the borders of the empire the Iranian tribes increased their military ability and political consolidation during the seventh century, until they became a fundamental element (and no longer an external one) of the Near Eastern framework. With the fall of the empire, the mountain-dwellers could once again spread onto the plains: after the great descent of the Medes (the determinant factor in the fall of the empire), other similar incursions were feared, including the reports, more or less imaginary, of Cimmerians and Scythians. And the powerful image of the 'northern hordes' that threaten the maintenance of order and continuity of life in the overrun lands, now takes shape.

The paradigm of the 'enemy from the north' was an ancient *topos* in Mesopotamia, whose entire northern flank adjoined the Zagros mountains, and it goes back to the fall of the dynasty of Akkad to the Guteans. In Palestine, the danger was more remote, but the paradigm was equally effective since, because of the configuration of the Levantine strip, most invasions of armies and foreigners could come only from the north. Thus, in this same paradigm the Assyrian and Babylonian armies were united with the nomadic invaders – numerous, cruel, and very swift on their horses.

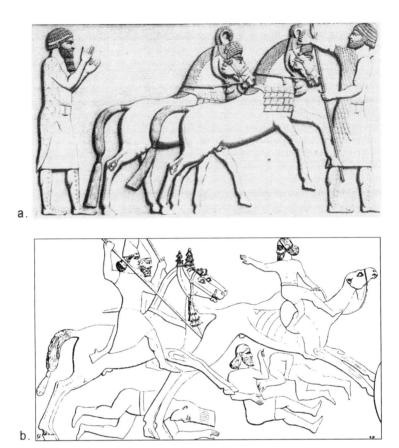

Figure 48. *Assyrian images of nomads: (a) Median horse-breeders; (b) Arabs on camels*

The relative improbability of a 'northern' nomadic threat makes even more remarkable the formation of a literary pattern of inexorable and destructive invasion whose strongest expression is found in the long passage from Ezekiel (38–39) about Gog of Magog, where it acquires an apocalyptic tone, describing a final event:

> Therefore, mortal, prophesy, and say to Gog: Thus says the Lord Yahweh: On that day when my people Israel are living securely, you will rouse yourself and come from your place out of the remotest parts of the north, you and many peoples with you, all of them riding on horses, a great horde, a mighty army; you will come up against my people Israel, like a cloud covering the earth. In the latter days I will bring you against my land, so that the nations may know me, when through you, O Gog, I display my holiness before their eyes (Ezek. 38.14-16).

The figurative power of Ezekiel's oracle has bestowed a long life on the 'Gog and Magog' motif (up to the Islamic and Christian Middle Ages) and inspired some famous literary expressions: it is enough to think of Alexander the Great and the iron wall built by him on the Caucasus to contain the menace beyond the civilized world.

The nomadic camel drivers of the desert are less fearsome than the nomadic horsemen of the northern mountains; they are less strange in their language and culture, and better integrated through their long-standing trade and interaction. They also dwell in close proximity, on the very borders of Palestine. They do make raids, but the trading image prevails – quite the opposite of the Medes, who also indulged in trade, but for whom the destructive image predominated. There is no doubt that the presence of Arabs in the Near East suddenly accelerates during the seventh century. Previously, both Assyrian and biblical reports referred to tribes whose homeland lay well inside the desert, and who are mostly presented as caravan leaders. The Assyrians received luxury goods from them, more in ceremonial gifts and trade than as a result of military victory. At the time of Ashurbanipal, however, they are depicted as a real menace: they enter into the anti-Assyrian coalition, they press upon the Syrian provinces, they need to be contained by campaigns that venture inside the desert, or, better, must be bound by oaths of loyalty sworn under pain of terrible curses. As for the Medes, the fall of the empire allowed the Arabs to spread into the Syro-Palestinian strip. Their bases remained in Arabia, at Teima and Duma, which in the sixth century reach the peak of their first cycle of expansion, and which Nabonidus (certainly not out of foolish stupidity) tried to enclose within the structure of the shaky Chaldean kingdom. However, their infiltration into the territories of Ammon, Moab and Edom was also serious, to judge from the oracle of Ezekiel:

> Thus says the Lord Yahweh: Because Moab said, 'The house of Judah is like all the other nations', therefore I will lay open the flank of Moab from the towns on its frontier, the glory of the country, Beth-jeshimoth, Baal-meon, and Kiriathaim. I will give it along with Ammon to the people of the East as a possession. Thus Ammon shall be remembered no more among the nations, and I will execute judgments upon Moab. Then they shall know that I am Yahweh (Ezek. 25.8-11).

Into the lands destroyed by the Babylonian armies, the Arab nomads thus infiltrated and took possession. They settled in southern Syria, in Gilead, and in Moab. The partial relocation of the Edomites into the Negev allowed them to become established in southern Transjordan as well. In post-exilic texts (such as Num. 31.1-12), Amalekites and Midianites are well represented, even dominating, within the territory of Moab. Now Kedar is no more a distant tribe, but an inner tile of the mosaic; and Ishmael is for Israel a 'relative' closer (a half-brother) than Moab and Ammon (second cousins). The genealogical scheme evidently does not reflect the monarchic era, but that of the Diaspora and return, with the Ishmaelites fully included within events in Palestine.

On the other hand, we have already seen (§3.3) that the Hebrew terminology for 'tribe' belongs to this phase, and that the large Arab tribal confederations of the seventh–sixth centuries (such as the Ishmaelites and Kedarites) provided the pattern for the creation (and its projection back to the founding moment of ethnogenesis) of the large confederation of twelve tribes of Israel, genealogically structured and acting in unison to invade the lands of the settled people.

Part II
AN INVENTED HISTORY

Chapter 13

RETURNEES AND 'REMAINEES':
THE INVENTION OF THE PATRIARCHS

1. *The Fall of Babylon and the Edict of Cyrus*

The exile (*gôlāh*), spent in a climate of resignation mixed with hope, did not last for ever. Jeremiah had at first exhorted the exiles to integrate themselves into the new milieu and start a new life with a positive attitude (see §11.2), dispensing with the vain hope that a more open attitude from the Babylonians (probably noted at the ascent of Awil-Marduk) could lead to the restitution of the temple furniture (Jer. 27.16-17). Finally he prophesied a period of 70 years (Jer. 25.11-12; 29.10), not for the duration of the exile, but for the Chaldean dynasty. He probably pronounced this prophecy when the imminent collapse of the Babylonian empire was universally expected: the 70 years fit rather neatly between 609, the Assyrian collapse, and 539, the conquest of Babylon by Cyrus.

The 70-year cycle of Yahweh's anger against his people is a motif already used to describe the anger of Marduk against his city of Babylon in the inscriptions of Esarhaddon (see the quotation in §7.6). It is the period of time needed to assure a full generational replacement of those responsible for the acts that caused the divine anger by their innocent offspring. According to Jeremiah (50–51), the fall of Babylon, seen as a kind of repetition of the fall of Nineveh and Assyria, will be caused – as usual – by barbaric hordes from the North (Jer. 50.41-43), at first (around 580–570) identified with the confederation of mountain tribes under the leadership of the Medes (Jer. 51.11, 27). This identification was later reread (and partly rewritten) with reference to the Persians under Cyrus. Babylon is in any case brought down in just the same way that it had caused the destruction of many other peoples, and Judah in particular – though in fact Cyrus did not destroy the city nor topple Marduk, as Jeremiah had announced, or hoped (50–51):

> Thus says the Yahweh of hosts:
> The broad wall of Babylon
> shall be leveled to the ground,
> and her high gates
> shall be burned with fire.
> The peoples exhaust themselves for nothing,
> and the nations weary themselves only for fire (Jer. 51.58).

Deutero-Isaiah, too, saw in the fall of Babylon a sure sign of the fulfilment of the divine anger, and so attributed to Cyrus the role of saviour. Writing at the same time as the events (a generation after Jeremiah), he knew well that times had changed since the old paradigm: Babylon would not be destroyed like Nineveh, and Cyrus was not a furious destroyer, but a rightful king sent by Yahweh in a miraculously peaceful mission:

> Thus says Yahweh to his anointed, to Cyrus,
> whose right hand I have grasped
> to subdue nations before him
> and strip kings of their robes,
> to open doors before him –
> and the gates shall not be closed:
> I will go before you
> and level the mountains,
> I will break in pieces the doors of bronze
> and cut through the bars of iron,
> I will give you the treasures of darkness
> and riches hidden in secret places,
> so that you may know that it is I, Yahweh, the God of Israel, who call you by
> your name (Isa. 45.1-3).

The arrival of Cyrus marked a moment of great hope for the exiles. Such a hope was not unmotivated, at least in Babylonia, because Cyrus introduced himself to the inhabitants of the town as the one to restore the local cult of Marduk, make concession and give 'freedom' to the people of Babylon, putting an end to the evil and impious acts of Nabonidus, the last Chaldean king. The Babylonian priests accepted the interpretation of the events suggested by Cyrus himself (*ANET*, 315-316): it was Marduk who had summoned the people from the north and the saviour-king Cyrus against Babylon. In the same way, Jewish priests living in Babylonia expressed a similar hope: Cyrus would act in the name of Yahweh, bringing freedom to Jewish people and restoring the cult of Yahweh. The 70 years of Jeremiah were completed exactly on time. The 'servant of Yahweh' enthusiastically announces a 'new exodus' from Babylonia, inspired by the mythical foundational deliverance from Egypt (Isaiah 49).

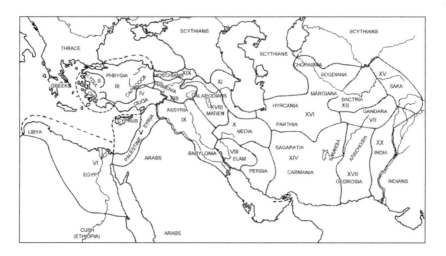

Figure 49. *The Persian empire at the time of Darius I. I-XX: list of the satrapies according to Herodotus 3.89-94*

The political situation was, however, quite different. Cyrus needed the support of the priests and people of Babylonia so as to conquer, almost unopposed, the most powerful kingdom of the time and establish his universal empire. He did not need the support of Jewish priests, and most probably he completely ignored their concerns for the Jerusalem temple. Moreover, the impact of Zoroastrian religion had little to do with hopes of redemption: we do not know whether Cyrus was in fact Zoroastrian, but in any case a monotheistic faith (especially in a dualistic form) is usually less tolerant and respectful of other religions than polytheism. Non-Zoroastrian gods would thus be placed on the dark side of falsehood, injustice and evil. But it is also true that the enlargement of the empire, its diversified structure, and its tendency to adopt local forms of government were factors that opened wider horizons and a certain freedom of worship – though the prophets who applauded the advent of Cyrus could not have been aware of that.

A couple of centuries later the idea circulated that Cyrus, immediately in the first year of his reign, had issued an edict authorizing the return of exiles and the reconstruction of the temple of Yahweh. This edict (whose text is reproduced in Ezra 1.2-4) is certainly a fake, as is clear from both textual analysis and its anachronisms. The same can be said of a second edict of Cyrus (Ezra 6.3-5), said to have been found in Persian archives in the time of Darius, which contains additional measures and technical and financial details for the construction of the new temple. These edicts were written and used, in much later times, in order to give prestige and imperial privileges to the temple already built in Jerusalem, and as an answer to the claims of the rival temple in Samaria.

The return, in fact, did not take place at the time of Cyrus, and Zechariah (active in the second year of Darius, 520) expresses the common feeling of frustrated hope:

> O Yahweh of hosts, how long will you withhold mercy from Jerusalem and the cities of Judah, with which you have been angry these seventy years? (Zech. 1.12).

By 520 the 70 years were already passed, even if reckoned from the deportation of 589. It was then, in fact, that an important return took place, under the leadership of Zerubbabel, who also began the reconstruction of the temple (see §16.1; 17.3).

More reliable – if not in actual wording at least in having a generally plausible historical context – are the edicts of Artaxerxes authorizing the return of a group led by Ezra (Ezra 7.12-26) and the authorization by the same king for the return of a second group under Nehemiah (Neh. 2.7-8). These took place in the mid-fifth century. We can take it for granted that the group led by Zerubbabel and Joshua in the time of Darius also had official permission. Although the redactors of the books of Ezra and Nehemiah had very poor knowledge of the chronology of the Achaemenid kings, we can assume that a return in small groups took place at least between 539 and 445. At first (in the time of Cyrus) these will have been informal, taking advantage of a political climate favourable to the repatriation of groups deported by the defeated dynasty; later on, they were formally authorized by the reigning emperors.

We will later examine the individual problems of the political organization that the returnees intended to create, the phases of rebuilding of the second temple, the emergence of priests as leaders of the people, and the formation of distinctive legal principles characterizing the new *ethnos* of 'Israel'. But the first question to consider is the interaction between the groups of returnees and the population they found in Palestine, and the huge problems that the return implied, of a legal and moral kind as well as for the self-identity of the new nation.

2. The Groups of Returnees

The groups of returnees could not have been very numerous, especially considering that their return took place over quite a long period – at least a century. Nebuchadrezzar had deported no more than 10,000 people in

598 and (we may guess) another 10,000 in 587. During the two generations of exile, those numbers could have doubled. But not all of them came back, perhaps only a minority. It is probable that others joined the group – maybe not always with proper genealogical credentials (see Ezra 2.59-63 = Neh. 7.61-65). In Babylonia during the exile, the leaders of the Jewish community (elders and priests) had recorded and updated lists of the legitimate members of the community. Ezekiel threatened his enemies as follows:

> they shall not be in the council of my people, nor be enrolled in the register of the house of Israel, nor shall they enter the land of Israel (Ezek. 13.9).

The mention of 'soil' (*'ădāmāh*, not *'ereṣ*!) brings to mind lists of families (houses), but also land holdings. It is obvious that these lists could also be emended and manipulated for political reasons, and anyone whose name was cancelled did not have a right to return. In such conditions it is quite difficult to make a reliable estimate.

Given this uncertainty, we have a document that apparently gives precise data: a list of returnees that appears, with slight variations, in Ezra 2 and Nehemiah 7. It is true that the two books are late and, as already mentioned, full of inaccuracies, both accidental (from ignorance) and deliberate. But the lists of 'Zionists' have a strong probability of being reliable, because they are in all likelihood derived from original documents. They probably combine several groups of returnees (Zerubbabel's and Joshua's, Nehemiah's, and several others) and perhaps the differences in numbers between the two versions arise through the continual updating of the files. It is a kind of document that, because of its high legal importance, could be completely authentic or completely invented. The numbers and place names give a quite realistic picture, so a verdict of authenticity seems preferable.

Without discussing the details (the numbers show some variation, some groups are not numbered and the actual figures do not correspond to the totals given), the lists contain about 25,000 laypersons and about 5,000 priests and temple workers, plus about 7,500 serfs: a total of approximately 40,000. If we take the list to be correct, we have about twice the number deported by Nebuchadrezzar.

But a topographical analysis is more interesting. First of all, the returnees come from (i.e. their grandfathers lived in) Jerusalem (this is true for everyone involved in the cult) and in the towns and villages of the kingdom of Judah (the tribal territories of Judah and Benjamin). The figures from minor settlements (excluding Jerusalem) are quite small, another sign of authenticity: for example, 123 from Bethlehem, 62 from Ramah and Geba, 122 from Michmash, 223 from Bethel and Ai, 345 from Jericho, and so on. Apart from those small groups identified by towns of origin (sometimes indicated as 'sons of' or 'men of'), most groups are regularly defined by clan name or eponym (again 'sons of', followed this time by a personal name), such as Parosh (2172) or Senaah (3630): do these all come from Jerusalem? And how were such large clans formed? In one case (Bigvai: 2,056) a group leader is named – that is, the person who has registered as his clan all members of the caravan of returnees he led. There are also quite large groups whose geographical origin is given: 2,812 from Pahath-Moab (the province of Moab) and, twice, 1,254 from Elam: how did these non-genealogical groups mix with the others, yet be accepted as fully Israelite? A few (650 people) are said not to have been able to prove their membership of Israelite clans, but so they were registered, though in a marginal position. Most of the lay returnees are registered purely in apparently kin-based categories, yet in fact the groups are derived simply from the logistics of the returnees' recruitment.

Anyway, at the end of the list (Ezra 2.70 = Neh. 7.72) it is said that the priests, levites and a proportion of the people (probably the large, non-topographically identified groups) settled in Jerusalem, while the temple slaves and Israelites who came from specific towns returned to their place of origin. If this is true, most of the returnees went to Jerusalem and only a few hundred people occupied the villages and towns nearby, within an area of about 20-25 km between Bethel and Jericho to the north and Bethlehem to the south. Nobody from Hebron or Beer-sheba went back there: it was well known that their territory was now firmly occupied by the Edomites. From the Shephelah only a group from Lod arrived: it was well known that the western plains were in the possession of the coastal cities. The land of Judah from which returnees came corresponds to the territory of the kingdom of Zedekiah, and not to the wider kingdom of Hezekiah, Manasseh and Josiah. The 'topographical' groups (owning deeds of possession of their patrimony) numbered a few hundred: most of the others had obscure geographical origins, and were concentrated in Jerusalem.

The reconstruction of a Jewish 'national core' was only partly realized with the return of the exiles: the process mostly took place over a longer period of time, during which they expanded and consolidated in their homes. In the resettled territory (Benjamin and northern Judah), if there were just a few returnees, there should also have been few remainees. There were two possible strategies for dealing with these: involving and including them, or rejecting them. We will see traces of strong disagreement on this matter, but the surviving sources were mostly produced by the 'rejection' party, which prevailed. The legal debate about land possession should have made quite a major impact: the returnees had property rights, but the remainees actually occupied the land. On these concrete issues the later sources are quite vague (especially those of priestly redaction), preferring to elevate the rejection of the 'remainees' to an ideological level, justifying it by their assimilation by marriage and in religious practice, with non-Yahwistic idolaters.

But in assessing the triumph of the returnees and the marginalization of the remainees we should above all bear in mind the social status and cultural influence of each group. The deportees all belonged to the palace milieu (i.e. to the 'political' class), or had worked in the Jerusalem temple (priests and scribes), or were landowners. The remainees were members of village communities, poor peasants and serfs, left by the Babylonians to work the land. The returnees, during their exile, had built up a 'strong' ideology, based on the new covenant, on Yahweh's exclusiveness, on the 'remnant that shall return' (*šĕ'ār-yāšûb* is the name given by Isaiah to his son: Isa. 7.3; see 10.21). They had fanatical determination, leaders and a paramilitary structure; they had an educated class (the scribes who returned introduced the Aramaic script into Palestine, replacing the Phoenician one previously in use), economic resources and the support of the imperial court. The remainees were illiterate and ignorant, scattered, with no leaders, poor and without hope, without any strategy and without a god. The result of that conflict could be foreseen from the outset.

3. *The 'People of the Land'*

To define the remainee peasants, the expression 'people of the land' (*'am hā'āreṣ*), began to be used by the returnees. The term had a long tradition; in the monarchic era it had designated that part of the population of the kingdom (a large majority) which did not belong to the palace entourage, to the 'servants of the king'. In legal and economic terms, it comprised the free population, who possessed its own means of production, was organized in families and local clans, and was politically subject to the palace, which had begun to control it through its bureaucratic organization. The 'people of the land' played an active part in political life only when a particular crisis occurred, when the dynastic succession was in danger and no one could guarantee the legitimate exercise of power: this was the case during the crisis that attended the usurpation of Athaliah and the murder of Amaziah (§6.2), the death of Josiah on the battlefield and the murder of

Amon (§8.3). In such cases, it was the people of the land (evidently through its representatives, 'elders' and clan-leaders) who acted as guarantors, stipulating or renewing a contract (*bĕrît*) with the new king. But apart from these instances where political power lapsed, the people of the land usually remained passive and confident in whatever the king did.

This use of the expression 'people of the land' for the subjects as a whole is still attested in the Persian period in Byblos – where no deportation, exile or return had ever taken place! – with Yehawmilk who wishes: 'May the Lady of Byblos give him favour in the eyes of the gods and in the eyes of the people of the land' (*SSI*, III, 25.9-10). But in Hebrew, in the context of the exile, the word changed its meaning: since the deportees were mainly members of the palace and temple elite, while most of the 'free' population had been left in Palestine, the remainees began to be called 'people of the land'. The connotations of the term were even more important than the technical meaning: the relation between 'people' and 'land' inevitably raised the question of who was the legitimate occupier of the land, and on which authority or credentials, human or divine (the question of the covenant arose again, as did the identification of the true 'remnant', see §11.4). The peasantry was regarded as a sort of physical appendix to the land, without voice or individual rights.

Once back in Judea, the returnees used the expression 'people of the land' to define the people who lived there: Judeans who had neither been deported nor emigrated, and non-deported Israelites of the north. All of them were Yahwists and members, broadly speaking, of the 'Israelite' community which was to be reconstructed. They lacked, however, all the cultic and ideological ideas elaborated during the exile. Thus the term 'people' began to acquire a connotation of exclusion, opposed to its traditional meaning, which had always indicated belonging: in the pre-exilic era, the word '*am* '(our) people' was usually opposed to *gôyîm* 'the (foreign) nations'.

In later post-exilic texts (Ezra, Nehemiah, Chronicles), the word assumes an ethnic flavour, marked by the use of the plural 'peoples of the land' or also 'peoples of the lands', to indicate nations different from Israel: Samaritans, Edomites, Ammonites and all the others who lived in a land that should belong to Israelites. They did not observe the sabbath and the other distinctive principles of the Yahwistic religion, were against the rebuilding of the temple, and opposed the returnees' programme of national and religious restoration. With these 'peoples of the land', firmly extraneous, no intermarriage was possible. This priestly definition is followed by the Rabbinic usage, indicating those who do not recognize nor observe the divine law.

4. The Mythical Foundation of the Resettlement

The conflict of political strategies and material interests between the clusters of returnees and local communities generated some mythical 'foundation charters' relating to entitlement to the 'land' as a whole. Just as at a personal level it was important to be able to show titles to property, or at least family genealogies specifying single clans and villages, the whole enterprise of the returnees needed to be based on their ability to refer to authoritative traditions assigning the property of the land of Canaan to the tribes of Israel, and then to identify the communities of returnees as the legitimate heirs of those tribes, and not the communities of remainees. It is quite significant that a linguistic shift took place from the term *nāḥălāh* 'hereditary property', typical of Deuteronomistic texts, to the term *'ăḥuzzāh* '(landed) property', typical of Priestly texts. Such a change apparently marks the transition from a judicial claim to an act of taking possession.

Although the literature that we have – inevitably rewritten from the point of view of the victors – is not adequate to reconstruct the different ideological positions that existed, it is clear that such a conflict took place, because the interests of the parties were too distant, and the strategies available to each party were also different. Apart from the obvious conflict between returnees and remainees, there were also differences within the two groups. Among the returnees, we can distinguish a more radical position, wanting the community of 'uncontaminated' returnees to be absolutely closed against the remainees who were irretrievably contaminated by the alien milieu, and a compromising one, positively considering the assimilation of groups that had the minimum ethnic and religious requirements. The 'softer' line probably prevailed with the first groups of returnees, so long as the monarchical option remained valid (and this shows some traces in texts, especially Deuteronomistic ones, which sharply distinguish between the massacre of 'alien' Canaanites and the assimilation of the 'people of the land'). But later, with the arrival of Nehemiah and Ezra and the prevalence of priestly ideology, the harder attitude prevailed. Among the locals different strategies could also have existed, with the non-Israelites probably supporting a policy of violent rejection (including military opposition), and the 'people of the land' who probably preferred assimilation (as we will see again below, §17.3 and 18.5).

The position that eventually prevailed, and so is largely represented in later texts, is that of violent opposition. The 'foundation myth' more suitable to this position is the conquest of the land promised to the returnees

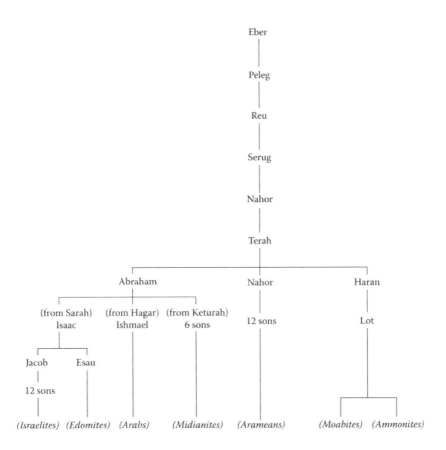

Table 9. *The patriarchal genealogies and the nations related by descent*

from Egyptian captivity, under the leadership of Joshua. We will examine this in the following chapter. But another relevant and authoritative 'foundation myth' was that of the 'patriarchs', the eponymous ancestors of the twelve tribes and their fathers, Abraham, Isaac and Jacob.

This second myth was too weak to establish the right to the conquest by the returnees, for several reasons. First of all, it referred to a very remote period, its legendary character was rather obvious, and it was therefore more suitable for a mythical than a legal claim. Second, it alluded to an infiltration, of a semi-nomadic type, by small groups of shepherds: this model did not exclude – indeed it required – the presence of other inhabitants in the same land. Finally, it made reference to a period of time which preceded the constitution of the people of Israel (and, even more, of a state of Israel) and the possession of specific territories by individual tribes.

The patriarchal 'foundation myth' was, on the contrary, perfectly suited to support position in favour of co-existence. Abraham had been 'a stranger and a sojourner' in the land of Canaan (Gen. 23.4 *gēr wĕtōšāb*) and was therefore sympathetic to the plight of strangers and sojourners. He had to purchase the piece of land where he wanted to put the family tomb, and he did so according to an oral contract reminiscent of the contracts of the Neo-Babylonian age (Genesis 23), paying, as it happens, an inflated price so as to stress his superior status in dealing with a very kind, but greedy seller. Isaac also had to buy a piece of land near Shechem to plant his tents (Gen. 33.18-20). The ownership of wells in the western Negev was disputed and later negotiated with the king of Gerar (Gen. 26.15-33). Each piece of land had to be bought individually. Only pastures and cattle belonged indisputably to the patriarchs, but in case of famine they had to come to agreements with rulers of the lands where they sought refuge, in the Shephelah or even as far as Egypt. The clear impression is conveyed of a society where coexistence and collaboration between groups is necessary.

The 'political landscape' emerging from the patriarchal narratives is, of course, quite unreal and rarefied: apart from Abimelech king of Gerar, who occurs more than once, and has a specific narratological function in the wife-sister stories, the political authorities of the territory are virtually absent or represented by non-existent characters (such as Shechem of Shechem) or at least suspect (as Melchizedek of Jerusalem; see below). The land appears rather 'empty', for two reasons. First, the authors were unable to describe, concretely and realistically, the political landscape of a period we would define as the Middle Bronze Age (when Palestinian urbanization reached its peak). But most of all, they were influenced by the situation confronting them in their own day: a demographically reduced territory experiencing a partial regression to a nomadic lifestyle and politically dependent on a ruler (the distant emperor) unable to play any active role in local events.

The influence of the returnees' point of view is clearly present, especially in the basic concept of promise (*šĕbû'āh*). It is noticeable that the divine promise concerns above all the multiplication of future descendants, so making explicit a concern to produce enough population to successfully occupy a land promised by God (or by the Persian emperor) but already settled by others:

> Reside (*gûr*) in this land as an alien, and I will be with you, and will bless you; for to you and to your descendants I will give all these lands, and I will fulfill the oath (*šĕbû'āh*) that I swore to your father Abraham. I will make your offspring as numerous as the stars of heaven, and will give to your

offspring all these lands; and all the nations of the earth shall gain blessing for themselves through your offspring, because Abraham obeyed my voice and kept my charge, my commandments, my statutes, and my laws (Gen. 26.3-5; but see also 12.2; 15.5; 17.6; 18.17-19; 22.16-18; etc.).

The archetypical migration of Abraham, from Ur of the Chaldees to Harran and then to Palestine, reflects the events of the return and the point of view of the returnees (or at least of their recruiters). Abraham embodied a sort of advertisement for those who planned to return from the land of the Chaldeans to Palestine, showing how to cope successfully with all the problems of living alongside different peoples and creating an economic and political niche for themselves.

But the impression remains that these stories also conserve some traces of the attitude of the remainees, though they have been assembled and reinterpreted in a document designed to suit the positions of the returnees. Thus, against the theory of a total annihilation of the 'others' comes the objection that it is not fair to kill people who have never done (us) any harm. The innocent Abimelech of Gerar explicitly asks: 'Will you slay also a righteous nation?' (Gen. 20.4). The objection is squashed with the answer that there are no innocent amongst the aliens (see the episode of Sodom), but at least a trace remains of the debate. In the story of Hagar, the Egyptian wife of Abraham (Gen. 16.3), no blame attaches to the patriarch's behaviour. When he travels together with Lot (Gen. 12.4), he makes several interventions (in the expedition against the kings of the East, Genesis 14, and then on the destruction of Sodom, Gen. 18.19) to rescue his nephew, the ancestor of those who will become fierce enemies of Israel. More generally, we may think of the 'family' relations described between the ancestors of Judeans and Arameans, Arabs and Edomites, Ammonites and Moabites. And most of all, to the future role of Abraham's descendants, as agents of a divine blessing extended to all peoples of the earth.

5. *The Setting of the Patriarchal Narratives*

The patriarchal world, which lies outside historical time, according to the genre of stories that portray it, is nevertheless composed in a continuous narrative, framed by a genealogical sequence and, most of all, intended as an essential block in a sequence of events (within the scheme of promise and fulfilment) that functions within the ideological foundation of Israel.

Figure 50. *The geography of the patriarchal sagas*

But to when can we date this continuous narrative, this organic interpretation of traditional stories? Pre-exilic prophets (and texts) do not know Abraham, and in general use the word 'fathers' to refer to the generation of the Exodus. They, do, however, know Jacob well (and, obviously, 'the house of Jacob') as referring to the northern kingdom and to the traditions collected there (see especially Hos. 12.2-6, 12-14). Amos also knows Isaac

(7.9, 16) and Joseph (5.6, 15; 6.6), always with reference to the northern kingdom. Jeremiah knows Rachel (the mother of Ephraim and Manasseh), who weeps and does not wish to be comforted.

Ezekiel too (20.5), begins his historical recognition of Israel's infidelities with the divine promise to lead the 'house of Jacob' out of the land of Egypt, and ignores (or at least does not consider) the previous promises of the patriarchal age. But exactly in Ezekiel's time the prophetic allusions to the patriarchs, including Abraham, start to multiply. From a diaspora perspective, Jeremiah (30.10; 46.27-28) sees Jacob living in peace, having come back from 'distant lands' that Yahweh gave to him; analogously, Second Isaiah (41.8, 44.21) has him return from 'the ends of the earth'. Micah (7.20) and Deutero-Isaiah again (29.22, 41.8) both know the pair Abraham and Jacob, but Jeremiah (33.26) also knows the complete sequence Abraham–Isaac–Jacob. A late passage in Isaiah, when the return has already taken place, seems to allude to debates between returnees and remainees, when it states (Isa. 63.16) 'though Abraham does not know us and Israel does not acknowledge us'.

While more and more allusions to the patriarchs appear in the exilic prophetic texts, the Deuteronomic historiography composes a continuous narration of their deeds, centred on the theme of the covenant. This elaboration reaches its most complete form with the Priestly redactor of the Pentateuch, the author of the patriarchal sagas in the form we read them today (apart from occasional later additions). Then, in the late post-exilic age, the fortunes of the patriarchs decline, and they are never mentioned in Ezra-Nehemiah or Chronicles: a 'hard' line against the remainees and aliens has prevailed. The systematization of the patriarchal sagas is therefore rather late, but it derives most of its information from traditions evidently originating in Palestine.

Abraham is originally (as we have said in §1.9) the eponym of the tribe of Banu-Raham attested in central Palestine in the twelfth century; this tribe later disappeared, but its name survived in tribal genealogies. Its range of operation corresponds to the itineraries of pastoral trans-humance: winter pastures in the Negev (between Hebron and Beer-sheba), summer grazing in the central highlands (Shechem and Bethel), with escape routes, in case of famine, to Egypt or to the Philistine plain (Gerar). The setting of Isaac is similar, from the encampment in the Negev (at Lahai-roi) to refuge in Gerar and eventually in Egypt. Jacob has his southern base camp in Beer-sheba, and in the north his points of reference are Bethel and Shechem, as well as Succoth and Penuel beyond the Jordan river. The places are marked by significant symbols of the pastoral cult (§1.9): the oak of

Mamre with its annexed 'patriarchal' tomb in Hebron (Gen. 12.18; 18.1; 23.19; etc.), the oak of Moreh with its annexed altar in Shechem (Gen. 12.6), the oak with an annexed 'patriarchal' tomb in Bethel, a tomb with a stela in Bethlehem and a 'tree of the oath' in Beer-sheba; one or more altars and a commemorative stela in Bethel, a border stela in Mizpah of Gilead. These are all extra-urban cult places.

The stories show a consistent aetiological relationship with the peculiarities of the landscape, which are explained through them. This is particularly true for the hyperarid and saline plain of Sodom and Gomorrah and particularly for the salt pillars (Gen. 19.26) and bitumen wells near the Dead Sea (Gen. 14.10), but also for the seven wells of Beer-sheba (Gen. 21.30-31) – and for all the topographic peculiarities of the cult places just mentioned. This connection also holds for popular etymologies of place names, from Beer-sheba to Penuel (Gen. 32.31), Succoth (Gen. 33.17) and many others. The stories are therefore of definitely Palestinian origin and are rather traditional, we could say 'timeless', with no specific relation to the migration of exiles, unlike Abraham's itinerary from Ur of the Chaldees through Harran and Shechem, which is evidently related to it (and even serves as its foundation).

The extra-Palestinian origin of the patriarchs, apart from anticipating the return of exiles, is above all the basis for the issue of marriage between cross-cousins, with the husband living in Palestine and the wife in Upper Mesopotamia (Harran and Paddan-Aram). Isaac marries his cousin Rebecca, Jacob his two cousins Leah and Rachel. The wives' family (the branch of Nahor and Laban) remained in Upper Mesopotamia, while the husbands' family (the Abrahamic branch) migrated to Palestine, but between the two parts of the family survives the notion of a common origin and even a privileged, if not exclusive, relationship. If we read this in the light of the post-exilic situation and of the relation between returnees and remainees, the story conveys a fairly clear message. Implied in the apparently normative exclusivist attitude ('I will not give my son a Canaanite wife'), there is in fact a strong invitation to encourage connexions between returnees and remainees, since the latter are Yahwists and share a common origin. On the contrary, the marriage of Esau with 'Hittite' and Arab wives is negatively evaluated, if not openly condemned.

6. *Interethnic Relations*

In this process of traditional stories reinterpreted by post-exilic readings, we find the proper context for narratives aiming to establish specific relations with neighbouring peoples. Note that in this case these are not imaginary peoples, like those populating the 'empty land' given to the twelve tribes, as in the historiography of the conquest (§14.2). They are rather those peoples who really contested the possession of Palestine in the fifth–fourth century with the returnees.

With the Edomites there is a close fraternal bond (Abraham and Lot are closely-related eponyms, as are Jacob and Esau), but also a delimitation, more precise than anywhere else, of the respective territories. Edomites have the Arabah and what is to the east of it, Israelites have Cisjordan (Genesis 13; 33), and also have a privileged position, only qualified by the prospect of a considerable expansion of the Edomites in the future (Gen. 27.39-40). But the return of Jacob from Mesopotamia and his meeting with Esau take place in a mood of profound uneasiness and fear of the former towards the latter. Jacob, having come back from a distant country, has to find a place in a land already occupied by the other, who has always been there. These precise specifications should clearly be understood in the light of Edomites infiltration west of the Arabah, which occurred during the exilic period and was consolidated later; and thus of the concern of the returnees over the kind of reception they would meet. The mixture of strong rivalry and close ties will be reinforced in subsequent periods by the adoption of Yahwism by the Edomites and a very unusual sharing of political destiny (even of rulers). It is also indicative of their hostility that the latest of the 'oracles against the nations', at a time when this literary genre had become obsolete because of the re-absorption into the Empire of the various ethnic groups, is dedicated exclusively to the Edomites (see in particular the brief and late book of Obadiah).

With the Arameans (represented by Laban) there are similar relations of common origin and affinity. The border marked in Gilead, between Mizpah and Mahanaim (Gen. 32.45–33.3) is apparently not related to the period of bloody warfare between Israel and Damascus; it is instead placed in a land 'empty' of local kingdoms. The Arameans of the patriarchal stories are not the fierce kingdom of Damascus, but distant tribes, in Upper Mesopotamia, and relations with them are peaceful.

Relations with the Arabs are based on the story of Ishmael, son – first-born, even – of Abraham (but from the slave-girl Hagar), who shows a clear affinity in several of his defining characteristics: Ishmael is the first to be circumcised (after Abraham) and his descendents are also circumcised – circumcision is, according to the author of the story (Gen. 17.11-14, 26), the only sign that Yahweh requires from his faithful. But at the same time Ishmael's descendants must be placed 'outside', in the desert: they can be considered brothers, but only if they remain elsewhere, where they will become numerous (by token of a 'promise', Gen. 21.18, very similar to that made to the Israelites) and occupy other lands. Here can be detected a clear echo of the Arab expansion in the sixth–fifth centuries, of their primary location in the desert, and an interest in enjoying positive relations with them.

The case of the Moabites and Ammonite is different: their myth of origin (Gen. 19.30-38) relates an incestuous relationship (Lot's daughters with their own father) which immediately disqualifies them, places them outside the cultic community and excludes them from any prospect of 'national' assimilation, unlike the Edomites. The fact is that Ammon and Moab had always contended for Transjordan in a struggle between similar societies: alternative because non-complementary. But, more specifically, the issue arose from the role played by the Ammonites against the returnees and their project of rebuilding the temple and the walls of Jerusalem.

The other border that needs to be defined is the western one, with the towns and cities of the Philistine coastal plains, represented in this case by Gerar. Unlike the demarcation with Edom, this border is left 'open' and marked by a sort of complementariness, in both landscape and economic issues. The key points here are the dispute between Isaac and Abimelech over the use of the wells in the western Negev (Gen. 26.15-22, see 21.25-30) and the stories of the relations between the patriarchs and the king of Gerar, which follow the novelistic scheme of the wife-sister – first applied to Abraham and Sarah (Genesis 20) and then to Isaac and Rebecca (26.1-11). Yet the outcome is an alliance between the patriarchal family and the Philistine city-state, which allows the Israelite element to use the pastures of the Shephelah, protected against attack.

7. Jerusalem and Shechem

In the patriarchal stories, Jerusalem appears only occasionally, and in a rather ambiguous way . The story of Abraham's victory against the five kings of the East (Genesis 14: a strange story, hardly attributable to local folklore) ends with his blessing by Melchizedek 'king of Salem' and 'priest of El Elyon', who receives from him a tithe from the booty:

> Blessed be Abram by El Elyon, maker of heaven and earth; and blessed be El Elyon, who has delivered your enemies into your hand! (Gen. 14.19-20).

Here we see an obvious priestly intervention, presenting this event as referring to the Jerusalem temple, to its Zadokite priests, to the temple tithes in effect in the post-exilic age. Note that if we expunge the suspect words

'Melchizedek king of Salem' not only would the narrative make perfect sense, but the author of the blessing would now be the king of Sodom (and this, given the end of the story, would be rather embarrassing!).

As for the remainder of Abraham's deeds (the Melchizedek episode remains narratologically quite isolated), just like the stories of Isaac and Jacob, not only do they show no interest in a central role for the Jerusalem temple, but they even initiate a host of cultic sites all over the land.

More attention is paid to Shechem, where the episode of the rape of Dinah occurs. A vendetta follows, despite the payment of recompense, an oath of fraternity, and acceptance of circumcision by the Shechemites (Genesis 34). At a first reading, the episode reflects a firm rejection of marriage with uncircumcised persons. But the text stresses so much the treachery and total slaughter that it seems to be a polemical response to those in favour of blood-revenge (not accidentally: *Ant.* 1.338-340 tells the same story, expunging completely the issue of circumcision). The policy of compromise is represented by Jacob himself (thus by the tribal leader), while the 'strict' line is represented by Simeon (the eponym of a tribe that had disappeared a long time before) and by Levi, that is, by the dominant priestly class of the post-exilic age.

It is clear that these stories about Jerusalem and Shechem have no connection with the two 'historical' Canaanite highland kingdoms, which according to the Deuteronomistic historiography emerge only after the institution of the monarchy (Shechem with Abimelech, Jerusalem with David), but they represent rather the post-exilic Jerusalem (and its temple) and Samaria, as political centres of the returnees. In the story of Dinah we encounter the problem of mixed marriages between members of the returnees and members of Palestinian communities. Under the (violated) pact between Isaac and Shechem, we read the relationship between Judeans and Samarians. The author suggests that circumcision (which implies the formal assumption of the cult of Yahweh) is a sufficient condition to make the connexion possible and that an overly strict position is morally unacceptable and not appropriate. In the words of Jacob to his sons:

> You have brought trouble on me by making me odious to the inhabitants of the land, the Canaanites and the Perizzites; my numbers are few, and if they gather themselves against me and attack me, I shall be destroyed, both I and my household (Gen. 34.30).

Once again, the point of view of the remainees, a policy of collaboration, the legitimacy of a plurality of cult places scattered across the land, and the possibility of mixed marriages, all seem to be the central message of the patriarchal stories.

8. The Joseph Story

The Joseph story (Genesis 37–48) is completely different in structure and setting. It is not a mosaic of different episodes, but a short novella with a single plot. Compared with the other patriarchal stories, it is less related to Palestinian topography – apart from the post-biblical tradition of the transfer and burial of the bones of Joseph from Egypt to Shechem. Joseph is also less connected with the tribal milieu: his ancestry of Ephraim and Manasseh is secondary and historically motivated (§5.1). The story of the sale of Joseph (by his jealous brothers) as a slave to a caravan of Ishmaelite or Midianite traders, and his further sale by them in Egypt, his ascent from slavery to counsellor and vizier of the Pharaoh, evidently belongs to the novelistic genre of entertainment, and was inserted at this point in the patriarchal sequence because it provided a suitable pretext for the story of the exodus/return from Egypt to Palestine of Israel's ancestors, who had in the meantime become a multitude, forming a real nation.

Many parallels to the sale of Palestinian slaves in Egypt can be found in the Late Bronze Age, when the biblical chronology places Joseph. For example, in a text from Ugarit (*Ug.*, V, 42) we read of a person 'who was sold to the Egyptians by his own companion, who abandoned him and took his goods'. Another text from Ugarit (*PRU*, V, 116) records that guarantors of a debt, if unable to pay the due sum, 'will be sold (as slaves) in Egypt'. But these are not very significant parallels, since they refer to a recurrent practice: Egypt was no doubt the main slave 'market' of the time and throughout the course of ancient history many Asiatic slaves were brought there.

But the main moral values of the Joseph story find their closest parallels in the time of the Persian empire. We may recall the story of Ahiqar, set in the Assyrian court, but redacted later (the 'Tale' of that name is dated to the fifth century), which recounts the deeds of a sage who, from humble origins, succeeds in becoming the favourite counsellor and vizier of Esarhaddon. Or the story of Democedes (*Herod.* 3.129-137), the Greek doctor brought as a slave to the court of Darius who became a table-companion of the king. Or, again, the stories of Daniel set in the court of the Babylonian kings, but whose redaction is much later: just like Joseph, through the interpretation of mysterious dreams, Daniel avoids his humble fate and becomes chief royal counsellor.

Today all scholars agree on a post-exilic date for the Joseph story and many of them underline its 'wisdom' character, based on the fact the Joseph's wisdom allows him to overcome difficulties and attain power:

wisdom lies in the interpretation of dreams, but also in chastely resisting the offers of Potiphar's wife and then, most of all, in planning economic measures to save the country from famine (the 'seven lean cattle': Gen. 41.18-21). On this last point a comparison may be useful with another famous sage of the sixth century, one of the 'seven sages' of Archaic Greece: Thales, who according to a tradition (still unknown to Herodotus) became rich because he had foreseen, through his astronomical and meteorological knowledge, a good olive crop. So, he rented all the oil-presses of the region, in order to hire them out later at a higher price, when demand would increase. The abilities of the two wise men are similar, but they act according to different models: Thales acts for personal interest and follows the rules of a market economy, while Joseph acts in the interest of the state and uses the methods of a redistributive economy.

The result of Joseph's administrative measures is the concentration of all land in the hands of Pharaoh, except for priestly lands, as the redactor (certainly coming from a priestly milieu) carefully remarks, safeguarding the economic autonomy of the temple from imperial administration. In this sense the story of Joseph (or rather a section of it) is an aetiological story, explicitly characterized as such by the sentence: 'and it is like this to this day' (Gen. 47.26), answering the question: why in Egypt do all the lands belong nominally to the Pharaoh while the landowners are in fact only lessees, who have to pay a very high rent? The answer is given from an 'Asiatic' point of view, on the assumption that cession of the rights of property by private citizens (which the 'utopian' law of the jubilee year aimed to avoid) happened usually because of an extreme economic crisis.

The Joseph story implies the presence of numerous groups of Palestinian immigrants in Egypt, living in a society whose economic institutions and practices were different. Therefore, it cannot have been imagined or written before the fifth century.

Chapter 14

RETURNEES AND ALIENS:
THE INVENTION OF THE CONQUEST

1. *The Phases of the Return*

The 'oaths' or 'promises' of Yahweh to Abraham and then Moses correspond, at the mythical level, to the legal function of the edicts of the Persian emperors: they provide legitimation for the return and bestow entitlement of property to the land. But at the practical level, the actual return of exiles and their takeover of Palestine required another model. The patriarchal traditions could be used by the returnees as a prefiguration of their presence in the country; but the remainees could equally appeal to them as a model of coexistence between complementary groups. These stories offered the returnees a 'weak' yet realistic model of return: in small groups, without direct conflict, by agreement with the residents and surrounding peoples, sharing the land and its resources. The traditions of the conquest offer a 'strong' model, preferred by the supporters of violent confrontation and of the exclusion of 'extraneous' people. These were logically (or at least narratively) connected to the 'exit from Egypt' that marked the liberation of the people from slavery in a foreign land.

But did an actual return take place along these 'strong' lines? Though there are doubts about the historical reliability of Ezra and Nehemiah (written a couple of centuries after the events they describe and betraying a strong ideological influence), it is clear that the return did not happen all at once and did not involve any particularly violent military conflict.

To begin with, the origin of the groups of returnees ought to correspond to the various locations of the exiles and immigrants already mentioned (that is, not only Babylon, but also Egypt and ex-Assyrian lands). Second, the return did not involve 'all' the people of Israel, but only some groups with specific and strong ideological motives to return; most Judeans remained scattered (and more or less well integrated) in the lands of the diaspora. A realistic portrait would show groups of volunteers organizing their own return, financially supported by diaspora communities, most of whom chose to stay where they were though they sympathized with the returnees' project. At the beginning of Ezra we find a significant description inserted into the context of Cyrus' edict – but certainly added later:

> and let all survivors, in whatever place they reside, be assisted by the people of their place with silver and gold, with goods and with animals, besides freewill offerings for the house of God in Jerusalem (Ezra 1.4).

Note that the text mentions returnees who come back after the temple has already been rebuilt, and describes their financial support as a form of cultic offering. Moreover, the text apparently lays this burden (with ambiguous wording) on the population in general, and not only Judeans. These changes to the edict are ideologically important, and have been made in order to preserve the global character of the return.

But, most important of all, the return did not take place in a single move, but in different phases over the course of a century at least. Some groups may have come back already in the Babylonian age, after the amnesty of Awil-Marduk. Others returned after 538, after the advent of Cyrus, thanks to the tolerant policy that the Achaemenid monarchy immediately adopted. Amongst these was probably a group led by Sheshbazzar, a member of the Judean royal family and uncle of Zerubbabel, with whom he becomes confused in later tradition (with the tendency to compress all the returnees into a single movement). The most coherent and determined group probably went back in 521, in the second year of Darius, because these initiated the energetic rebuilding of the Second Temple (the first Passover was celebrated there in 515; Ezra 6.19). This group was under a mixed leadership of high rank: Zerubbabel, remaining heir of 'David's house', representing the monarchy, and Joshua, high priest of the Zadokite line, representing the priesthood.

Other groups arrived in the time of Artaxerxes (his 20th year = 446), according to the accounts of Ezra's and Nehemiah's activities. And other groups arrived even later, drawn by the success in the rebuilding of the temple, the fortification of Jerusalem and the autonomy granted to the province of Judah (Yehud) by the Persian administration.

This portrait of partial return in small groups over a long period of time shows that the 'strong' model of a single, violent conquest of Canaan under the leadership of Joshua must have been applied at a time when the return was already underway. It was probably the manifesto of a group of particularly determined returnees, perhaps the group leaded by Zerubbabel – in which case it belongs to a quite late strand of Deuteronomist historiography. But above all, it is not intended as a 'foundation model', reflecting the return that really had occurred, but rather as a blueprint of the character that the return should have. The story narrated in Joshua is not only unreliable in its reconstruction of a mythical 'conquest' in the twelfth century, but also unrealistic for reconstructing the return in the sixth–fifth centuries. It is a utopian manifesto, intended to support a project of return that never took place in such terms.

2. *Palestine in the Achaemenid Age*

Before presenting the motives and ideological justifications for the conquest, we must paint a general picture of the settlements in Palestine in the Achaemenid age, and in particular the fifth century, which is the crucial period. When the Achaemenid Empire began, Palestine had been devastated and depopulated by the destruction and deportations of the Assyrians and later the Babylonians (§9.5). This population decline, the most serious since the urbanization of the country in the mid- third millennium, was rectified by the Persian kings in two ways. They made strenuous efforts to stimulate the coastal area, but the inland areas of the country were apparently of less interest to the imperial administration, which seems to have had no intention to invest great resources there: it therefore encouraged, with material support, initiatives aimed at local recovery, such as those organized by Judeans.

As a consequence of this relatively neglectful attitude, the archaeological picture reveals only a modest economic recovery. In Jerusalem, the 'city of David' was re-occupied, but the Mishneh quarter built by Hezekiah remained abandoned. Quite small settlements are attested in Samaria (VI), Shechem (V), Ramat Rahel (IV B), with some fortresses/residences such as Tell el-Hesi and Lachish (I). We find a certain distribution of amphorae with the typical *yhd* stamp (the name of the Persian province of Judah, see §15.1). There is also a recovery of settlements in the central Jordan valley (Deir 'Alla V-II; Tell es-Sa'idiya II) and on the edges of the Judean desert (Jericho, Tel Goren IV). A quite modest scene, on the whole. The most recent archaeological estimates of the population of Judah are very low (especially if compared with the Biblical data of 40,000 returnees): about 12,000 people between 550–450, and 17,000 between 450–330. Samaria also appears quite depressed, with a population which may be calculated as 42,000 (in the eighth century there were about 51,000).

The coastal area shows a radically transformed picture: everywhere strong growth is attested (in both sites of continuous occupation and new settlements), thanks to imperial initiatives: fortresses, administrative centres, cities rebuilt on an orthogonal plan (Dor, Tel Magadim), commercial stores and the first artificial harbours in the Levant (Acco, Dor, Athlit, Apollonia, not to mention the major Phoenician towns in the north, like Arwad and Tyre). It is important to note the strong Phoenician participation in this development, evidenced by their typical building technique (large 'pillars' alternating with small stone filling), by the diffusion of Phoenician pottery (especially Phoenician trade amphorae) in the far south, by the presence of Phoenician ostraca, and by objects (both decorative and cultic) in the Egyptian-Phoenician style. There is also an abundance of imported Greek pottery, which shows overseas commercial links and perhaps the presence of Greek mercenaries.

The development of Phoenicia was concentrated in the north, on the four autonomous kingdoms of Arwad, Byblos, Sidon and Tyre, where archaeology reveals really imposing building activity: temples (for example the temple of Eshmun in Sidon), military structures (walls and fortresses in Byblos and Arwad) and harbours (Tyre and Arwad). From written sources we know of the interest of the Achaemenid emperors in the development of Phoenician fleets and cities (Herod. 3.19; 7.89, 96, 100). However, this development also involved Palestine, because we know that Sidon obtained from the Persian king possession of Dor and Jaffa (*SSS*, III, 29) and Tyre the possession of Acco and Ashkelon (cf. the *Periplous* of Skylax). Tyre exercised a strong influence over Galilee, which became more and more independent of Samaria, following a process already begun at the time of the Assyrian conquest. The diffusion of Phoenician or Egyptian-style objects along the whole Palestinian coast is a clear indication of this process.

Proceeding from north to south, the archaeological picture of strong resurgence is documented in Nahariya (III-II), Acco, Tell Keisan, Tell Abu Hawam (II), Shiqmona (on Mt Carmel), Tell Megadim, 'Atlit (II), Dor, Tel Mevorakh, Tel Mikhmoret, Apollonia-Arsuf, Makmish, Tel Michal, Tell Qasile (VI), Jaffa, Ashdod (V), Ashkelon and Tell Ruqeish. From its coastal settlements, the Phoenician-Persian presence penetrated inland, in two zones especially: the extreme north and extreme south, avoiding the central highlands, which were less populated and so less commercially attractive. In the north, Galilee became the rural hinterland for the Phoenician cities from Tyre to Acco, whose influence can be seen in the local cults (Mizpeh Yammim, see §17.4); the same is true for that part of the Jezreel plain nearest to the plain of Acco, with the settlements of Jokneam, Tel Qashish and Tel Qiri. To the extreme south, Phoenician-Persian presence is attested at first in the area of Tell Jemme, Tel Sera' and Tel Haror, and then down to the Beer-sheba valley (Tel 'Ira, Beer-sheba, Arad), with fortresses and post-stations for the control of the east-west caravan-routes. We know that Gaza in particular operated as the Mediterranean terminal of the South-Arabian caravan routes and the city flourished in proportion with that traffic, which in the Persian age increased considerably.

This division of the country between a densely populated coastal area, with its dynamic growth, well integrated in the commercial and political activity of the period, and an inland zone that shows only very slow and arduous signs of recovery – a division rather similar to that at the end of the Late Bronze Age – is the true historical context of Judean resettlement in Jerusalem and in the central highlands.

3. The 'Intruders'

The groups of Judean returnees to Palestine, prompted by Achemenid imperial edicts, found a region that only partially corresponded to their expected vista of an empty and available land: in fact it was inhabited by more or less coherent groups of various origin. These were farmers who had remained in their lands all the while, escaping deportation; deportees from different places, living there since the Assyrian age; neighbouring peoples who had taken advantage of the partial vacuum to expand their territory (the coastal towns) or to move in (the Edomites); and finally, mixed groups, resulting from various processes of cohabitation or integration.

The ideological rejection of the right of these other groups to occupy Palestine (connected to the theory of the promise) could not, however, negate their existence. The settlement of returnees was therefore justified by the story of an ancient conquest, set at the time of transition from the Late Bronze Age to the Iron Age, when the tribes became sedentary and the ancient inhabitants were exterminated. Lists began to be written (largely standardized, but with some variants), which included 'Canaanites and Hittites, Amorites and Perizzites, Hivites and Jebusites' and others. The coexistence of so many different peoples in a restricted space is striking: it is a situation inconceivable before the ethnic melting pot created by the cross-deportation measures of the Assyrians. But most of all it is absolutely clear that these lists do not mention the *real* historical inhabitants of the Iron Age: Phoenicians and Philistines, Edomites, Moabites and Ammonites, Arameans and Arabs. Instead, most of the names in the lists are fictional, corresponding to peoples that never existed.

'Canaanites' is the only term that is not anachronistic when appplied to the end of the Bronze Age. In the fourteenth–thirteenth centuries Canaan (*Kinaḥnu*) was the name of Palestine, and also the name of the Egyptian province whose capital was in Gaza and which roughly corresponded to Palestine. From the geographical name of Canaan, which we find already in the fourteenth–thirteenth century sources, the name 'Canaanites' for 'inhabitants of the land of Canaan' was derived. The term did not imply any ethno-linguistic or political unity, which in fact did not exist. In the fifth–fourth centuries the term still existed: it was usually employed to mean Phoenicians, but could describe the population of Palestine in general. Its use particularly in the narrative of the conquest corresponds to this generic meaning, though we cannot exclude the existence of some memory that the expansion of the tribes had taken place in competition with an entity which could be defined as 'Canaan' or 'Canaanites'.

The word 'Hittites' has a rather different history and it is completely anachronistic. We know that the Hittites were a people of Central Anatolia who in the sixteenth–thirteenth centuries had a powerful and aggressive kingdom, occupying for a time even part of Syria. In the past, some scholars have supposed that some Hittites really had settled in Palestine: but this theory has no basis, and contrasts sharply with what we know for certain about the limits of Hittite expansion. The use of the term 'Hittites' in the Old Testament has a different origin. Since the thirteenth century the Assyrians had been confronting the Hittite empire on the banks of the Upper Euphrates, and therefore gave the name 'Hittite (Hatti)-land' to the region west of the river. In the ninth–eighth centuries, they still had to face, across the same river, the kingdoms that we call 'Neo-Hittite' (Carchemish, Kummukh, Melid, etc.) and continued to call the region beyond the Euphrates (i.e. Syria) *Hatti*. In the eighth–seventh centuries the term was used extensively, without any ethno-linguistic connotation, to indicate all of Syria and Palestine. The Babylonians inherited this use of *Hatti* for Syria-Palestine and it continued until the Persian age, when it was replaced by the term Eber-Nari 'Trans-River', indicating the lands west of the Euphrates (though *Hatti* survives in literary texts until the Hellenistic age). Thus, the biblical authors, in the sixth-century Babylonian milieu, found the term *Hatti* referring to Palestine and (just as they derived the name 'Canaanites' from the geographical term Canaan) so deduced the existence of a people called 'Hittites'.

The case of 'Amorites' is rather similar. In the remote past (2300–1800), these had been a people, or rather a group of pastoral tribes of Syria. There was still a kingdom of Amurru in Syria in the fourteenth century. But in later times, we find only the Babylonian use (adopted by the Assyrians) of the word *Amurru* to indicate the West, one of the four quarters of the world: consequently, Syria-Palestine is called *Amurru* in historical texts and especially in the archaizing and cosmological language of omens. Already in the court of Nineveh there were difficulties in establishing a correspondence between *Amurru* and a specific historical reality, but the equation Amurru = Hatti was the first and most obvious option:

> This eclipse which occurred in the month Tebet, afflicted the West-land; the king of the West-land will die and his country decrease or, according to another tradition, perish.

> Perhaps the scholars can tell something about the (concept) 'Westland' to the king, my lord. Westland means the Hittite country (Syria) and the nomad land or, according to another tradition, Chaldea. Someone of the kings of Hatti, Chaldea or Arabia will carry this sign' (*SAA*, X, 351).

The biblical nation of 'Amorites' is therefore a construction similar to 'Hittites', which Biblical authors probably came to know from Babylonia in the sixth century.

'Perizzites' are a different case. The word in fact simply means 'inhabitants of villages', that is, farmers, not living in towns. For the elites of the towns, and for nomadic peoples too, farmers were almost part of the landscape, a fixed and unchanging element of remote antiquity. They had to be there well before 'our' arrival.

The *Rephaim* are a different case again: they are the deceased, the spirits of dead, in the religious conceptions of the Canaanites. Before being dead they must have been alive – or so the Judeans, who were extraneous to those ideas, probably thought. They should thus have been a people, one that exists no more, but lived in Palestine before our arrival. They are localized especially in Bashan, a land containing many megalithic funerary monuments. It was probably from a reflection of the sometimes imposing size of megalithic dolmens (from the prehistoric age) and of some 'cyclopean' walls (among Bronze Age ruins) that the existence of a population of Anakim, legendary 'giants' (Deut. 9.1-2; Josh. 11.21-22) was inferred. In Rabbath Ammon the legendary 'iron bed' (perhaps a basalt slab covering over a dolmen?) of king Og of Bashan could be seen: it was 9 cubits long and 4 cubits wide (Deut. 3.11).

Of other names – Jebusites, Hivites, Girgashites – we know nothing and may presume that they originated from placenames or strictly local traditions. In their totality, those lists of presumed pre-Israelite peoples of Palestine are built up through completely artificial speculation, with no connection whatsoever (apart from the term 'Canaan') with the historical reality of the time of the archetypical conquest (thirteenth century) or of the resettlement of returnees (fifth century).

Since the point of these names was to prove that such peoples had been completely annihilated, the safest choice was to select fictional names. In some cases the device is explicitly admitted: in Transjordan the elimination of the imaginary Rephaim and Amorites is celebrated (Num. 21.21-35; Deut. 3.1-17), while the survival of historical Moabites and Ammonites is recognized. In the Negev the ghostly 'giants' are annihilated (Josh. 11.21-23), but the Philistines and Amalekites must live on. Those who do not exist are exterminated – and the fact that they do not exist demonstrates the fact that they have been exterminated!

4. *The Exodus Motif*

The other important block in the archetypical legitimation of the possession of Canaan is the theory of arrival from outside and military conquest, in fulfilment of the divine promise. The sagas of the 'patriarchs' offered an inadequate legitimation, because they were too remote and were localized only in a few symbolic places (tombs, sacred trees). A much more powerful prototype of the conquest of the land was created by the story of exodus (*ṣē't*, and other forms of *yāṣā'* 'go out') from Egypt, under the guidance of Moses, and of military conquest, under the leadership of Joshua.

The main idea of the sequence 'exit from Egypt → conquest of Canaan' is relatively old: already before the formulation of the Deuteronomistic paradigm, the idea that Yahweh had brought Israel out from Egypt is attested in prophetic texts of the eighth century (Hosea and Amos). In Amos the formulation has a clearly migratory sense:

> Did I not bring Israel up from the land of Egypt, and the Philistines from Caphtor and the Arameans from Kir? (Amos 9.7).

In Hosea, the exit from Egypt and return there are used instead as a metaphor (underlined by reiterated parallelism) for Assyria, in the sense of submission or liberation from imperial authority. Because of its political behaviour, and also for its cultic faults, Ephraim (= Israel, the Northern Kingdom, where Hosea issues his prophecies) risks going back to 'Egypt', which is now actualized as Assyria:

> Ephraim has become like a dove
> silly and without sense;
> they call upon Egypt, they go to Assyria (Hos. 7.11).

> Though they offer choice sacrifices
> though they eat flesh,
> Yahweh does not accept them.

Now he will remember their iniquity,
and punish their sins;
they shall return to Egypt (Hos. 8.13; see 11.5).

They shall not remain in the land Yahweh;
but Ephraim shall return to Egypt,
and in Assyria they shall eat unclean food (Hos. 9.3).

Ephraim...they make a treaty with Assyria,
and oil is carried to Egypt (Hos. 12.2 [ET 1]).

In these eighth-century formulations, the motif of arrival from Egypt was therefore quite well known, but especially as a metaphor of liberation from a foreign power. The basic idea was that Yahweh had delivered Israel from Egyptian power and had given them control – with full autonomy – of the land where they already lived. There was an agreed 'memory' of the major political phenomenon that had marked the transition from submission to Egypt in the Late Bronze Age to autonomy in Iron Age I.

We should bear in mind that the terminology of 'bringing out' and 'bringing back', 'sending out' and 'sending in', the so-called 'code of movement', so evident in Hosea, had already been applied in the Late Bronze Age texts to indicate a shifting of sovereignty, without implying any physical displacement of the people concerned, but only a shift of the political border. Thus, to take one example, the Hittite king Shuppiluliuma describes his conquest of central Syria in the following way:

> I also brought the city of Qatna, together with its belongings and possessions, to Hatti... I plundered all of these lands in one year and brought them [literally: 'I made them enter'] to Hatti (*HDT* 39-40; cf. *ANET*, 318).

And here is another example, from an Amarna letter:

> All the (rebellious) towns that I have mentioned to my Lord, my Lord knows if they went back! From the day of the departure of the troops of the king my Lord, they have all become hostile (*EA* 169, from Byblos).

Egyptian texts also describe territorial conquest in terms of the capture of its population, even if in fact the submitted people remain in their place. This is an idiomatic use of the code of movement (go in/go out) to describe a change in political dependence.

But when, towards the end of the eighth century, the Assyrian policy of deportation began (with the physical, migratory displacement of subdued peoples), then the (metaphorical) exodus from Egypt was read in parallel with the (real) movement from Israel of groups of refuges from the north to the kingdom of Judah (Hos. 11.11). The inevitable ambiguity of the metaphor of movement gave way to a 'going out' which was unambiguously migratory, though it maintained its moral-political sense of 'liberation from oppression'. The first appearance of this motif occurs, significantly, in the Northern kingdom under Assyrian domination.

Thus in the seventh century the so-called exodus motif took shape in proto-Deuteronomistic historiography. The expression 'I (= Yahweh) brought you out from Egypt to let you dwell in this land that I gave to you' (and similar expressions) became frequent, as if alluding to a well-known concept. Evidently this motif, influenced by the new climate of Assyrian cross-deportations, and the sight of whole populations moving from one territory to another, was now connected to the patriarchal stories of pastoral transhumance between Sinai and the Nile Delta, to stories of forced labour of groups of *ḥabiru* (*'pr.w*) in the building activities of the Ramessides, and to the more recent movements of refugees between Judah and Egypt: such movement was therefore no longer understood as a metaphor, but as an allusion to an actual 'founding' event: a real 'exodus', literally from Egypt.

Just as in Hosea the Exodus motif already provided a metaphor for the Assyrian threat, so in prophetic texts of the exilic age the exodus became (more consistently) a prefiguration of the return from the Diaspora – at first, fleetingly, from the Assyrian, to a (still independent) Jerusalem; then firmly, from the Babylonian disapora:

> Therefore, the days are surely coming, says Yahweh, when it shall no longer be said, 'As Yahweh lives who brought the people of Israel up out of the land of Egypt,' but 'As Yahweh lives who brought out and led the offspring of the house of Israel out of the land of the north and out of all the lands where he had driven them.' Then they shall live in their own land' (Jer. 23.7-8; 16.14-15).

At the conclusion of the whole process, in the sixth–fifth centuries the entire story of exodus and conquest of Canaan had been re-elaborated in the light of the real events of Babylonian deportation and return of exiles, thus in effect a 'new exodus', prefigured by the mythical one. Because of the location of the deported people, the exodus motif was likewise applied – with no change – to the departure of Abraham from Ur of the Chaldees:

> I am Yahweh who brought you from Ur of the Chaldeans, to give you this land to possess (Gen. 15.7).

To this phase of elaboration of the exodus motif belongs the generational scheme of 'sin/punishment', according to which responsibility for unfaithfulness towards Yahweh could not be reconciled with possession of the land and so removal of the inhabitants became a process of purification. And to this phase belongs, most of all, the vision of an Israel, already existing as a nation, consisting of twelve tribes, marching in columns like an army, devoted to the only god Yahweh, trusting in (though sometimes unfaithful to) the 'covenant' that prescribes the rights and duties of the chosen people. Some groups imagined, and even structured, the new exodus as an enterprise undertaken by a sort of paramilitary organization, with a high degree of hostility towards the indigenous groups.

The vision of a people marching through the desert owes something to such a paramilitary scheme; but it also depends (perhaps a lot) on the experience of imperial deportation. The divine promise 'I will let you dwell in a land where milk and honey flow' significantly parallels the statement of the Assyrian *rab-šāqē* (§7.6) about giving those who submit the opportunity to dwell in a fertile and productive land. It also signifies the fear expressed by those on the march of not finding in their destination the conditions promised or hoped for – such a fear reflects the mental state of someone who, in the Diaspora, had to decide whether or not to face the risk of return. And, most of all, the lists and censuses of the people divided into family groups and clans (Num. 2; 26) reflect the kind of administrative units into which groups of deportees were divided, so as to check their number (and the inevitable losses during the transfer process) and their final destinations. We are undoubtedly talking about descriptions of procedures not conceivable before the exilic age, and probably applied to the return of the exiles as organized in the Persian age. It should be noted that in the case of the returnees from Babylon too a very similar list is given, clearly reflecting an administrative origin (Ezra 2 = Nehemiah 7).

The people on the march have a decision-making structure based on an assembly rather than a kinship system ('*ēdāh* or *qāhāl*) with a tent of the assembly ('*ohel mô'ēd*); the divisions into thousands, hundred and tens again represents a military and not a family structure (Deut. 1.15). The tribal census aims in fact to establish and assign appropriate portions of land in the country of arrival (Num. 26.53-54, *nāḥălôt*). The 'military' organization of the twelve tribes during their march through the desert (as described in Numbers 10) has little to do with pastoral transmigrations and can rather be compared with the movement, under military escort, of communities of deportees and returnees.

5. *Moses, the Desert and the Itineraries*

The link between the 'exodus' from Egypt and 'arrival' in Canaan is, notoriously, among the most artificial and complicated in the entire corpus of traditions included in the Old Testament: scholars are in broad agreement that the itinerary of the exodus and the topographical setting of the giving of the Law are very late elements (from the post-exilic age), inserted to create a logical and narrative link between the two elements of the promise: the exit from Egypt and the possession of the land. (Such a link, by the way, was automatic when the image had been used metaphorically, without an implication of migration). Moses is never mentioned (apart from Mic. 6.4, a statement of very doubtful authenticity) before the post-exilic age; Sinai is mentioned a couple of times (Judg. 5.5; Psalm 68), but with no connection to the covenant between God and the people.

The late date of its composition implies that the description of the journey through the desert (*midbār*) is as it could have been imagined (in Babylon or in Jerusalem) by some Judean groups living in a town. The image of the desert, in the Exodus-Numbers complex, does not come from a pastoral society, seen as a place where the tribes live comfortably, but has the character of 'place of refuge' or 'land of exile', projecting a very uneasy urban perspective. The way is difficult and risky, full of dangers and lacking water:

> who led you through the great and terrible wilderness, an arid wasteland with poisonous snakes and scorpions, a thirsty place with no water (Deut. 8.15, amending the NRSV).

This passage betrays an anxiety similar to that provoked by the logistical problem of crossing the desert, as felt by the Assyrian armies, for example in the case of Esarhaddon's expedition to Baza:

> a remote district, a desert plain of salty land, a region of drought…(with) snakes and scorpions which cover the soil like ants (*IAKA*, 56-57).

The armies of the monarchy of Judah had also crossed the desert, for example, during the expedition against Moab: and the search for the water made by Moses, who makes it come out from the rock (Exod. 17.1-6), recalls the search for water described by the 'prophets' who were together with the army on such occasions:

> Thus says Yahweh, 'I will make this wadi full of pools.' For thus says Yahweh, 'You shall see neither wind nor rain, but the wadi shall be filled with water, so that you shall drink, you, your cattle, and your animals' (2 Kgs 3.16-17).

The miracle of Moses purifying the salty water (Exod. 15.22-25) also recalls the similar miracle by Elisha (2 Kgs 2.19-22).

The difficulties of the crossing of the desert are concentrated in the motif of the seditious murmuring of the people against Moses (Exod. 15.24, 16.2, 17.3; Num. 11.4-5, 14.2-3, 20.2-3). Similarly, the doubts about occupying Canaan are expressed in the motif of the scouts most of whom (except Joshua and Caleb) give discouraging news (Numbers 13). In both cases, the people wonder whether it was a mistake to follow Moses (= the priests), leaving Egypt (= Babylon) to look for a harsher and more difficult land, occupied by a hostile and aggressive population. It is clear that the two motifs of rebellion and of the scouts reflect debates that presumably took place between those who encouraged a return and those who expressed doubts or simply preferred to remain in a land of exile that appeared enjoyable and prosperous.

In describing the crossing of the desert, depicted as a hard and hostile landscape, mostly unknown, the Biblical authors used sections of 'itineraries' that probably belonged to military and trading routes, and perhaps also pilgrimage routes to sacred sites in the desert. All those itineraries quite obviously repeat ancient transhumance routes, because in the desert the tracks are always indicated by wells, mountain passes and fords. Analysis of the Exodus itinerary is difficult: most of the place names are attested only here and even the location of Sinai is debatable. Some main tracks can be traced: the north-south route, from the Gulf of Aqaba to the plain of Moab through the 'desert of Edom' and the 'desert of Moab', runs inside the desert zone, not because Edomites and Moabites opposed the Israelites' passage, but because that was the course of the main caravan route, where the plateau is not interrupted (as it is to the west) by deep valleys difficult to cross. The transverse route (west-east) from Kadesh-barnea to Aqaba also follows the important caravan route connecting the major north-south route to the Mediterranean terminal in Gaza. The sections from the eastern Delta to Sinai and to the Arabah should also have been well-known routes, because they led to the turquoise and copper mines. The section from Kadesh-barnea to Sinai most probably reflects a pilgrimage itinerary. At this general level it is impossible to go into more detail.

But the description of the trek of the Israelites from Egypt to Palestine serves chiefly as a framework for sections of prescriptions, which occupy most of the text and have nothing to do with a tale of a migration that never took place. The growth (through successive redactions) of these sections, which give details of the Law, each one set in some specific stopping place on the way, is due to their logical setting between the 'covenant' and the arrival in Canaan: but the origin and composition of all those texts has nothing to do with the narrative of the conquest.

6. *The Difficult Settlement in Canaan*

If the story of the conquest of Canaan offers a model for its reoccupation by the returnees of the early Persian age, the character of Joshua, the 'charismatic' leader of the archetypical event, should be a model for the leaders who guided the returnees in their settlement in Palestine. Perhaps it is not accidental that the name Joshua is also borne by one of the priestly leaders of the returnees (Ezra 2.2; 3.2 etc.), associated with a 'monarchic' leader, Zerubbabel, to whom it was evidently anachronistic to make reference in a pre-monarchic age. Perhaps already taken as a model by Josiah, Joshua was an obvious choice for the leaders of the return.

Rather paradoxically, we have no information about the military aspects of the resettlement of the returnees from Babylon; or the slightest detail of any relevance that would imply the book of Joshua as a 'mythic foundation'. In the confused and artificial chronology of Ezra and Nehemiah, some central question nevertheless emerge, such as the rebuilding of the walls of Jerusalem and the opposition of a coalition of enemies (Neh. 1.10, 19; 6.1) led by the Persian governor of Samaria, Sanballat (Bab. *Sinuballit*), but including also Tobiah the Ammonite (called 'servant' because he was a Persian functionary?) and Geshem the Arab (this name is attested in the royal dynasty of Qedar, see Tell Mashkuta inscription, *SSI*, II, 25). The narration centres on the character of Nehemiah, and is thus set in the time of Artaxerxes; but the rebuilding of the walls was very probably an immediate necessity for the first groups of returnees, and the task was spread over a quite long period and in different phases. In fact, Nehemiah goes to Jerusalem to restore walls that had been damaged in a specific incident (alluded to in Neh. 1.3, 17), certainly not during the Babylonian destruction of 150 years earlier.

While the rebuilding of the Temple (§17.3), the prestigious focus of religious activity, was opposed by neighbouring peoples, but supported by the 'remainees' (rejected and labelled as 'enemies' by the supporters of the 'hard line'), in the case of the walls, only opposition is mentioned. It was probably an operation aimed at securing the returnees adequate protection from external attack, and thus giving the necessary security to reconstitute the nation. The opponents had a good opportunity to create alarm in the Persian court over an operation that could easily be presented as an act of 'rebellion', and in the Achaemenid archives there were in fact some documents (the Babylonian Chronicles, what else?) attesting that Jerusalem had always been a city rebellious towards imperial authority:

> You will discover in the annals that this is a rebellious city, hurtful to kings and provinces, and that sedition was stirred up in it from long ago. On that account this city was laid waste. We make known to the king that, if this city is rebuilt and its walls finished, you will then have no possession in the province Beyond the River (Ezra 4.15-16).

But the leaders of the returnees, having a number of supporters at the Persian court and being themselves personally in touch with the emperors, could respond by producing official decrees from Cyrus (probably false, as we have seen), Darius and Artaxerxes himself (Ezra 5–6) authorizing the return, the rebuilding of the temple and therefore, implicitly or explicitly, the reconstitution of a national entity as well: for this purpose, walls were absolutely necessary.

So the walls were rebuilt, and the coalition of enemy kings defeated, mostly through legal means, but probably also with military action that it was subsequently deemed wiser to omit from the historiographical accounts.

7. Joshua and the 'Holy War'

The Biblical narrative of the 'founding' conquest is clearly an artificial construction, aiming to underline the unity of action of all twelve tribes. There are many clear internal contradictions, arising from a clumsy use of different, chronologically distinct traditions. Some traditions of strictly local relevance (like the Calebites in Josh. 15.13-19) were evidently supported by an authority that made it impossible to exclude them. Similar traditions, clearly connected with the transhumance routes between the Negev and central highlands, better describe an arrival into Palestine from the south (following the 'normal' direction from Egypt), but were removed so as to manufacture an arrival of all the people from an easterly direction.

The nucleus of the whole narrative (Joshua 6–8) refers to the conquest, after the crossing of the Jordan, of only the territory of Benjamin and Ephraim. The stories of the victory over the 'Amorite' kings of the south (Joshua 10) and the victory over Hazor in the north (Joshua 11) are clearly separated. The juxtaposition of three different episodes is used to give the impression of a total conquest. The distribution of the land by casting lots (Num. 33.50–34.15) is completely artificial and cannot correspond to any historical process of settlement (it could, however, have been used instead as a device for the returnees of the Persian age). The description of tribal territories (Joshua 13–19), with the differences between north and south that we have already seen (§8.3) can only be read in the light of events that happened much later than the events described.

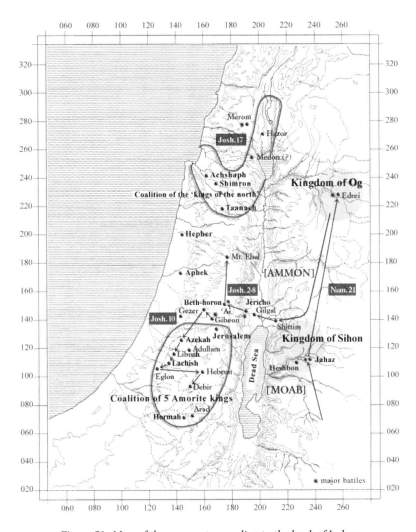

Figure 51. *Map of the conquest according to the book of Joshua*

There are so many incongruous and stereotypical features in the narrative of the book of Joshua that it can only be read in the light of a (Deuteronomistic) redactor considering the problems of his own time, especially the question of the possession of Canaan by the returnees from Babylon. This redactor chose to relate a unified conquest in the interests of the unity of these returnees and their strong opposition towards the remainees. The basic choices were not obvious: the returnees were, and could only be, from Judah and Benjamin (Ezra 1.5), that is, from that nucleus of former Judah conquered by Nebuchadrezzar, two tribes out of twelve. And throughout the land lived a variety of peoples, not all of them 'extraneous' in the same way, because they included Israelites (Yahwists) who had not been deported, in both south and north, with whom a policy of compromise could reasonably be pursued. But the narrative seems to reflect an extremist policy, one of the possible options for the leading groups who proposed to reconstruct a new Israel.

The paradigm adopted in the book of Joshua is 'holy war', clearly belonging to a Deuteronomistic matrix, but with deep roots in Syro-Palestinian ideology from the period of Assyrian pressure (§6.6). Deuteronomist historiography applied it retrospectively to the whole history of the relations between Israel and the 'other' peoples, not only for the conquest period, but also for the Judges and early monarchic eras. The basic concepts of holy war are the following: God is with us, he fights for us and assures us of victory; the enemies, even when apparently stronger, lack this support and are doomed to defeat; military action must be preceded by the appropriate votive-cultic preparation, and any fault or negligence in this respect will be punished by defeat; the booty is to be reserved for God (who is the author of victory) and therefore must be ritually destroyed (*ḥērem*) without any material gain being derived. In conclusion, if the people are faithful to God, they will certainly win. And, *vice versa*: if defeated, the reason must be sought in their unfaithfulness.

The practice of *ḥērem* is entirely suitable for a project envisaging complete substitution of 'extraneous' peoples by 'chosen' ones, who can take possession of a land already furnished with everything necessary for settlement (towns, houses, fields), provided the previous dwellers are eliminated without mercy; and it guarantees the total devotion to Yahweh of members of the new community that will be built:

> When you went over the Jordan and came to Jericho, the citizens of Jericho fought against you, and also the Amorites, the Perizzites, the Canaanites, the Hittites, the Girgashites, the Hivites, and the Jebusites; and I handed them over to you. I sent the hornet ahead of you, which drove out before you the two kings of the Amorites; it was not by your sword or by your bow. I gave you a land on which you had not labored, and towns that you had not built, and you live in them; you eat the fruit of vineyards and oliveyards that you did not plant (Josh. 24.11-13).

In the priestly version, too, the idea of a country ready to inhabit after the elimination of the previous inhabitants, is firmly established, even if the emphasis is on cultic purification instead:

> When you cross over the Jordan into the land of Canaan, you shall drive out all the inhabitants of the land from before you, destroy all their figured

stones, destroy all their cast images, and demolish all their high places. You shall take possession of the land and settle in it, for I have given you the land to possess (Num. 33.51-53).

The idea of the conquest as a total replacement (by extermination) of the preceding population by another cannot have been imagined before the beginning of imperial deportations. But in the terms formulated, it becomes a completely utopian vision, in its utter extremism, and cannot belong either to the original ethnogenesis nor to the time of return from exile. It is rather an ideal project, with no clear relationship to a practical strategy, and represents the ideology of those who formulated rather than an event that actually took place.

8. *The Landscape and Aetiology*

Apart from being occupied by phantom peoples, destined for physical elimination to give way to new occupants, Palestine was also full of cities in ruin, offering scope for aetiological stories that explained their condition through the deeds of ancient heroes. Note that the *ḥērem* offered a precise aetiological explanation for ruins that had not been reoccupied: an explicit case is Hormah, in the territory of Simeon, whose name alludes to the destiny of the cursed city (Num. 21.1-3).

The archetypical conquest by Joshua offered the most obvious setting for such explanations, which were spread by popular lore and family instruction, as illustrated by the description of a father answering his son's questions:

> When your children ask in time to come, 'What do those stones mean to you?' then you shall tell them that the waters of the Jordan were cut off in front of the ark of the covenant of Yahweh. When it crossed over the Jordan, the waters of the Jordan were cut off. So these stones shall be to the Israelites a memorial forever (*zikkārôn 'ad-'ôlām*)' (Josh. 4.6-7).

The most famous example is Jericho and its walls. In the narrative of Joshua 6 the city is captured by ceremonial rather than military action: the sacred ark is brought in procession around the walls seven times: on the seventh circuit, the walls collapse to the sound of trumpets and the city is captured. The results of archaeological excavations have shown that the walls of Jericho were much more ancient than the time of Joshua, when the town was simply abandoned (and remained so for a long time). This is a typical aetiological story, aiming to explain why the city remained ruined for so long. The 'explanation' is that the town was destroyed in the legendary age of the conquest by the men of Joshua and was furthermore subject to a curse pronounced in the name of Yahweh: 'Cursed before Yahweh be anyone who tries to build this city!' (Josh. 6.26). The details of the fall of Jericho obviously belong to the genre of legendary saga and contain no real historical memory.

The same is true for the city of Ai, whose name means 'ruin, remains' (the place name is in fact a common name, preceded by the article: *hā-'āy* 'the ruin', like the corresponding Arabic place name *et-Tell*) and had been abandoned at the end of the Early Bronze Age, a thousand years before Joshua. The aetiological character of the story (who destroyed this huge town? When? How? Why?) is quite clear. The literary character of the narrative (Joshua 7–8) is also very interesting. There is at first the motif of the failed attempt, or the lost battle, due to a ritual failure (the same motif is attested in Babylonian literature, in the case of Naram-Sin), after which success will follow, thanks to divine support, once the fault has been removed. There follows the account of a strategy in battle that is exactly the opposite of a 'normal' one. Usually the attacker has to break the defensive line and the defenders go back inside the walls to bear the siege. In the case of Ai, however, the defenders become the attackers of a defensive line created by the besiegers. The exit of the besiegers into the open country is the opposite of the normal direction of defenders, towards the protected area, the city. Another inversion of the scheme may be noted in the capture of the town, after the defenders' success, with the fire determining the final defeat instead of being the consequence of it. The sequence sin-defeat-expiation-victory and the use of an 'inverted' tactic are told twice, in very similar terms: in the case of Ai and in the capture of Gibeah (Judges 20), confirming that it belongs to a literary and legendary 'repertory': the historical value of these stories is in fact extremely meagre.

Other aetiological elements can be found in the Joshua conquest stories: a circle of twelve stones (presumably remains of some prehistoric monument) are explained as an 'eternal memorial' of the crossing of the Jordan by the twelve tribes (Josh. 4.1-9, see above). A great heap of stones (possibly a prehistoric funerary monument) is explained by the story of the stoning of the wicked Achan (Josh. 7.26). Some large stones at the entrance of a cave (Josh. 10.27) are explained by the torture and execution of five Amorite kings who found refuge in it. A tall stone stela beneath the oak in the sacred precinct of Shechem, testifies to an oath of covenant between Yahweh and the people (Josh. 24.25-27) – and so on. In all these cases, the landscape feature (which 'is still there to this day') is appealed to as proof of the truth of the story. This completely subverts the logical sequence: after the takeover of Judah by the returnees comes their appropriation of the significant signs and symbolic places scattered over the territory, which become proofs of the archetypical conquest and, consequently, justification for a historical one.

9. *Compromise and Cohabitation*

Not all the 'extraneous' groups were eliminated, and so requiring archetypal stories of their destruction. Other groups were assimilated, which needed different explanations. The only one narrated in length concerns the Gibeonites (Joshua 9), who tried to escape the elimination reserved for all the local inhabitants by saying that they had come from elsewhere. Thus they secured a treaty that saved them from danger. When the trick was revealed, the assembly and the nobles of Israel decided to keep the pact, but make the Gibeonites slaves, serving as woodcutters and water carriers for the temple of Yahweh – and this is their task to this day, says the author of the text (9.27). It is clear that the story originates as an explanation of why, in the second temple, the Gibeonites were subject to this *corvée* in the Jerusalem sanctuary.

A more relevant case of assimilation involves Shechem, which in the story in Joshua 24 has an important role as the seat of the grand assembly concluding the conquest, with the 'covenant' between Yahweh and all the people. By contrast, the Jerusalem of Adoni-zedek is one of the defeated Amorite kingdoms. It is clear that the Deuteronomist historiographer wants to keep his account consistent with the later history of the two cities (see §4.2), denoting Shechem as a symbol of assimilation and Jerusalem as one of conquest – with interesting repercussions (for those who read the story in the post-exilic age) on the roles of Samaria (supporting assimilation) and the new Jerusalem (separatist) over remainees and aliens.

If surviving enclaves in the interior were modest, the problem of the surrounding peoples was, on the contrary, quite evident, even in the eyes of a redactor who wished to present the conquest as substantially complete. The 'imaginary' peoples were completely exterminated: the five Amorite kings after the battle of Gibeon (Josh. 10.1-39), the 'giant' Anakim in the Negev (Josh. 11.31-32), the Amorite Sihon of Heshbon (Deut. 2.26-37; Num. 21.21-31) and the Rephaim or Perizzite Og king of Bashan (Deut. 3.1-11; Num. 21.33-35). But 'real' peoples remained: the Philistines in their pentapolis, the Phoenicians on the northern coast, the Edomites, Moabites and Ammonites in Transjordan. Moreover, if we look at the distribution of the settlements in the fifth century (as examined in §2), we see that in general the 'residual lands' – those not conquered by Joshua – mostly correspond to the territory that was most densely inhabited and affluent in the Persian age. The Deuteronomist redactor could not deny the persistence of these 'historical' peoples, because the evidence of the historical period during which the kings of Israel and Judah had to fight against them was too substantial and important. And since the situation at the time of the return of the exiles was even worse, it was impossible to claim possession of all the 'land of Israel'; yet, even with the exclusion of the neighbouring territories, the account demonstrates great optimism and an extraordinary determination.

10. *Ideal Borders and Residual Lands*

Another way of defining territorial control is by establishing external boundaries. Here many different conceptions come together, diverging in type (both realistic description and consciously utopian conceptions), in date and in the period they originally refer to. The more extensive, and thus less realistic formulation marks the two borders by two rivers (typical liminary elements): the Euphrates to the north and the so-called 'brook of Egypt' (i.e. the wadi Arish) to the south. This larger definition is based on the presumed Davidic-Solomonic empire, but corresponds, not to any realistic historical situation, but rather to the borders of the Persian satrapy of Transeuphrates (*ebir nāri*, or *'ăbar nahărāh* 'beyond the river' – from a Babylonian perspective). In the Persian age, assigning to the Solomonic empire the dimensions of the whole satrapy had clearly provocative political implications.

Less provocative, and probably based on more ancient traditions, was the siting of the northern border of Canaan at the 'entrance of Hamath', or rather in the locality *Lebo-Hamath*, known also from extra-Biblical texts and to be located in the Lebanese Beq'a. The entire passage Num. 34.1-12, which describes the borders of Canaan, shows possible correspondence with the Egyptian province of Canaan in the fourteenth–thirteenth centuries. The extent of the land of Canaan was probably fixed at that time, under the influence of Egyptian administrative divisions and the spread of the urban-agricultural area, and later remained as a standard definition. But its relevance to the question of Israel's borders consists only in the fact that, in the first instance, it is the land of Canaan that is promised by Yahweh to the chosen people.

The most frequent formula 'from Dan to Beer-sheba' indicates the northernmost and southernmost extent of the territory occupied by an Israelite population, and so corresponds to the totality of tribal territories. In this sense, it is a quite realistic definition, which projects back in time (to the age of the founding conquest) a unity in fact gained over the centuries and in the post-exilic age no longer valid – perhaps lost forever. This extent is not based on any political model, but on tribal occupation, and thus on the covenant between Yahweh and all the people: it is the territory that Yahweh gives to Israel and Israel has to gain by fighting, but most of all by showing its loyalty. In this case too, in evaluating the effect of 'from Dan to Beer-sheba' on the political realities of the fifth-fourth century, we must realise that it corresponds roughly to the province (a sub-division of the satrapy) whose capital was in Samaria and which included minor administrative units, like the city-temple of Jerusalem.

The utopian character of Israel's borders may be seen also in its conjunction with the notion of the lands that 'still have to be conquered' (Judg. 1.1–2.5; 2.20-23), an expression of the gap between the project and its realization, something presented as a temporary accident, to be solved in time but blamed on Israel's failure to follow Yahweh's instructions.

No doubt the tribal divisions as recorded in Judges 13–19, have a strong realistic character: the lists of villages, the descriptions of the borders as points of reference in topography and landscape, are not utopian. These divisions may go back to some specific administrative structure in a kingdom including (or intended to include) all the named territories under its control (Solomon's kingdom, for the most traditionalist historiography, or more probably the kingdom of Josiah, for the reasons given in §8.3), but probably also reflects the traditional tribal demarcations, which were therefore pre-exilic. Based on a long history of settlement, these territorial partitions were on their turn effective in predicating for the whole pre-exilic age a tribal organization that in reality needed a long time to take shape, but had finally reached a stable form. Yet it is also clear that in the post-exilic age most of the traditional tribes had disappeared (apart from Judah and Benjamin) and no longer had any territorial connections.

Let us consider, by contrast, the strongly utopian character of the territorial description in Ezekiel (Ezekiel 48): twelve portions of land, all of the same dimensions, all running from the extreme east to the extreme west, one after the other from north to south, with the temple at their centre. Whoever created this image had no idea of the real historical distribution of the tribes, or else deliberately ignored it because he considered it as completely dismantled, needing to be established again *de novo*. In this case, it is not a question of one or other region missing from the conquest, but rather of a total territory considered as an empty space, a geometrical, we would say 'Euclidean', space to be divided into equal portions, as in a survey exercise.

Chapter 15

A NATION WITHOUT A KING:
THE INVENTION OF THE JUDGES

1. *The Achaemenid Administrative Organization*

Since Persian domination had taken place without any particular traumas, its administration of Palestine has been supposed more or less to adopt the system already existing in neo-Babylonian times. Unfortunately, we do not know as much about the Babylonian system as the Assyrian, which may have been used as a model only in general terms, given the very different way in which Assyrians and Babylonians looked after their provinces. Because of the size of their empire, the Achaemenids certainly set up an administrative organization involving several levels, with a more complicated hierarchy than the Babylonians, but the ancient sources are not entirely consistent on this point.

At first the entire Babylonian empire was annexed as one single satrapy. At a later stage, under Darius I, this satrapy (too large and too important) was divided into two, and the Trans-Euphrates satrapy ('Across-the-river', bab. *Ebir Nāri*, aram. *'Abar Nahărāh)* had Damascus as its capital, where a Persian satrap lived. The satrapy's territory was then divided into provinces, probably more numerous along the densely inhabited coast (there are numerous remains of Persian palaces in Sidon, Arwad and Byblos), while the inland plateaux of Palestine were all entrusted to a governor based in Samaria.

In the course of time, however, Judah too, with Jerusalem as its capital, rose to the status of a province, with its governors usually chosen among the members of local ethnic group (from Zerubbabel to Nehemiah). The size of the province may have varied over time, but was certainly small: the area where the returnees lived (more or less from Bethel and Jericho in the north to Bet-Sur in the south), plus rather arid areas to the east, as far as the Dead Sea. It did not include the Shephelah, nor could it have reached the coast. The province was divided into administrative districts (*pelek),* in turn divided into semi-districts: probably with Jerusalem and

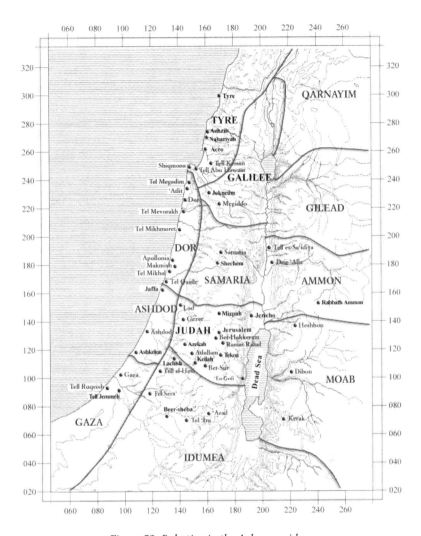

Figure 52. *Palestine in the Achaemenid era*

Gibeon in the north-centre, Bet-hakkerem in the south-centre, Mizpah and Jericho in the north, Keilah and Zanoah in the south-east and Bet-Sur and Tekoa in the south-west.

Like other provinces, Judea (*Yĕhûd*) minted its own coins (for local use) and the seals found there include official ones (also with the words *Yhd* or *Yhwd*) and some belonging to public officials (bearing their names and sometimes a title such as *phw'* 'governor', or *spr* 'scribe'). However, both bullae and seals nearly all come from the antique market and include many forgeries; hence it is not prudent to use them. A precise understanding of the system and its variations is made even more difficult because the imperial Aramaic words for 'governor' (*peḥāh*) and for 'province' (*mĕdīnāh*) also appear to be used at more than one level of hierarchy.

Under this administrative structure, the local communities kept their representative bodies, both restricted ('elders' and 'judges') for dispensing justice, and plenary ('*ēdāh*, *qāhāl* are typical words used in the post-exile language), plus a variety of political leaders according to local tradition. Some city-states had their own reigning dynasties, as we know for the Phoenician coast thanks to inscriptions of the kings of the Persian period in Sidon (Eshmun'azar I and II, Tabnit: *SSI*, III, 27-28) and Byblos (Yehawmilk: *SSI*, III, 25). This is also confirmed by classical sources like Herodotus (7.97). We should note that during the fourth and third centuries the 'autonomous' cities (those with their own kings) along the Phoenician coast (Arwad, Byblos, Tyre, Sidon) and in Philistia (Ashdod, Ashkelon, Gaza) also minted high denomination coins bearing their own emblems and distributed regionally, while Samaria and Jerusalem only minted small value coins with the imperial emblems, for local use.

Other 'kingdoms' had an ethnical-tribal nature, especially in Transjordan, where our information mainly concerns the 'kings' of the Ammonites, and in the Arab world mainly the 'kings' of Qedar (in particular from the Tell Maskhuta inscription *SSI*, II, 25). These local political structures were obliged to coexist (especially in the city-states) alongside the third-level Persian administrative structures.

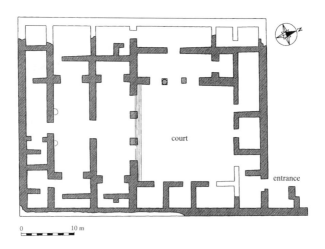

Figure 53. *Palestinian building of the Persian period: the administrative palace at Lachish*

The situation in Judah was complicated, at least initially, by the coexistence of the remaining local communities and those who had returned from Babylon (and perhaps other places) and also by the particular importance of the temple in Jerusalem. The main nucleus of returnees had been led (and this is no coincidence) by Zerubbabel, a royal descendent, and Joshua, from the line of high priests. The Judeans were presented with various options: (1) remaining organized with their own judges and elders, administratively dependent on Samaria, a situation approved by the remainees but certainly not liked by the returnees; (2) organizing themselves into a kingdom, revitalizing the Davidic dynasty as in the pre-exilic era, in line with popular expectations and the ambitions of the royal house; or (3) assuming the status of a temple-city, following the Babylonian model, a plan taking shape among the clergy, which would have received greater approval (certainly more than the monarchic option) by the Persian overlords. The choice (which was to be the temple model) was made after some time, as the outcome of events that have left few traces, and following debates that nevertheless are substantially documented. Let us now analyse these three options: the judges (in this chapter), the monarchy (in Chapter 16) and the temple-city (in Chapter 17).

2. The Context and Chronology of the Book of Judges

From 587, first under the Babylonian kings and then the first Achaemenid emperors from Cyrus to Darius, for almost a century (at least until 515, when the second temple was consecrated), Judah remained without a formal political authority, with all its local affairs run by judges and elders. Although it lasted for a shorter period of time, there was an analogous situation in Tyre, where between the deportation of the local king to Babylon (following the siege by Nebuchadrezzar) and his return (when pardoned by Awil-Marduk) the area was governed by 'judges' (*dikastaí*) of whom we have a list (*C. Ap* 1.157). We therefore have evidence for a 'period of judges' in a fully historical era (i.e. a historically documented period), but this is in the sixth century.

However, the 'period of the judges' in Israel's history refers to a quite different timeframe, preceding and not following the monarchy, and recounted in the book of Judges. The reasoning used by the Deuteronomistic historian is a clear and simple one: after Joshua had destroyed all the Canaanite kingdoms, and before the advent of an Israelite monarchy, first under Saul and then David, the country obviously had no king and was entrusted (as normally happened in such cases) to the care of 'judges' (*šōfĕṭîm*) over all matters of local government.

The creation of a period 'with no king' for the whole of Palestine is con-
trived, and contradicted by references to the existence of kings at that time
in the Book of Judges itself and by archaeology (in the persistence of palace
constructions in cities such as Megiddo). But the Deuteronomistic historian meant that there were no *Israelite* kings; that the tribes were not ruled
by the surviving foreign kings (Canaanite or Philistine), and that therefore
they needed 'judges'. He had neither the documentation nor any ideological interest for presenting a situation in which (as always) there were kings
in the cities alongside tribes in the countryside and elders and judges in the
villages managing daily affairs.

As described in Judges, the functions and figures of the judges correspond to a very slight extent to the substantially judicial role played by
elders and judges in local communities. Instead of councils of wise heads
of families appointed to enforce justice and settle local issues, we have
military leaders assuming the role of protecting the people of Israel from
the dangers posed by aggressive surrounding populations. It is clear that
the author of the book wished to project the problems of his time into the
'protohistoric' or 'legendary' past of national origins, in the formative stages
of the Israelite ethnic group; and he did this using materials of doubtful
credibility.

Basically the book speaks of twelve judges, which commentators have
divided into six 'minor judges' and six 'major judges'. There are no stories
provided for the minor judges (Shamgar, Tola, Jair, Ibshan, Elon and
Abdon), not even the identity of their oppressors, but only the length of
their term of office (in three cases) and their burial places (in five cases).
As far as the major judges are concerned (Othniel, Ehud, Barak, Gideon,
Jephthah and Samson), the text is expansive, with stories enriched in vary-
ing degrees with fairytale details, cunning tricks and moral lessons.

The chronological outline is quite artificial, with 'round' periods in mul-
tiples of six or ten, both for the oppressions and for the judges' terms of
office; the recurrent '40 years' for the periods of oppression is simply the
length of a human life. In adding up the oppressions and liberations of the
major judges we reach a total of 271 years, and if we add the periods of
office of the minor judges (provided for only three of them) the era would
have lasted more than 300 years. Taken seriously, this total is clearly too
long when set alongside the conventional historical chronology: with a
'conquest' in about 1250 one would have Samuel in 950, very close to the
Sheshonq expedition! This discrepancy has given rise to a variety of proposals, all unnecessary when we take account of the totally schematic
nature of the figures, the fictitiousness of the stories and the overall utopian scheme.

3. *Historical and Utopian Elements*

The book's entire narrative structure is set out in a repetitive and schematic manner, in accordance with the leading principles of Deuteronomist historiography. The people of Israel experience a series of crises, 'oppressions' that Yahweh inflicts upon it as punishment for its wavering loyalty. However, after a long period of oppression, Yahweh 'repents' or 'is compassionate' and sends a judge to save the people and destroy its enemies, after which they enjoy peace for a certain number of years. The message is clear, and by now also well known – the people's misfortunes are the result of its sins: redemption lies in Yahweh, and if we are faithful, no one will be able to resist us. Between the covenants with Moses and David runs a continuous series of divine interventions on behalf of his people throughout a period that one could describe as a 'trial run', a period of assessing the people's capability of remaining faithful in spite of the temptations provided by neighbouring peoples and the harshness of foreign oppression.

Table 10. *Chronology of the Book of Judges*

Years of oppression	Oppressors	Judge/liberator	Length of judgeship	Years of peace
08	Edom	Othniel		40
18	Moab	Ehud		24
20	Hazor	Deborah/Barak		40
07	Midianites	Gideon		40
		Tola	23	
		Jair	22	
18	Ammonites	Jephthah	06	
		Ibshan	07	
		Elon	10	
		Abdon	08	
40	Philistines	Samson	20	

However, in addition to this basic message, one finds another more specific and no less important one: occasional rule such as that of the judges can only result in occasional redemption, with an alternation of betrayal and repentance, protection and abandonment:

> Whenever Yahweh raised up judges for them, Yahweh was with the judge, and he delivered them from the hand of their enemies all the days of the judge; for Yahweh would be moved to pity by their groaning because of those who persecuted and oppressed them. But whenever the judge died,

they would relapse and behave worse than their ancestors, following other gods, worshiping them and bowing down to them. They would not drop any of their practices or their stubborn ways (Judg. 2.18-19).

Only a monarchy could have provided (and might yet once again) a definitive solution. It is enough to quote the recurrent reminder 'In those days there was no king in Israel; all the people did what was right in their own eyes' (Judg. 17.6 and 21.25) to understand the pro-monarchic attitude that inspired the person who wrote these stories.

There are kings in the Book of Judges, but these are kings of neighbouring peoples, 'oppressors' – Philistines and Canaanites, Ammonites and Moabites – while Israel remained without a king and as such felt clearly inferior. Almost as if to answer a possible objection, the author has added the story about Abimelech, king of Shechem, who as the son of the judge Gideon and a Canaanite mother is half-Israelite. With this story – presented as one of a failed monarchy, but also mentioning the process of assimilation between Israelites and Canaanites – we are on more reliable historical ground (see §4.2). This is also true of the war against Hazor, which duplicates (although in a different topographical context) the earlier story set in the time of the conquest: it should really be set in the earliest stages of Israelite monarchic development.

Hence a (small) number of recollections of 'pre-monarchic' historical events seems to have found a place in Judges, although their form and chronology is extremely doubtful, because of the author's problems in placing within a time frame events about which he had not, and could not have, reliable information. However, for everything else it is difficult to isolate historically plausible events – except of course the obvious generic setting of conflicts with the Philistines (Samson) and the Ammonites (Gideon). Nor can one envisage that the author, living so much later, was provided with written sources on these events, which are self-evidently situated in an environment or a period without state organization, and hence without archives or celebrative inscriptions.

4. Legendary and Fairy-tale Elements

Being obliged to supply events and characters for a period without written sources, the author(s) of Judges had to draw on a repertory of traditional stories with the usual legendary and mythological features found in such cases. Most of these sagas were set in an era before the arrival of the Israelites (the patriarchal sagas, see §§13. 4-5) or during the conquest (aetiological stories of destruction, see §14.8). Sagas featuring Israelites already

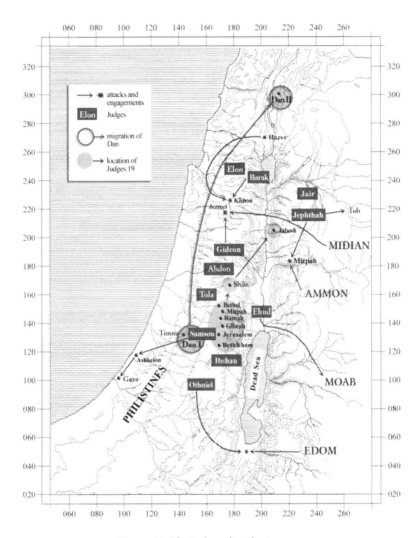

Figure 54. *The Judges: distribution map*

living in the area, heroes fighting neighbouring populations, were therefore set in the Judges period. These folk-tales are hard to analyse or date, since they have been reinterpreted many times over the course of their history. All in all they certainly do not provide a picture of twelfth-century Israel. Rather, they depict how exilic and post-exilic Israel imagined its formative period in the land of Canaan, transferring values and problems mostly relevant to their own time, though partly based on material that may well have been ancient. In particular, the proper names in Judges undoubtedly reflect linguistic (imperfect verbs, hypocrostics in –*ōn*/*ān*) as well as religious archaisms (relatively few theophoric names, of which only a couple are Yahwist) which are unlikely to have been falsified at a later date.

This idea of a narrative repertory is hinted at by a number of interesting features, such as repetitions of the same theme, already mentioned in regard to the patriarchal stories (in particular the sister/bride and stolen inheritance). The story of the 'inhospitable city', which instead of welcoming the wayfarer abuses him in every possible way, also occurs in very similar versions – when Lot spends the night in Sodom (Genesis 19) or the Levite at Gibeah (Judges 19), both containing a moral aetiology (the destruction of the inhospitable city). The story of the 'inverted siege', where the defenders adopt the attackers' tactics, is found in the conquest of Ai (Joshua 8) and of Gibeah (Judges 19–29), both describing military stratagems. Is there any sense in attempting to date these stories? Was there ever a historical event behind their origins?

It is more constructive to try to unravel the reinterpretations and the stratifications that these stories reveal. For example, in the story of the Levite in Judges 19–21, the change of 'Levite' from tribe to priestly caste, the portrait of the popular 'assembly' and the insecurity experienced in travelling over a distance betray an obvious post-exilic setting. Yet they do not obliterate previous reinterpretations (such as the anti-Benjaminite stance and more specifically anti-Saul sentiments attributable to the first monarchic era), nor the saga's aetiological kernel – the celebration at Shiloh during which the followers of Benjamin ceremonially kidnapped their brides:

> 'There must be heirs for the survivors of Benjamin, in order that a tribe may not be blotted out from Israel. Yet we cannot give any of our daughters to them as wives.' For the Israelites had sworn, 'Cursed be anyone who gives a wife to Benjamin.' So they said, 'Look, the yearly festival of Yahweh is taking place at Shiloh, which is north of Bethel, on the east of the highway that goes up from Bethel to Shechem, and south of Lebonah.' And they instructed the Benjaminites, saying, 'Go and lie in wait in the vineyards, and watch; when the young women of Shiloh come out to dance in the dances, then come out of the vineyards and each of you carry off a wife for himself from the young women of Shiloh, and go to the land of Benjamin. Then if their fathers or their brothers come to complain to us, we will say to them, 'Be generous and allow us to have them; because we did not capture in battle a wife for each man. But neither did you incur guilt by giving your daughters to them' (Judg. 21.17-22).

Certain stories have an obvious fairy-tale nucleus; the Samson episode in Judg. 14.12-20 is based on the theme of the impossible riddle ('my

secret is locked within myself' as Turandot would say); the Ehud story
(Judg. 3.15-30) based on the theme of the killer ambassador (rather like
Mutius Scevola), the Jephthah story (Judges 11) on the theme of the oath
that rebounds on the swearer ('Should we win I will offer to God the first
person I meet': he meets his daughter) – all these themes occur repeatedly
in the fairy tales of many peoples. Ibshan's '30 sons and 30 daughters'
(Judg. 12.8-10) who bring him 30 daughters-in-law and 30 sons-in-law, or
Abdon's '40 sons and 30 grandchildren who rode on 70 donkeys' (Judg.
12.13-15) also have obvious fairy-tale features. The same theme appears in
the story of Jair, with the addition of an aetiological and etymological play
on his name, which combines the words 'donkey' and 'city':

> He had thirty sons who rode on thirty donkeys ('*ăyārîm*); and they had thirty
> towns ('*ārîm*), which are in the land of Gilead, and are called Havvoth-jair to
> this day (Judg. 10.4).

A number of such folk stories possess a generic fairy-tale flavour; others,
however, are more deeply rooted in the landscape and the calendar. We
have already mentioned the ceremonial abduction of the girls at Shiloh,
described quite fully in all its aspects and motives. Jephthah's daughter,
too, is mourned each year for four days by all the girls in Israel (Judg.
11.39-40). The insistence on the judges' burial places (for some this is the
only information we have) suggests that the stories about them were linked
to tales (or festivities) that came into being around extremely ancient funerary monuments. This legacy of places, memories, sagas and tales had no
doubt already been created in the pre-exile era; one can however imagine
the care with which those returning retraced and valorized these signs of
the past when they re-occupied that same territory.

The geographical setting provided for the judges and their stories is
also revealing, since it is concentrated in areas re-occupied in the post-
exile era and where there was conflict with neighbouring populations
(the central plateaux of Ephraim and Benjamin); conflict with remainees
and foreigners (the Levite and the Benjaminites); the Shephelah and conflicts with Philistine cities (the stories about Samson and Shamgar); battles with the Edomites (Othniel), with the Moabites (Ehud) and above all
with the Ammonites and Midianites in Gilead (Gideon, Jephthah). In the
north we have only the figure of Elon (and nothing is narrated about him)
and Deborah and Barak's battle against Hazor (for its historical plausibility see §4.3). Judah is markedly absent, as if the sagas were intended rather
to mark the territory on its borders, rather than on the more securely
possessed centre.

5. *The Twelve Tribe System*

The historiographical tradition places the normative function of the league of twelve tribes during the Judges period, following their feats of conquest. The artificial nature of the number twelve has always been acknowledged, given that the names on the lists vary but always amount to twelve. Besides, all formal lists with a fixed number of equal members necessarily do a degree of violence to a tribal reality that must have been fluid and variously unbalanced. In the past (following M. Noth) it was thought that a formalization membership of twelve pointed to an organization that actually existed, like the Greek and Italian 'amphictionies' organized around a main sanctuary and perhaps with monthly service (one month for each tribe). The amphictyonic model, however, does not work: a central sanctuary is a royal feature and never existed at the time of a tribal league; there is no mention of rotation service, nor would there have been any reason for this. It is better to suppose that a formally structured league never actually operated, and was only created by the historiographer to represent, at least in the past, the organic unity of tribal groups that now appeared in reality to have been disrupted.

As we have already seen (§3.3), the tribes certainly had a real history and a known pre-exile location. The model of a large tribal confederation, of which there is little evidence in ancient times, was probably conceived during a historical phase (the sixth century) when powerful examples of such organizations existed, especially among the full nomads of the Arab world: the Ishmaelites and the Kedarites were large tribal groups with 'ethnic' characteristics, while the tribes in the period straddling the Late Bronze and Iron I Age were small and not very powerful, being linked to individual cities and living in a strictly local context.

On various occasions (from Solomon, §4.6, to Josiah, §8.3) we have seen how the definitions of tribal, clan and village borders were reshaped as administrative districts within the state. Rather than the administrative adoption of pre-existing tribal realities, these were probably cases of formal establishment of previously fluid entities. The very concept of 'tribe' should be better clarified, so as to understand its ongoing development and its formalization. There are two models of tribal identity: genealogical, which is 'true' for the great camel-riding tribes especially; and territorial, which emerges from lists of clans belonging to tribes, which is 'true' especially for agro-pastoral groups.

Table 11. *Tribal lists in the Bible*

Song of Deborah (Judges 5) ninth century	Blessing of Moses A (Deuteronomy 33) eighth century	Blessing of Moses B (Deuteronomy 33) seventh century	Ezekiel (48.1-29) sixth century	Ezekiel (48.30-35) sixth century
Ephraim (1)	Joseph (4)	Ephraim (5)	Ephraim (5)	Joseph (4)
Machir (3)		Manasseh (6)	Manasseh (4)	
Benjamin (2)	Benjamin (3)	Benjamin (4)	Benjamin (8)	Benjamin (5)
Zebulon (4)	Zebulon (5)	Zebulon (7)	Zebulon (11)	Zebulon (9)
Issachar (5)	Issachar (6)	Issachar (8)	Issachar (10)	Issachar (8)
Reuben (6)	Reuben (1)	Reuben (1)	Reuben (6)	Reuben (1)
Gilead (7)	Gad (7)	Gad (9)	Gad (12)	Gad (10)
Dan (8)	Dan (8)	Dan (11)	Dan (1)	Dan (6)
Asher (9)	Asher (10)	Asher (12)	Asher (2)	Asher (11)
Naphtali (10)	Naphtali (9)	Naphtali (10)	Naphtali (3)	Naphtali (12)
	Judah (2)	Judah (2)	Judah (7)	Judah (7)
		Levi (3)		Levi (3)
			Simeon (9)	Simeon (7)
Total: 10	Total: 10	Total: 12	Total: 12	Total: 12

NB: the numbers in parentheses indicate the order of enumeration

In the post-exilic era, the correspondence between the tribes and their territory must have almost totally disintegrated. The obvious priestly innovation of giving the status of a tribe to the Levites interferes with the list, but does not imply spatial dislocation, since this tribe has no territory. Such an intrusion into the list produces some of the more obvious variations, while others are produced by several minor elements. It would be oversimplifying to say that the addition of Levi is compensated by combining Ephraim and Manasseh in Joseph (to the detriment of the Samaritan area). Other instances of disintegration or even disappearance are 'founded' in benedictions and curses put into the mouths of Jacob and other patriarchs. We would be correct in suspecting that certain 'vanished' tribes were memories that were now difficult to cope with.

The tribe of Simeon, for example, may have been introduced in order to maintain that the loss of the more southern territories had not affected Judah. The migration of Dan from the Shephelah to the Upper Jordan valley (Judges 18) appears designed to claim rights over an area previously only briefly included in the kingdom of Israel (since it was first Sidonian, then Aramean and finally Assyrian), and simultaneously to explain its disappearance from the original area (annexed to the Philistine cities).

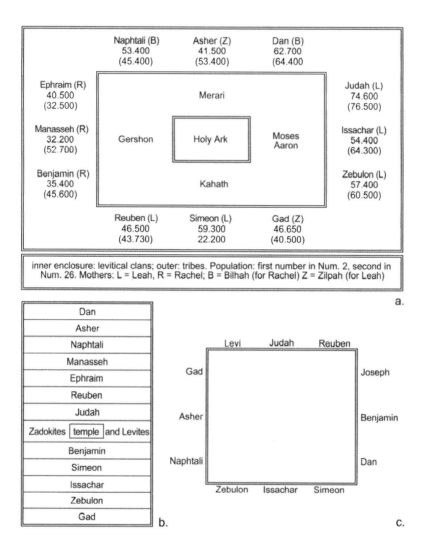

Figure 55. *The disposition of the twelve tribes: idealistic scheme: (a) Exodus encampment (Numbers 2 and 26); (b) allocation of the land (Ezekiel 48.1-29); (c) the gates of the future Jerusalem (Ezekiel 48.30-35).*

Those texts, definitely written during the exile, such as Ezekiel 48, or in the post-exilic period, such as Numbers-Leviticus, seem to have lost all knowledge of where the various tribes had been situated, arranging them artificially (divided into four quarters, north-south-east-west), mixing into this rearrangement a hierarchical order (the sons of Leah/Rachel/the maid-servants), that partly reflects the historical prestige they had acquired.

Basically, the generally agreed conclusions seem to be as follows: (1) 'tribes', in the sense of geographical groups of local communities considering themselves relatives by descent, always existed, but were continuously re-formed in the light of historical events; (2) in a basically agricultural and sedentary territory, the tribes experienced interference from the administrative organization of the kingdoms they belonged to; (3) their formal organization in a 'league' of twelve tribes, with equal territory, drawn by lot in a conquered and 'empty' land, is clearly utopian (and in reality never existed) and of late date (conceived in accordance with the post-exile reoccupation).

6. *Intertribal Space*

The historically credible facts derivable from the book of Judges (in particular the action against Hazor: see §4.3) show the tribes acting in agreement but only partially and occasionally, as dictated by events. The book's editorial framework easily confers a pan-tribal set-up to any episode simply by adding the words 'the whole of Israel' or 'the children of Israel' or such inclusive terms. However, the only episode in which there is a detailed description of the 'league' acting as a united political body is the war against Benjamin in the wake of Gibeah's crime against the woman of the visiting Levite. This narrative is extremely interesting: although it cannot be used as a basis for understanding how the tribes interacted in the pre-monarchic era, it is undoubtedly useful for appreciating how they were imagined in the post-exile period as having done so. The story contains elements of very ancient traditions (tenaciously preserved because of being tied to local cults) as well as features that relate to post-exilic problems over a territory with a difficult ethnic-political geography.

Obviously – the story is set in a time before David – there is no king, no capital city nor central administration, and no central sanctuary. There were, however, places of common encounter. Bethel was the seat of the 'tabernacle' or 'ark' of the covenant with Yahweh (*'ărôn běrît Yhwh*), the place where Yahweh's oracle was consulted and a census of the population taken. Mizpah was where the assembly (*qāhāl*) was held. Shiloh was a military camp but also a place of 'festivities/pilgrimages' (*ḥag*) to honour Yahweh. There were places of asylum (the 'rock of Rimmon', Judg. 20.47), that in other texts of later date will acquire greater importance as 'asylum cities' (Numbers 35; see §17.6).

Assembly decisions were taken by acclamation, through oaths that compelled or prohibited (such as 'None of us will go to his tent, none of us will return to his house!'). Decisions were made by drawing lots (*'ālāh běgôrāl*). The oracle was asked three times with increasing insistence: the first time it was simply requested (*šā'al*), the second time it was requested with a cry, and the third time sacrifices were offered in addition, and only then was a positive answer obtained. A summons to assembly could take the form of an 'object', or be symbolic:

> When he had entered his house, he took a knife, and grasping his concubine he cut her into twelve pieces, limb by limb, and sent her throughout all the territory of Israel. Then he commanded the men whom he sent, saying, 'Thus shall you say to all the Israelites, "Has such a thing ever happened since the day that the Israelites came up from the land of Egypt until this day? Consider it, take counsel, and speak out"' (Judg. 19.29-30).

While the use of a human victim's body is astonishing and abnormal, a story about Saul (1 Sam. 11.7) shows that a summons through pieces of cattle could be a 'normal' form. Each tribe, bringing its piece, met in the assembly, reconstituting the complete body. There existed, in fact, a rhythm in meeting and dispersing, dictated by the need to act together for a community spread throughout the territory. Dispersion was necessary in leading a normal life, exploiting all of the territory's resources; meetings were necessary for making decisions and acting in times of crisis requiring the combined participation of all tribes. A large variety of means of communication were used: messages, either verbal or in the form of objects, explicit and ritual, everyday and important, intentional and unintentional, smoke signals (in the ploy used to conquer Gibeah), even implied messages, such as that from the Levite requesting hospitality simply by sitting in the square at Gibeah without speaking a word or doing anything.

Issues of hospitality seem to have been of great importance when travelling through unsafe territory, because of different affiliations. Each person was safe within his own tribal territory, avoiding as hostile the territory of other groups, and taking care to follow normal procedure when visiting territory belonging to other tribes. The travelling Levite, coming from Judah, would not have dreamed of stopping in 'Jebusite' Jerusalem and looked instead for hospitality in Gibeah of Benjamin. However, hospitality followed precise rules and timing. The Levite, having stayed too long with his father-in-law, reached Gibeah when it was already dark and he was not welcomed, except by a resident who was not a Benjaminite. He met with sexual abuse from the inhabitants and saved himself only by handing over his wife, who was raped to death – a horrendous tale to which the league reacted with war and by exterminating the Benjaminites. To circumvent the oath that 'No one will give a daughter in marriage to Benjamin', the survivors were permitted to survive by means of a massacre at Jabesh and then a ritual kidnapping of the girls at Shiloh. The lesson was that there was a correct model of behaviour (hospitality, solidarity, intertribal marriage); if the rules were not respected, an 'anti-model' was enacted (war, kidnapping). However, what was not tolerated was the interruption of relations, or an absence of relations, that would make these tribes outsiders, the same as foreigners.

The scenario of a diversified territory, dangerous to cross, of relationships that represented a balance between maximum security and maximum interaction, of regular meetings and dispersions, is set in a 'founding' pre-monarchic past. It is, however, clear that both author and reader have also – and chiefly – the post-exile situation in mind, with the returnees spread throughout the whole territory, partly governed by them and partly in the hands of foreign, and clearly hostile, people, as well as partly controlled by groups that they were related to but who were not very trustworthy. It is no coincidence that the historical scene, restricted to the area between Bethlehem and the Benjaminites centres, coincides precisely with the territory that the Babylonian returnees occupied on their arrival.

Chapter 16

THE ROYAL OPTION:
THE INVENTION OF THE UNITED MONARCHY

1. *The Dying Rays of the House of David*

The monarchy, personified in the last descendants of the 'house of David', remained the foundation of hopes for redemption throughout the sixth century. This was initially a predictable option, so deeply rooted was the identification between the royal house and national independence. The plan to rebuild Israel, in its old territory, and in the same manner as before, could only imagine putting the legitimate king back on the throne (Jehoiachin, or after his death, his legitimate heir). The monarchic option, however, encountered both ideological and practical opposition. Ideologically, the negative verdict on past experience could only weigh heavily, and did so increasingly as the idea developed that national disaster was of course to be blamed on all the citizens, but above all on its monarchs. Compare the assessment of the 'house of David's' failure later expressed by Third Isaiah (Isaiah 56–59) with the trust still displayed by First Isaiah. If hope for redemption was to be based on greater loyalty to Yahweh, not only a 'new covenant', but also a new kingship must be conceived, not repeating the mistakes of the past, just (assured by a more important role for the people's representatives), and pious (assured by a political role for the priesthood).

At the practical level, imperial support for a markedly political, and not just religious, renewal was by no means a foregone conclusion. There was certainly no lack within the empire of vassal kings, and the Achaemenids effectively allowed Zerubbabel to return to Jerusalem, knowing well that he was the heir to the local dynasty and a candidate for its return to power. However, this imperial authorization may either have been conditional, or the person designated did not prove equal to the task. The monarchy probably became involved in – and ruined by – the problematic choice between the 'soft' and 'hard' approach towards the remainee

Judeans and the ex-Assyrians in the north. The monarchy, if it wanted to establish a powerful and unified Israel, had in principle to support strategies of participation. But, concerned with maintaining the new Israel uncontaminated by the surrounding environment, the priests supported a strategy of selective delimitation. The fact remains that Zerubbabel played some kind of a role until the new temple was inaugurated, a typically royal duty according to ancient tradition. After this, he disappeared. And one may suspect a *coup d'état* against him; after his disappearance there is no specific mention of him and records of the events may have been censored.

As for the two prophets Haggai and Zechariah, contemporaries of these events, the first seems to have assumed a decidedly pro-monarchy position. Although acknowledging the dual leadership of the 'governor of Judah', Zerubbabel, and the 'high priest' Joshua , along with a complementary role for a third party, the 'remnant of the people' (Hag. 2.2), his messianic message is centred on Zerubbabel:

> I am about to shake the heavens and the earth, and to overthrow the throne of kingdoms; I am about to destroy the strength of the kingdoms of the nations, and overthrow the chariots and their riders; and the horses and their riders shall fall, every one by the sword of a comrade. On that day, says Yahweh of hosts, I will take you, O Zerubbabel my servant, son of Shealtiel, says Yahweh, and make you like a signet ring (Hag. 2.21-23).

The setting is apocalyptic, but the political terms are cautious, so as not to offend imperial prerogatives. The choice, however, is a precise one.

Zechariah assumed a different position. Although acknowledging Zerubbabel's merit as a 'builder' (Zech. 4.6-10), he added a critical allusion ('not by an army, nor by might, but by my spirit'). And it is rather Joshua who plays the leading role in the vision of a purification and investiture ceremony, in which the temple appears to assume the prerogatives of sole leadership, a prerogative that once belonged to the royal palace:

> Thus says Yahweh of hosts: If you will walk in my ways and keep my requirements, then you shall rule my house and have charge of my courts, and I will give you the right of access among those who are standing here. Now listen, Joshua, high priest, you and your colleagues who sit before you! For they are an omen of things to come: I am going to bring my servant the Branch. For on the stone that I have set before Joshua, on a single stone with seven facets, I will engrave its inscription, says Yahweh of hosts (Zech. 3.7-9).

Table 12. *Judah in the Persian period, 540–330*

Persia	Judah		Events
	Governors	High Priests	
550 Cyrus 556–529			538 Cyrus' edict
	Zerubbabel	Joshua	520 return of exiles
Cambyses 529–522			(Zerubbabel)
			515 inauguration of
			temple
500 Darius I 522–486	Bagoas	Joakim	455 Return of exiles
Xerxes I 486–465			(Nehemiah)
450 Artaxerxes I (465–423	Nehemiah 445–433	Eliashib 455–425	
	430–425		
Xerxes II 423		Jehoiada 425–410	425 Samaritan
Darius II 423–404			schism
400 Artaxerxes II 404–358	Ezra 398–390	Johanan 410–370	
Artaxerxes III 358–338			
350 Arses 338–336		Jaddua 370–323	
Darius III 336–330			333–332 Alexander
			the Great

Later events show that after the inauguration of the temple the 'house of David' no longer played any political role, while we know that the priests assumed leadership of the Jewish community and of the new temple-city. In the course of a few years, between 520 (when Zerubbabel arrived in Jerusalem full of hope) and 515 (when the temple was inaugurated at Passover), a real revolution took place in the age-old tradition in Syria-Palestine that had always seen the temple annexed to the royal residence.

2. The Pro- and Anti-Monarchy Debate

While the final outcome is heavily suppressed by the priestly historiography, the pro- and anti-monarchy debate itself, which took place during the exile and lasted a few decades, has instead left important traces, especially in the rewriting of the past. We cannot exclude the possibility that a number of issues in this debate already had a long history in the monarchic era, a history that can be linked to repeated displays of tribal independence, resistant to submission to the palace. It is worth remembering the recurrent quotation of this pro-independence slogan:

'We have no portion in David,
no share in the son of Jesse!
Everyone to your tents, O Israel
...Look now to your own house, O David' (2 Sam. 20.1; 1 Kgs 12.16).

But there is no doubt that the debate in the Deuteronomistic History emerges in a situation where supporting or denigrating the monarchy was an unavoidable part of the vital issue of the monarchist option for national redemption.

The debate, in its more explicit terms, is retrojected to the time when Israel first adopted kingship, in the days of Abimelech and Saul. When Abimelech was crowned at Shechem, we are given Jotham's fable (Jotham was the only one of Gideon's sons to survive the massacre ordered by Abimelech). The fable speaks of trees searching for a king: they first approached the olive tree, which refused because it was too busy producing oil; then the fig-tree and then the vine, always receiving a refusal, until in desperation they turned to the useless, thorny bush that accepted the offer immediately, with ill-concealed arrogance. In truth this fable is not especially appropriate to the situation, but must have been a well-known folk-tale, a parable against power and the powerful, emanating from working people.

The controversy became more urgent in the episode where Samuel, asked by the people to choose a king (who was to be Saul) thought he should expose the defects of kingship. The opposition of the 'prophet' Samuel's coincides with Yahweh's, since the popular request for a king indicates a lack of trust in the divine leader (and thus his prophets or priests):

These will be the ways of the king who will reign over you: he will take your sons and appoint them to his chariots and to be his horsemen, and to run before his chariots; and he will appoint for himself commanders of thousands and commanders of fifties, and some to plough his ground and to reap his harvest, and to make his implements of war and the equipment of his chariots. He will take your daughters to be perfumers and cooks and bakers. He will take the best of your fields and vineyards and olive orchards and give them to his courtiers. He will take one-tenth of your grain and of your vineyards and give it to his officers and his courtiers. He will take your male and female slaves, and the best of your cattle and donkeys, and put them to his work.He will take one-tenth of your flocks, and you shall be his slaves (1 Sam. 8.11-17).

But the people, though warned that they would no longer be allowed to complain if all this came true, answered, undeterred:

> No! but we are determined to have a king over us, so that we also may be like other nations, and that our king may govern us and go out before us and fight our battles (1 Sam. 8.19-20).

This passage, apparently offering arguments both for and against, one portrait showing a greedy king and another a national leader, is clearly on the whole anti-monarchy: it considers the monarchic option not only inconvenient but also trivial – desirable and understandable for 'all (other) nations' (*kol-haggôyîm*) but useless for those who can rely instead on direct contact with a divine ruler. In fact, those in favour of the priestly option decry the desire for normality, the desire 'to be like all other nations' as a clear intent to abandon Yahweh and adopt idolatry:

> What is in your mind shall never happen – the thought, 'Let us be like the nations, like the tribes of the countries, and worship wood and stone.' As I live, says the Lord Yahweh, surely with a mighty hand and an outstretched arm, and with wrath poured out, I will be king over you. I will bring you out from the peoples and gather you out of the countries where you are scattered, with a mighty hand and an outstretched arm, and with wrath poured out (Ezek. 20.32-33).

In his plan for a future Israel, Ezekiel reserves for the 'prince' (*nāśî'*, a word he uses to avoid 'king'), a portion of the land and resources to prevent him from oppressing the people (45.7-8; 48.21). The king is hence reduced to an institutional impediment, a legacy of the past, impossible to remove and thus a king one must neutralize.

The other passage reflecting the Deuteronomic idea of kingship comes from the same author as the debate between Samuel and the people, the only passage within the Deuteronomic legislation that concerns the king and his role. After expressing in the form of negative recommendations the same problems that Samuel had expressed as predictions ('he must not multiply his horses...he must not multiply his wives...he must not multiply his silver and his gold...'), he lays down 'constitutional' terms to submit the king to the control of the Law – in effect, of the priests:

> When he has taken the throne of his kingdom, he shall have a copy of this law written for him in the presence of the levitical priests. It shall remain with him and he shall read in it all the days of his life, so that he may learn to fear Yahweh his God, diligently observing all the words of this law and these statutes (Deut. 17.18-19).

From the eternal and unconditional 'Davidic' form of kingship, a monarchy is reached conditioned by observance of the Law, supervised by the priests. The king-priest has its archetypical foundations in Melchizedek, king of Jerusalem in the days of Abraham (§13.7), and Psalm 110 (an enthronement rather than a messianic composition) proclaims the new king 'a priest for ever on the model of Melchizedek'. Besides specific Judean events, we should also bear in mind contemporary trends, conditioned by the restricting presence of the Persian 'king of kings': At Sidon, king Tabnit (c. 500) declared himself 'priest of Ashtart and king of the Sidonians' (*khn. 'štrt.mlk.ṣdnm: SSI*, III, 27), and his successor Eshmun'azar II (c. 480) was the son of the king and of the priestess of Ashtart (who were siblings). Under these conditions, the priesthood could have accepted a new form of sovereignty, one naturally reduced to playing a ceremonial role. This is the image of the king that emerges from the historiography of Chronicles (when the city-temple and priests as leaders were fully established): the king was a 'cult functionary', praised because he built or restored the temple, implemented cultural reforms, and guaranteed the resources for maintaining the cult.

3. *The Mythical Foundations: Unity as Archetype*

Before the priestly solution was reached, creating that 'kingdom of priests and holy nation' (*mamleket kōhănîm wĕgôy qādôš*) of the priestly author (Exod. 19.6), Deuteronomist historiography needed to revisit the past monarchic history throughout, fully accepting its role and praising its merits as well as condemning its disloyalty. It is probable, but now difficult to prove precisely (without presupposition), that the proto-Deuteronomist school at the court of Josiah judged the monarchy as a positive institution (but attacking the idolatry of individual kings); while the Deuteronomist historiography dating to the exilic period, after the fall of the monarchy, had no qualms about adding passages highly critical of it. As for 'democratic' tendencies within the Deuteronomist school, describing the role of the 'judges' and the 'city elders', these elements could have been contributed by refugees from the north, but will have been reinforced in the Diaspora communities.

Once instituted, the monarchy was nevertheless legitimate. In fact, every possible legitimization imaginable was bestowed on the first king, Saul: he was chosen by Yahweh, anointed by Samuel, acclaimed by the people, praised by the army. However, since historiographic traditions about Saul soon took on negative (and unalterable) characteristics, reflecting pro-Davidic editing, the course of kingship, according to the Deuteronomist (and then the Chronicler) started with David and continued until the exile.

It seems obvious to us that the monarchy should start with David, since it was David who made Jerusalem his capital and everything that precedes the unification of Judah and Jerusalem is but part of the prehistory of the Judean monarchy. However, according to ancient historical tradition the political and administrative requirement was not enough; the real founding event was provided by the 'covenant' established by Yahweh with David, a covenant that properly confirmed what had been basically established earlier, at least with Moses, if not even Abraham. The terms of this 'covenant' (faithfulness in return for prosperity) then determined the entire course of events, and since Yahweh was always loyal, the kingdom's fortunes and misfortunes were determined by the king's behaviour and his kingdom's progressive deterioration through persistent unfaithfulness.

In its earliest manifestation, newly created by Yahweh and not yet degenerate, at least apart from minor unfaithfulness, the kingdom must have been at the apex of its expansion and power. And since the century-old division of the two Yahwehist kingdoms of Judah and Israel, each living its parallel history, was considered as an early and clear sign of degeneration, the prototypical kingdom must have been united, and embracing all twelve tribes, all those worshipping the one true God. This is a clear mark of how pro-monarchic historiography, from Hosea to Zerubbabel, envisaged not the simple revitalization of the kingdom of Judah, but the creation of a single realm, the 'whole of Israel', including the north.

They imagined (one could rather say they established as an irrefutable fact) a kingdom united under David and Solomon, covering the entire Trans-Euphrates satrapy, centred on the royal dynasty and the temple of Yahweh, invincible in war and characterized internally by justice and wisdom. Already a millennium earlier (and thus no more than an analogy), undergoing a profound institutional crisis and military weakness, the Hittite king Telipinu had postulated an original model kingdom, extending from 'sea to sea', characterized by internal unity and military power, that could once again be recovered by adopting the correct behaviour and operative principles. The retrospective model proves false when compared with contemporary sources of the times, which speak of intense internal strife, plots and factions. Similarly, David's and Solomon's model-kingdoms, to judge from what is reliable in their sources, not only seem to have experienced furious battles over the succession, but were also rather small and fairly normal for the times, with a rather modest capital city.

Telipinu's text helps us understand the apologetic mechanisms used to refute charges of illegitimacy and abuse of power that emerged in a situation of institutional chaos, with rebellions and battles for succession. In particular, the way in which the Hittite king avoided accusations of complicity in the murder of pretenders to the throne is similar to the way David avoided accusations of having played a part in the deaths of Abner (2 Sam. 3.22-39), Ishbaal (ch. 4), Absalom (ch. 18) and many others.

In discussing the United Monarchy within a historically reliable context (§4.5-6) we mentioned a number of historiographic devices used to turn this into a model kingdom. A number of local wars against small Aramean kingdoms in the north-east may have been magnified in the light of later Israelite-Damascene wars and of the power Damascus had achieved. A number of documents (especially Solomon's 'twelve districts') may have been transferred from later administrations or plans (Josiah). A number of buildings (and not only the temple, but also fortified cities) may have been attributed to the most prestigious kings in popular tradition. All that was needed was the addition here and there of an 'all Israel' to give the reader the impression of a large and united realm.

Once established, such a model kingdom inevitably became embellished with all sorts of anecdotes or fables, with the leading role played by a king who was brave in battle, or famous and wise, or oppressive. It was easy to decorate details that were otherwise authentic, but far more banal, with colourful fictional features. For example, opening up trading links with the Yemen in the tenth century is not anachronistic; but the story of the Queen of Sheba's visit is much too like a fairy-tale in style and in use of narrative themes to be regarded as anything other than a romance from the Persian era. Then there is the tale of Uriah the Hittite, whom the king had put to death so as to marry his beautiful wife, a story that might have taken place under David or any other king. Nathan's parable takes the tale out of any historical context and perhaps provides the story's original nucleus:

> There were two men in a certain city, the one rich and the other poor. The rich man had very many flocks and herds; but the poor man had nothing but one little ewe lamb, which he had bought. He brought it up, and it grew up with him and with his children; it used to eat of his meager fare, and drink from his cup, and lie in his bosom, and it was like a daughter to him. Now there came a traveler to the rich man, and he was loath to take one of his own flock or herd to prepare for the wayfarer who had come to him, but he took the poor man's lamb, and prepared that for the guest who had come to him (2 Sam. 12.1-4).

We can hardly believe that a story like that of David and Uriah, so degrading for the king, could have appeared in any official text imaginable in the tenth century (archival documents, reports, celebrative inscriptions, or whatever), produced by a palace school for the benefit of the king. These stories are unreliable not because one wishes to minimize David or Solomon's historicity, nor because they are *per se* anachronistic or impossible, but because one cannot see by which channels they could have been recorded and passed on in the form they now have.

They are, however, fully part of the picture of what people in the 'Deuteronomistic' age (between Josiah and Zerubbabel) thought David and Solomon's United Monarchy was like. Unless we exercise a lack of criticism or employ an excess of credulity, they cannot be part of our realistic historical reconstruction of that kingdom during the tenth century.

4. *Dynastic Continuity and Stories of Succession*

If the 'covenant' between Yahweh and the people of Israel was that made with David, then dynastic continuity was a fundamental factor. Only David's legitimate and direct successors were the heirs of that covenant. Should the 'house of David' be supplanted, that ancient bond would no longer be valid. The 'founding charter' of Yahweh's promise to David can be found in 'Nathan's prophecy' and in David's answer (2 Samuel 7). On the one side David proposed to build the temple as a house 'worthy of God' (2 Sam. 7.2); on the other, God simultaneously wished to create the 'house of David', not in the physical sense (David had just finished building himself a royal palace), but as a dynasty that was to last forever:

> Your house and your kingdom shall be made sure forever before me; your throne shall be established forever (2 Sam. 7.16).

'Forever' of course was implicitly conditioned by David's promise. For as long as there was a 'house of God' there would also be a 'house of David'. Such a condition cannot have existed in David's time, when the temple was not yet built (and would not be built) and the dynasty was still simply a hypothesis. It belonged to the exilic period: the destruction of the temple coincided with the deportation of the royal house, and to rebuild the one it was necessary to rebuild the other. Even the promise

> And I will appoint a place for my people Israel and will plant them, so that they may live in their own place, and be disturbed no more; and evildoers shall afflict them no more, as formerly (2 Sam. 7.10).

appears anachronistic in the time of David, when the 'first' settlement had taken place three centuries earlier (and without the need for a royal dynasty), while it clearly alludes to the 'second' settlement (or its plan). The link between the royal house, the temple, the people and the land was the basis of the project of redemption.

Having established this solid and necessary link, the Deuteronomist then paid considerable attention to the history of Judah as an uninterrupted succession within the house of David, simultaneously emphasizing the dynastic fragmentation of the northern kingdom. The historical sources were not lacking, for the historiographer's *a posteriori* concern actually coincided with that of every king: proving (to God and to the people) that his enthronement was legitimate and dynastic continuity was assured. Those who succeeded in the regular manner (the heir to the throne being the chosen son) had nothing to worry about: the people's acceptance was automatic. If, however, the succession was irregular, or even just controversial, the new king was obliged to present his credentials, to justify himself, usually in the form of a celebrative inscription (a written transcript of what the king said orally). The ancient East is full of such 'apologias' by usurpers, declaring themselves to be the legitimate heirs, or by victors in wars of succession, explaining how God was on their side. As far as Judah is concerned, these inscriptions are lost, but traces remain in the narrative texts that drew upon them.

We have seen (§6.2) that there is a case of obvious dynastic discontinuity (the enthronement of Joash by the priest Jehoiada, with the agreement of the 'people of the land'), and the historian's narrative clearly derives from the usurper's arguments. Other cases mainly concern illegitimate succession within the royal family. In the case of Uzziah, Hoshea and Jehoahaz, following the violent deaths of their predecessors, the 'people of the land' played a fundamental role in choosing or accepting the new king. Real 'stories of succession', emphasizing internal conflict and the positions of the opposing parties, relate the passage from David to Solomon (1 Kgs 1.1–2.11) and from Solomon to Jeroboam (1 Kings 11–13).

These stories are quite detailed, a fact that nevertheless makes us even more suspicious and sceptical of the possibility that the historian could have employed genuine sources. Certainly not the original 'apologias' of the winners, though these may have remained visible until 587, but at least popular oral tales deriving from those 'apologias'. Various historical developments between the tenth-century events and their post-exile redaction have contributed to the moulding of these traditions. For example, the narrative of David's unification of Judah and Israel was influenced by contemporary anti-Saul and anti-Benjamin controversies, but also by later debates at the end of Solomon's reign (during the 'division') and in the time of Josiah (during his 'unification'). One can identify a number of elements, but the stratification and the weaving of traditions are such that analysis becomes extremely difficult.

To these possible 'authentic' sources and stratified traditions the post-exilic historian added a great deal of fairy-tale syle material (of the 'intrigue at the king's court' type) – tales of harems and rivalry between old and young wives, feuds and vendettas, oppression and repentance, generosity and cruelty, which make the tales of succession about David and Solomon, as we have them now, genuine historical novels, obviously selecting the most famous characters in the entire dynasty for the leading roles in dramas that actually fit better in the literary framework of the sixth and fifth centuries than in that (which was at the most only epigraphic) of the tenth century.

5. *Wisdom and Justice*

A prestigious dynasty needs to have well-established relations not only with God, but also with the people and the court. Concern with such relations emerges clearly in the Iron Age through an emphasis on 'wisdom' (*ḥokmāh*) and 'justice' (*ṣĕdāqāh*) as qualities distinguishing a good king. While the need for justice concerned the entire population, wisdom was more specifically linked to the court environment. And while justice was displayed – apart from anecdotes such as the 'Judgment of Solomon' in 1 Kgs 3.16-28 – in legal enactments, with populist aspects such as the care of orphans and widows, poor and marginalized, for wisdom we have specific books (which we technically term 'sapiential'), foremost among them the book of Proverbs.

Like other sapiential texts clearly from a later date (Ecclesiastes is third century and Wisdom first century BCE), Proverbs is attributed by tradition to Solomon, due to his reputation rather than to precise historical links. It is difficult, practically impossible, to date Proverbs, but this does not mean that one should necessarily classify its contents as 'late'. Rather, they belong to a literary genre known in very ancient written collections, from Mesopotamia to Egypt, usually in the form of 'teachings' from father to son or teacher to pupil, but also from the king to his heir. Oral transmission remained a powerful channel (proverbs were known and always quoted by heart), but the written collections are part of normal writing activities at court and may well be ancient.

The biblical book of Proverbs itself is a collage of various collections, presumably from different periods: a first collection of 'Solomon's Proverbs' (Prov. 10–22.16), a 'second collection', also attributed to Solomon but written under Hezekiah (25–29), the 'sayings of the wise' (Prov. 22.17–24.34), the 'sayings of Agur' (30.1-14) and the 'sayings of Lemuel' (31.1-9)

– two Arabs from the tribe of Massa. The framework, with its long praise of personified Wisdom, is certainly Hellenistic; however, the internal collections could easily date back to the monarchic era, and there is nothing implausible about one of them being attributed to Hezekiah.

The contents, however, are very ordinary, and hardly indicative of the behaviour and power relationships at court, as emphasized in Egyptian and Mesopotamian collections. A few of these, from the Wisdom of Amenemope (*LPAE*, 579-96) to that of Ani (*LPAE*, 302-313), closer in time to Solomon, can be interpreted as proper 'manuals' for the correct and moral behaviour of officials in that dangerous world that is the royal palace. The biblical Proverbs are much more principles of everyday wisdom, with an optimistic tone. They oppose the wise/just man to the stupid/evil one, and trust that God will remunerate justice and punish the evil. They praise wealth, but only if accompanied by generosity. They distrust women and foreigners. They invite obedience and endurance, work and sobriety, honesty and prudence. They express, so to speak, the common wisdom of the people, with no conceptual framework that offers a distinctive cultural picture of an environment or a period. It may be that the 'wise men' (i.e. the palace scribes) at Solomon's or Hezekiah's court collected folk sayings, contributing nothing themselves. The collection is certainly more comprehensible, however, if it was created when the royal palace no longer existed and the community identified itself with marketplace gossip and neighbourhood jealousy.

6. *From Royal to Eschatological Messianism*

In every civilization of the ancient East, the king's basic role was to ensure the correct relationship between the divine and human worlds, and thus guarantee his reign justice and prosperity. The enthronement of a new king was celebrated as the beginning of a new era of peace and happiness. Here is an example of a hymn for the enthronement of Ramses IV (c. 1150):

> A happy day! Heaven and earth are joyful,
> because you are the great Lord of Egypt!
> Those who fled return to their cities,
> those in hiding emerge,
> those who were hungry joyfully replenish themselves,
> those who were naked dress in fine linen,
> those who wore rags now dress in white garments,
> the imprisoned are freed, the unhappy happy,
> those who disturbed this nation are now peaceful (cf. *LPAE*, 450).

And here is what an Assyrian official wrote for the enthronement of Ashurbanipal (c. 670):

> Righteous days, years of justice,
> copious rains, huge floods, a fine rate of exchange...
> The old men dance, the young men sing,
> the women and girls are merry and rejoice.
> Women are married and provided with ear-rings;
> Boys and girls are brought forth, the births thrive.
> The king, my lord, has revived the one who was guilty and condemned
>   to death.
> You have released the one who was imprisoned for many years.
> Those who were sick for many days have got well.
> The hungry have been sated, the parched have been anointed with oil,
>   the needy have been covered with garments (*SAA*, X, 226.9-12, 16-3).

It is obvious that occasional and propagandist elements, typical of coronation days (amnesties, food distribution, festivities), were used to create a
picture of more general values and desires. In the Ugaritic poem of Keret
(c. 1350) a inverse picture was painted, using the same ingredients to
describe a king no longer capable of correctly carrying out his duties:

> You have not tried the case of the widow
> You have not judged the cause of the powerless!
> You have not banished those who plunder the child of the poor:
> You do not feed the orphan in your presence,
> Nor the widow behind your back!
> Like a bedfellow is illness,
> (your) concubine is disease!
> Step down from your:
> I shall be king;
> From your kingship:
> I shall be enthroned (*RTU*, 241; cf. *ANET*, 149).

The ancient oriental ideas about kingship were also common, then, in the
land of Canaan on the eve of Israel's emergence. It is entirely likely that the
enthronement ritual in the kingdoms of Israel and Judah involved similar
statements glorifying the new king, trusting in renewed prosperity and
justice, statements with strong populist characteristics and so aimed at
ensuring that the new king would win popular favour. It was pointed out
long ago (by members of the Scandinavian school) that a number of Psalms
(in particular 2, 18, 45, 72, 110) appear well-suited to an enthronement
ceremony, and therefore should date back to the monarchic period. One
example is sufficient here:

Give the king your justice, O God,
and your righteousness to a king's son.
May he judge your people with righteousness,
and your poor with justice...
May he defend the cause of the poor of the people,
give deliverance to the needy...
May the kings of Tarshish and of the isles
render him tribute,
may the kings of Sheba and Seba
bring gifts.
May all kings fall down before him,
all nations give him service.
For he delivers the needy when they call,
the poor and those who have no helper.
He has pity on the weak and the needy,
and saves the lives of the needy.
From oppression and violence he redeems their life;
and precious is their blood in his sight...
May prayer be made for him continually,
and blessings invoked for him all day long.
May there be abundance of grain in the land;
may it wave on the tops of the mountains;
may its fruit be like Lebanon;
and may people blossom in the cities
like the grass of the field (Psalm 72).

The psalms in question are known as 'messianic' because they are especially linked to the epithet of the king as 'anointed' (*māšīaḥ*) by God. But it remains to be seen whether these compositions were only recited on unique occasions – the enthronement ceremony, or sometimes perhaps for the birth of an heir – or repeated annually at the New Year festivals.

Following the national catastrophe, the end of monarchy and the exile, the ritual exultation uttered for a new king was transformed into the hope of salvation (always in terms of justice, prosperity and peace) placed in a potential king, who would act as a saviour and avenger, bringing national redemption. We can partly follow this evolution through the 'messianic' prophecies during the period of political crisis, from the exile and finally from the post-exile period. Already at the time of the disaster that struck the northern kingdom, the prophecies of Micah (5.2-7) and especially First Isaiah attribute a king-messiah role to an offspring of the house of David, within the framework of the redemptive gathering of Israelite survivors to Judah. The famous passage about the shoot from the stump of Jesse (Isa. 11.1-4) has already been mentioned (§11.1).

In Jeremiah, in a Jerusalem threatened by the Babylonians (between the first and second siege), hope was always placed in the Davidic dynasty, though projected into a perhaps near future and not applied to the present king:

> The days are surely coming, says Yahweh, when I will raise up for David a righteous Branch, and he shall reign as king and deal wisely, and shall execute justice and righteousness in the land. In his days Judah will be saved and Israel will live in safety. And this is the name by which he will be called: 'Yahweh is our righteousness' (Jer. 23.5-6).

The name given to the king-messiah, 'Yahweh is our justice' could only have been a polemical allusion to the current king, Zedekiah (whose name meant 'Yahweh is my justice').

During the Babylonian exile, messianism assumed different forms and directions. No doubt the traditional link between the house of David and hope for redemption remained, and was expressed politically in a more practical manner in the support for Zerubbabel in Zechariah's messianic prophecies (Zechariah 8–9). But there were also those like Second Isaiah who thought that the house of David had accumulated too many faults, was now out of consideration, and that the role of messiah was more suited to the Persian emperor. Obviously the idea (already suggested in *Ant.* 11.5-6) that Cyrus was inspired by Isaiah's prophecies is, to say the least, improbable. Finally there were those like Ezekiel who include rare references to royal messianism within the framework of a totally temple and priestly redemption – and when these occur he seems to want to avoid using the word 'king' (see §11.1), emphasizing instead the subordination of the 'shepherd' and 'prince' to Yahweh:

> I will set up over them one shepherd, my servant David, and he shall feed them: he shall feed them and be their shepherd. And I, Yahweh, will be their God, and my servant David shall be prince among them (Ezek. 34.23-24).

As the link between royal leadership and the hope for renewal diminished, the very nature of messianism changed. First, as a result of the profound crisis, there was a tendency to emphasize not the triumphal aspects of the coronation, but the negative reality. Second, there was a tendency to measure expectations more at the personal-existential than the political-national level. Both tendencies are well illustrated by the so-called 'servant of Yahweh' in Second Isaiah (Isa. 42.1-7; 49.1-9; 50.4-9), who is finally depicted in the guise of the 'righteous sufferer' (52.13 and 53.12) rather than of the messiah. But the prophecy of redemption strikes a tone that is strictly messianic:

Thus says Yahweh, the Redeemer of Israel and his Holy One, to one deeply
despised, abhorred by the nations, the slave of rulers,
'Kings shall see and stand up,
princes, and they shall prostrate themselves...
In a time of favour I have answered you,
on a day of salvation I have helped you;
...to establish the land,
to apportion the desolate heritages;
saying to the prisoners, 'Come out,'
to those who are in darkness, 'Show yourselves.'
They shall feed along the ways,
on all the bare heights shall be their pasture;
they shall not hunger or thirst... (Isa. 49.7-10).

Third, the messianic role shifted from the king to the whole people of
Israel, or to Jerusalem, the centre of attraction for the whole world. Here is
a passage from Third Isaiah:

Nations shall come to your light,
and kings to the brightness of your dawn.
Lift up your eyes and look around;
they all gather together, they come to you;
your sons shall come from far away,
and your daughters shall be carried on their nurses' arms.
Then you shall see and be radiant;
your heart shall thrill and rejoice,
because the abundance of the sea shall be brought to you,
the wealth of the nations shall come to you (Isa. 60.3-5).

One feels the effects of a diaspora now spreading to distant lands, of dreams
of wealth and power that can no longer reside in a messiah with regal characteristics. The messianic thread that started with the immediate celebration of the new king, full of imminent expectation, had now created the
foundation for long-term expectations, specifically eschatological, whether
at a personal level or a collective national or a universally human one.

Chapter 17

THE PRIESTLY OPTION:
THE INVENTION OF THE SOLOMONIC TEMPLE

1. Palestinian and Babylonian Temples

With its prospect of a powerful and pan-Israelite kingdom, the monarchic option was purely utopian: effectively the royal house no longer had any momentum, an independent kingdom was incompatible with the imperial situation, and those who returned came only from Judah and Benjamin. At times, utopias win the day, but in this case the vision was retrograde and conservative, an attempt to return to a now obsolete past. It was defeated by another utopia, the priestly vision, projected into the future and pursued with great determination. In theory this envisaged God's direct sovereignty: *Yahweh mālak*, 'God reigns', as the Psalms say, once royal but now adapted to this new ideology:

> Yahweh opens the eyes of the blind.
> Yahweh lifts up those who are bowed down;
> Yahweh loves the righteous.
> Yahweh watches over the strangers;
> he upholds the orphan and the widow,
> but the way of the wicked he brings to ruin.
> Yahweh will reign forever,
> your God, O Zion, for all generations (Ps. 146.8-10).

However, in practice the kingdom of God should be created by giving priests a political role and organizing the Judean community as a temple-city – a totally innovative solution in the history of Palestine.

In Palestine, and throughout the Levant, temples had always played a strictly cultic role. 'Houses' of various city gods (hence conceived as their dwellings), these temples were quite small, with a simple architectural structure comprising a vestibule, a sanctuary and an inner sanctum. Above all, they were not surrounded by outbuildings – the storehouses, shops, archives and rooms for the priests usually found in Egypt and Mesopotamia or even Anatolia, where the temple functioned as a redistribution centre and a basis of the country's economy.

The Syro-Palestinian temple played no political role; it was a sort of annexe to the royal palace and within the framework of that complex organization provided merely the ceremonial worship that the city addressed to one or more of its gods. The priests were palace employees and maintained by the king. This did not mean that organizing the cult had no political implications; it had many important ones: guaranteeing popular support for the king and assuring the people of good relations between their leaders and the gods. However, since the priesthood depended on the king (and the king played the leading role in the major religious ceremonies), this political role played by the temple was in fact controlled covertly by the king himself.

In economic life, too, the temple played a role, but ceremonial rather than productive. The temple owned no land, nor slaves to work it, but it held festivals (perhaps including fairs) and took care of sacrifices, receiving sacrificial victims from worshippers, dividing their meat among the officiants. It also received offerings, which were in part hoarded (the temple was the palace's 'treasury'), and partly spent on the ceremonial activities that punctuated the rhythm of community life. The people's participation in worship may have been extensive, but it took place outside the temple, which had no courtyard or other suitable spaces for accommodating the faithful inside.

In Babylonia, the exiles came into contact with a very different kind of temple. Temples in Babylon and Borsippa, in Nippur and Uruk, were complex organizations, endowed with considerable economic and political power. They were architecturally imposing: in addition to the 'house of the god', the sanctuary that contained the god's statue and which was relatively small, the temple complex also included all of the outbuildings mentioned earlier. There were large storerooms for the harvest produce, their wealth to be used in maintenance work on canals and on the land, as well as for temple personnel; they were also redistributed in the form of loans with preferential interest rates. There were artisans' workshops, scribal schools and housing for the priests. The temple also had large courtyards for the faithful to assemble. Priests and temple scribes were a distinct managerial class, organizing the economy of the city and its territory, especially in cities (also important) that were not capitals and so had no royal palace.

The tradition of the 'temple-city' dates back to the Sumerian world of the third millennium (and even earlier, to the 'late-Uruk' world of the fourth) but remained active throughout the history of Lower Mesopotamia. During the neo-Babylonian period, it was further revitalized when the temples provided the resources and direction for the agricultural re-colonization that characterized this period. Thanks to administrative texts from Uruk, covering the period between the end of the Chaldean dynasty and the beginning of Persian domination, we have information about the enormous amount of land owned by the temple (it is calculated that the Eanna temple owned most of the cultivated and irrigated land in Uruk), how it was managed, and its role in the country's overall economy. The Babylonian temple received considerable amounts of taxes ('tithes'), grants to cultic personnel, and individuals offering themselves under vows ('oblates': *širku*, feminine *širkatu*) for menial work. The 'exemptions' or 'privileged autonomy' (*kidinnūtu*) conferred on temple-cities by Babylonian kings were politically important, and the Achaemenids adopted them as an effective means of managing large city communities, preserving an appropriate balance between local autonomy and imperial control.

Returning to Jerusalem to rebuild the old Solomonic temple, the Judean priesthood (called 'Zadokite' because they were descendents of Zadok, one of David's priests) had this model in mind, one that worked well in relation to emperors, compensated for the weakness of the surviving Davidic monarchy, and ensured that priests had a means of managing the new national community, including its political decisions and above all legislative and social policies.

2. The Myth of the 'First Temple'

As often happens in such cases, a very radical project was planned and presented as a return to original practice, taking the Solomonic temple as a model, and conceiving a historical account that proved the ideological and historical centrality of the temple throughout the history of Israel. Here the Deuteronomistic History had already drawn a sketch at the outset, in the time of Josiah and his centralizing reform of the cult of Yahweh in the Jerusalem temple, when a suitable historical tradition had been created. Josiah, however, a real and ambitious king, could only follow local models that subordinated the temple to the king: so he understood the temple as an annexe to the palace, with centralization as a way to eliminate potential rival temples that were more difficult for the king to control. But the high priest Joshua, who returned to Jerusalem with Zerubbabel to rebuild the temple and re-found the community, must have had a clear idea of the new model and also some of the anti-monarchic implications, at least, for economic improvement and political hegemony. At the end of this trajectory, we need only compare the history of Judah as told by the Deuteronomist and the Chronicler to perceive the shifting of emphasis from the history of a regal dynasty to the history of a temple.

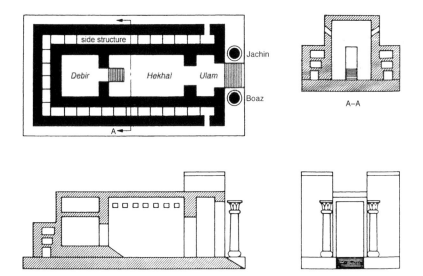

Figure 56. *Solomon's temple: reconstruction*

The architectural elements of the returnees' plans found their clearest expression in the description of the Solomonic temple and palace (1 Kings 6–7). We have already seen (§4.6) that tenth-century Jerusalem would hardly have found room for a complex of such size; according to the measurements provided by the Book of Kings, the palace building covered 1,000 square metres, but if we include enough space for walking round, and separating it from other buildings, plus its fortified wall, it would have occupied half of the 'city of David'. The temple was described as being similar in size to the palace, but with its 'inner courtyard' it covered a hectare, and if it also possessed an outer courtyard it would have covered the entire area on which the second temple was to be built.

However, it is not only the size that seems scarcely credible for the Solomonic era. A royal palace in tenth-century Jerusalem would have been built along the lines of the final palaces of the Late Bronze Age (such as that in Megiddo) or perhaps following the model of the first Syrian *bit ḫilāni* (like those in Zinjirli). But the building described is totally different from either (1 Kgs 7.1-8). It comprises a vast hall supported by four lines of columns (the so-called 'forest of Lebanon', because of the cedar wood), and there are two smaller buildings on the shorter sides: on one side the vestibule for ceremonial activities (judgment and audience), on the other, the king's private residence, facing another one for the queen. We need only draw a plan of this to see that it is the description of an Achaemenid

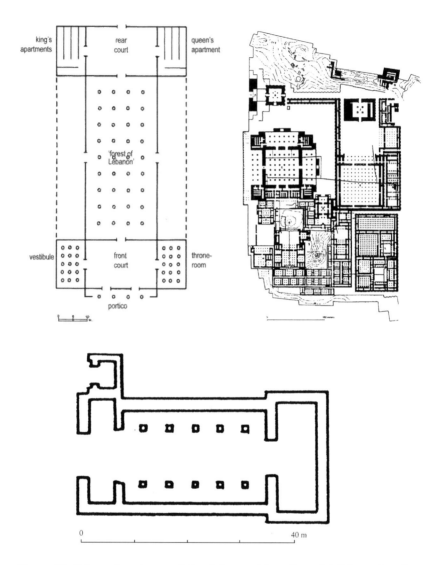

Figure 57. *Solomon's palace and the Achaemenid* apadāna: *(a) Solomon's palace (hypothetical reconstruction following 1 Kings 7.1-8); (b) Terrace of Persepolis with the* apadāna *of Darius; (c) Provincial* apadāna *of Byblos*

palace, centred around the large columned hall called the *apadāna*. The royal palace attributed to Solomon actually represents the plan of a palace in the Persian style, datable to the sixth and fifth centuries, similar in style to those in Susa or Persepolis.

The temple (1 Kgs 6.2-22), in an elongated shape comprising, in succession, a vestibule (*'ûlām*, measuring 20 cubits by 10), a main room (*hêkāl*, 20 by 40), and an inner sanctum (*děbîr*, 20 by 20 containing the ark of Yahweh with the tables of the Law), follows the architectural rules of Syrian-Palestinian temples, as we would expect, considering the conservative nature of places of worship; however, it stands entirely inside an inner courtyard, and probably also an outer one, clearly echoing the large fenced spaces of neo-Babylonian sanctuaries. Its decoration, in particular the enormous capitals, and its internal furnishings, especially the cult furniture in bronze, as briefly described in the text, are similar to those of the Iron Age, but the dimensions look suspicious: the enormous columns and capitals remind one of the architecture of the Persian period rather than the early Iron Age.

The exiles certainly had a good memory (and probably archival documents) of the first temple, and tried to reproduce it in their plans, but with larger dimensions and using precious materials (all in stone and wood, without the mudbrick partly employed for walls of the Solomonic era). However, the 'first temple' they had in mind was not Solomon's, but probably that rebuilt by Josiah and destroyed by Nebuzaradan and the Chaldean troops. They could only suppose that the temple had remained unchanged for four centuries, from when it was first built until its destruction. Note that every time the Deuteronomist historian mentions temple furnishings given as tribute or spoils, he always calls them 'Solomon's', as if they had seven lives.

The description in 1 Kings, with its mixture of memory and architectural planning, of authentic and anachronistic data, should still be assessed as quite realistic when compared with the visionary and architecturally impossible plan proposed by Ezekiel (Ezekiel 40–44), entirely projected into the future but based on a multiplicity of huge outer courtyards and working annexes with auxiliary activities, such as the prophet can only have seen in Babylon, but which the unchangeable holiness of a sacred building projects both backwards to the Solomonic prototype and forwards to the new temple still to be built.

3. *The Building of the 'Second Temple' and Establishment of Priestly Leadership*

There is no reason to doubt that Solomon had built a temple to Yahweh in Jerusalem. This achievement must have been the most original and authentic basis of his reputation as a model king, later embellished in various anecdotes. There may have been one or more inscriptions from this just

and wise king, celebrating the memorable building, inscriptions that remained visible for centuries. The suitably furnished temple then underwent all the misfortunes that normally attend the life of a sanctuary:
treasures and furnishings stolen or used for other purposes (as necessity
required) and later replaced by donations from kings or from the people,
walls repaired due to normal wear or after occasional destruction, but
also modified in response to the cult's changing requirements. Chapels
and altars could have been added or removed, access for the worshippers
regulated or even forbidden. We have only to bear in mind the hints given
about reforming kings such as Hezekiah and Josiah to appreciate how the
architecture and the functioning of the first temple were anything but
immutable.

The destruction in 587 was described as radical, and so it must have
been, within the limits of the destructive technology of the time: looted
and burned, the building remained roofless and with its walls partially
destroyed. It remained, however, a holy place for the survivors; the entire
city had in fact also been destroyed (walls, palace, and even private homes),
but was still occupied by squatters who did their best to repair the ruins. A
brief passage from Jeremiah (41.5) tells us that cultic activities took place
here even during the Chaldean period, known well enough to attract a
flow of worshippers from surrounding areas. Some scholars hypothesize
that the book of Lamentations was read there every year to commemorate
the destruction.

The returnees, led by Zerubbabel and Joshua, immediately took possession of the temple ruins and did their best to reorganize the altar to carry
out the fundamental cultic rituals according to the 'Mosaic' rules drawn up
in Babylon. They obviously drove out the priests who had maintained the
cult during the years of exile and thus came into conflict with the 'people
of the land' – (the remainees), who had continued to use the ruined temple
as a focal point. These people, called 'the enemies of Judah and Benjamin'
(Ezra 4.2), offered to cooperate in rebuilding the temple, giving as their
reasons the community of belief and continuity of cult:

> Let us build with you, for we worship your God as you do, and we have been
> sacrificing to him ever since the days of King Esar-haddon of Assyria who
> brought us here.

But their proposal was rejected, with the formal argument that imperial
authorization to rebuild only extended to the returnees. The remainees
therefore began hostilities, and appealed to the satrap of Trans-Euphrates,
Tattenai. However, the imperial court confirmed the authorization and
Tattenai allowed the work to proceed, and even cooperated in it. There are

certainly other authentic cases in which Achaemenid kings supported local cults (Darius endorses local cults in an inscription near Magnesia; the Xanthos trilingual inscription of Artaxerxes III grants exemptions to the local temple; the Elephantine 'Passover papyrus', etc.).

The story given in the book of Ezra is a confused one, the sequence of events does not correspond with the Persian kings named (and used to provide dates). If we accept its sequence of kings, we should conclude that reconstruction started during the second year of Darius and ended in his sixth year (515) with a solemn Passover celebration that marked the ceremonial conclusion of the return from exile. The returnees had now been joined by some of the remainees who had detached themselves from the 'people of the land'. The prophecies of Haggai and Zechariah relate to these events, which culminated (as seen in §16.1) with the disappearance or alienation of Zerubbabel and the assumption of full power by the high priest Joshua.

A generation later, however, in the time of Artaxerxes, we still find remainees and immigrants from former Assyrian provinces actively hostile to the temple community, making armed attacks and renewed appeals to the imperial court through the governor of Samaria, Rehum. The 'official correspondence' between Rehum and Artaxerxes, though of doubtful authenticity, reflects a plausible scenario. The temple-city had now been built, was in fact being fortified, and the loyal officials believed it was their duty to warn the imperial court about sedition and secession:

> May it be known to the king that the Jews who came up from you to us have gone to Jerusalem. They are rebuilding that rebellious and wicked city; they are finishing the walls and repairing the foundations. Now may it be known to the king that, if this city is rebuilt and the walls finished, they will not pay tribute, custom, or toll, and the royal revenue will be reduced. Now because we share the salt of the palace and it is not fitting for us to witness the king's dishonour, therefore we send and inform the king (Ezra 4.12-15, which is followed by the passage quoted in §14.6).

Again, however, the good offices of the influential Judeans at the Persian court, or the court's own more subtle strategy, resulted in permission to continue.

In fact, a few years later (the twentieth year of Artaxerxes, 445) Nehemiah, a Judean and high ranking official at the Persian court, managed to have himself sent to Jerusalem as the royal delegate to help with the building of the walls and the reorganization of the community. The hostility of the anti-Judean coalition, led by Sanballat, governor of Samaria, the Arab Geshem and the Ammonite Tobiah, had inflicted considerable damage,

burning doors and damaging walls. Nehemiah travelled to Jerusalem, over-
came the hostility of Samaria, and using imperial resources (wood from
the royal park), mobilizing the Judeans and cooperating with the high priest
Eliashib, he succeeded in having the walls quickly rebuilt. Remains of Nehemiah's walls have been found around the 'city of David' (the oldest district
and the only one inhabited in the Persian era), built higher on the slope
than the previous one.

Nehemiah then devoted himself to reorganizing the temple-city, which
from this moment on became detached from the province of Samaria and
so acquired complete autonomy. The realignment effected by Nehemiah
was essentially fiscal and administrative, but it also addressed the problem
of mixed marriages and the community's rejection of those without the
necessary requirements. We will discuss this in the next chapter. Note that
a parallel with Nehemiah's mission is provided by the Egyptian scribe and
priest Udjahorresnet (*LPAE*, 560-563), who in the days of Cambyses and
Darius managed to get himself sent to Sais to restore the temple of Neith
and to reorganize its worship and its administrative-legal provisions. The
autobiography inscribed on Udjahorresnet's statue also provides us with a
model of what Nehemiah's 'memoirs' may have been like in their original
epigraphic form.

It is not clear whether Nehemiah's reforms involved continuation of the
dual leadership of governor and high priest. The succession of governors
accorded the title (*pehāh*), Zerubbabel, Bagohi, Nehemiah, was interrupted
when the latter returned to the Persian court (in about 425). The sequence
of high priests, however, continued – even though these persons are not
known for any major initiatives, as befitted the highest representative
of what was effectively a priestly aristocracy, with its collegiality, internal
hierarchies, and its mechanisms of cooption and advancement, all of which
made it a genuine and powerful governing class. The leading representative of this class in fact held a position that was more one of representation
than of decision-making.

The process by which the priests took power occurred during the very
first years of the fourth century, when (allowing for the chronological uncertainty mentioned earlier) another imperial envoy, the scribe and priest
Ezra travelled to Jerusalem. His task was probably conceived by the Persians as a legislative one, considering the reference in Artaxerxes' decree
(Ezra 7) to the 'the law of God in Heaven' as an actual text ('which you
hold in your hands' hence a written document), accepted as such by the
emperor himself. Something similar is known to have happened in Egypt,
according to the 'Demotic Chronicle' (see *LPAE*, 803-814, which nev-

ertheless omits the relevant passage), according to which Darius ordered the satrap of Egypt to summon all the wise men for the purpose of writing down the laws of the land and ensuring that they were followed.

Appointed, then, to draw up the country's laws, and enforce them with imperial authorization, Ezra expanded the theological and political implications of his mandate considerably. Claiming total non-cooperation with 'the people of the land' and the supreme authority of the law of God (ratified by the emperor, but locally enforced unconditionally), Ezra initiated a new phase in Judean history. The temple-city, closed to the surrounding populations but open to believers of the same religion from the diaspora, was governed by the priesthood as the only legitimate representative of the Law. The drafting of the Law ended with Ezra, as did the historiographical enterprise; prophets ceased their activity and the priesthood in Jerusalem assumed full power.

4. Alternative Temples

The plurality of cults and places of worship that had dominated Palestine until the end of the seventh century had been initially restricted by the reforms of Josiah and then by the circumstances of the exile and return. According to the biblical texts, during the Persian period only the cult of Yahweh could have existed within the whole of Palestine, and in Judah only one temple stood, in Jerusalem. Famous ancient sanctuaries, such as Bethel, belonged to the past. The dominant religion tolerated only sites of sacred memory, spread across the land, in rural settings: the burial places of patriarchs, age-old trees, commemorative stones – all reinterpreted by the pre-Davidic history of the chosen people.

Regardless of the dogmatic statements of the biblical texts, all written or rewritten from a monotheistic and mono-temple point of view, the data provided by archaeology provide less precise but nevertheless significant confirmation. A map of the Palestinian temples during the Persian period shows their distribution along the coast (Makmish and Tel Mikhal), inhabited by the descendants of the Philistines and the Phoenicians and governed by the provinces of Tyre, Dor, Ashod and Gaza. Inland, only a few are known, in Galilee (Mizpe Yammin), beyond the sphere of influence of Jerusalem and Samaria, and belonging rather to the hinterland of Tyre.

The obvious links that had always existed between religious influence, cultic practices (the influx of worshippers to the central sanctuary), and political control had been further emphasized by the new configuration of the city-state which institutionalized these links more firmly and in forms never used before. It was therefore normal that the province of Judah, the hinterland of the city-state of Jerusalem, should be totally orientated towards the new temple of Yahweh. It would have been difficult for Samaria to accept this scenario passively. The province had already had to accept the loss of its status as a second level province (below the first hierarchic level of satrapy), exerting control over third level structures such as Judah. It could not now accept becoming subordinated to Jerusalem in a specific but important aspect such as the site of the official cult. Although on numerous occasions they affirmed, even stressed, their Yahwistic faith, the Samari(t)ans needed an alternative temple of their own.

The issue of mixed marriages provided an opportunity. There are two versions of this episode, relating similar events but with some different names (and chronologies). Nehemiah writes (13.28) that he expelled one of the sons of the supreme priest Jehoiada (the son and successor of Eliashib), because he had married, and refused to repudiate, the daughter of Sanballat, governor of Samaria. Josephus writes (*Ant.* 11.304-312) that a certain Manasseh, the high priest Jaddua's brother, having married and refused to repudiate a daughter of Sanballat, was expelled and found refuge with his father-in-law, who offered him the high priesthood of a Yahwistic temple, a rival to the one in Jerusalem, to be created or enlarged in Samaritan territory, at Shechem, which had always been the religious centre of that region.

The connection between these two accounts is obvious, and the biblical chronology (Jehoiada was the high priest c. 425–410) is preferable to that of Josephus (Jaddua coexisted with a Sanballat appointed governor by Darius III c. 335–325), if only because the Samaritan Pentateuch diverges from that of Jerusalem and so the schism must have taken place before Ezra. Thus, towards the end of the fifth century, a temple of Yahweh took shape in Shechem, on Mount Gerizim (see Deut. 27.4), entrusted to a Zadokite priest, and therefore with credentials as good as Jerusalem. A different historiographical tradition also emerged. While the Samaritans were able to accept the Law (hence their Pentateuch) in its contents and basic values, they most certainly could not accept the historiographical reconstruction that repudiated and effectively censured the deeds of all the kings of Israel (in the northern kingdom) in favour of the kings of Judah – a historiography that deliberately claimed the superiority of Judah and Jerusalem, the eternal validity of the Davidic alliance and the just end of the kingdom in the north due to its irredeemable sins. After the Samaritan schism, Judean historiography (as represented by the Chronicler, around the mid-fourth century) would have emphasized opposition to the north even more strongly, transforming it into real rejection. Chronicles replaces the parallel history of the two dynasties as presented by the Deuteronomist school by an exclusive history of Judah.

The Samaritan historiographical tradition, preserved in rather late sources, presents an alternative history starting with Joshua (the pan-Israelite hero of the conquest) who founds in Shechem a kingdom and a temple to Yahweh, ending with the Samaritans' return from the Assyrian exile at a date much earlier than when the Jews returned from their Babylonian exile (this idea is also found, but restricted to only one priest, in the Judean tradition as well: see 2 Kgs 17.26). However, Jerusalem's prestige and tradition were founded on a great deal more than the modest history of the old kingdom of Judah. They were based on the crucial developments by prophets, historians and priests in the elitist environment of the Babylonian exile. These were founded on an experience that the Israelites in the north could not have known in Samaria or in the places to which they were dispersed.

Papyri and bullae found in a cave in the wadi Daliya (north of Jericho) provide precious information about fourth-century Samaria, immediately before the Macedonian conquest. These are contracts and letters in Aramaic, in which a Sanballat, a descendent (perhaps the third) of the person of the same name in Nehemiah's time, is mentioned as the 'governor of Samaria. The onomastics are mainly Yahwistic, but there are also some foreign examples.

5. *The Temple-City*

We have already seen (§14.2) how the territory of Palestine, whose demography and settlement had reached their lowest point during the Babylonian occupation, began to recover during the Persian period, though differently in the fully developing coast and the clearly stagnating inland hill-country. This is the context into which we have to consider the slow and arduous growth of Jerusalem, which was protected to a certain extent by the Persian authorities and by the flow of donations to the temple from areas outside Judah (see Zech. 6.10). The sacrificial offerings (Deut. 18.1-5) of the firstborn (*běkôr*) of cattle, and firstfruits (*rē'šît*), were eaten by the priests and the offerers together. However, the 'tithes (*ma'ăśēr*) of wheat, wine and oil' of Judah (Neh. 13.12; see Mal. 3.6) were taxes intended to support temple staff as well as helping the needy. Following the Babylonian model, the temple in Jerusalem assumed a role that was in a sense that of a 'bank', granting loans on preferential terms – a stabilizing factor in the population's uncertain socioeconomic situation.

Not enough is known about Judah's administrative organization: the biblical texts speak mostly about cultic matters and only briefly mention fiscal and judicial arrangements. The most informative material is contained in the seal-impressions bearing the word *Yhd* and sometimes the names of the governors (*phw'*). Although the largest collection (assumed to be an 'archive', published by Avigad during the 1970s) is suspected as a forgery, some other finds seem authentic. Using a degree of caution, we can reconstruct a line of 'governors' following Zerubbabel and Nehemiah (Elnathan, Jehoezer, Ahzai), then a Bigvai who is the Bagohi (= Bagoas) known from the Elephantine papyri. But it is uncertain whether after Nehemiah's return to Susa (c. 430) appointments of real 'governors' or perhaps Persian 'delegates' were still being made. The biblical texts indicate that power was firmly in the hands of priestly class, at least after Ezra's reforms (c. 395). Beyond the biblical data, the line of high priests can be reconstructed from data provided by Josephus: one should also note that the biblical sequence of pre-exilic priests in 1 Chron. 5.30-41) and Josephus' list in *Ant.* 10.152-153 are in agreement only from the time of Josiah; before this they are entirely different, indicating an uncertain tradition, if not actual invention.

The province (*mĕdīnāh*) of Judah was divided into nine districts (*pelek* see §15.1) led by a prefect (*śar*). In the capital, self-government, especially judicial, was guaranteed by a college of 'elders' (*zĕqēnīm*) that dealt with daily affairs. However the important legislative and executive decisions were entrusted to an 'assembly' (*qāhāl*) in which all the heads of families (*rā'śê hā'ābôt*) in Judah took part, to which the summons was compulsory (Ezra 10.7-8; and see Judg. 20.1-2; 21.8-9). The right/duty to take part in this assembly involved legitimate membership of the community, and was subject to quite delicate selection criteria, on account of the population's ethnic complexity, the diversity of its origins and full acceptance of divine law.

While this organization with its districts, prefects, elders and assemblies, took care of everyday life, and was probably the same as in all other provinces, the centrality of the temple of Yahweh, absolute and even abnormal in proportion to the territory, plus the Judean criteria for ethnic-religious self-identification, conferred the real leadership of the community on the priests. They exercised this leadership by accruing to themselves numerous economic functions, but chiefly through their monopoly of the interpretation of the Law, which gave them the power to regulate all the important community issues. The figure of the 'high priest' (*kōhēn haggādōl, kōhēn hārō'š*) acquired its extremely important profile only during the post-exile period, acquiring functions and a status that were of course retrospectively applied to previous periods. However, the priests of the monarchic period (David's Zadok, Joash's Jehoiada, Josiah's Hilkiah), had been leaders of priestly 'corporations', officials dependent on the king, and the title applied to them looks anachronistic (they were probably *rab kōhănîm*, following the Canaanite custom) – not to mention founding figures, such as Aaron (created from the problem of the Levites, discussed below) or Samuel, who seems to combine the functions of 'judge', 'prophet' and post-exilic 'high priest'.

6. *Priests and Levites*

The question of who was entitled to exercise a priestly role was as important as the selection of authentic Judeans. The basic criteria were certainly evidence of descent from eponymous or 'founding' personalities from ancient times. There was no priestly 'vocation' (like the prophets): one was born as such and then bequeathed the position to one's children. Those born priests were invested when they started to officiate in sacrifices and other acts of worship. The priests *(kōhănîm)* were identifiable by a special garment (*'ēphôd*) and the pouch on their chest in which they kept the objects of oracular predictions (*'ûrîm* and *tummîm*).

High priests had to belong to the line of Zadok, which went back to Aaron and later through the high priests in the temple, descendants of David's Zadok and his son Azariah, Solomon's priest, continuing without interruption until the Babylonian deportation under Jehozadak (the genealogy in 1 Chron. 5.27-41 differs from the data given in Kings). However, the presence of another priest of David, Abiathar son of Ahimelek, who survived the massacre of all the priests ordered by Saul in the city of Nob (1 Samuel 22), proves, by its persistent memory, how it was possible to entertain alternatives even at a later stage.

The issue was even more important for normal priests, a significant part of the population. Of those returning and registered in the lists (see §13.2) about ten percent are priests. The group of returnees was certainly controlled by Zadokites, but both in exile and then in Judah, also obliged to confront other priestly elements: the priests from the north who moved down to Judah at the end of the seventh century, with their own important ideological contribution (§7.4), and the priests of the remainees (§17.3). The details of the confrontation can only partly be reconstructed. A number of groups were probably rejected, but others were accepted and criteria for descent broadened on the basis of the era of Moses and Aaron. The expression used to indicate priests 'sons of Zadok' was now replaced by 'sons of Aaron'.

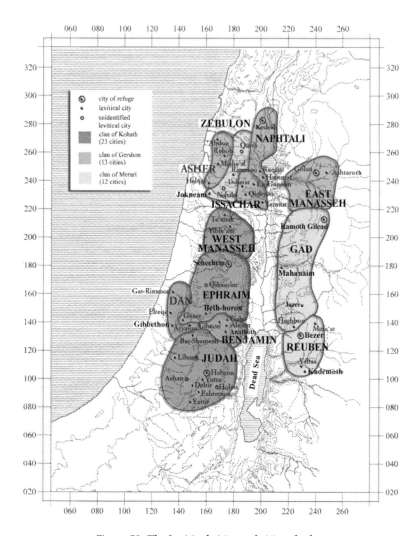

Figure 58. *The Levitical cities and cities of refuge*

Finally, the increased duties (administrative and fiscal, political and judi-cial) of the priesthood within the framework of the temple-city required more non-priests to work in the temple. There were temple slaves, oblates *(nĕtînîm)*, and specialized workers (singers, porters), and, as mentioned earlier, also those who collected wood and water (the Gibeonites of Josh. 9.27). But in particular there was a group of 'Levites' of whom only a small number were registered in the lists of returnees (only 74, all belonging to the clan of the high priest Joshua). The etymology of 'Levites' *(lēvi,* plural *lĕwīyîm)* is obscure, or at least complicated; it includes the meaning of 'added' (to the priests) and 'given, entrusted' (as confirmed by popular etymologies in Genesis and Num. 3.12; 8.16): hence additional personnel, recruited, at least in the beginning, through procedures similar to the oblates.

During the pre-exile monarchic period, Levites do not appear to have played any particular role. They are pictured during the Judges period (as, e.g., in Judges 19) as being a few individuals dispersed over the land, while they are discussed at length during the events of Exodus and following (Exodus–Numbers–Leviticus), representing obvious 'foundational' retrojections of a role acquired only in the post-exile period, and quite deliberately referred to a historically unverifiable era. Unlike the *nĕtînîm*, who were occasional oblates, unable to create a power-group, the Levites, hereditary oblates and organized in their own genealogical tribe, ended up by being acknowledged as one of Israel's twelve tribes (with a son of Jacob and Leah as ancestor), more closely associated with Judah (where the temple was), but given a social status reflecting their non-territorial tribal characteristics: they played no role in the division of the territory because they were devoted to Yahweh, replacing the firstborn (Num. 3.12; 8.16), and instead of land they received the tithe as a personal contribution (Num. 18.21-24). In addition, they were not only concentrated in Jerusalem, but lived throughout the territory, since in (or rather next to) the 48 'Levitical cities' including the 'cities of refuge' (for accidental murderers), they were reserved living and grazing areas. The rules in Num. 35.2-8 are rather abstract, as is the distribution of cities across the land belonging to the old 'tribal league', which cannot be imagined as anything but a utopian creation in the post-exilic period. The cities of refuge were six, three neatly distributed in Cisjordan (Kedesh in Naphtali in the north, Shechem in the centre, Hebron in the south), but the same number (too many) in Transjordan (Bezer in Reuben, Ramoth in Gilead and Golan in east Manasseh). The 48 Levitical cities are described more realistically (Joshua 21 = 1 Chronicles 6): the dominant clan of Kohath (more directly linked to Aaron) received 13 cities in Judah and 10 in Samaria, Gershon received 13 in Galilee, Merari 12 in Transjordan and Upper Jordan.

The Levites' rise in status, as fulfilling an important function, is well represented by the fact that their tribal genealogies were created so as to include Aaron, and hence the entire line of Zadok priests. However, the obvious discrepancies between the various versions (all from a later period) of Levite genealogies (Gen. 46.11; Exod. 6.16-25: Num. 26.57-60; 1 Chron. 5.27–6.38) all show the complicated and controversial features of an *a posteriori* reconstruction. Nevertheless, this genealogical contrivance reflects what became the standard usage of 'Levites' (beside the more correct 'priests and Levites') to indicate the entire group of those responsible for the cult.

However, the Levitical rise in status, from a category of ministers with auxiliary functions, recruited from outside, to a dominant component of the priesthood itself, required that they took on duties more closely linked to worship. The immense amount of rewriting of texts dealing with this does not permit more than an outline of the development. In the first, pre-exile phase, perhaps linked to the arrival of priests from the north in the days of Hezekiah and Josiah, the Levites must have been accepted as auxiliary staff having ancillary tasks rather than any involvement in worship – being thus somewhat penalized for coming from sanctuaries that were perhaps not very rigorously Yahwistic. A second step occurs in the earliest post-exile phase, documented in the great vision of Ezekiel 40–48, whose historical context is suggested by the fact that the Israelites had already returned to Palestine (foreigners were 'among them' and not *vice versa*), the 'prince' still played an important role next to the priest, and the temple was imagined rather than built. There is here a clear hierarchical distinction between the role of the 'Levites' (44.10-14) and the 'Levitical priests' (44.15-31). The priests cooked the meat for God, while the Levites did it for the people; the first served in the inner sanctuary, the second outside, and only the priests were required to observe the extremely strict rules protecting what was holy (including themselves) from contamination. Priests and Levites had separate rooms (40.45-46), kitchens (46.20-24), and prebendary lands (45.4-5).

The third step comes once the temple has been built, culminating in the time of the Chronicler, when the Levites assumed cultic duties very similar to those of the priests, while still carrying out maintenance, especially administrative and financial, duties (1 Chron. 26.20; 2 Chron. 31.11-12). We should note that the sources do not always reflect a linear development: Deuteronomy already in practice identifies priests and levites (10.8-9; 18.1-8), while Leviticus-Numbers assigns them practical tasks, reserving the cult for Aaron's descendents only: different positions that partly coexisted in evident conflict. At least one episode in the conflict between the old priestly aristocracy and the increasingly powerful Levites is probably preserved in the protest against Moses by the Levite Korah and 250 authoritative members of the congregation *(nĕśî'ê 'ēdāh)* who seem to be speaking on behalf of a widespread discontent among the people:

> 'You have gone too far! All the congregation are holy, everyone of them, and Yahweh is among them. So why then do you exalt yourselves above the

assembly of Yahweh?'... Then Moses said to Korah, 'Hear now, you Levites! Is it too little for you that the God of Israel has separated you from the congregation of Israel, to allow you to approach him in order to perform the duties of Yahweh's tabernacle, and to stand before the congregation and serve them? He has allowed you to approach him, and all your brother Levites with you; yet you seek the priesthood as well!' (Num. 16.3, 8-19).

It is a reasonable guess that the basis and context of the Levites' ambitions and demands lies in the fact that they managed the tithes and the temple's financial resources. A degree of 'commercialization' of the priestly office in the second temple, unavoidable in the light of the many economic implications of a flow of donations and sacrificial victims, tithes and services, contracts and commerce, was both the cause and the consequence of the Levites' unstoppable rise in the cultic hierarchy.

Chapter 18

SELF-IDENTIFICATION:
THE INVENTION OF THE LAW

1. *The Covenant and the Law, God and the People*

Israel's history is marked, at least from the neo-Assyrian to the Persian periods (from Josiah to Ezra as far as personalized references are concerned), by a series of recurrent 'treaties' (covenants) stipulated between Yahweh and the people. The Deuteronomistic emphasis on the covenant, dating back to the times of Josiah, owes a great deal to the Assyrian loyalty treaty. In addition to the historically verified 'assemblies', in which the people were called upon to ratify a covenant with Yahweh (*běrît Yahweh*), such as those summoned by Josiah himself (and perhaps earlier by Hezekiah), by Zerubbabel, Nehemiah, and Ezra, other covenants and assemblies were conceived and considered as 'foundational', located in the very distant past, ranging from Abraham's covenant, through Moses' on Sinai and the assembly in Shechem in the time of Joshua, to the 'promise' *(šěbû'āh)* made to David (in Nathan's prophecy).

Over the course of time – both invented and real time – one observes an evolution. From being a covenant/oath whose purpose was Israel's acceptance of exclusive loyalty *(ḥesed)* to the only real God (Yahweh) in exchange for his benevolence *(ḥēn* 'grace'), it changed, when this exclusiveness was no longer questioned, involving greater specificity in stipulations of behaviour: a change from a political and theological treaty to one more strictly legal and linked to the cult. Within this change, the literary genre and the ancient Near Eastern backdrop also mutate: while the political-theological covenant was clearly inspired by the vassal treaty (the neo-Assyrian in particular), the legal-cultic laws are inspired by the so-called ancient-oriental 'lawcodes' which have a totally different function and structure.

The protagonists in these treaties also changed. During the monarchic period there was no doubt that the king played a major role, and the political component consisted of replacing the human sovereign (the emperor) with a divine sovereign, although the people's consent was considered fundamental for such an important decision. With the end of the monarchy and political autonomy, those instigating the covenant had a lower level of institutional authority, while the role played by the people became that of the leading player. The covenants projected backwards in time were accordingly given a non-monarchic institutional setting and featured charismatic personalities, while reserving a major role for the people.

The people's role was always emphasized, using the context of an 'assembly' for the drafting of the law, but also, more specifically, in requiring public readings of these laws, as in particular under Josiah (2 Kgs 23.2) and Ezra (Neh. 8.4-18). The public readings (to be repeated every seven years according to Deut. 31.10-13) were countered by a degree of 'secrecy' with respect to the written text, which was kept in the inaccessible Ark (Deut. 31.24-26), or discovered by chance in the temple's archives (Judg. 24.26), or rendered symbolic in Shechem by means of an aniconic stone with no inscription – a secrecy that indicates and indeed suggests pious falsifications, also providing the clergy with the monopoly of correct readings and interpretations. This monopoly was challenged not so much by the people (or the assembly in the institutional sense), but by the prophets, spokesmen for the people's expectations. To Miriam and Aaron who were protesting against Moses' monopoly of the divine message ('Has Yahweh spoken only through Moses? Has he not spoken through us also?' Num. 12.2), the answer that the priestly author put in Yahweh's mouth involves the prophets:

> When there are prophets among you, I, Yahweh, make myself known to them in visions; I speak to them in dreams. Not so with my servant Moses; he is entrusted with all my house. With him I speak face to face – clearly, not in riddles; and he beholds the form of Yahweh (Num. 12.6-8).

The status of those addressed in the covenant was also linked to the definition of what Israel was: Abraham's covenant implied a kin-based definition, and a validity not limited to Israel (for other peoples also descended from Abraham). The Shechem treaty referred to a tribal league, coinciding with a united Israel that more or less corresponded to Zerubbabel's (albeit utopian) vision. David's covenant, like Josiah's, referred to a well-defined political nucleus (the kingdom of Judah), although that could be expanded to a pan-Israelite perspective. The most suitable model on which to build the post-exile period's prospects (hence the substance of Nehemiah's and Ezra's reforms) was undoubtedly that set in the tribal era: not Joshua's formulation (both because the latter was concretized by territorial allocation and because it was linked to a centre in the north) but that of Moses, when

Israel was a united but abstract concept, wandering in the unreal spaces of the 'desert'.

The events of the exodus, and the person of Moses (from the Sinai covenant to that on the plains of Moab) thus came to be associated not only with the fundamental definition of the covenant (loyalty in exchange for prosperity) but also with all the other casuistically detailed formulations that constituted ancient Israel's legislative corpus found in Exodus–Deuteronomy: the *tôrāh*, 'Law', which historically came to completion in the days of Ezra, but according to legend was attributed to the archetypal legislator Moses. It is a varied and complex body of texts, with many contradictions, within which smaller (and organic) legal collections can be identified, linked with various episodes in the long exodus, but certainly formulated and drafted in different periods.

Unlike ancient Near Eastern society, where a legislative corpus was usually linked to the initiative of a king firmly on the throne (from Ur-Nammu in Ur to Hammurabi in Babylon) the Israelite legislative corpus arose in a different situation: conceived mainly during a (real) period of political destructuring, it was retrojected into another (imaginary) period when the structuring had not yet taken place. The ancient Near Eastern codes had a celebrative purpose, describing how well the current kingdom worked (and therefore how prosperous it was), thanks to the prudent activities of the king in power, while Israelite legislative material had, instead, a prospective function, describing what should be done to achieve a prosperity that had not yet been acheieved.

2. The Legendary Foundation: Moses and Sinai

The extraordinary insistence on national self-identification through observance of a divinely-given law is typical of Israel, and answers the precise needs of a nation lacking the normal geopolitical coordinates. Respect for the Law could in fact take place even in social groups scattered over the territory and dependent on different political organizations (but in any case not their own). Self-identification through observance of the Law was certainly linked to the exile and post-exile periods: initially with a wish to maintain cohesion within a community risking dispersion, and later with the will to recreate a nation based on shared values (religious and moral).

Nevertheless, the introduction of the Law cannot be presented as an invention pure and simple. On the one hand, it had to be based on ancient models, because moral and legal norms were typically traditional and persisted over time. On the other hand the development of legal provisions and their formalizing inevitably attended the nation's entire history: there must have always been laws, albeit differently related to political power. We must therefore first analyse the archetypal reference, and then the actual historical stratified contexts of these moral and judicial provisions.

We should bear in mind that in all its formulations and re-elaborations, Israel's law has never been attributed to any royal initiative, which must in fact have been the norm for the entire monarchic period. We have mentioned (§16.2) that in the whole of Deuteronomy the only passage referring to kingship is brief and extremely critical. In the entire history of the ancient Near East, the king always issued codes and edicts – and it could not have been otherwise. In Israel, even Josiah's reform, the most drastic royal legislative intervention, was presented as the 'rediscovery' (and in the temple!) of an ancient code; hence the royal participation was minimized in favour of the archetypal reference.

A law that needed to be both non-monarchic (because it was needed precisely to found a nation without a king) but ancient (for the obvious reasons of authentication) could only be set in a pre-monarchic period. And since it created a national self-identification regardless of geographical location, it was set in a period during which the people of Israel already existed but had not yet taken possession of Palestine. A 'legislative' process, conferring this people with an identity, accompanied the 'demographic' process of transforming the patriarchal family into a nation.

Moses was the founding figure, the personality that led the people from Egypt to the borders of Palestine. Moses' personal history is very mythical: his birth and non-suppression remind one of the stories of Cyrus (Herodotus 1.108-121) and Sargon of Akkad (*ANET*, 119), tales that could have been known in the Babylon of the exilic period. Even the Egyptian features seem rather late, and scholars have mostly seen Moses as figure used (rather artificially) to link the patriarchal legends with the great theme of the conquest of the promised land. While narratively this link is based on the so-called 'exodus' – the journey from the land of exile and 'captivity' to the 'promised land' – thematically it is based on the Law: on the idea that at the origin of a people there had to be a set of rules for living together, and hence a 'legislator'.

As we shall see, the legal texts were different in scope and in chronological setting; however, from a narrative perspective the Decalogue above all linked Moses organically with the more systematic elaborations. Their physical transfer (in two stone tablets) by Yahweh to Moses and from Moses to the people was set at Sinai, and so related to the southern tribes' presumably ancient traditions, to their transhumance routes and their mountain sanctuaries, to Yahweh's southern origin, to the uninhabited land between Egypt and Palestine.

3. The Stratification of the Law

The legislative corpus is preserved entirely in 'late' documents, from the exilic and post-exilic periods; this does not mean that all the material they contain is also from a late period. Their chronology can be partly recovered by an internal analysis, from the social context that their contents reflect, and by correlation with historical and prophetic texts. A diachronic sequence has long been established, scholars still diverge widely on various points.

Behind the monotheistic, at the earliest Josianic, alterations, we have already observed (§3.5) that the Decalogue – in its Deuteronomic (Deut. 5.6-21) and Priestly (Exod. 20.2-17) versions – contains extremely ancient material, set close to the crisis of the Late Bronze–Iron Age transition. We have seen (§3.6) that the 'Book of the Covenant' (Exod. 20.22–23.33) may also be pre-monarchic, perhaps connected to the Shechem assembly. It has even been proposed that its laws should be attributed to the 'Canaanite' world, a view contradicted by the strongly non-monarchic characteristics of the society described in it and its clear social-economic polemic.

The 'Deuteronomic Code' (at least its strictly legislative part, chs. 12–26) might consist of, or derive from, Josiah's reform corresponding to the law found in the temple, as in the hypothesis formulated by De Wette (1805) that has subsequently remained one of the anchor-points of the entire chronological structure of the Pentateuch. This hypothesis should, however, at least be chronologically qualified in respect of obvious post-exile interventions that also marked the writings of the entire Deuteronomistic school.

With the 'Holiness Code' (Leviticus 17–26) we are already at the beginning of the exilic period, the time of Ezekiel (there are clear stylistic and phraseological similarities), in the milieu of the Zadokite priesthood, as indicated by the great concern for ritual and sacrificial procedures, the status of the priesthood and the definition of criteria for discriminating between pure and impure. The provisions (clearly of priestly origin) classified as the 'Priestly Code', but effectively subdivided into various collections concerning sacrifices (Leviticus 1–7: *'olāh*, 'holocaust', 'burnt offering' and *zebaḥ šĕlāmîm*, 'whole' or 'peace' offerings'), priesthood (Leviticus 1–7), criteria of purity (Levitcus 11–16) are clearly from the post-exilic period. It may be that this block is connected with Ezra's law. A similarly late date should be attributed to other legislative and ritual material found in Exodus and Numbers, and to the entire reorganization of this material (including the Holiness Code) in the form that we now have it. It was only in the time of Ezra (beginning of the fourth century) that the Law was established in the form in which it was passed down, but a little earlier (end of the fifth century) the Samaritan schism provoked numerous but generally insignificant variations.

These repeated interventions in the legislative corpus, this insistent returning to the same themes, to correct or add a few details, seem to conflict with the obvious idea that the Law, especially if divine, had been given once and for all. Yet it is not without interest that throughout the great legislative era, during the exilic period, there was a recurrent search, or demand, for a 'new covenant' *(bĕrit hădāšāh)*, or 'eternal covenant' (Ezek. 37.26; Isa. 55.3-5) – linked no longer to the departure from Egypt but from Babylon, and, bearing in mind the failure of the first one, written on hearts rather than taught by priests:

> The days are surely coming, says Yahweh, when I will make a new covenant with the house of Israel and the house of Judah. It will not be like the covenant that I made with their ancestors when I took them by the hand to bring them out of the land of Egypt – a covenant that they broke, though I was their husband, says Yahweh. But this is the covenant that I will make with the house of Israel after those days, says Yahweh: I will put my law within them, and I will write it on their hearts; and I will be their God, and they shall be my people. No longer shall they teach one another, or say to each other, 'Know Yahweh,' for they shall all know me, from the least of them to the greatest, says Yahweh; for I will forgive their iniquity, and remember their sin no more (Jer. 31.31-34).

Events took a different direction: the new covenant – judging by the legal texts that were actually drawn up in the post-exilic period – far from expressing a more intimate, more spiritual feeling, became instead increasingly ritualistic and occupied with detailed regulation. Comparing over time the ancient remains of pre-exilic legislation (the Decalogue and Book of the Covenant) with the Deuteronomic Code and then the priestly codes, one perceives an increasing amount of, and an increasing interest in, rules for rituals and sacrifices, purity, festivities and sacred ornaments. The great 'ethical' prophets had spoken of the need for spiritual renewal, but then the priests and levites drafted the new laws.

In the corpus available to us there is a complete prevalence of 'late' post-exile legal and ritual provisions: something like 95 percent of the total (approximately), with numerous repetitions or re-elaborations between one code and another. It is neither possible nor useful here to analyse all these provisions and their evolution over time. We will, however, try to provide observations on some of the most historically significant issues.

4. Social Legislation

The interest in regulating purity and cult rituals, which was quite unlike ancient Near Eastern codes, was undoubtedly considerable for the priestly class that wrote these texts, but perhaps of little concern to the ordinary people, who were kept away from these rituals. On the other hand we do have laws that have a direct social impact, although these also receive religious confirmations and implications. Social provisions deal with the sphere of 'justice' (*ṣĕdāqāh*) in the sense of maintaining a fair balance within the community and safeguarding personal status. This stability was threatened by economic processes, which the ruling authorities had usually remedied with amnesties or release, as in the age-old Mesopotamian tradition of the *mīšarum* edict (*mīšarum* also means 'justice' in this sense) and the *(an)durārum* (which means 'liberation' from bonds of servitude).

Social unrest was generated by the process of indebtedness, endemic in peasant societies in the ancient Near East, including Palestine; this was met by paying interest and mortgaging property (homes and land) and personal service ('debt slavery'). These processes were highly corrosive for the socioeconomic system, destroying the theoretical model of a fabric of families that were all free (with their own productive means) and of equal status; and also because they increased the number of servants in the latifundia, basically without limit. Unlike the Old Babylonian edicts, the provisions for 'justice' in the biblical legislation had a utopian character: loans with interest were forbidden, and periodical remission granted, with the release of debtors and the return of land to the families. Under a monarchy, such remission took place (like amnesties) when a new king was enthroned; without the monarchy, however, they occurred at regular intervals: a 'sabbatical year' every seven years and a 'jubilee year' every 50 (7 × 7) years. The absolute predictability of these dates underlines the utopian characteristics of the provision, as foreseen by the legislators themselves, who can only recommend an attitude of pious goodwill:

> Be careful that you do not entertain a mean thought, thinking, 'The seventh year, the year of remission, is near,' and therefore view your needy neighbour with hostility and give nothing; your neighbour might cry to Yahweh against you, and you would incur guilt. Give liberally and be ungrudging when you do so, for on this account Yahweh your God will bless you in all your work and in all that you undertake. Since there will never cease to be some in need on the earth, I therefore command you, 'Open your hand to the poor and needy neighbour in your land' (Deut. 15.9-11).

But besides predictability, that could have been faced by evaluating pawned property or personal service on the time remaining until the sabbatical year, the utopian nature of the provisions is manifest in the willingness to face a disorder by eliminating the effects and not the causes. During the best-known case of a royal amnesty, the one proclaimed by Zedekiah in a Jerusalem threatened by siege, Jeremiah's plea for an early return to the previous situation, seeing how impossible it was for released debtors to avoid falling back into debt, is significant:

> Thus says the Yahweh, the God of Israel: I myself made a covenant with your ancestors when I brought them out of the land of Egypt, out of the house of slavery, saying, 'Every seventh year each of you must set free any Hebrews who have been sold to you and have served you six years; you must set them free from your service.' But your ancestors did not listen to me or incline their ears to me. You yourselves recently repented and did what was right in my sight by proclaiming liberty to one another, and you made a covenant before me in the house that is called by my name; but then you turned around and profaned my name when each of you took back your male and female slaves, whom you had set free according to their desire, and you brought them again into subjection to be your slaves (Jer. 34.13-16).

This passage draws the basic contours of the entire issue: reference to a 'founding' provision in a very distant past, which was never applied; revival of the provision to deal with an emergency; recognition of its impracticability; restriction of benefits to compatriots ('Judean brothers'); and the provision's religious character.

The founding provision from a distant past was linked (as a counterpart) to the release from servitude to Egypt, and may not be pure make-believe (see the comments in §3.6) since it alludes closely to conditions in the Late Bronze Age and uses the words 'Hebrew slave' in the sense of *ḫabiru*. However, if a provision of this kind had been envisaged during the formative period of the Israelite ethnic group, in the anti-palace atmosphere that marked the crisis of the twelfth century, nothing for certain ever came of it. Its (re)application in an emergency, however, proves that the inspiring principle was known and favoured among the people. It is also interesting to observe that the Zedekiah amnesty, which took place in 590, is strictly coeval by Solon's legislation in Athens, which also envisaged tax relief (*seisáchtheia*) followed by freedom – under evident Near Eastern influence.

In the early post-exilic period the emergency reappeared on a broader scale, and the utopian legislation involving remission re-emerged in various forms. It appeared as a specific provision in the time of Nehemiah, following great pressure from the people:

For there were those who said, 'With our sons and our daughters, we are many; we must get grain, so that we may eat and stay alive.' There were also those who said, 'We are having to pledge our fields, our vineyards, and our houses in order to get grain during the famine.' And there were those who said, 'We are having to borrow money on our fields and vineyards to pay the king's tax. Now our flesh is the same as that of our kindred; our children are the same as their children; and yet we are forcing our sons and daughters to be slaves, and some of our daughters have been ravished; we are powerless, and our fields and vineyards now belong to others' (Neh. 5.2-5).

The fifth-century Judeans had no idea they were using almost literally the same words of protest used by the peasants in Byblos during the fourteenth century:

Our sons and daughters, our pawns, are gone, having been sold in the land of Yarimuta in exchange for wheat to keep us alive (*EA* 74 = *LA* 135; one of several cases).

While the problem persisted, the context changed. Legislative provisions in fact reappeared, adapted however to the new ethnic awareness, and to the new situation of mixed ethnicity. The beneficiaries were now the 'Hebrews' not as *ḥabiru* but as 'Israelites', and money should also be invested in buying back any Jews who had become the slaves of foreigners – a totally different problem from the release of debtors in servitude, acknowledging their status as free men regardless of ethnic origin.

In post-exilic Judah the problem of restoring land to its legitimate owners, whether in the sabbath year or jubilee, was compounded by the issue of land ownership rights, as between 'returnees', who still held ownership rights, and remainees, who had occupied those lands with the (explicit or tacit) permission of the local Babylonian administration. It was also complicated by the question of inheritance by a daughter, who might transfer the family property to other tribes, a transfer that the jubilee amnesty apparently might have made definitive (Num. 36.4). These implications are not very clear, and poorly attested; they do, however, show us that renewing provisions based on traditional principles of periodical remission gave rise to interesting debates and conflicts, as was inevitable in a society whose social fabric had been permanently ruptured.

The various codes make inconsistent provisions on this topic. According to the 'Book of the Covenant' (Exod. 21.2-6) the 'Hebrew slave' was to be freed after six years, that is, calculated on its own cycle. In the 'Deuteronomist Code' (Deut. 15.1-18) the cycle is identical for the entire community and involves the *simultaneous* liberation *(šĕmiṭṭāh)* of slaves and land restoration. In the 'Priestly Code' (Lev. 25.2-17; 23-25), as well as a sabbatical year there was also a jubilee year *(yôbēl)* for reinstatement of land *(dĕrôr,* from the Babylonian *da/urāru* 'liberation').

It is pointless now to try to link the rare historically known cases of liberation edicts with the utopian provisions of Deuteronomy and other post-exile codes, in order to calculate how many missed jubilees there were between Zedekiah and Nehemiah. The legislation simply confirmed the ethical-social principles and customs according to which all those in the community of free status and owning family land, had the right for this status and property to be safeguarded from the consequences of debt and debt-servitude. This utopia was realized on only a few occasions, under the pressure of acute crises, and only to emphasize even more clearly the inevitability of the disasters threatening the country's traditional social-economic structure.

5. *Matrimonial Legislation*

Within the framework of family law, the most controversial issue was that of 'mixed' marriages, always viewed with suspicion, both because of the issue of controlling the family heritage which, when the husband was the first to die, was managed by the widow – watched suspiciously by the members of his clan – and because of differences in customary behaviour. It is enough to recall the recurrent denigration of the 'alien woman' *('iššāh zārāh)* or 'foreign woman' *('iššāh nokrīyāh)* visible in the book of Proverbs. Under the monarchy a multitude of foreign wives was a privilege reserved to kings: praised by them as a mark of international prestige, but criticized by the prophets, expressing the mood of the people and seeing this as a way for idolatrous cults to be introduced.

In Israel, as normally in traditional societies, matrimonial laws maintained a balance between endogamy, which better ensured a clear line of inheritance, and exogamy, which broadened the spectrum of choice and afforded greater scope in the event of a crisis. Where settlement was stable, the villagers did not have many problems, choosing wives from the same village or clan, thus becoming ever more closely related through repeated intermarriage. The preferred choice of paternal cousins (daughter of the father's brother) is the most common in the anthropological inventory. But the behavioural models become complicated when the community, rather than stable and localized, becomes scattered and intermixed with foreigners. We can recall the patriarchal principle (illustrated by the marriages of Isaac and Jacob) of seeking paternal cousins even if these lived far away, rather than marrying 'Canaanite' or 'Hittite' women who lived in the same area (Gen. 24.3; 37; 26.34-35; 27; 46-28.1); or the Mosaic law (Num. 36.5-12) stating that one should marry within the same tribe so as not to disperse the patrimony.

The issue exploded into a fundamental crisis in the post-exile period, when the strong ethnic self-identification (in opposition to other ethnic groups) that had matured during the exile had to face settling in multi-ethnic territories where a strong tendency (which was at the very least tolerated) prevailed to inter-marry. Opposition to mixed marriages from the priests among the returnees was motivated not by patrimonial considerations but rather religious ones – and these motives were projected back into the monarchic and pre-monarchic periods. Well aware of the dominant influence of mothers in the upbringing of children, the priests feared that the spread of mixed marriages would inevitably compromise the stability and exclusivity of the Yahwistic faith and cult.

Mixed marriages were therefore branded as acts of 'contamination' (see later comments on this subject) as a union with elements deemed unacceptable because of their religion, involving cult practices considered immoral and perverted. The ban on taking foreign daughters-in-law for sons, and giving daughters in marriage to foreign husbands was increasingly applied. There were, however, different views on this, and the story of the Moabite Ruth, the perfect bride who became David's great-grandmother, proves that some thought a foreign woman could be accepted positively, on condition she behaved unimpeachably, following Israelite customs and showing affection and respect for her adopted family. Elsewhere, the definitive global provision banning marriages with Moabites prevailed (Deut. 23.4 = Neh.13.1-2), and stories were told (far less poetic than Ruth's) about the immoral nature of relations with Moabite women (Num. 25.1 describes these as *zĕnôt*, 'fornication'; see also Num. 13.15-18 and Deut. 23.4).

The Deutronomistic law, clearly post-exilic on this point, is quite clear:

> Make no covenant with them and show them no mercy. Do not intermarry with them, giving your daughters to their sons or taking their daughters for your sons, for that would turn away your children from following me, to serve other gods. Then the anger of Yahweh would be kindled against you, and he would destroy you quickly (Deut. 7.2-4).

But the practice of mixed marriages continued, and the debate went on. On one side the priests' position advocated even the repudiation of foreign wives, while on the other voices were raised in favour of a more humane attitude, recognizing the value of pity and love. Malachi, a strong critic of the inimical priestly strategy ('Have we not all the one Father? Has not the one God created us?', 2.10), showed his sensitivity to the moral unease and emotional tragedy of repudiating a wife – without distinction between

Israelite and foreign – with whom one has entered an covenant, lived with and had children:

> Because Yahweh was a witness between you and the wife of your youth, to whom you have been faithless, though she is your companion and your wife by covenant. Did not one God make her? Both flesh and spirit are his. And what does the one God desire? Godly offspring. So look to yourselves, and do not let anyone be faithless to the wife of his youth. For I hate divorce, says Yahweh, the God of Israel (Mal. 2.14-16).

Since people continued to enter mixed marriages, the priestly leadership reached a decision concerning the repudiation of all foreign wives as well as children born from these 'contaminated' families. (Ezra 9–10; also see Neh. 13.23-30). The terrible scene with the people all assembled, crying and trembling under the pouring rain, listening to the words of this new provision implicitly echoes precisely what Malachi had feared:

> You have trespassed and married foreign women, and so increased the guilt of Israel. Now make confession to Yahweh the God of your ancestors, and do his will; separate yourselves from the peoples of the land and from the foreign wives' (Ezra 10.10-11).

The 'guilty', a little over one hundred (75 percent lay and 25 percent priests and temple workers) recanted and 'sent them away, both the women and the children' (10.3, 44), if only to remain members of a community now closed, not only on religious but also ethnic grounds.

6. Identity Markers

In imperial iconography (from Egyptian to Assyrian and Persian), the various subject populations were portrayed with distinctive garments and hairstyles. In Assyrian reliefs, which are the most precise, one can distinguish a Judean/Israelite from a Philistine, a Syrian or an Arab. In the 'babel' of exile, the Judeans were instantly recognizable by these external characteristics. However real these were, national self-identification was perhaps based on less obvious but more important aspects: cooking customs, circumcision, Sabbath observance (and yearly festivities), differences in religious and funerary practices. During the exile period, having lost national political autonomy, all these elements acquired greater importance in corporate self-identification. Also in a negative sense, a rejection of certain things that are 'not done in Israel' (Judg. 19.30; 2 Sam. 13.12) served to define the invisible border (so important in a mixed multi-ethic environment) created by different ethical codes of behaviour that usually distinguish 'us', correct and decent people, from the immoral and deviant 'them'.

Circumcision, although not an exclusive mark, was considered an explicit sign of devotion to Yahweh. Its founding myth relates it to Abraham's covenant (Gen. 17.10-14), perhaps acknowledging the widespread practice of this custom by non-Israelites as well. Various passages include among the circumcised the peoples of Transjordan, Arabs and Egyptians. However in these other populations, circumcision was simply an external mark, without the religious meaning thought to adhere exclusively to the Israelites, circumcised not only in the flesh, but also in their hearts (Gen. 9.24-25; see also Deut. 10.16; 30.6). Circumcision was therefore necessary and sufficient, for cohabiting strangers, such as slaves or alien residents (Ezek. 12.43-48), and, following a more open-minded school of thought, even for foreign husbands, as in the story of Dinah and Shechem (Genesis 34). It is in exile that the custom became a distinctive mark (Babylonians, Elamites and Persians were not circumcised) and also gained a religious symbolic significance that ensured its persistence, while it progressively became less used among the other peoples.

Sabbath observance became equally fundamental – a distinctive custom not only due to a different calendar from other people, but above all for the rigid ban on any work (*šabbāt* means 'cessation of all activity'). Its mythical foundation went back even to the creation of the world (Gen. 2.2-3; see Exod. 20.11); it is also linked (through the number seven) to traditional sayings ('for six days...but on the seventh'), and had been adopted in Israel from an early period (it is already mentioned in the Decalogue and in the Book of the Covenant). In exile it may have been influenced by the Babylonian calendar, which often considered the quarter-moon days (7th, 14th, 21st and 28th) of the lunar month as unlucky for all activities. The importance of the Sabbath, however, was certainly not intended to be merely negative (a ban on all work) but above all socially positive, enshrining the right to rest, even for slaves, after a week of work, as well as in a religious sense (a time devoted to Yahweh). In exile, however, its importance increased, because this was the only festival that could be celebrated without need of a sanctuary; it was then that it became a distinctive religious rite over and above a well-deserved day of rest.

Its strict observance, however, conflicted with economic and professional interests, as well as the need to buy supplies and sometime to defend oneself: both praise and criticism can be found in the prophets:

> If you refrain from trampling the sabbath,
> from pursuing your own interests on my holy day;
> if you call the sabbath a delight
> and the holy day of Yahweh honourable;
> if you honour it, not going your own ways,

serving your own interests, or pursuing your own affairs;
then you shall take delight in Yahweh (Isa. 58.13-14).

Thus says Yahweh: For the sake of your lives, take care that you do not bear
a burden on the sabbath day or bring it in by the gates of Jerusalem. And do
not carry a burden out of your houses on the sabbath or do any work, but
keep the sabbath day holy, as I commanded your ancestors (Jer. 17.21-22).

Nehemiah ordered the city gates to be closed so as to compel people to observe the Sabbath (13.14-22), and in the words of the priestly legislation, breach of the Sabbath was punished by stoning to death (Num. 15.32-36; Exod. 31.14-15; 35.2-3).

The annual festivals also evolved during the exilic period and the return. In ancient times the Book of the Covenant scheduled three festivals, all agrarian, during which the people went and gathered (*ḥag*) at the sanctuaries; the festival of Unleavened Bread (*maṣṣōt*), another celebrating the cereal harvest (*qāṣîr*), and a third for the fruit harvest (*'āsîph*). These were part of the Canaanite calendar whose New Year fell in the autumn. In Deuteronomy the spring festival was called Passover *(pesaḥ)* and linked to the exodus from Egypt; the harvest festival was called 'Weeks' (*šābū'ôt*), and the fruit harvest was renamed 'booths' or 'tabernacles' *(sukkôt)*. With the exile and the adoption of the Babylonian calendar (with the new year at the spring equinox), the three festivities fell on the night of the full moon of the first month ('Passover', followed by a week of unleavened bread), 50 days later ('Weeks') and on the night of the full moon of the seventh month ('Booths'). Obviously, in returning to Judah all these great festivals (*ḥaggîm*) became centralized in Jerusalem. Other festivities, of great importance for Judaism would be introduced at a later date: 'Atonement' (*Kippurîm*), 'Dedication' (*Ḥănukkāh*), and 'Destinies' (*Pûrîm*).

7. Purity and Contamination

Regulations concerning diet and cult, based as they are on the idea of 'contamination' and 'impurity' (*ṭŭmĕ'āh*, adjective *ṭāmē'*), deserve separate treatment. They are correlated variously with the concept of 'holiness' (*qōdeš*). The basic criteria appear to be the need to keep different elements separate and distinct: contamination (as in the case of simple dirt) is the improper adhesion of matter that is extraneous, or has become so. The issue of culinary taboos may appear unimportant, but these are significant because they represent an attempt to organize cooking customs in an overall rational system, following general principles. The better-known rules for slaughtering and cooking animals are the ban on cooking a kid in its mother's milk (Deut. 14.21; Exod. 23.19; 34.26), and eating meat with the blood (Deut. 12.16). Complex concepts are obviously involved here too, ranging from the opposition solid/liquid to the moral issue of life/death.

The complex taxonomy of edible and non-edible animals was inspired by the presence together of elements that on principle should be kept separate. Hence ruminants were pure (and so edible) if they had cloven hooves (corresponding to the ideal image of a ruminant), but impure if they had whole hooves like camels, or were non-ruminants with cloven hooves like pigs (Lev. 11.3-8; Deut. 14.3-8). Typical fish with fins and scales were edible, but animals similar to fish yet without fins and scales were not. Animals that fly but have four legs were impure, with the exception of locusts (Lev. 11.20-23). Four-footed animals that normally walk with their bellies off the ground are pure: but if they crawled they were impure (Lev. 11.29-30; 41-42), and so on. Practical agricultural techniques or customs were reinterpreted according to purity/contamination criteria; hence the ban on yoking together an ox and a donkey (Deut. 22.5), or growing different plants in the same field (Deut. 22.9). As for human social customs, men were forbidden to wear women's clothes and *vice versa* (Deut. 22.5); and even textiles of wool and linen mixed were forbidden (Deut. 22.11).

Similar principles and analogies regulated purity rules in the realm of physiology too: contact with internal body liquids (sperm, blood, saliva) made one impure, and this applied to both normal and abnormal emissions as well as all sexual practices (both legitimate and illegitimate). Hygienic rules dictated by experience (contact with corpses or persons with contagious diseases) became ritual taboos: those who touched impurity became themselves impure (though sometimes only 'until that evening'). Precautions against leprosy (Leviticus 13–14) and other skin diseases were considered as important as those protecting one from totally imaginary taxonomic impurities. Only water, among all the liquids, did not contaminate; on the contrary, it purified, and contamination was removed by repeatedly washing the person, the clothes and anything involved or exposed to contact.

What was taboo for humans could, on the other hand, be acceptable for the divinity: drinking blood was forbidden (Lev. 7.26), but it was poured in libation on the altar (Lev. 1.5; 7.2); eating fat was forbidden (Lev. 7.22-25), but it was burned on the altar (Lev. 3.3-5; 7.3-5). This introduces a major criterion of separation between the human and divine sphere. The divine sphere was certainly *per se* positive, however it could not be the object of any form of human contact (even visual, from a distance): a human would be contaminated. Between the sacred sphere and the normal human world stood the priest, protecting humans from contact with the holy (Num. 18.1-7); he was obliged to undergo a solemn investiture (Leviticus 8–9) and even more strict purity procedures (Leviticus 21) not only when performing the cult but even before that, in the selection of priests. Physical imperfections, whether congenital or resulting from physical injury (such as broken bones, Lev. 21.19) barred men from the priesthood; and sins, whether personal or by relatives, led to terrible punishment (Lev. 21.9).

These purity criteria, including the provisions for exclusion or punishment, and for re-acceptance, were a very powerful instrument for controlling the entire community. It is no coincidence that the rules on impurity and holiness increased in number, detail and severity during the post-exilic period, when the community, deprived of civil leadership, survived through its solidarity with the temple and the vindictive and inaccessible God who lived there.

8. *Proselytism or Exclusivity*

Having returned from exile, pure and extremely careful to avoid contamination, the returnees found themselves in a country, Palestine, widely contaminated by people, practices, divinities and cults that were impure. The 'people' were idolaters whose behaviour observed no purity rules. The 'Canaanite' cults involved scandalous fertility rituals, with abominable sexual practices (the 'sacred prostitution' of both men and women) and sacrifices of the newborn (the so-called *mōlek* practised in the *tōfet*). Care for the dead involved dangerous contact with the world of death. Direct access to the divine through necromancy, possession and divination, was forbidden by a fundamental injunction (Exod. 22.17; Lev. 20.6, etc.) but was also reprehensible in the manner in which it was practised. The iconic representations of the divinity themselves transformed into a material object (made by a human being) what was meant to be inaccessible and unknowable. Contamination was so widespread that the land itself had to be considered defiled.

An overall purification was necessary, through holy wars and the *ḥērem*: all alien populations were to be eliminated, as well as all idolatrous cults. Deuteronomy's 'rules of war' clearly express the difference between external wars, to which the customs of selective massacre common to the ancient Near East applied, and the wars against Canaanites that required a generalized massacre:

When you draw near to a town to fight against it, offer it terms of peace. If it accepts your terms of peace and surrenders to you, then all the people in it shall serve you at forced labour. If it does not submit to you peacefully, but makes war against you, then you shall besiege it; and when Yahweh your God gives it into your hand, you shall put all its males to the sword. You may, however, take as your booty the women, the children, livestock, and everything else in the town, all its spoil. You may enjoy the spoil of your enemies, which Yahweh your God has given you. Thus you shall treat all the towns that are very far from you... But as for the towns of these peoples that Yahweh your God is giving you as an inheritance, you must not let anything that breathes remain alive. You shall annihilate them – the Hittites and the Amorites, the Canaanites and the Perizzites, the Hivites and the Jebusites – just as Yahweh your God has commanded, so that they may not teach you to do all the abhorrent things that they do for their gods, and you thus sin against Yahweh your God. (Deut. 20.10-18).

In practice, as we have already seen (§§14, 2-4), this radical elimination took place only 'historiographically', with imaginary populations, while the real population survived alongside and within the Judean community. The eradication of Canaanite cults (the destruction of the *bāmôt* with their *'ăšērôt)* was rewritten as a process that involved repeated unsuccessful attempts, a persistent habit that unfortunately proved impossible to eradicate.

With neighbouring populations, relationships of total exclusion or partial acceptance (so long as the minimum requirements of accepting Yahwism were met) were developed With non-Israelite residents relations were necessary for the organization of society. There were also foreigners passing through, or even permanently residing there, such as the Phoenician merchants with their financial strength (Neh. 13.15-16), whose separate status was acknowledged on condition they did not contaminate the Judean community with egregiously different practices. But there were also foreigners who were well-integrated, albeit socially alienated and economically subordinate, whose work was vital. The category of the *gēr*, 'alien resident' of foreign origin was used, designating people with a free status (unlike foreign slaves) but dislocated and accommodated within Israelite families for their working activities. The status of *tôšab* 'resident', often in the pairing *gēr wĕtôšab* was similar: it appears to be a more generic word but is basically a synonym. The problem of integrating these people was recurrent, and various forms of assimilation were permitted; for example they could celebrate Passover if circumcised (Exod. 12.48-49) and could offer sacrifices. The times during which Abraham had been a *gēr* in Hebron (Gen. 23.4), Moses in Midian (Exod. 2.22) or the whole of Israel in Egypt

(Exod. 22.20; 23.9) were recalled to encourage a reasonable benevolence. Although not permitted to own land, they were allowed to glean the harvest (Lev. 19.9-10; 23.22; Deut. 24.19-21; and the story of Ruth); in this they are compared to widows and orphans as a class in need of charity and protection:

> (Yahweh) who executes justice for the orphan and the widow, and who loves the strangers, providing them food and clothing. You shall also love the stranger, for you were strangers in the land of Egypt (Deut. 10.18-19).

Their complete assimilation was also considered or hoped for, in particular in Ezekiel's vision of a future Israel, in which foreign residents would have access to land ownership:

> So you shall divide this land among you according to the tribes of Israel. You shall allot it as an inheritance for yourselves and for the aliens who reside among you and have begotten children among you. They shall be to you as citizens of Israel; with you they shall be allotted an inheritance among the tribes of Israel. In whatever tribe aliens reside, there you shall assign them their inheritance, says the Lord Yahweh (Ezek. 47.21-23).

On a more strictly religious level, even Second Isaiah openly declared his approval of acceptance – for the greater glory of God and to enlarge his kingdom – not only of the 'resident' (*gēr*), but also of the 'enemy/foreigner' (*nokrî*) and the 'nations' (*gôyîm*) (Isa. 42.1-6; 45.14-17, 20-25; 49.6; 55.3-5; 60).

As well as the issue of mixed marriages, the question of equal rights was central to the general strategic choice facing the Judean community: between an exclusive religion or proselytism (*gēr* is translated as *proselytos* by the LXX). A couple of generations after Ezekiel, Third Isaiah became the champion of proselytism: foreigners also attended the temple in Jerusalem (Isa. 56.7-19) and helped to build it (Isa. 56.10); foreigners and eunuchs were warmly welcomed (Isa. 56.3-7). This strategic dilemma, with its roots in the exile and return, would be passed on to Judaism and Christianity. While the more realistic and political strategy of 'closing' the community was in the medium term victorious, the more ambitious and utopian strategy of universal openness left a messages of high and everlasting spiritual value:

> I will appoint Peace as your overseer
> and Righteousness as your taskmaster.
> Violence shall no more be heard in your land,
> devastation or destruction within your borders; (Isa. 60.17-18)

they shall beat their swords into ploughshares,
and their spears into pruning hooks;
nation shall not lift up sword against nation,
neither shall they learn war any more;
but they shall all sit under their own vines and under their own fig trees,
and no one shall make them afraid;
for the mouth of Yahweh of hosts has spoken (Mic. 4.3-4).

EPILOGUE

Chapter 19

LOCAL HISTORY AND UNIVERSAL VALUES

1. *The Fourth-Century Scenario: The 'Second Temple' and the Diaspora*

Just as it proved difficult to set a date for the beginning of this ancient history of Israel, it is equally difficult to establish a final date. This history is not contained between two dates, or two events, but rather between two processes, each lasting a given period of time. The process involving so-called 'ethnogenesis' began with the invasion of the 'Sea Peoples' in about 1180 and lasted for a couple of centuries, though it was rooted in the socioeconomic and political situation of the Late Bronze Age. The beginning of the twelfth century as the crucial turning point and founding moment, not only for the kingdoms of Judah and Israel but for all Levantine political formations at the beginning of the Iron Age seems therefore reasonable as well as widely shared choice.

Taking the early-fourth century – let us use 398 as a symbolic date – as the final date for our history requires more explanation. Ezra's mission (which can be precisely dated to 398, despite a number of problems) represents another appropriate turning point, the beginning of Judaism. The finalization of the drafting of the Law, the end of prophetism, the end of Deuteronomistic historiography, the rise to power of the priesthood in Jerusalem, national self-identification based on religion rather than politics – these are all interlinked phenomena, which were to develop and continue at least until the destruction of the 'second temple' in 71 CE. This additional half-millennium of history obviously deserves another book, a different approach and another author. It is a period entirely characterized by relations between the Temple and the Diaspora, and totally unlike the era of monarchic autonomy to which the earlier events belong. Incidentally, the divine promise to Abraham to multiply greatly the people of Israel and spread them all over the world was achieved not through victory and independence, as vaguely indicated by the author of the promise, but on the contrary, through defeat, dispersion and imperial submission. The ferment of ideological creativity that characterized the Persian era, and which would result in Judaism, derived mainly from the long experience of imperial domination (from the Assyrians onwards), of deportations, and of (attempted) political de-culturation.

Would it not therefore have been simpler and more accurate to bring the book to an end with the 70 years of Babylonian exile, leaving the whole of the early post-exilic phase to be linked to what followed, rather than what came previously – and thus adopt the traditional periodization of 'first temple' and 'second temple'? I did not find this acceptable, both for historical reasons and, even more basically, for historiographical ones. The entire ideological process of the Persian era had a retrospective character, referring to previous events while simultaneously providing them with a meaning – certainly an additional meaning, yet one that became an integral and indispensable part of those events.

If it is legitimate, indeed necessary, to have the history of Judaism beginning with the exile, it is equally legitimate and necessary to end Israel's historical events with their post-exilic ideological re-elaboration. Like a two-faced Janus, that re-elaboration looks simultaneously backwards and forwards, and is an integral and fundamental part of the preceding as well as the subsequent events.

2. The Great Caesuras

The historical caesuras we have chosen as most suitable for delimiting Israel's history must be compared to other more widespread caesuras in the history of the ancient Near East. The periodization chosen for Israel will probably prove all the more correct in that it fits in with a general analysis of the entire area within which that particular history occurred. History in general, and especially ancient history, is marked by similar caesuras that become clearly (including archaeologically) visible, resulting from crucial demographic and settlement changes, as well as technological innovation, but also involving elements of socioeconomic and socio-political adaptation as well as cultural change. These are crisis periods, separating longer lapses of time that show more uniform and progressive change, the slow but secure growth of population and economic resources, greater stability in territorial occupation by human communities, and relatively less traumatic relations between social groups and among individuals.

The first caesura is clear-cut and well known: that which put an end to the Syrian-Palestinian society of the Late Bronze Age at the beginning of the twelfth century. This caesura, which, as we have seen (§2.1), can be analyzed into various ideological and material elements, embraced the entire eastern Mediterranean and most of the Near East, and was profound enough to mark the transition from the Bronze to the Iron Age, two periods that, quite apart from their nineteenth-century technologically-based labels, took distinctively different shapes. The existence of this caesura is widely accepted: there is no account of ancient oriental history that does not use it as a division marker. For Israel it indicates the beginning of our 'normal history': Israel's so-called 'ethnogenesis' takes place precisely at the end of that crisis, at the same time as the similar ethnogenesis of neighbouring populations.

The second caesura, closing the trajectory of 'normal history', is, by contrast, not so commonly acknowledged in history books of the ancient Orient. The sixth-century crisis is as it were obscured by the imposition of a political scheme on the events, following the ancient device of 'succession of empires' – Babylonia succeeding Assyria and then Persia succeeding Babylonia. And yet it would be enough simply to analyze, as we customarily do in proto-historical situations like the previous caesura, the demographic-settlement picture in order to see immediately the signs of a crisis, if not of a real and proper collapse. The catalyst here was different from that in the previous crisis (deportation instead of invasion), but the level of human suffering, if quantifiable, must have been similar if not greater. The demographic collapse and settlement crisis are not merely signs of something else: they are in themselves significant historical phenomena. In the case of the sixth century, they are accompanied by a complete reorganization of sociopolitical relations and religious and cultural concepts, resulting in a crisis as important as that which brought the Bronze Age to an end. I have used (§10-1) the concept 'axial age' to allude to the many innovations in the religious and political fields marking this caesura.

The first caesura was effective above all in the sectors of technological innovation, settlement organization and ethno-political configuration and in fact resulted in the 'ethno-genesis' and subsequent 'normal history'. The second caesura was effective most of all in the ideological sector, and thus resulted in the creation of ethical monotheism, historiographical revision, Law and Prophets; in a word, invented history. The more general Near Eastern historical context thus seems to give support and plausibility to the periodization and the characterization that we have adopted for ancient Israel.

3. *The Historiographical Debate*

It would not be possible or appropriate here to review the history of the last century of scholarship on Israel's ancient history. An adequate account of the various trends – or even of current positions – would require a whole new book. Several such reviews have in fact already been provided. However, it is useful to at least suggest how the idea of the 'two-faced Janus' can help to eliminate to some extent the historiographical stalemate that has come about as a result of more decisive positions in current scholarship.

On one hand the traditionalist approach, both reluctant and unable to renounce the historical re-elaboration created by the Judean intellectual elite during the exile and post-exilic period as an integral and indispensable basis for interpreting the history of the pre-exilic eras, ends up by denying in effect the very substance (although not the technical details) of the modern critical approach. All traditional histories of ancient Israel adopt (as mentioned in the Introduction) this 'biblical' scheme, even when pretending, or assuming, to have received the results of historical criticism. Hence, all such books have a chapter on the Patriarchs, perhaps in order to deny their historicity, yet unable to renounce 'the patriarchal period' (be it legendary or historical) as a setting for the beginning of Israel's history. They all have chapters about the exodus and Moses, perhaps to state the lateness of the traditions, but still without taking the fundamental step of placing their analysis in the period where their composition belongs. Obviously all these books have a chapter about the conquest, perhaps to debate its nature in the light of archaeology. And then they all have a Judges period and a United Monarchy period. In doing this, and thus accepting and endorsing all the themes of the Persian period's historiographical re-elaboration as the only ones capable of making sense of earlier historical events, the traditional approach ignores profounder lessons of historical criticism.

On the other hand, the most recent critical approach, especially in respect of the utopian-retrospective characteristics of the United Monarchy, drastically refuses to accept the late re-elaborations as authentic sources, finding itself with a history of pre-exile Israel so impoverished that it becomes reasonable to ask whether it is possible to write a history of ancient Israel at all. If the events of the tiny kingdoms of Judah and Israel have no greater value or evidence than those of the contemporary kingdoms of Carchemish or Hamath, of Sidon or Moab or Gaza, then all that remains is to write a history of Syria-Palestine in Iron Age II, a topic of interest only to specialists, to professional historians. Those who propose this appear not to consider sufficiently the fact that late elaborations usually impose modern ideological characteristics on what is ancient material. While taking for granted that the more obvious and safer method aims at recovering the ideologies of the authors, the historian still has the duty to investigate what, if anything, has remained of that ancient information, and through which channels and with which distortions their transmission and re-elaboration took place.

The greater the temporal distance between an event and its historical re-elaboration, the greater the need to investigate and identify the basic links and analyze these case by case. It may be that in some cases (perhaps in many cases) the investigation will have a negative result, concluding that the event never took place, is pure invention, or has been so distorted as to be considered falsified. In other cases, however, it is possible to find such a link, to manage to read – as in a palimpsest – the ancient event underlying the recreated one, as well as the original ideology under the re-elaborated one. This difficult but necessary work is part of a historian's task.

4. *From Trivial Event to Significant Re-elaboration*

If a historical analysis is organized in this way, it can only lead to a twofold reconstruction, as illustrated by the division of this book into two parts. The two parts, 'normal history' and 'invented history', should be read as supporting each other. The mistake (in my opinion) made by traditionalists consists in wanting to load 'normal history' with all the ideological values that pertain to the later re-elaboration, rendering it rather abnormal, anachronistic and 'unique'. The innovators' mistake or limitation consists rather in neglecting to what extent the later re-elaboration is rooted in the preceding events, thereby leaving the elaboration unexplained and the events insignificant.

The historian's legitimate and proper ambition is to connect these two parts, giving life to a historical trajectory that makes overall sense. 'Normal history' is not without ideological values, just as 'invented history' is not without real events and authentic references. On one hand the nearly thousand-year duration of the entire trajectory requires us to emphasize the drastic changes that occurred over the course of time; hence to differentiate the horizons of the Late Bronze age, of the Early Iron Age, the independent Levantine kingdoms of Iron Age II, the imperial intrusion with its repercussions and local resistance, the horizons of domination and dispersion and of reconstruction on new foundations and new values. On the other hand it is also true that one identifies certain trends that tenaciously resist the passing of time, starting with the imprinting provided by the pharaonic ideology and the social crisis of the Late Bronze era, to the later priestly elaborations.

There is a third scenario overlying the two scenarios of 'normal' and 'invented' history, that of the modern historical reconstruction, necessarily adding its own contribution, including a methodological approach (ranging from criticism of sources to the more overall meaning of historical processes), additional information (archaeological and epigraphical) unavailable to ancient re-elaborators, its own topics of interest (for example technological, demographic, anthropological and others), unavailable to the actors in those events. This third scenario is inevitable and normal in all historical work, true for any subject that might be chosen, and any conditions the historical product may have provided. This book was written between 2001 and 2002, by an author born in 1939, whose historical methodology was formed between 1965 and 1975. Things would be different if the dates were moved five or ten years in either direction.

But the book would, above all, be different if the subject did not say something today, not only to the author, but also to the readers it is written for – something connected with fundamental problems facing the individual conscience and the international community, problems of political coexistence, religious tolerance, ethnic interaction, socioeconomic choices and cultural traditions. Something different than what the same subject meant ten, or one hundred years ago (or to what it will mean in ten or one hundred years from now), and yet part of an ongoing process that should be (and must be) the object of historical analysis. The book therefore, here and there, I would say almost absent-mindedly, alludes to these problems, taking them for granted, considering them to be well known, but also terribly important.

BIBLIOGRAPHY

General Bibliography and Research Tools

Bibliography on the ancient history of Israel and on the Old Testament is immense, often repetitive and in most cases to be regarded as theological rather than historical in its subject and method. In the present bibliography I will generally restrict myself (apart from some indispensable works of reference), to works published in the last 25 years (where previous bibliography can easily be found).

Among the many histories of Israel, see in particular M. Noth, *History of Israel*, London: A. & C. Black, 1951; and J.A. Soggin, *An Introduction to the History of Ancient Israel*, London: SCM Press; Philadelphia: Westminster Press, 1993. Also useful are J.H. Hayes and J.M. Miller (eds.), *Israelite and Judean History*, London: SCM Press; Philadelphia: Westminster Press, 1994² [1977]; G.W. Ahlström, *The History of Ancient Palestine*, Sheffield: Sheffield Academic Press, 1993 (very traditional), *The World History of the Jewish People. First Series: Ancient Times*, II-IV, VIII, Tel Aviv-Jerusalem: Massada Press, 1970–1979; only on the origins, R. de Vaux, *The Early History of Israel*, I-II, London: Darton, Longman & Todd; Philadelphia: Westminster Press, 1978. On chronology, G. Galil, *The Chronology of the Kings of Israel and Judah*, Leiden: E.J. Brill, 1996. On the history of the ancient Near East, M. Liverani, *Antico Oriente. Storia, società, economia*, Rome: Laterza, 1988.

Among the works on the history of Israelite religion, see Y. Kaufmann, *The Religion of Israel: From the Beginnings to the Babylonian Exile*, Chicago: University of Chicago Press; London: Allen and Unwin, 1960 (very conservative); G. Fohrer, *History of Israelite Religion*, Nashville, TN: Abingdon Press, 1972; London: SPCK, 1973; J.H. Tigay, *You Shall Have No Other God: Israelite Religion in the Light of Hebrew Inscriptions*, Atlanta, GA: Scholars Press, 1986; R. Albertz, *A History of Israelite Religion in the Old Testament Period*, I-II, London: SCM Press, 1994. Also some biblical 'theologies' include useful historical parts, see in particular G. von Rad, *Old Testament Theology*, I-II, Edinburgh: Oliver & Boyd, 1962; W. Eichrodt, *Theology of the Old Testament*, I, London: SCM Press; Philadelphia: Westminster Press, 1961.

On institutions, R. de Vaux, *Ancient Israel: Its Life and Institutions*, London: Darton, Longman & Todd, 1961 is a useful reference work up to 1960. On society, see P.M. McNutt, *Reconstructing the Society of Ancient Israel*, Louisville, KY: Westminster/John Knox Press; London: SCM Press, 1999 (with a diachronic approach); R.E. Clements (ed.), *The World of Ancient Israel: Sociological, Anthropological and Political Perspectives*, Cambridge: Cambridge University Press, 1989 (with a synchronic approach). On material culture and family structures see now P.J. King and L.E. Stager, *Life in Biblical Israel*, Louisville, KY: Westminster/John Knox Press; London: SCM Press, 2001; see also O. Borowski, *Agriculture in Ancient Israel*, Winona Lake, IN: Eisenbrauns, 1987. For convenient references on institutions, places, and characters biblical encyclopedias can also be useful, such as D.N. Freedman (ed.), *The Anchor Bible Dictionary*, I-VI, New York: Doubleday, 1992; G.A. Buttrick (ed.), *The Interpreter's Dictionary of the Bible*, I-IV, Nashville, TN: Abingdon Press, 1962; G.W. Bromiley (ed.), *The International Standard Bible Encyclopaedia*, I-IV, Grand Rapids: Eerdmans, 1979–1988; *Suppléments au Dictionnaire de la Bible*, Paris: Letouzey et Ané, 1928–1996; *Encyclopaedia Judaica*, I-XVIII, Jerusalem: 1971–1982.

Manuals of Palestinian archaeology: Y. Aharoni, *The Archaeology of the Land of Israel*, London: SCM Press; Philadelphia: Westminster Press, 1982; H. Weippert, *Palästina in vorhellenistischer Zeit*, München: Beck, 1988; A. Mazar, *Archaeology of the Land of the Bible 10,000–586 B.C.E.*, New York: Doubleday, 1990; E. Stern, *Archaeology of the Land of the Bible. 2. The Assyrian, Babylonian and Persian Periods*, New York: Doubleday, 2001.

Architecture: F. Braemer, *L'architecture domestique du Levant à l'âge du fer*, Paris: Editions Recherche sur les civilisations, 1982; G.R.H. Wright, *Ancient Buildings in South Syria and Palestine*, I-II, Leiden: E.J. Brill, 1985; A. Kempinski and R. Reich (eds), *The Architecture of Ancient Israel from the Prehistoric to the Persian Periods*, Jerusalem: Israel Exploration Society, 1992.

Urbanism: Z. Herzog, *Archaeology of the City: Urban Planning in Ancient Israel and its Social Implications*, Tel Aviv: Emery and Claire Yass Archaeology Press, 1997; W.E. Aufrecht, N.A. Miran and S.W. Gauley (eds.), *Urbanism in Antiquity*, Sheffield: Sheffield Academic Press, 1997 (in particular the contributions by W.G. Dever, 172–93 and E. Ben Zvi, 194–209).

On single archaeological sites, see the respective entries in in E. Stern (ed.), *The New Encyclopedia of Archaeological Excavations in the Holy Land*, I-IV, New York and London: Simon & Schuster, 1993.

Ceramics: R. Amiran, *Ancient Pottery of the Holy Land*, New Brunswick: Rutgers University Press, 1969. Bullae: N. Avigad and B. Sass, *Corpus of West Semitic Stamp Seals*, Jerusalem: Israel Academy of Sciences and Humanities, 1997.

Historical geography: F.M. Abel, *Géographie de la Palestine*, I-II, Paris: Librarie Lecoffre, 1933–38 remains useful; more concisely, Y. Aharoni, *The Land of the Bible: A Historical Geography*, London: Burns & Oates, 1967 (for ancient periods), and M. Avi-Yonah, *A History of Israel and the Holy Land*, New York: Continuum, 2001–2003 (for later periods); very practical: M. du Buit, *Géographie de la Terre Sainte*, I-II, Paris: Editions du Cerf, 1958. On ancient cartography see S. Mittmann and G. Schmitt (eds.), *Tübinger Bibelatlas*, Stuttgart: Deutsche Bibelgesellschaft, 2001. For modern cartography, the *Survey of Israel 1:250.000* (in two sheets, ed. 1997), is more than enough for what we need. The many existing 'bible atlases' are often imprecise and too 'popular'; but see Y. Aharoni and M. Avi-Yonah, *The Carta Bible Atlas*, Jerusalem: Carta, 2002; more concise is H.G. May, *Oxford Bible Atlas*, Oxford: Oxford University Press, 1985.

Introductions to the Old Testament: O. Eissfeldt, *The Old Testament: An Introduction*, Oxford: Basil Blackwell, 1965; J.A. Soggin, *Introduction to the Old Testament*, London: SCM Press, 1989[3].

On any biblical books it is possible to find several commentaries, which I will not include in the following bibliography. On terminology it is always useful to consult the two excellent lexicons by G.J. Botterweck and H. Ringgren (eds.), *Theological Dictionary of the Old Testament*, I-XIII, Grand Rapids: Eerdmans, 1974–2004; E. Jenni and C. Westermann (eds.), *Theological Lexicon of the Old Testament*, I, Peabody, MA: Hendrickson, 1997. On personal names: R. Zadok, *The Pre-Hellenistic Israelite Anthroponymy and Prosopography*, Leuven: Peeters, 1988; J.D. Fowler, *Theophoric Personal Names in Ancient Hebrew*, Sheffield: Sheffield Academic Press, 1988.

Chapter 1. Palestine in the Late Bronze Age (Fourteenth–Thirteenth Centuries)

1. *Landscape and Resources.* (A) In general: Y. Karmon, *Israel: A Regional Geography*, Chichester: Wiley-Interscience, 1971; in a wider Near Eastern framework: J. Dresch, *La Méditerranée et le Moyen Orient. II. Le Moyen Orient arabe*, Paris: Presses universitaires de France, 1956; X. de Planhol, *Les fondements géographiques de l'histoire de l'Islam*, Paris: Flammarion, 1968 is still valid; but now there is P. Sanlaville, *Le Moyen-Orient arabe*, Paris: Armand Collin, 2000. Botany: M. Zohary, *Vegetation of Israel and Adjacent Areas*, Wiesbaden: Reichert, 1982. (B) On Late Bronze Age: J. Sapin, 'La géographie humaine de la Syrie-Palestine au deuxième millénaire av. J.C.', *JESHO* 24 (1981), 1-62 (25); (1982), 1-49, 113-86; M.B. Rowton, 'Dimorphic Structure and Topology', *OA* 15 (1976), 17-31.

2–3. *Geopolitical Fragmentation* and *Discontinuity of Settlements.* See A. Alt, 'Das Stützpunkysystem der Pharaonen an der phönikischen Küste und im syrischen Binnenland', in *KS*, III, 107-140; G. Buccellati, *Cities and Nations of Ancient Syria*, Rome: University of Rome, 1967; I. Finkelstein, 'The Territorial-Political System of Canaan in the Late Bronze Age', *UF* 28 (1996), 221-55.

4. *Egyptian Domination.* (A) Egyptian imperialism: B. Kemp, 'Imperialism and Empire in New Kingdom Egypt', in P. Garnsey and C. Whittaker (eds.), *Imperialism in the Ancient World*, Cambridge: Cambridge University Press, 1978, 7-57; P.J. Frandsen, 'Egyptian Imperialism', in M.T. Larsen (ed.), *Power and Propaganda*, Copenhagen: Akademisk Forlag, 1979, 167-90; J.M. Galan, *Victory and Border*, Hildesheim: Gerstenberg, 1995. On relations between Egypt and Levant: D.B. Redford, *Egypt, Canaan, and Israel in Ancient Times*, Princeton, NJ: Princeton University Press, 1992. (B) Economic aspects: S. Ahituv, 'Economic Factors in the Egyptian Conquest of Canaan', *IEJ* 28 (1978), 93-105; N. Na'aman, 'Economic Aspects of the Egyptian Occupation of Canaan', *IEJ* 31 (1981), 172-85. (C) Administrative organization: W. Helck, *Die Beziehungen Ägyptens zu Vorderasien*, Wiesbaden: Otto Harrassowitz, 1962, esp. 248-52; J.M. Weinstein, 'The Egyptian Empire in Palestine: A Reassessment', *BASOR* 241 (1981), 1-28; R. Hachmann, 'Die ägyptische Verwaltung in Syrien während der Amarnazeit', *ZDPV* 98 (1982), 17-49; W.J. Murnane, *The Road to Kadesh*, Chicago: University of Chicago, 1985, 3-23; M. Liverani, 'A Seasonal Pattern for the Amarna Letters', in T. Abusch, *et al.* (eds.), *Lingering over Words: Studies in Honor of W.L. Moran*, Atlanta, GA: Scholars Press, 1990, 337-48. 'Residencies': E.D. Oren, '"Governor's Residencies" in Canaan under the New Kingdom', *Journal of the Society for the Study of Egyptian*

Antiquities 14 (1984), 37-56. (D) Diachrony: M. Liverani, 'Ramesside Egypt in a Changing World', in *L'impero ramesside*, Rome: University of Rome La Sapienza, 1997, 101-115; M.G. Hazel, *Domination and Resistance: Egyptian Military Activity in the Southern Levant, ca. 1300–1185 BC*, Leiden: E.J. Brill, 1998.

5. *Egyptian Ideology*. See M. Liverani, 'Contrasti e confluenze di concezioni politiche nell'età di el-Amarna', *Revue d'Assyriologie* 61 (1967), 1-18; *idem*, 'Political Lexicon and Political Ideologies in the Amarna Letters', *Berytus* 31 (1983), 41-56; *idem*, 'Formule di auto-umiliazione nelle lettere di el-Amarna', in M.G. Angeli Bertinelli and L. Piccirilli (eds.), *Linguaggio e diplomazia*, Rome: Giorgio Bretschneider, 2001, 17-29. On 'great king': P. Artzi and A. Malamat, 'The Great King. A Preeminent Royal Title in Cuneiform Sources and the Bible', in M. Cohen, D.C. Snell and D.B. Weisberg (eds.), *The Tablet and the Scroll: Near Eastern Studies in Honor of William W. Hallo*, Bethesda: CDL Press, 1993, 28-38.

6. *The Palace and its Central Role*. See R. Gonen, 'Urban Canaan in the Late Bronze Period', *BASOR* 253 (1984), 61-73; M. Liverani, 'La royauté syrienne de l'âge du bronze récent', in P. Garelli (ed.), *Le palais et la royauté*, Paris: P. Geuthner, 1974, 329-56. Economic aspects: M. Heltzer, *The Internal Organization of the Kingdom of Ugarit*, Wiesbaden: Otto Harrassowitz, 1982; M. Liverani, 'Economia delle fattorie palatine ugaritiche', in *Dialoghi di Archeologia*, NS 1.2 (1979), 57-72. Demography: W.R. Garr, 'Population in Ancient Ugarit', *BASOR* 266 (1987), 31-43.

7. *Economic Prosperity and Commercial Exchanges*. See M. Liverani, 'Elementi "irrazionali" nel commercio amarniano', in *OA* 11 (1972), 297-317; C. Zaccagnini, *Production and Consumption in the Ancient Near East*, Budapest: Eötvös Loránd University, 1989; F. Pintore, *Il matrimonio interdinastico nel Vicino Oriente durante i secoli XV-XIII*, Rome: Istituto per l'Oriente, 1978; M. Heltzer and E. Lipiński (eds.), *Society and Economy in the Eastern Mediterranean, c. 1500–1000 B.C.*, Leuven: Peeters, 1988; N.H. Gale, *Bronze Age Trade in the Mediterranean*, Jonsered: P. Åströms förlag, 1991; M. Liverani, *Guerra e diplomazia nell'antico Oriente 1600–1100 a.C.*, Rome: Laterza, 1994.

8. *Villages and Collective Bodies*. See H. Reviv, 'On Urban Representative Institutions and Self-Government in Syria Palestine in the Second Half of the Second Millennium B.C.', *JESHO* 12 (1969), 283-97; M. Liverani, 'Communautés de village et palais royal dans la Syrie du IIème millénaire', *JESHO* 18 (1975), 146-64; *idem*, 'Ville et campagne dans le royaume d'Ugarit: essai d'analyse économique', in J.N. Postgate (ed.), *Societies and Languages of the Ancient Near East: Studies in Honour of I.M. Diakonoff*, Warminster: Aris & Phillips, 1982, 250-58; *idem*, 'The Role of the Village in Shaping the Ancient Near Eastern Rural Landscape', in L. Milano (ed.), *Landscapes Territories Frontiers and Horizons in the Ancient Near East*, I, Padova: Sargon, 2000, 37-47. On patriarchal sanctuaries: M. Liverani, 'Le chêne de Sherdanu', *VT* 27 (1977), 212-16.

9. *'External' Nomads*. See M. Weippert, 'Semitische Nomaden des zweiten Jahrtausend', *Bibl* 55 (1974), 265-80, 427-33. Suteans: M. Heltzer, *The Suteans*, Napoli: Istituto Uni-

versitario Orientale, 1981. Shasu: R. Giveon, *Les Bédouins Shosou des decuments égyptiens*, Leiden: E.J. Brill, 1971. Banu-Raham: M. Liverani, 'Un'ipotesi sul nome di Abramo', *Henoch* 1 (1979), 9-18. Topological factors: M.B. Rowton, 'The Topological Factor in the Habiru Problem', in *Studies in Honor of B. Landsberger*, Chicago: Oriental Institute, 1965, 375-87; *idem*, 'Dimorphic Structure and the Problem of the 'Apiru-'Ibrim', *JNES* 45 (1976), 13-20.

10. *Socioeconomic Tensions.* (A) Habiru: A. Alt, 'The Settlement of the Israelites in Palestine', in *Essays on Old Testament History and Religion*, Oxford: Basil Blackwell 1966, 135-69; G.E. Mendenhall, 'The Hebrew Conquest of Palestine', *BA* 25 (1962), 66-87; *idem*, *The Tenth Generation*, Baltimore: The Johns Hopkins University Press, 1973, 122-41; M. Liverani, 'Farsi Habiru', *Vicino Oriente* 2 (1979), 65-77; O. Loretz, *Habiru-Hebräer: Eine sozio-linguistische Studie über die Herkunft des Gentiliziums 'ibrî vom Appellativum Habiru*, Berlin: W. de Gruyter, 1984. (B) Riots and tensions: M. Liverani, 'Il fuoruscitismo in Siria nella tarda età del bronzo', *Rivista Storica Italiana* 77 (1965), 315-36; *idem*, 'Implicazioni sociali nella politica di Abdi-Ashirta di Amurru', *Rivista degli Studi Orientali* 40 (1965), 267-77; P. Artzi, ' "Vox populi" in the el-Amarna Tablets', *Revue d'Assyriologie* 58 (1964), 159-66; A. Altman, 'The Revolutions in Byblos and Amurru during the Amarna Period', in P. Artzi (ed.), *Bar-Ilan Studies in History*, Ramat Gan: Bar-Ilan University Press, 1978, 3-24; J.M. Halligan, 'The Role of the Peasant in the Amarna Period', in D.N. Friedman and D.F. Graf (eds.), *Palestine in Transition*, Sheffield: Almond Press, 1983, 15-24; M.L. Chaney, 'Ancient Palestinian Peasant Movements and the Formation of Premonarchic Israel', in D.N. Friedman and D.F. Graf (eds.), *Palestine in Transition*, Sheffield: Almond Press, 1983, 39-90.

Chapter 2. The Transition (Twelfth Century)

1. *A Multifactor Crisis.* (A) On biblical theory on settlement and its modern interpretation, the following surveys remain fundamental: J. Bright, *Early Israel in Recent History Writing*, London: SCM Press, 1956; M. Weippert, *The Settlement of the Israelite Tribes in Palestine*, London: SCM Press, 1971; and most of all A. Alt, 'The Settlement of the Israelites in Palestine', in *Essays on Old Testament History and Religion*, Oxford: Basil Blackwell, 1966, 135-69. (B) 'Sociological' theory: G.E. Mendenhall, 'The Hebrew Conquest of Palestine', *BA* 25 (1962), 66-87; N.K. Gottwald, *The Tribes of Yahweh: A Sociology of the Religion of Liberated Israel*, Sheffield: Sheffield Academic Press, 2nd edn, 1999 (Maryknoll, NY: Orbis Books, 1979); N.P. Lemche, *Early Israel*, Leiden: E.J. Brill, 1985. (C) For more recent approaches and debates: B. Halpern, *The Emergence of Israel in Canaan*, Chico, CA: Scholars Press, 1983; R. Coote and K.W. Whitelam, *The Emergence of Early Israel in Historical Perspective*, Sheffield: Almond Press, 1987; T.L. Thompson, *Early History of the Israelite People*, Leiden: E.J. Brill, 1992; S. Ahituv and E.D. Oren (eds.), *The Origin of Early Israel*, Beer-Sheva: Ben-Gurion University, 1998.

2. *Climatic Factors and Migrations.* (A) Climatic change: for a recent bibliographical survey, see P. Sanlaville, *Le Moyen-Orient arabe*, Paris: Armand Collin, 2000, 188-91; on the twelfth century, see J. Neumann and S. Parpola, 'Climatic Change and the Eleventh-Tenth-Century Eclipse of Assyria and Babylonia', *JNES* 46 (1987), 161-82. (B)

Invasion by 'Sea Peoples': A. Strobel, *Die spätbronzezeitliche Seevölkersturm*, Berlin: W. de Gruyter, 1976; B. Cifola, 'Ramses III and the Sea Peoples', *Orientalia* 57 (1988), 275-306; O. Margalit, *The Sea Peoples in the Bible*, Wiesbaden: Otto Harrassowitz, 1994; O. Eliezer, *The Sea Peoples and their World: A Reassessment*, Philadelphia: University of Pennsylvania, 2000. (B) Philistines: T. Dothan, *The Philistines and their Material Culture*, New Haven: Yale University Press, 1982; *eadem*, 'Initial Philistine Settlement: From Migration to Coexistence', in S. Gitin, A. Mazar and E. Stern (eds.), *Mediterranean Peoples in Transition*, Jerusalem: Israel Exploration Society, 1998, 148-60; J.F. Brug, *A Literary and Archaeological Study of the Philistines*, Oxford: British Archaelogical Reports, 1985; I. Finkelstein, 'The Date of the Settlement of the Philistines in Canaan', *Tel Aviv* 22 (1995), 213-39; G. Garbini, *I Filistei: gli antagonisti di Israele*, Milano: Rusconi, 1997.

3. *The Collapse of the Regional System.* Regional system: M. Liverani, *Guerra e diplomazia nell'antico Oriente 1600–1100 a.C*, Rome: Laterza, 1994. Crisis: M. Liverani, 'The Collapse of the Near Eastern Regional System at the End of the Bronze Age: The Case of Syria', in M. Rowlands, M.T. Larsen and K. Kristiansen (eds.), *Centre and Periphery in the Ancient World*, Cambridge: Cambridge University Press, 1987, 66-73; J. Strange, 'The Transition from the Bronze Age to the Iron Age in the Eastern Mediterranean and the Emergence of the Israelite State', *SJOT* 1 (1987), 1-19.

4. *The Palace Crisis.* (A) Megiddo: D. Ussishkin, 'The Destruction of Megiddo at the End of the Late Bronze Age and its Historical Significance', *Tel Aviv* 22 (1955), 240-67; I. Finkelstein, 'The Stratigraphy and Chronology of Megiddo and Beth-Shan in the 12th–11th Centuries B.C.E.', *Tel Aviv* 23 (1996), 170-84. (B) Hazor: V. Fritz, 'Das Ende der spätbronzezeitlichen Stadt Hazor Stratum XIII und die biblische Überlieferung in Josua 11 und Richter 4', in *UF* 5 (1973), 123-38; A. Ben-Tor, 'The Fall of Canaanite Hazor', in S. Gitin, A. Mazar and E. Stern (eds.), *Mediterranean Peoples in Transition*, Jerusalem: Israel Exploration Society, 1998, 456-67; Ch. Schafer-Lichtenberger, 'Hazor: A City State between the Major Powers', *SJOT* 15 (2001), 104-122; D. Ben-Ami, 'The Iron Age I at Tel Hazor in Light of the Renewed Excavations', *IEJ* 51 (2001), 148-70.

5. *The Growth of the Tribal Element.* (A) Concept of nomadism: T.L. Thompson, 'Palestinian Pastoralism and Israel's Origins', *SJOT* 6 (1992), 1-13. (B) Merenptah Stele: H. Engel, 'Die Siegstele von Marnepta', *Bibl* 60 (1979), 373-99; L.E. Stager, 'Merenptah, Israel and the Sea People', *Eretz-Israel* 18 (1985), 56-64; G.W. Ahlström, *Who Were the Israelites?*, Winona Lake, IN: Eisenbrauns, 1986; J. Bimson, 'Merenptah's Israel and Recent Theories of Israel's Origins', *JSOT* 48 (1990), 3-19; N.P. Lemche, *The Canaanites and their Land*, Sheffield: Sheffield Academic Press, 1991. (C), Battle of Gibeon: B. Margalit, 'The Day the Sun Did Not Stand Still. A New Look at Joshua X 8-15', *VT* 42 (1992), 466-91.

6. *Technological Change.* (A) Iron: J.C. Waldbaum, *From Bronze to Iron*, Göteborg: Aström, 1978; T.A. Vertime and J.D. Muhly (eds.), *The Coming of the Age of Iron*, New Haven, CT: Yale University Press, 1980; P. McNutt, *The Forging of Israel: Iron Technology, Symbolism and Tradition*, Sheffield: JSOT Press, 1990. (B) Alphabet: B.E. Coless,

'The Proto-Alphabetic Inscriptions of Sinai', *Abr-Nahrain* 28 (1990), 1-52; *idem*, 'The Proto-Alphabetic Inscriptions of Canaan', *Abr-Nahrain* 29 (1991), 18-66; B. Sass, *Studia Alphabetica: On the Origin and Early History of the Northwest Semitic, South Semitic and Greek Alphabets*, Freiburg: Universitätsverlag; Göttingen: Vandenhoeck & Ruprecht, 1991. First abecedaries: A. Demsky, 'A Proto-Canaanite Abecedary Dating from the Period of the Judges and its Implications for the History of the Alphabet', *Tel Aviv* 4 (1977), 14-27; A. Lemaire, *Les écoles et la formation de la Bible dans l'ancien Israël*, Freiburg: Universitätsverlag; Göttingen: Vandenhoeck & Ruprecht, 1981. Further developments: S. Warner, 'The Alphabet: An Innovation and its Diffusion', *VT* 30 (1980), 81-90; I.M. Young, 'Israelite Literacy: Interpreting the Evidence', *VT* 48 (1998), 239-53, 408-22. (C) Pits and terraces: D.C. Hopkins, *The Highlands of Canaan*, Sheffield: Almond Press, 1985; S. Gibson and G. Edelstein, 'Investigating Jerusalem's Rural Landscape', *Levant* 17 (1985), 139-55; S. Gibson, 'Agricultural Terraces and Settlement Expansion in the Highlands of Early Iron Age Palestine', in A. Mazar (ed.), *Studies in the Archaeology of the Iron Age in Israel and Jordan*, Sheffield: Sheffield Academic Press, 2001, 113-46.

7. *Widened Horizons.* See several contributions in the collective volume by S. Gitin, A. Mazar and E. Stern (eds.), *Mediterranean Peoples in Transition, Thirteenth to Early Tenth Centuries* BCE, Jerusalem: Israel Exploration Society, 1998; and see also §4.1.

Chapter 3. The New Society (c. 1150–1050)

1. *Distribution of Settlements.* Synthesis by I. Finkelstein, *The Archaeology of the Israelite Settlement*, Jerusalem: Israel Exploration Society, 1988; V. Fritz, 'Die Landnahme der israelitischen Stämme in Kanaan', *ZDPV* 106 (1990), 63-77; *idem, Die Entstehung Israels im 12. und 11. Jahrhundert v.Chr.*, Stuttgart: W. Kohlhammer, 1996. On single regions. (A) Central highlands: I. Finkelstein, 'The Land of Ephraim Survey 1980–1987', in *Tel Aviv* 15-16 (1988–89), 117-83: I. Finkelstein, Z. Lederman and S. Bunimowitz, *Highlands of Many Cultures: The Southern Samaria Survey, the Sites*, Tel Aviv: Institute of Archaeology, 1997. (B) Galilee and Yezre'el: Z. Gal, 'The Late Bronze Age in Galilee: A Reassessment', *BASOR* 272 (1988), 79-84; *idem, Lower Galilee During the Iron Age*, Winona Lake, IN: Eisenbrauns, 1992. (C) Negev: R. Cohen, 'The Iron Age Fortresses in Central Negev', *BASOR* 236 (1980), 61-79; I. Finkelstein, 'The Iron Age "Fortresses" of the Negev Highlands: Sedentarization of the Nomads', *Tel Aviv* 11 (1984), 189-209; V. Fritz, 'Conquest or Settlement? The Settlement of Nomadic Tribes in the Negeb Highlands in the 11th Century B.C.', in M. Heltzer and E. Lipiński (eds.), *Society and Economy in the Eastern Mediterranean c. 1500–1000 BC*, Leuven: Peeters, 1988, 313-40; D. Jericke, *Die Landnahme im Negev*, Wiesbaden: Otto Harrassowitz, 1997; L.E. Axelsson, *The Lord Rose up from Seir: Studies in the History and Traditions of the Negev and Southern Judah*, Lund: Almqvist & Wiksell, 1987. (D) Transjordan: R.H. Dornemann, *The Archaeology of Transjordan in the Bronze and Iron Ages*, Milwaukee: Milwaukee Public Museum, 1983; J.A. Sauer, 'Transjordan in the Bronze and Iron Ages: A Critique of Glueck's Synthesis', *BASOR* 263 (1986), 1-26; R.G. Boling, *The Early Biblical Community in Transjordan*, Sheffield: Almond Press, 1988.

2. *Forms of Settlement.* Y. Shiloh, 'The Four-Room House. Its Situation and Function in the Israelite City', *IEJ* 20 (1970), 180-90; *idem*, 'Elements in the Development of Town Planning in the Israelite City', *IEJ* 28 (1978), 36-51; *idem*, 'The Casemate Wall, the Four Room House, and Early Planning in the Israelite City', *BASOR* 268 (1997), 3-15; Chang Ho Ji, 'A Note on the Iron Age Four-Room House in Palestine', in *Orientalia* 34 (1997), 381-413. Cult places: A. Zertal, 'An Early Iron Age Cultic Site on Mount Ebal', *Tel Aviv* 13-14 (1986–87), 105-165. Jars: M. Ibrahim, 'The Collared-Rim Jar of the Early Iron Age', in P.R.S. Moorey and P.J. Parr (eds.), *Archaeology in the Levant, Essays for K. Kenyon*, Warminster: Aris & Phillips, 1978, 116-27.

3. *The Ethnogenesis of 'Proto-Israelites'.* Ethnical identity of village settlers: I. Finkelstein, 'Ethnicity and Origin of the Iron I Settlers in the Highland of Canaan', *BA* 59 (1996), 198-212; *idem*, and N. Na'aman (eds.), *From Nomadism to Monarchy: Archaeological and Historical Aspects of Early Israel*, Jerusalem: Israel Exploration Society, 1994; E. Bloch-Smith and B.A. Nakhai, 'A Landscape Comes to Life: The Iron Age I', *BA* 62 (1999), 62-92, 101-127; U. Zwingenberger, *Dorfkultur der frühen Eisenzeit in Mittelpalästina*, Göttingen: Vandenhoeck & Ruprecht, 2001. Hypercritical approach: M. Skjeggestad, 'Ethnic Groups in Early Iron Age Palestine', *SJOT* 6 (1992), 159-86. More in general on the problem of ethnic identification: K.L. Sparks, *Ethnicity and Identity in Ancient Israel*, Winona Lake, IN: Eisenbrauns, 1998; S. Grosby, *Biblical Ideas of Nationality*, Winona Lake, IN: Eisenbrauns, 2002.

4. *The Dislocation of 'Tribes'.* (A) On this subject there is a rich bibliography; among others, see A. Alt, *Das System der Stammesgrenzen im Buche Josua* (1927), in *KS* I, 193-202; E. Cortese, *Josua 13–21. Ein priesterschriftlicher Abschnitt im deuteronomistischen Geschichtswerk*, Göttingen: Vandenhoeck & Ruprecht, 1990; Z. Kallai, 'The Twelve-Tribe Systems of Israel', *VT* 47 (1997), 53-90; J.-D. Macchi, *Israël et ses tribus selon Genèse 49*, Göttingen: Vandenhoeck & Ruprecht, 1999; cf. §15.5. (B) On single tribes: K.-D. Schunck, *Benjamin*, Berlin: W. de Gruyter, 1963; M. Ottosson, *Gilead: Tradition and History*, Lund: C.W.K. Gleerup, 1969; H.D. Neef, *Ephraim: Studien zur Geschichte des Stammes Ephraim*, Berlin: W. de Gruyter, 1995; U. Shorn, *Ruben and das System der zwölf Stämme Israels*, Berlin: W. de Gruyter, 1997; H. Donner, 'The Blessing of Issachar (Gen. 49:14-15), as a Source for the Early History of Israel', in *Le origini di Israele*, Rome: Accademia Nazionale dei Lincei, 1987, 53-63; N. Na'aman, 'The Inheritance of the Sons of Simeon', *ZDPV* 96 (1980), 136-52.

5. *Intertribal Solidarity.* Social and family structure: L.E. Stager, 'The Archaeology of Family in Ancient Israel', *BASOR* 260 (1985), 1-35; S. Bendor, *The Social Structure of Ancient Israel: The beit 'ab from the Settlement to the End of Monarchy*, Jerusalem: Simor, 1996; J.D. Schloen, *The House of the Father as Fact and Symbol*, Winona Lake, IN: Eisenbrauns, 2001. Tribal attitudes: see A. Ruwe, 'Das Zusammenwirken von "Gerichtsverhanlung", "Blutrache" und "Asyl"', *ZABR* 6 (2000), 190-221.

6. *Judicial Norms.* (A) A still fundamental study is A. Alt, 'The Origins of Israelite Law', in *Essays on Old Testament History and Religion*, Oxford: Basil Blackwell, 1966, 79-132. On the Decalogue, see also J.J. Stamm and M.E. Andrew, *The Ten Command-*

ments in New Research, London: SCM Press, 1967; E. Nielsen, *The Ten Commandments in New Perspective*, London: SCM Press, 1968; A. Phillips, *Ancient Israel's Criminal Law: A New Approach to the Decalogue*, Oxford: Oxford University Press, 1970; C. Levin, 'Der Dekalog aus Sinai', *VT* 35 (1985), 165-91; F.L. Hossfeld, *Der Dekalog. Seine späten Fassungen, die originale Komposition und seine Vorstufen*, Göttingen: Vandenhoeck & Ruprecht, 1982. (B) On the fifth commandment: M. Liverani, 'Onora il padre e la madre nei testi di Emar e Ugarit', *Storia e Dossier* 2.14 (1988), 22-26; on parents' care: E. Otto, 'Biblische Alterversorgung im altorientalischen Rechtsvergleich', *ZABR* 1 (1995), 83-110; M. Stol and S.V. Vleeming, *The Care of the Elderly in the Ancient Near East*, Leiden: E.J. Brill, 1998.

7. *Social Demands*. (A) On the Book of the Covenant: S.M. Paul, *Studies in the Book of the Covenant in the Light of Cuneiform and Biblical Law*, Leiden: E.J. Brill, 1970; J.M. Sprinkle, *The Book of the Covenant: A Literary Approach*, Sheffield: Sheffield Academic Press, 1994. (B) Release of 'Hebrew slaves': G.C. Chirichigno, *Debt-Slavery in Israel and the Ancient Near East*, Sheffield: Sheffield Academic Press, 1993; A. Schenker, 'The Biblical Legislation on the Release of Slaves', *JSOT* 78 (1998), 23-41; I. Cardellini, *Die biblischen 'Sklaven'-Gesetze im Lichte des keilschriftlichen Sklavenrechts*, Bonn: Hanstein, 1981 (omitting important aspects and parallels). Against Near Eastern parallels (and against '*ibrîm* as *ḫabiru*): A. Phillips, 'The Laws of Slavery: Exodus 21.2-11', *JSOT* 30 (1984), 51-66. (C) On religion in the formative period, see the classic essay of A. Alt, 'The God of the Fathers', in *Essays on Old Testament History and Religion*, Oxford: Basil Blackwell, 1966, 3-77; F.M. Cross, 'Yahweh and the Gods of the Patriarchs', *HTR* 55 (1962), 225-59; more recently W. Bluedorn, *Yahweh versus Baalism. A Theological Reading of the Gibeon-Abimelech Narrative*, Sheffield: Sheffield Academic Press, 2001; J. Tropper, 'Der Gottesname *Yahwa*', *VT* 51 (2001), 81-106.

8. *Urban Continuity and Canaanite-Philistine Symbiosis*. T. Dothan, 'Aspects of Egyptian and Philistine Presence in Canaan', in E. Lipiński (ed.), *The Land of Israel: Crossroad of Civilizations*, Leuven: Peeters, 1985, 55-75; S. Gitin and T. Dothan, 'The Rise and Fall of Ekron of the Philistines', *BA* 50 (1987), 197-222; A. Raban, 'The Philistines in the Western Jezreel Valley', *BASOR* 284 (1991), 17-27; B.J. Stone, 'The Philistines and Acculturation: Culture Change and Ethnic Continuity in the Iron Age', *BASOR* 298 (1995), 7-32; I. Finkelstein, 'The Philistine Countryside, *IEJ* 46 (1996), 225-42; C.S. Ehrlich, *The Philistines in Transition: A History from ca. 1000–730 BCE*, Leiden: E.J. Brill, 1996; S. Gitin, 'Philistia in Transition: The Tenth Century BCE and Beyond', in S. Gitin, A. Mazar and E. Stern, *Mediterranean Peoples in Transition*, Jerusalem: Israel Exploration Society, 1998, 162-82. Still important is A. Alt, 'Zur Geschichte von Beth-Sean 1500–1000 v.Chr.' in *KS*, I, 246-55; *idem*, 'Megiddo im Übergang vom kanaanäischen zum israelitischen Zeitalter' (1944), in *KS*, I, 256-73.

9. *The Permanence of Egyptian Presence*: M. Bietak, 'The Sea Peoples and the End of the Egyptian Administration in Canaan', in J. Aviram (ed.), *Biblical Archaeology Today 1990*, Jerusalem: Israel Exploration Society, 1993, 292-306; M.G. Hasel, *Domination and Resistance: Egyptian Military Activity in the Southern Levant, ca. 1300–1185 B.C.*, Leiden: E.J. Brill, 1998; J.M. Weinstein, 'Egyptian Relations with the Eastern Mediter-

ranean World at the End of the Second Millennium BCE', in S. Gitin, A. Mazar and
E. Stern (eds.), *Mediterranean Peoples in Transition,* Jerusalem: Israel Exploration
Society, 1998, 188-96. Cf. also O. Goldwasser, 'Hieratic Inscriptions from Tel Sera' in
Southern Canaan', *Tel Aviv* 11 (1984), 77-93.

10. *Ethnic States and City-States: Two Cultures.* M. Liverani, 'Dal "piccolo regno" alla
"città-stato"', in E. Acquaro (ed.), *Alle soglie della classicità: il Mediterraneo tra tra-
dizione e innovazione: studi in onore di Sabatino Moscati,* Pisa: Istituti editoriali e
poligrafici internazionali, 1996, 249-59; *idem,* 'Stati etnici e città-stato: una tipologia
storica per la prima età del ferro', in M. Molinos and A. Zifferero (eds.), *Primi popoli
d'Europa,* Firenze: Dipartamento d'Archeologia, Universitá degli Studi de Bologna,
2002, 33-47; A.H. Joffe, 'The Rise of Secondary States in the Iron Age Levant', *JESHO*
45 (2002), 425-67. On ethnicity, see §3.3. The two cultures: G. London, 'A Comparison
of Two Contemporaneous Lifestyles of the Late Second Millennium BC', *BASOR* 273
(1989), 37-55.

Chapter 4. The Formative Process (c. 1050-930)

On the 'formative' process: (A) B. Halpern, *The Constitution of the Monarchy,* Chico,
CA: Scholars Press, 1981; F. Frick, *The Formation of the State in Ancient Israel,* Shef-
field: Almond Press, 1985; I. Finkelstein, 'The Emergence of Monarchy in Israel. The
Environmental and Socio-Economic Aspects', *JSOT* 44 (1989), 43-74; *idem* and
N. Na'aman (eds.), *From Nomadism to Monarchy: Archaeological and Historical
Aspects of Early Israel,* Jerusalem: Israel Exploration Society, 1994 (with many important contributions and the historical syntesis by Na'aman); V. Fritz and P.R. Davies
(eds.), *The Origins of the Ancient Israelite States,* Sheffield: Sheffield Academic Press,
1996; D. Edelman (ed.), 'Toward a Consensus on the Emergence of Israel in Canaan',
SJOT 2 (1991); N.P. Lemche, 'The Origins of the Israelite State', *SJOT* 12 (1998), 44-
63; D. Master, 'State Formation Theory and the Kingdom of Israel', *JNES* 60 (2001),
117-31. (B) 'Low' archaeological chronology: I. Finkelstein, 'The Archaeology of the
United Monarchy: An Alternative View', in *Lev* 28 (1996), 177-87; see also *idem,*
'Hazor and the North in the Iron Age: A Low Chronology Perspective', *BASOR* 314
(1999), 55-70; A. Ben-Tor, 'Hazor and the Chronology of Northern Israel: A Reply to
I. Finkelstein', *BASOR* 317 (2000), 9-15; *idem* and D. Ben-Ami, 'Hazor and the
Archaeology of the Tenth Century BCE', *IEJ* 48 (1998), 1-37; D. Predsson, 'Jezreel: Its
Contribution to Iron Age Chronology', *SJOT* 12 (1998), 86-101; P. Bunimowitz and
A. Faust, 'Chronological Separation, Geographical Segregation, or Ethnic Demarcation?
Ethnography and the Iron Age Low Chronology', *BASOR* 322 (2001), 1-10.

1. *The Palestinian Mosaic in a Widened Horizon.* (A) On main peoples see §§5.4–5, 6.3.
Geshur: R. Arav and M. Bernett, 'The *bit hilani* at Bethsaida: Its Place in Aramaean/
Neo-Hittite and Israelite Palace Architecture in the Iron Age II', *IEJ* 50 (2000), 47-81.
(B) The widened horizon: Mediterranean navigation: S. Sherratt and A. Sherratt, 'The
Growth of the Mediterranean Economy in the Early First Millennium B.C.', *World
Archaeology* 24.3 (1993), 361-78. Early caravan routes: M. Liverani, 'Early Caravan
Trade between South Arabia and Mesopotamia', *Yemen* 1 (1993), 111-16; more gener-

ally, R.W. Bulliet, *The Camel and the Wheel*, Cambridge, MA: Harvard University Press, 1990. Ishmaelites: E.A. Knauf, *Ismael*, Wiesbaden: Otto Harrassowitz, 1989. Midianites: J. Sawyer and D. Clines (eds.), *Midian, Moab and Edom*, Sheffield: JSOT Press, 1983; E.A. Knauf, *Midian*, Wiesbaden: Otto Harrassowitz, 1988.

2. *The Central Highlands and the Role of Jerusalem and Shechem.* N. Na'aman, 'Canaanite Jerusalem and its Central Hill Country Neighbours in the Second Millennium B.C.', *UF* 24 (1992), 275-91; *idem*, 'The Contribution of the Amarna Letters to the Debate on Jerusalem's Political Position in the Tenth Century B.C.E.', *BASOR* 304 (1996), 17-27; H. Reviv, 'The Government of Shechem in the el-Amarna Period and in the Days of Abimelech', *IEJ* 16 (1966), 252-57; G.E. Wright, *Shechem: The Biography of a Biblical City*, New York: McGraw-Hill, 1965; J.A. Soggin, 'Il regno di Abimelek in Sichem (Giudici 9), e le istituzioni delle città-stato siro-palestinesi dei secoli XV-XI a.C.', in *Studi in onore di E. Volterra*, VI, Milano, n.p., 1973, 161-89; K. Jaroš, *Sichem*, Göttingen: Vandenhoeck & Ruprecht, 1976; J. Pitt-Rivers, *The Fate of Shechem or the Politics of Sex*, Cambridge: Cambridge University Press, 1977; E. Jans, *Abimelek und sein Königtum*, St Ottilien, n.p., 2001.

3. *The North: The Plain of Megiddo and Galilee.* (A) On royal domains see N. Na'aman, *Pharaonic Lands in the Jerzreel Valley*, in M. Heltzer and E. Lipiński (eds.), *Society and Economy in the Eastern Mediterranean, c. 1500–1000 B.C.*, Leuven: Peeters, 1988, 178-85. (B) Song of Deborah: G. Garbini, 'Il Cantico di Debora', *La Parola del Passato* 33 (1978), 5-31; B. Halpern, 'The Resourceful Israelite Historian: The Song of Deborah and Israelite Historiography', *HTR* 76 (1983), 379-402; A. Caquot, 'Les tribus d'Israël dans le cantique de Debora', *Semitica* 36 (1986), 47-70; C. Grottanelli, 'The Story of Deborah and Barak: A Comparative Approach', *Studi e Materiali di Storia delle Religioni* 53 (1987), 145-62; H.D. Neef, 'Der Sieg Deboras und Barak über Sisera', *ZAW* 101 (1989), 28-49; J.W. Watts, *Psalm and Story: Inset Hymns in Hebrew Narrative*, Sheffield: Sheffield Academic Press, 1992; J.C. de Moor, 'The Twelve Tribes in the Song of Deborah', *VT* 43 (1993), 483-93. Interesting contributions by L.E. Stager, 'Archaeology, Ecology, and Social History: Background Themes to the Song of Deborah', *VT* Suppl. 40 (1988), 221-34; *idem*, *The Song of Deborah*, *BAR* (1989), 51-64.

4. *The Centre: The 'Charismatic' Kingdom of Saul.* (A) D.M. Gunn, *The Fate of King Saul*, Sheffield: JSOT Press, 1980; H. Donner, *Die Verwerfung von König Saul*, Wiesbaden: Otto Harrassowitz, 1983; W.L. Humphries, 'From Tragic Hero to Villain: A Study of the Figure of Saul', *JSOT* 22 (1982), 95-117; T. Seidl, 'David statt Saul. Göttliche Legitimation und menschliche Kompetenz des Königs', *ZAW* 98 (1986), 39-56; G. Bettenzoli, 'Samuel und Saul in geschichtlicher und theologischer Auffassung', *ZAW* 98 (1986), 338-51; D.V. Edelman, *King Saul in the Historiography of Judah*, Sheffield: Sheffield Academic Press, 1991; K.D. Schunk, 'König Saul. Etappen seines Weges zum Aufbau eines israelitischen Staates', *BZ* 36 (1992), 195-206; K. van der Toorn, 'Saul and the Rise of Israelite State Religion', *VT* 43 (1993), 519-42; D.V. Edelman, 'Saul ben Kish in History and Tradition', in V. Fritz and P.R. Davies (eds.), *The Origins of the Ancient Israelite States*, Sheffield: Sheffield Academic Press, 1996, 142-59; W. Dietrich, *Die frühe Königszeit in Israel*, Stuttgart: W. Kohlhammer, 1997; S. Kreuzer, '"War Saul

auch unter den Philistern?" Die Anfänge des Konigtums in Israel', *ZAW* 113 (2001), 57-73. Legendary elements: C. Grottanelli, 'Possessione carismatica e razionalizzazione statale nella Bibbia ebraica', *Studi Storico-Religiosi* 1 (1977), 263-88; *idem*, *Sette storie bibliche*, Brescia: Paideia, 1998. 'Chiefdom' more than 'kingdom': J.W. Flanagan, 'Chiefs in Israel', *JSOT* 20 (1981), 47-73. (B) Towns related to Saul: D.G. Schley, *Shiloh: A Biblical City in Tradition and History*, Sheffield: Sheffield Academic Press, 1989; P.M. Arnold, *Gibeah, The Search for a Biblical City*, Sheffield: Sheffield Academic Press, 1990; K.D. Schunck, 'Erwägungen zur Geschichte und Bedeutung von Mahanaim', *Zeitschrift der deutschen morgenländischen Gesellschaft* 113 (1963), 34-40; J. Blenkinsopp, *Gibeon and Israel*, Cambridge: Cambridge University Press, 1972.

5. *The South: The Kingdom of David between Reality and Utopia*. (A) For a traditional vision, a still important study is A. Alt, 'The Formation of the Israelite State', in *Essays on Old Testament History and Religion*, 171-237; *idem*, '*Das Grossreich Davids'*, *KS*, 66-75. More recent synthesis: W. Dietrich, 'David in Überlieferung und Geschichte', *Verkundigung und Forschung* 22 (1977), 44-64; J.W. Flanagan, *Davids Social Drama: A Hologram of Israel's Early Iron Age*, Sheffield: Almond Press, 1988; T. Veijola, *David: Gesammelte Studien zu den Davidüberlieferungen des Alten Testaments*, Helsinki: Finnische Exegetische Gesellschaft, 1990; B. Halpern, 'The Construction of the Davidic State', in Fritz and Davies, *Origins*, (cited above), 44-75; N. Na'aman, 'Sources and Composition in the History of David', in Fritz and Davies, *Origins*, 170-86; K.L. Noll, *The Face of David*, Sheffield: Sheffield Academic Press, 1997. (B) On the dimensions of the kingdom, still maximalist A. Malamat, *Das davidische und solomonische Königreich*, Wien: Österreichischen Akademie der Wissenschaften, 1983; the reduction started with G. Garbini, 'L'impero di David', in *Annali della Scuola Normale Superiore di Pisa*, 3.13 (1983), 1-20. (C) Ascent: F. Langlamet, 'David et la maison de Saül', *RB* 86 (1979), 194-213, 385-436, 481-513; *RB* 87 (1980), 161-210; *RB* 88 (1981), 321-32. (D) Census and warrior list: N. Wyatt, 'David's Census and the Tripartite Theory', *VT* 40 (1990), 352-60; P. Särkiö, 'The Third Man – David's Heroes in 2 Sam 23,8-39', *SJOT* 7 (1993), 108-124. (E) Failed construction of the temple: P.B. Dirksen, 'Why Was David Disqualified as Temple Builder? The Message of 1 Chronicles 22.8', *JSOT* 70 (1996), 51-65; B.E. Kelly, 'David's Disqualification in 1 Chronicles 22.8', *JSOT* 80 (1998), 53-61.

6. *The Kingdom of Solomon, between Administration and Legend*: (A) D. Ussishkin, 'King Solomon's Palaces', *BA* 36 (1973), 78-105; thematic volume in *BASOR* 277/278 (1990); G.J. Wightman, 'The Myth of Solomon', *BASOR* 277 (1990), 5-22; A.R. Millard, 'Texts and Archaeology: Weighing the Evidence. The Case for King Solomon', *PEQ* 123 (1991), 19-27; J.M. Miller 'Solomon: International Potentate or Local King', *ibidem*, 28-31; V. Fritz, 'Monarchy and Re-urbanization: A New Look at Solomon's Kingdom', in Fritz and Davies, *Origins*, 187-95; J.K. Handy (ed.), *The Age of Solomon: Scholarship at the Turn of the Millennium*, Leiden: E.J. Brill, 1997 (a complete and well organized survey); G.N. Knoppers, 'The Vanishing Solomon: The Disappearance of the United Monarchy from Recent Histories of Ancient Israel', *JBL* 116 (1997), 19-44; H.M. Niemann, 'Megiddo and Solomon: A Biblical Investigation in Relation to Archaeology', *Tel Aviv* 27 (2000), 61-74. (B) Justice and wisdom: a good bibliography in K.I. Parker, 'Solomon as Philosopher King? The Nexus of Law and Wisdom in 1 Kings 1–11',

JSOT 53 (1992), 75-91; 'Solomonic Judgement': J. Lasine, 'The Riddle of Solomon's Judgement', *JSOT* 45 (1989), 61-86. Justice in Iron Age inscriptions: M. Liverani, 'Συδυκ η Μισωρ', in *Studi in onore di E. Volterra*, VI, Milano, 1971 (cited above), 55-74; H. Niehr, 'The Constitutive Principles of Establishing Justice and Order in Northwest Semitic Societies,' *ZABR* 3 (1997), 112-30. (C) Beginning of South-Arabian trade: M. Liverani, 'Early Caravan Trade between South-Arabia and Mesopotamia', *Yemen* 1 (1992), 111-15. Sea commerce: G. Bunnens, 'Commerce et diplomatie phéniciennes au temps de Hiram Ier', *JESHO* 19 (1976), 1-31. (D) Officers: T. Mettinger, *Solomonic State Officials*, Lund: C.W.K. Gleerup, 1971; E.W. Heaton, *Solomon's New Men: The Emergence of Ancient Israel as a National State*, London: Thames & Hudson, 1974; U. Rüterswörden, *Die Beamten der israelitischen Königszeit*, Stuttgart: W. Kohlhammer, 1985; N.S. Fox, *In the Service of the King: Officialdom in Ancient Israel und Judah*, Cincinnati: Hebrew Union College Press, 2000. (E) Egyptian influence: D.B. Redford, 'Studies in the Relations between Palestine and Egypt during the First Millennium B.C.', in *idem, Studies on the Ancient Palestinian World*, Toronto: University of Toronto Press, 1972, 141-56; P.S. Ash, *David, Solomon and Egypt: A Reassessment*, Sheffield: Sheffield Academic Press, 1999; B.U. Schipper, *Israel und Ägypten in der Königszeit*, Göttingen: Vandenhoeck & Ruprecht, 1999. (F) On the twelve districts: A. Alt, *Israels Gaue unter Salomo* (1913), in *KS*, II, 76-89; F. Pintore, 'I dodici intendenti di Salomone', *Rivista degli Studi Orientali* 45 (1970), 177-207; P.S. Ash, 'Solomon's? District? List', *JSOT* 67 (1995), 67-86.

7. *Sheshonq's Campaign*. K.A. Kitchen, *The Third Intermediate Period in Egypt*, Warminster: Aris & Phillips, 1973, 294-300, 432-37. For the reconstruction of the campaign, I follow Y. Aharoni. More recently: N. Na'aman, 'Israel, Edom and Egypt in the Tenth Century B.C.E.', *Tel Aviv* 19 (1992), 79-93; G. Ahlström, 'Pharaoh's Shoshenk's Campaign in Palestine', in A. Lemaire and B. Otzen (eds), *History and Traditions of Early Israel: Studies Presented to Eduard Nielsen*, Leiden: E.J. Brill, 1993, 1-16. Reductive: F. Clancy, 'Sheshonq's Travels', *JSOT* 86 (1999), 3-23. Most recently, I. Finkelstein, 'The Campaign of Sheshonq I to Palestine: A Guide to the 10th Century BCE Polity', *ZDPV* 118 (2002), 109-135.

Chapter 5. The Kingdom of Israel (c. 930–740)

1. *Uncertain Beginnings and Consolidation*. W.I. Toews, *Monarchy and Religious Institutions in Israel under Jeroboam I*, Atlanta, GA: Scholars Press, 1993. Historiographic condemnation of the 'secession': J. Debus, *Die Sünde Joroboams*, Göttingen: Vandenhoeck & Ruprecht, 1967; G.N. Knoppers, *Two Nations under God: the Deuteronomistic History of Solomon and the Dual Monarchies*, I-II, Atlanta, GA: Scholars Press, 1993–94.

2. *Samaria and the 'House of Omri'*. A. Alt, 'Der Stadtstaat Samaria', in *KS*, III, 258-302; S. Timm, *Die Dynastie Omri*, Göttingen: Vandenhoeck & Ruprecht, 1982.

3. *The Dynasty of Jehu*. B. Halpern, 'Yaua, Son of Omri, Yet Again', *BASOR* 265 (1987), 81-85; Y. Minokami, *Die Revolution des Jehu*, Göttingen: Vandenhoeck & Ruprecht, 1988; T.J. Schneider, 'Rethinking Jehu', *Biblica* 77 (1996), 101-107; N. Na'aman, 'Jehu Son of Omri: Legitimizing a Loyal Vassal by his Lord', *IEJ* 48 (1998), 236-38.

4. *Wars and Alliances within the Regional System.* (A) L.G. Herr, 'The Iron Age II Period: Emerging Nations', *BA* 60 (1997), 115-83; A. Faust, 'Ethnic Complexity in Northern Israel during the Iron Age II', *PEQ* 132 (2000), 2-27. (B) Phoenicians: H.J. Katzenstein, *The History of Tyre*, Beersheva: Ben Gurion University Press, revised 1997²; G. Garbini, *I Fenici. Storia e religione*, Napoli: Istituto Universitario Orientale, 1980; M.E. Aubet, *The Pheonicians and the West: Politics, Colonies and Trade*, Cambridge: Cambridge University Press,1994; F. Briquel-Chatonnet, *Les relations entre les cités de la côte phénicienne et les royaumes d'Israël et de Juda*, Leuven: Peeters, 1992. (C) Arameans: P.E. Dion, *Les Araméens à l'âge du fer*, Paris: Lecoffre, 1997; C.-J. Axskjöld, *Aram as the Enemy Friend*, Lund: C.W.K. Gleerup, 1998; E. Lipiński, *The Aramaeans*, Leuven: Peeters, 2000.

5. *The Aramean Hegemony.* (A) W. Pitard, 'The Identity of the Bir-Hadad of the Melqart Stela', *BASOR* 272 (1988), 3-21; I. Eph'al and J. Naveh, 'Hazael's Booty Inscriptions', *IEJ* 39 (1989), 192-200; A. Lemaire, 'Hazael de Damas, roi d'Aram', in D. Charpin and F. Joannès (eds.), *Marchands, diplomates et entrepreneurs. Etudes offertes à P. Garelli*, Paris: Éditions Recherche sur les civilisations, 1991, 91-108; W. Pitard, *Ancient Damascus*, Winona Lake, IN: Eisenbrauns, 1995; N. Na'aman, 'Rezin of Damascus and the Land of Gilead', *ZDPV* 111 (1995), 105-117; M. Weippert, 'Israélites, Araméens et Assyriens dans la Transjordanie septentrionale', *ZDPV* 113 (1997), 19-38; K.L. Noll, 'The God Who Is among the Danites', *JSOT* 80 (1998), 3-23. (B) Tel Dan Stela: A. Biran and J. Naveh, 'An Aramaic Stele Fragment from Tel Dan', *IEJ* 43 (1993), 81-98; *ibid.*, 'The Tel Dan Inscription: A New Fragment', *IEJ* 45 (1995), 1-18; W.M. Schniedewind, 'Tel Dan Stela: New Light on Aramaic and Jehu's Revolt', *BASOR* 302 (1996), 75-90; A. Lemaire, 'The Tel Dan Stela as a Piece of Royal Historiography', *JSOT* 81 (1998), 3-14; G. Galil, 'A Re-Assessment of the Fragments of the Tel Dan Inscription and the Relations between Israel and Aram', *PEQ* 133 (2001), 16-21. (C) Balaam: J. Hoftijzer and G. van der Kooij, *The Balaam Text from Deir Alla Re-Evaluated*, Leiden: E.J. Brill, 1991; S.C. Layton, 'Whence Comes Balaam? Num 22,5 Revisited', *Bibl* 73 (1992), 32-61; M. Dijkstra, 'Is Balaam also among the Prophets?', *JBL* 114 (1995), 43-64.

6. *Policy-making and Prophecy.* (A) Assyrian policy-making: I. Starr, *Queries to the Sungod: Divination and Politics in Sargonid Assyria*, Helsinki: Helsinki University Press 1990; B. Pongratz-Leisten, *Herrschaftswissen in Mesopotamien*, Helsinki: Neo-Assyrian Text Corpus Project, 1999; J. Pečirková, 'Divination and Politics in the Late Assyrian Empire', *Archiv Orientální* 53 (1985), 155-68; T. Abusch, 'Alaktu and Halakhah: Oracular Decision, Divine Revelation', *HTR* 80 (1987), 15-42. On political procedures, see also N.K. Gottwald, *The Politics of Ancient Israel*, Louisville, KY: Westminster/John Knox Press, 2001. (B) Near Eastern prophecy (esp. Assyrian): M. deJong Ellis, 'Observations on Mesopotamian Oracles and Prophecies', *JCS* 41 (1989), 127-186; J. Høgenhaven, 'Prophecy and Propaganda: Aspects of Political and Religious Reasoning in Israel and the Ancient Near East', *SJOT* 1 (1989), 125-41; J.-G. Heintz (ed.), *Oracles et prophéties dans l'antiquité*, Strasbourg: Centre de recherche sur le Proche-Orient et la Grèce antiques, 1997; M. Nissinen, *References to Prophecy in Neo-Assyrian Sources*, Helsinki: Neo-Assyrian Text Corpus Project, 1998. (C) Biblical prophecy: F.H. Cryer, *Divination in Ancient Israel and its Near Eastern Environment: A Socio-Historical*

Investigation, Sheffield: Sheffield Academic Press, 1994; J. Blenkinsopp, *Sage, Priest, Prophet: Religious and Intellectual Leadership in Ancient Israel*, Louisville, KY: Westminster/John Knox Press, 1995; *idem*, *A History of Prophecy in Israel*, Louisville, KY: Westminster/John Knox Press, 1996; L.L. Grabbe, *Priests, Prophets, Diviners, Sages: A Socio-Historical Study of Religious Specialists in Ancient Israel*, Valley Forge, PA: Trinity Press International, 1995; A. Laato, *History and Ideology in the Old Testament Prophetic Literature*, Stockholm: Almqvist & Wiksell, 1996; R.E. Clements, *Prophecy and Covenant*, London: SCM Press, 1965; *idem*, *Old Testament Prophecy: From Oracles to Canon*, Louisville, KY: Westminster/John Knox Press, 1996; H.M. Barstad, 'No Prophets? Recent Developments in Biblical Prophetic Research and Ancient Near Eastern Prophecy', *JSOT* 57 (1993), 39-60. (D) Amos: H.M. Barstad, *The Religious Polemics of Amos*, Leiden: E.J. Brill, 1984; D.U. Rottzoll, *Studien zur Redaktion und Komposition des Amosbuch*, Berlin: W. de Gruyter, 1996. (E) Elijah and Elisha: J.M. Miller, 'The Elisha Cycle and the Account of the Omride Wars', *JBL* 85 (1966), 441-54; L. Bronner, *The Stories of Elijah and Elisha*, Leiden: E.J. Brill, 1968; R.P. Carroll, 'The Elijah-Elisha Sagas', *VT* 19 (1969), 400-415; R.B. Coote (ed.), *Elijah and Elisha in Socioliterary Perspective*, Atlanta, GA: Scholars Press, 1992; W.J. Bergen, *Elisha and the End of Prophetism*, Sheffield: Sheffield Academic Press, 1999; M. Beck, *Elia und die Monolatrie*, Berlin: W. de Gruyter, 1999; N. Na'aman, 'Prophetic Stories as Sources for the Histories of Jehoshaphat and the Omrides', *Bibl* 78 (1997), 153-73; M. Roncace, 'Elisha and the Woman of Shunem', *JSOT* 91 (2000), 109-127.

7. *Religion: Baalism and Yahwism*. S. Dalley, 'Yahweh in Hamath in the 8th Century B.C.: Cuneiform Material and Historical Deductions', *VT* 40 (1990), 21-32; J.A. Emerton, 'The House of Baal in 1 Kings XVI 32', *VT* 47 (1997), 293-300; M. Gleis, *Die Bamah*, Berlin: W. de Gruyter, 1997.

8. *City-building, Architecture, Crafts*. (A) Urbanization: I. Finkelstein, 'Omride Architecture', *ZDPV* 116 (2000), 114-138; A. Faust, 'Socioeconomic Stratification in an Israelite City: Hazor VI as a Test Case', *Levant* 31 (1999), 179-90; H. Williamson, 'Tel Jezreel and the Dynasty of Omri', *PEQ* 128 (1996), 41-51; T.L. McClellan, 'Town Planning at Tell en-Nasbeh', *ZDPV* 100 (1984), 53-69. Pre-Omride Samaria: L.E. Stager, 'Shemer's Estate', *BASOR* 277 (1990), 93-107. (B) Settlement: M. Broshi and I. Finkelstein, 'The Population of Palestine in Iron Age II', *BASOR* 287 (1992), 47-60; A. Zertal, 'The Heart of the Monarchy: Patterns of Settlement and Historical Considerations of the Israelite Kingdom of Samaria,' in A. Mazar (ed.), *Studies in the Archaeology of the Iron Age in Israel and Jordan*, Sheffield: Sheffield Academic Press, 2001, 38-64.

9. *Administration and Economy*. A. Faust, 'The Rural Community in Ancient Israel during Iron Age II', *BASOR* 317 (2000), 17-39. Social polemics of the prophets: B. Lang, 'The Social Organization of Peasant Poverty in Biblical Israel', *JSOT* 24 (1982), 47-63; J.A. Dearman, *Property Rights in the Eighth-Century Prophets*, Atlanta, GA: Scholars Press, 1988. Samaria Ostraca: A.F. Rainey, 'Toward a Precise Date for the Samaria Ostraca', *BASOR* 272 (1988), 69-74. Crisis: S. Lasine, 'Jehoram and the Cannibal Mothers', *JSOT* 50 (1991), 27-53.

Chapter 6. *The Kingdom of Judah (c. 930-720)*

1. *The 'House of David'.* N. Na'aman, 'Azariah of Judah and Jeroboam II of Israel', *VT* 43 (1993), 227-34; G.N. Knoppers, 'Reform and Regression: The Chronicler's Presentation of Jehoshaphat', *Bibl* 72 (1991), 500-524.

2. *Dynastic Changes.* M. Liverani,' L'histoire de Joas', *VT* 24 (1974), 438-53; P. Dutcher-Walls, *Narrative Art, Political Rhetoric: The Case of Athaliah and Joash*, Sheffield: Sheffield Academic Press, 1996: W.B. Barrick, 'Another Shaking of Jehoshaphat's Family Tree', *VT* 51 (2001), 9-25. Dynastic ideology: T. Ishida, *The Royal Dynasties in Ancient Israel*, Berlin: W. de Gruyter, 1997; Z. Ben-Barak, 'Succession to the Throne in Israel and in Assyria', *Orientalia Lovaniensia Periodica* 17 (1986), 85-100. On Azariah: H. Tadmor, 'Azriyau of Yaudi', *Scripta Hierosolymitana* 8 (1961), 232-71.

3. *The Formation of Transjordanian States.* (A) In general: R.H. Dornemann, *The Archaeology of Transjordan in the Bronze and Iron Ages*, Milwaukee: Milwaukee Public Museum, 1983; A. Hadidi (ed.), *Studies in the History and Archaeology of Transjordan*, I-III, Amman: Department of Antiquities, 1982-1987; P. Bienkowski (ed.), *Early Edom and Moab*, Sheffield: Sheffield Academic Press, 1992. (B), Ammon: U. Hübner, *Die Ammoniter*, Wiesbaden: Otto Harrassowitz, 1992; A. Zertal, 'Three Iron Age Fortresses in the Jordan Valley and the Origin of the Ammonite Circular Towers', *IEJ* 45 (1995), 253-73; B. MacDonald and R.W. Younker (eds.), *Ancient Ammon*, Leiden: E.J. Brill, 1999. Epigraphy: W.E. Aufrecht, *A Corpus of Ammonite Inscriptions*, Lewiston, NY: Edwin Mellen Press, 1989. (C) Moab: S. Timm, *Moab zwischen den Mächten*, Wiesbaden: Otto Harrassowitz, 1989; U. Worschech, *Die Beziehungen Moabs zu Israel und Ägypten*, Wiesbaden: Otto Harrassowitz, 1990; *The Archaeology of Moab*, BA 60.4 (1997). Mesha Stela: J.A. Dearman (ed.), *Studies in the Mesha Inscription and Moab*, Atlanta: Scholars Press, 1989; N. Na'aman, 'King Mesha and the Foundation of the Moabite Monarchy', *IEJ* 47 (1997), 83-92; B. Routledge, 'The Politics of Mesha', *JESHO* 43 (2000), 221-56. (D) Edom: J.R. Bartlett, *Edom and the Edomites*, Sheffield: Sheffield Academic Press, 1989; I. Finkelstein, 'Edom in the Iron I', *Lev* 24 (1992), 159-72; N. Na'aman, 'Israel, Edom and Egypt in the 10th Century B.C.E.', *Tel Aviv* 19 (1992), 71-93; D.V. Edelman (ed.), *You Shall Not Abhor an Edomite for He is your Brother*, Atlanta, GA: Scholars Press, 1995.

4. *Economy and Material Culture.* R. Kessler, *Staat und Gesellschaft im vorexilischen Juda (vom 8. Jahrhundert bis zum Exil)*, Leiden: E.J. Brill, 1992 (very useful also for the following period); A. Faust, 'The Rural Community in Ancient Israel during the Iron Age II', *BASOR* 317 (2000), 17-39; A. Ofer, 'The Monarchic Period in the Judean Highlands: a Spatial Overview', in A. Mazar (ed.), *Studies in the Archaeology of the Iron Age in Israel and Jordan*, Sheffield: Sheffield Academic Press, 2001, 14-37. L. Singer-Avitz, 'Beer-sheba – A Gateway Community in Southern Arabian Long-Distance Trade in the Eighth Century B.C.E.', *Tel Aviv* 26 (1999), 3-74.

5. *Yahwism and Prophetic Activity in the South.* (A) Micah: C.S. Shaw, *The Speeches of Micah: A Rhetorical-Historical Analysis*, Sheffield: Sheffield Academic Press, 1993;

B.M. Zapff, *Redaktionsgeschichtliche Studien zum Michabuch*, Berlin: W. de Gruyter, 1997; M.R. Jacobs, *The Conceptual Coherence of the Book of Micah*, Sheffield: Sheffield Academic Press, 2001; R. Kessler, 'Zwischen Tempel und Tora. Das Michabuch im Diskurs der Perserzeit', *BZ* 44 (2000), 21-36. (B) Hosea: G.I. Emmerson, *Hosea: An Israelite Prophet in Judean Perspective*, Sheffield: Sheffield Academic Press, 1984; H.D. Neef, *Die Heilstradition Israels in der Verkündigung des propheten Hosea*, Berlin: W. de Gruyter, 1987; D.R. Daniels, *Hosea and Salvation History: The Early Traditions of Israel in the Prophecy of Hosea*, Berlin: W. de Gruyter, 1990; E.K. Holt, *Prophesysing the Past: The Use of Israel's History in the Book of Hosea*, Sheffield: Sheffield Academic Press, 1995; Y. Sherwood, *The Prostitute and the Prophet: Hosea's Marriage in Literary-Theological Perspective*, Sheffield: Sheffield Academic Press, 1996; A.A. Keefe, *Woman's Body and Social Body in Hosea*, Sheffield: Sheffield Academic Press, 2001. (C) First Isaiah, see below. (D) Epigraphy: Kuntillet Ajrud: A. Lemaire, 'Date et origine des inscriptions hébraiques et phéniciennes de Kuntillet 'Ajrud', *Studi Epigrafici e Linguistici* 1 (1984), 131-43. Khirbet el-Qom: A. Lemaire, 'Les inscriptions de Khirbet el-Qôm', *RB* 84 (1977), 595-608. On Asherah: T. Binger, *Asherah: Goddesses in Ugarit, Israel and the Old Testament*, Sheffield: Sheffield Academic Press, 1997; S.M. Olyan, *Asherah and the Cult of Yahweh in Israel*, Atlanta, GA: Scholars Press, 1988; J.E. Taylor, 'The Asherah, the Menorah and the Sacred Tree', *JSOT* 66 (1995), 29-54.

6. *The Common Ideology of the Ninth-Eighth Centuries.* A. Albrektson, *History and the Gods: An Essay on the Idea of Historical Events as Divine Manifestations in the Ancient Near East and in Israel*, Lund: C.W.K. Gleerup, 1967; A. Lemaire, 'Joas de Samarie, Barhadad de Damas, Zakkur de Hamat. La Syrie-Palestine vers 800 av. J.C.', *Eretz-Israel* 24 (1993), 148*-57*; idem, 'Oracles, politique et littérature dans les royaumes araméens et transjordaniens (IXe-VIIIe s. av.n.è.)', in J.G. Heinz (ed.), *Oracles et prophéties dans l'Antiquité*, Strasbourg: Centre de recherche sur le Proche-Orient et la Grèce antiques, 1997, 171-93; D.I. Block, *The Gods of the Nations: Studies in Ancient Near Eastern National Theology*, Winona Lake, IN: Eisenbrauns, 1988; A. Kunz, 'Zum rechtlichen Hintergrund der ammonitisch-aramäischen Militärkoalition', *ZABR* 6 (2000), 127-54.

Chapter 7: The Impact of the Assyrian Empire (c. 740–640)

1. *The Conquest of the North.* (A) Assyrian empire in general: F.M. Fales, *L'impero assiro*, Rome: Laterza, 2001. Western expansion: R. Lamprichs, *Die Westexpansion des neuassyrischen Reichs*, Neukirchen: Neukirchener Verlag, 1995. On ideological aspects, see P. Machinist, 'Assyria and its Image in the First Isaiah', *JAOS* 103 (1983), 719-37. (B) Shalmaneser III (cf. §5.3): S. Yamada, *The Construction of the Assyrian Empire*, Leiden: E.J. Brill, 2000. (C) Adad-nirari III: H. Tadmor, 'Adad-nirari III in Syria', *Iraq* 35 (1973), 57-64; idem, 'The Historical Inscriptions of Adad-nirari III', *ibid.* 141-50; N. Na'aman, 'Forced Participation in Alliances in the Course of the Assyrioan Campaigns to the West', in M. Cogan and I. Eph'al (eds.), *Ah, Assyria... Studies in Assyrian History and Ancient Near Eastern Historiography presented to H. Tadmor*, Jerusalem: Magnes Press, 1991, 84-89; M. Weippert, 'Die Feldzüge Adadniraris III. nach Syrien', *ZDPV* 108 (1992), 42-67. (D) Tiglat-pileser III: H. Tadmor and M. Cogan, 'Ahaz and Tiglat-Pileser in the Book of Kings', *Bibl* 60 (1979), 499-509; J.M. Asurmendi, *La guerra*

siro-efraimita, Valencia: Institución San Jerónimo para la Investigación Bíblica, 1982; R. Bickert, 'König Ahas und der Prophet Jesaja', *ZAW* 99 (1987), 361-83; N. Na'aman, 'The Deuteronomist and Voluntary Servitude to Foreign Powers', *JSOT* 65 (1995), 37-53; R. Tomes, 'The Reason for the Syro-Ephraimite War', *JSOT* 59 (1993), 55-71; G. Galil, 'A New Look at the Inscriptions of Tiglath-pileser III, *Bibl* 81 (2000), 511-20. (E) Conquest of Samaria: H. Tadmor, 'The Campaigns of Sargon II of Assu'r, *JCS* 12 (1958), 22-40; S. Timm, 'Die Eroberung Israels (Samaria), 722 v.Chr. aus assyrisch-babylonischer Sicht', *Die Welt des Orient* 20/21 (1989–90), 62-82; B. Becking, *The Fall of Samaria*, Leiden: E.J. Brill, 1992; N. Na'aman, 'The Historical Background to the Conquest of Samaria', *Bibl* 71 (1990), 206-25; J.H. Hayes and J.K. Kuan, 'The Final Years of Samaria', *Bibl* 72 (1991), 153-81; and recently the survey by K. Lawson Younger, 'The Fall of Samaria in Light of Recent Research', *CBQ* 61 (1999), 461-82.

2. *Pressure on the South.* H. Spickermann, *Juda unter Assur in der Sargonidenzeit*, Göttingen: Vandenhoeck & Ruprecht, 1982; N. Na'aman, 'The Brook of Egypt and Assyrian Policy on the Border of Egypt', *Tel Aviv* 6 (1979), 68-90.

3. *Patterns of Deportation and Provincialization.* (A) Deportations: B. Oded, *Mass Deportations and Deportees in the Neo-Assyrian Empire*, Wiesbaden: Otto Harrassowitz, 1979; N. Na'aman, 'Population Changes in Palestine Following Assyrian Deportations', *Tel Aviv* 20 (1993), 104-24; N. Na'aman and R. Zadok, 'Assyrian Deportations to the Province of Samerina', *Tel Aviv* 27 (2000), 159-88; H. Limet, 'Les exploitations agricoles en Transuphratène ai Ier millénaire à la lumière des pratiques assyriennes', *Trans* 19 (2000), 35-50. (B) Province organization: A. Alt, 'Das System der assyrischen Provinzen auf dem Boden des Reiches Israel' (1929), in *KS*, II, 188-205; O. Lipschitz,' The Date of the "Assyrian Residence" at Ayyelet ha-Shahar', *Tel Aviv* 17 (1990), 96-99; J.D. Macchi, 'Megiddo à l'époque assyrienne', *Trans* 7 (1994), 9-33.

4. *Growth and Prosperity in the Kingdom of Judah.* (A) M. Broshi, 'The Expansion of Jerusalem in the Reigns of Hezekiah and Manasseh', *IEJ* 24 (1974), 21-26; E. Stern, 'Israel at the Close of the Period of the Monarchy: An Archaeological Survey', *BA* 38 (1975), 26-53; D.W. Jamieson-Drake, *Scribes and Schools in Monarchical Judah*, Sheffield: Sheffield Academic Press, 1991. (B) Particular aspects: Y. Shiloh, 'South Arabian Inscriptions from the City of David, Jerusalem', *PEQ* 119 (1987), 9-18; D. Ussishkin, 'The Rectangular Fortress at Kadesh-Barnea', *IEJ* 45 (1995), 118-27; E. Stager, 'Farming the Judean Desert during the Iron Age', *BASOR* 221 (1976), 145-58. (C) '*lmlk*' stamps: P. Welten, *Die Königs-Stempel*, Wiesbaden: Otto Harrassowitz, 1969; D. Ussishkin, 'The Destruction of Lachish by Sennacherib and the Dating of the Royal Judean Storage Jars', *Tel Aviv* 4 (1977), 28-60; N. Na'aman, 'Hezekiah's Fortified Cities and the *Lmlk* Stamps', *BASOR* 261 (1986), 5-21; G. Barkay and A.G. Vaughn, '*Lmlk* and Official Seal Impressions from Tel Lachish', *Tel Aviv* 23 (1996), 61-74; *idem*, 'New Readings of Hezekian Official Seal Impressions', *BASOR* 304 (1996), 29-54; N.S. Fox, *In the Service of the King: Officialdom in Ancient Israel und Judah*, Cincinnati: Hebrew Union College Press, 2000; R. Kletter, 'Temptation to Identify: Jerusalem, *mmšt* and the *lmlk* Stamps', *ZDPV* 118 (2002), 136-49. (D) Socioeconomic problems: D.N. Premnath, 'Latifundialization and Isaiah 5.8-10', *JSOT* 40 (1988), 49-60.

5. *Hezekiah's Reforms and the Prophetic Debate.* (A) Hezekiah: M. Hutter, *Hiskija, König von Juda*, Graz: Institut für Ökumenische Theologie und Patrologie an der Universität Graz, 1982; A. Laato, 'Hezekiah and the Assyrian Crisis in 701 BC', *SJOT* 1 (1987), 7-21; I.W. Provan, *Hezekiah and the Book of Kings*, Berlin: W. de Gruyter, 1988; N. Na'aman, 'Hezekiah and the Kings of Assyria', *Tel Aviv* 21 (1994), 235-54. Hezekiah's inscriptions: S. Norin, 'The Age of the Siloam Inscription and Hezekiah's Tunnel', *VT* 48 (1988), 37-48; A. Faust, 'A Note on Hezekiah's Tunnel and the Siloam Inscription', *JSOT* 90 (2000), 3-11; F.M. Cross, 'A Fragment of a Monumental Inscription from the City of David', *IEJ* 51 (2001), 44-47. (B) Sennacherib's campaign: N. Na'aman, *'Sennacherib's "Letter to God" on his Campaign to Judah'*, *BASOR* 214 (1974), 25-39; F.J. Gonçalves, *L'expédition de Sennacherib en Palestine*, Louvain-la-Neuve: Universite catholique de Louvain 1986; W.R. Gallagher, *Sennacherib's Campaign to Judah*, Leiden: E.J. Brill, 1999; J. Goldberg, 'Two Assyrian Campaigns against Hezekiah', *Bibl* 89 (1999), 360-90. (C) Siege of Lachish: D. Ussishkin, 'Excavations at Tel Lachish', *Tel Aviv* 5 (1978), 1-97; 10 (1983), 97-185; 23 (1996), 3-60; *idem*, 'The "Lachish Reliefs" and the City of Lachish', *IEJ* 30 (1980), 174-95; S. Gitin and T. Dothan, 'A Royal Dedicatory Inscription from Ekron', *IEJ* 47 (1997), 1-16. (D) Assyrian expeditions to Egypt: H.-U. Onasch, *Die assyrischen Eroberungen Ägyptens*, Wiesbaden: Otto Harrassowitz, 1994. (E),(Proto-)Isaia: B.S. Childs, *Isaiah and the Assyrian Crisis*, London: SCM Press, 1967; W. Dietrich, *Jesaja und die Politik*, München: Kaiser Verlag, 1976. (F) Proto-Deuteronomy: A.K. Jenkins, 'Hezekiah's Reform and Deuteronomic Tradition', *HTR* 72 (1979), 23-43; I. Provan, *Hezekiah and the Books of Kings*, Berlin: W. de Gruyter, 1988; B. Halpern, *The First Historians*, San Francisco: Harper & Row,1988; A. Lemaire, 'Vers l'histoire de la rédaction des Kivres des Rois', *ZAW* 98 (1986), 221-36.

6. *Imperial Ideology and Local Strategies.* (A) Assyrian ideology: M. Cogan, *Imperialism and Religion*, Missoula, MT: Scholars Press, 1974; *idem*, 'Judah under Assyrian Hegemony', *JBL* 112 (1993), 403-414; M. Liverani, 'The Ideology of the Assyrian Empire,' in M.T. Larsen (ed.), *Power and Propaganda*, Copenhagen: Akademisk Forslag, 1979, 297-317; B. Oded, *War, Peace and Empire*, Wiesbaden: Otto Harrassowitz, 1992; E. Otto, 'Die besiegten Sieger', *BZ* 43 (1999), 180-203. (B) Prophecies against the nations: H. Donner, *Israel unter den Völkern*, Leiden: E.J. Brill, 1964 (First Isaiah, Hosea, Micah); B. Gosse, 'Le recueil d'oracles contre les nations du livre d'Amos et l'"histoire deuteronomique"', *VT* 38 (1998), 22-40.

7. *Loyalty and Protection: The Emperor and the God.* (A) Assyrian 'covenant': H. Tadmor, 'Alleanza e dipendenza nell'antica Mesopotamia e in Israele', in L. Canfora *et al.*, (eds.), *I trattati nel mondo antico*, Roma: Bretschneider, 1990, 17-36; M. Liverani, 'Terminologia e ideologia del patto nelle iscrizioni reali assire', *ibid.*, 113-47. (B) Comparison with Deuteronomy: R. Frankena, 'The Vassal-Treaties of Esarhaddon and the Dating of Deuteronomy', *Oudtestamentische Studiën* 14 (1965), 122-54; H.U. Steymanns, *Deuteronomium 28 und die* adê *zur Thronfolgeregelung Asarhaddons*, Göttingen: Vandenhoeck & Ruprecht, 1995; E. Otto, 'Treu und Gesetz', *ZABR* 2 (1996), 1-52. (C) Biblical ideology of the covenant: E. Kutsch, *Verheissung und Gesetz*, Berlin: W. de Gruyter, 1973; and the survey by E. Otto, 'Die Ursprünge der Bundestheologie

im Alten Testament und im Alten Orient', *ZABR* 4 (1988), 1-84 (and other articles in the same volume). (D) Covenant terminology: D.J. McCarthy, *Treaty and Covenant*, Rome: Biblical Institute Press 1963, 1978²; P. Kalluveettil, *Declaration and Covenant*, Rome: Biblical Institute Press, 1982.

Chapter 8: Pause between Two Empires (c. 640–610)

1. *The Collapse of the Assyrian Empire.* S. Zawadzki, *The Fall of Assyria and Median-Babylonia Relations in Light of the Nabopolassar Chronicle*, Poznan: Adam Mickiewicz University Press, 1988; M. Liverani, 'The Fall of the Assyrian Empire: Ancient and Modern Interpretations', in S. Alcock (ed.), *Empires: Perspectives from Archaeology and History*, Cambridge: Cambridge University Press, 2001, 374-91. On Medes, M. Liverani, 'The Medes at Esarhaddon's Court', *JCS* 47 (1995), 57-62; *idem*, *The Rise and Fall of Media*, (in press).

2. *An Interval of Freedom.* (A) Tyre: I.M. Diakonoff, 'The Naval Power and Trade of Tyre', *IEJ* 42 (1992), 168-93; M. Liverani, 'The Trade Network of Tyre According to Ezek. 27', in *Ah, Assyria... Studies in Assyrian History and Ancient Near Eastern Historiography presented to H. Tadmor*, Jerusalem: Magnes Press 1991, 65-79. (B) Ammon: R. Kletter, 'The Rujm el-Malfuf Buildings and the Assyrian Vassal State of Ammon', *BASOR* 284 (1991), 33-50.

3. *Josiah and the Unification Project.* (A) On the policy of Josiah: A. Alt, 'Judas Gaue unter Josia' in *KS*, II, 276-288; W.E. Claburn, The Fiscal Basis of Josiah's Reform, *JBL* 92 (1973), 11-22; V. Fritz, 'The List of Roboam's Fortresses in 2 Chr 11,5-12. A Document from the Time of Josiah', *Eretz-Israel* 15 (1981), 46-53; D.L. Christensen, 'Zephaniah 2,4-15: A Theological Base for Josiah's Program of Political Expansion', *CBQ* 46 (1984), 669-82; N. Na'aman, 'The Kingdom of Judah under Josiah', *Tel Aviv* 18 (1991), 3-71. (B) Archaeological indicators: R. Kletter, 'Pots and Polities: Material remains of Late Iron Age Judah in Relation to its Political Borders', *BASOR* 314 (1999), 19-54. Desert of Judah: L.E. Stager, 'Farming in the Judean Desert during the Iron Age', *BASOR* 221 (1976), 145-58. Negev: I. Beit-Arieh, 'The Edomite Shrine at Horvat Qitmit in the Judean Negev', *Tel Aviv* 18 (1991), 93-116; I. Finkelstein, 'Horvat Qitmit and the Southern Trade in the Late Iron Age II', *ZDPV* 108 (1992), 156-70; Ph. Mayerson, 'Toward a Comparative Study of a Frontier', *IEJ* 40 (1990), 267-79.

4. *The Discovery of the Law.* N. Lohfink, 'Culture Shock and Theology', *Biblical Theology Bulletin* 7 (1977), 12-22; W. Dietrich, 'Josia und das Gesetzbuch', *VT* 27 (1977), 13-35; B.J. Diebner and C. Nauerth, 'Die Invention des *sfr twrh* in 2 Kon 22', *Dielheimer Blätter zum Alten Testament* 18 (1984), 95-118; R.H. Lowry, *The Reforming Kings*, Sheffield: Sheffield Academic Press, 1991; E. Eynikel, *The Reform of King Josiah and the Composition of the Deuteronomistic History*, Leiden: E.J. Brill, 1996; Th. Römer, 'On "Book-Finding" and Other Literary Strategies', *ZAW* 109 (1997), 1-11.

5. *A Single God in a Single Temple.* (A) Centralization of the cult: E. Reuter, *Kultzentralisation. Entstehung und Theologie von Dtn 12*, Frankfurt: Hain, 1993; N. Lohfink, 'Kultzentralisation und Deuteronomium', *ZABR* 1 (1995), 117-48. (B) Archaeological

data: D. Ussishkin, 'The Date of the Judean Shrine at Arad', *IEJ* 38 (1988), 142-57. (C) Epigraphic data: P. Bordreuil, F. Israel and D. Pardee, 'Deux ostraka paléo-hébreux de la collection Sh- Moussaieff', *Semitica* 46 (1996), 49-76.

6. *The Deuteronomistic History.* Still fundamental is M. Noth, *The Deuteronomistic History*, Sheffield: Sheffield Academic Press, 1981; M. Weinfeld, *Deuteronomy and the Deuteronomic School*, Oxford 1972; F.M. Cross, *Canaanite Myth and Hebrew Epic*, Cambridge, MA: Cambridge University Press, 1973, 274-89; R.D. Nelson, *The Double Redaction of the Deuteronomistic History*, Sheffield: Sheffield Academic Press, 1981; J. van Seters, *In Search of History: Historiography in the Ancient World and the Origins of Biblical History*, New Haven, CT: Yale University Press, 1983; M. O'Brien, *The Deuteronomistic History Hypothesis: A Reassessment*, Göttingen: Vandenhoeck & Ruprecht, 1989; E. Otto, *Das Deuteronomium. Politische Theologie und Rechtsreform in Juda und Assyrien*, Berlin: W. de Gruyter, 1999; L.S. Schearing and S-L. McKenzie (eds.), *Those Elusive Deuteronomists*, Sheffield: Sheffield Academic Press, 1999; A. de Pury, T. Römer and J.D. Macchi (eds.), *Israel Constructs its History: Deuteronomistic Historiography in Recent Research*, Sheffield: Sheffield Academic Press, 2000; G.N. Knoppers and J.G. McConville (eds.), *Reconsidering Israel and Judah: Recent Studies on the Deuteronomistic History*, Winona Lake, IN: Eisenbrauns, 2000.

7. *Failure and its Aftermath.* (A) Manasseh: P. Keulen, *Manasseh through the Eyes of the Deuteronomists*, Leiden: E.J. Brill, 1996; K. Schmid, 'Manasse und der Untergang Judas', *Bibl* 78 (1997), 87-99; B. Halpern, 'Why Manasseh is Blamed for the Babylonian Exile', *VT* 48 (1998), 473-514. (B) Jeremiah: R.P. Carroll, *From Chaos to Covenant: Uses of Prophecy in the Book of Jeremiah*, London: SCM Press, 1981; E.K. Holt, 'Was Jeremiah a Member of the Deuteronomist Party?', *JSOT* 44 (1989), 109-22. (C) Zephaniah: P.H. House, *Zephaniah: A Prophetic Drama*, Sheffield: Almond Press, 1988; E. Ben-Zvi, *A Historical-Critical Study of the Book of Zephaniah*, Berlin: W. de Gruyter, 1991.

Chapter 9. The Impact of the Babylonian Empire (c. 610–585)

1. *Nebuchadrezzar and the Imperial Reconquest.* D.J. Wiseman, *Nebuchadrezzar and Babylon*, London: Oxford University Press, 1985; W.G. Lambert, 'Nebuchadnezzar King of Justice', *Iraq* 27 (1965), 1-11; P. Coxon, 'Nebuchadnezzar's Hermeneutical Dilemma', *JSOT* 66 (1995), 87-97; O. Lipschits, 'Nebuchadrezzar's Policy in "Hattu-Land" and the Fate of the Kingdom of Judah', *UF* 30 (1998), 467-87. On particular issues: B. Porten, 'The Identity of King Adon', *BA* 44 (1981), 36-52; J. Day, 'The Problem of "So, King of Egypt"', *VT* 42 (1992), 289-301; A.J. Katzenstein, 'Gaza in the Neo-Babylonian Period', *Trans* 7 (1994), 35-49.

2. *Local Strategies and the Oracles against the 'Nations'.* N.K. Gottwald, *All the Kingdoms of the Earth*, New York: Harper & Row, 1964; F. Huber, *Jahwe, Juda und die anderen Völker beim Propheten Jesaja*, Berlin: W. de Gruyter, 1976; F. Fechter, *Bewaltigung der Katastrophe. Untersuchungen zu ausgewählten Fremdvölkersprüchen im Ezechielbuch*, Berlin: W. de Gruyter, 1992; K.L. Sparks, *Ethnicity and Identity in Ancient Israel*, Winona Lake, IN: Eisenbrauns, 1988.

3. *The Internal Political Debate.* A. Schenker, 'Nebukadnezzars Metamorphose: vom Unterjocher zum Gottesknecht', *RB* 89 (1982), 498-527; T. Krüger, *Geschichtskonzepte im Ezechielbuch*, Berlin: W. de Gruyter, 1989; C. Hardmeier, *Prophetie im Streit vor dem Untergang Judas*, Berlin: W. de Gruyter, 1990; H.-J. Stipp, *Jeremia im Parteienstreit*, Frankfurt: Hain, 1992.

4. *From Vassal State to the Final Destruction.* (A) Zedekiah: J. Applegate, 'The Fate of Zedekiah: Redactional Debate in the Book of Jeremiah', *VT* 58 (1998), 137-60, 301-308; H.J. Stipp, 'Zedekiah in the Book of Jeremiah', *CBQ* 58 (1996), 627-48. Jerusalem Bullae: N. Avigad, *Hebrew Bullae from the Time of Jeremiah*, Jerusalem: Israel Exploration Society, 1976; Y. Shiloh, 'A Group of Hebrew Bullae from the City of David', *IEJ* 36 (1986), 16-38; R. Deutsch, *Messages from the Past*, Tel Aviv: Archaeological Center, 1999; F. Bianchi, *I superstiti della deportazione sono là nella provincia*, I, Napoli: Istituto universitario orientale, 1993. (B) Gedaliah: E. Janssen, *Juda in der Exilzeit*, Göttingen: Vandenhoeck & Ruprecht, 1956; O. Lipschits, 'The History of the Benjamin Region under Babylonian Rule', *Tel Aviv* 26 (1999), 155-90; J. Zorn, J. Yellin and J. Hayes, 'The *m(w)ṣh* Stamp Impressions and the Neo-Babylonian Period', *IEJ* 44 (1994), 161-83; H.-J. Stipp, 'Gedolja und die Kolonie von Mizpa,' *ZABR* 6 (2000), 155-71.

5. *One-way Deportations and Demographic and Cultural Collapse.* (A) Destruction: E. Kutsch, 'Das Jahr der Katastrophe: 587 v.Chr.', *Bibl* 55 (1974), 520-45. (B) Edomites in Negev: see I. Beit-Arieh, 'New Data on the Relationship between Judah and Edom toward the End of the Iron Age', in S. Gitin and W. Dever (eds.), *Recent Excavations in Israel: Studies in Iron Age Archaeology*, Winona Lake, IN: Eisenbrauns, 1989, 125-31; J.R. Bartlett, 'Edom and the Fall of Jerusalem', *PEQ* 114 (1982), 13-24.

Chapter 10. The Axial Age

1. *The Individual and the 'Distant Power'.* See M. Liverani, *Antico Oriente*, Rome: Laterza, 1988, 938-42.

2. *The Question of Monotheism.* (A) On Yahwistic religion, among the rich bibliography see in particular: E.A. Knauf, 'Yahwe', *VT* 34 (1984), 467-72; T.L. Thompson, 'How Yahweh Became God', *JSOT* 68 (1995), 57-74; R. Albertz, *A History of Israelite Religion in the Old Testament Period*, I, Nashville: Westminster/John Knox Press, 1994 (and review article by W.G. Dever in *BASOR* 301 (1996), 83-96); M. Weippert, *Yahwe und die anderen Götter*, Tübingen: Mohr, 1997. (B) Monotheism: M. Smith, *Palestinian Parties and Politics that Shaped the Old Testament*, New York: Columbia University Press, 1971; B. Lang, *Monotheism and the Prophetic Minority*, Sheffield: Almond Press, 1983; W. Dietrich and M.A. Klopfenstein (eds.), *Ein Gott allein? YHWH-Verehrung und biblischer Monotheisms*, Göttingen: Vandenhoeck & Ruprecht, 1994; D.V. Edelman (ed.), *The Triumph of Elohim: From Yahwisms to Judaisms*, Kampen: Kok Pharos, 1995; J. de Moor, *The Rise of Yahwism: The Roots of Israelite Monotheism*, Leuven: Peeters, 1997; R.K. Gnuse, *No Other Gods: Emergent Monotheism in Israel*, Sheffield: Sheffield Academic Press, 1997; J. Pakkala, *Intolerant Monolatry in the Deuteronomistic History*, Göttingen: Vandenhoeck & Ruprecht, 2000. Questionable is the recent survey by

W. Propp, 'Monotheism and "Moses"', *UF* 31 (1999), 537-75. (C) Pesian elements: M. Smith, 'II Isaiah and the Persians', *JAOS* 83 (1963), 415-21; G. Garbini, 'Universalismo iranico e Israele', *Henoch* 6 (1984), 293-312. (D) Aniconism: C. Dohmen, *Das Bilderverbot*, Bonn: Hanstein, 1985; T. Mettinger, *No Graven Image?*, Stockholm: Almqvist & Wiksell, 1995; K. van der Toorn (ed.), *The Image and the Book*, Leuven: Peeters, 1997; A. Berleijung, *Die Theologie der Bilder*, Göttingen: Vandenhoeck & Ruprecht, 1998; O. Keel and C. Uehlinger, *Gods, Goddesses, and Images of God in Ancient Israel*, Minneapolis, MN: Fortress Press, 1998; N. Na'aman, 'No Anthropomorphic Graven Image', *UF* 31 (1999), 391-415; Th. Podella, '*Bild und Text*', *SJOT* 15 (2001), 205-256. (E) Syncretism: G.W. Ahlström, *Aspects of Syncretism in Israelite Religion*, Lund: C.W.K. Gleerup, 1963; *idem, An Archaeological Picture of Iron Age Religions in Palestine*, Helsinki: Finnish Oriental Society, 1984. (F) Cult of the dead: E. Bloch-Smith, *Judahite Burial Practices and Beliefs about the Dead*, Sheffield: Sheffield Academic Press, 1992. Prohibition of necromacy: J. Tropper, *Nekromantie*, Neukirchen–Vluyn: Neukirchener Verlag, 1989. (F) Babylonian henotheistic tendencies: W.G. Lambert, 'The Historical Development of the Mesopotamian Pantheon', in H. Goedicke and J. Roberts (eds.), *Unity and Diversity*, Baltimore: The Johns Hopkins University Press 1975, 191-200 (citing 197-98).

3. *From Ceremonial Worship to Ethical Religion*. See the general works on religion mentioned in the introductory bibliography.

4. *Collective and Personal Responsibility.* J.S. Kaminsky, *Corporate Responsibility in the Hebrew Bible*, Sheffield: Sheffield Academic Press, 1995; R.A. Freund, 'Individual vs. Collective Responsibility', *SJOT* 11 (1997), 279-304; recently, K. Schmid, 'Kollektivschuld? Der Gedanke übergreifender Schuldzusammenhänge im Alten Testament und in Alter Orient', *ZABR* 5 (1999), 193-222; R.A. Di Vito, 'Old Testament Anthropology and the Construction of Personal Identity', *CBQ* 61 (1999), 217-38. Criticism of divine justice: K.P. Darr, 'Ezekiel's Justification of God', *JSOT* 55 (1992), 97-117; C. Patton, '"I Myself Gave Them Laws That Were Not Good"', *JSOT* 69 (1996), 73-90.

Chapter 11. The Diaspora

1. *The Fate of the Political Elite*. E. Weidner, 'Jojachin, Konig von Juda in babylonischen Keilinschriften', in *Mélanges Syriens offerts à R. Dussaud*, Paris: Gembloud, 1939, II, 923-25. In general on the period of the exile, see the synthesis by M. Dandamayev and E. Bickerman in *The Cambridge History of Judaism*, Cambridge: Cambridge University Press, 1984, I, 326-58.

2. *Adapting to New Circumstances.* (A) E. Janssen, *Juda in der Exilzeit*, Göttingen: Vandenhoeck & Ruprecht, 1956; M. Cogan, 'Life in the Diaspora', *BA* 37 (1974), 6-12; R. Zadok, *On West Semites in Babylonia during the Chaldean and Achaemenian Periods*, Jerusalem: Wanaarta, 1977; *idem, The Jews in Babylonia during the Chaldean and Achaemenian Periods*, Haifa: University of Haifa, 1979; *idem*, 'The Nippur Region during the Late Assyrian, Chaldean and Achaemenian Periods', *Israel Oriental Studies* 8 (1978), 266-332; I. Eph'al, 'The Western Minorities in Babylonia in the 6th–5th Cen-

turies BC', *Or* 47 (1978), 74-90; B. Oded, 'Observations on the Israelite/Judaean Exiles in Mesopotamia', in K. van Lerberghe and A. Schoors (eds.), *Immigration and Emigration within the Ancient Near East*, Leuven: Peeters, 1995, 205-212; L. Grabbe, ' "The Exile" under the Theodolite: Historiography as Triangulation', in L. Grabbe (ed.), *Leading Captivity Captive*, Sheffield: Sheffield Academic Press, 1998, 80-100. (B) On the Murashu archives: M. Stolper, *Entrepreneurs and Empire: The Murašû Archive, the Murašû Firm, and Persian Rule in Babylonia*, Leiden: E.J. Brill, 1985; M. Coogan, *West Semitic Personal Names in the Murašû Documents*, Atlanta, GA: Scholars Press, 1976; G. van Driel, 'The Murašûs in Context', *JESHO* 32 (1989), 203-229. Judean cities in Babylonia: F. Joannès and A. Lemaire, 'Trois tablettes cunéiformes à onomastique ouest-sémitique', *Trans* 17 (1999), 17-34. (C) Religious aspects: E.W. Nicholson, *Preaching to the Exiles*, Oxford: Oxford University Press, 1970; T.M. Raitt, *A Theology of Exile*, Philadelphia: Westminster Press, 1977; R.W. Klein, *Israel in Exile: A Theological Interpretation*, Philadelphia: Westminster Press, 1979; D.L. Smith, *The Religion of the Landless*, Bloomington: Meyer-Stone, 1989; C.R. Seitz, *Theology in Conflict: Reactions to the Exile in the Book of Jeremiah*, Berlin: W. de Gruyter, 1989. (D) On linguistic aspects, see the synthesis and bibliography by J. Naveh and J.C. Greenfield in *The Cambridge History of Judaism*, Cambridge: Cambridge University Press, 1984, I, 115-29.

3. *Deportees and Emigrants.* (A) L.L. Grabbe (ed.), *Leading Captivity Captive: 'The Exile' as History and Ideology*, Sheffield: Sheffield Academic Press, 1998; J. Sapin, 'La main-d'oeuvre migrante en Transeuphratène achéménide', *Trans* 19 (2000), 13-33. (B) Egyptian Diaspora: E. Bresciani and B. Porten in *The Cambridge History of Judaism*, Cambridge: Cambridge University Press, 1984, I, 358-400. (C) Papyri from Elephantine: B. Porten, *Archives from Elephantine*, Berkeley: University of California Press, 1968; Y. Muffs, *Studies in the Aramaic Papyri from Elephantine*, Leiden: E.J. Brill, 1969; P. Grelot, *Documents araméens d'Egypte*, Paris, Editions du Cerf, 1972; also K. van der Toorn, 'Anat-Yahu, Some Other Deities, and the Jews of Elephantine,' *Numen* 39 (1992), 80-101; R. Contini, 'I documenti aramaici dell'Egitto persiano e tolemaico', *Rivista Biblica* 34 (1986), 73-109; P. Bedford, 'Jews at Elephantine', *Australian Journal of Jewish Studies*, 13 (1999), 6-23. Systematic edition: B. Porten and A. Yardeni, *Textbook of Aramaic Documents from Ancient Egypt*, I-IV, Jerusalem: Hebrew University, 1986–1999.

4. *Who Is the 'Remnant'?* G.F. Hasel, *The Remnant*, Berrien Springs, MI: Andrews University Press, 1972; W.E. Müller, *Die Vorstellung vom Rest im Alten Testament*, Neukirchen–Vluyn: Neukirchener Verlag, 1973; O. Carena, *Il resto di Israele: Studio storico-comparativo delle iscrizioni reali Assire e dei testi profetici sul tema del resto*, Bologna: Edizioni Dehoniane, 1985; J. Hausmann, *Israels Rest*, Stuttgart: W. Kohlhammer, 1987.

5. *The Prophecy of Return and the 'New Covenant'.* (A) On Babylon: D.S. Vanderhooft, *The Neo-Babylonian Empire and Babylon in the Latter Propehts*, Cambridge, MA: Harvard University Press, 1999. (B) Deutero-Isaiah: H.M. Orlinski and N.H. Snaith, *Studies in the Second Part of the Book of Isaiah*, Leiden: E.J. Brill, 1967; D. Baltzer, *Ezechiel und Deuterojesaja: Berühmungen in der Heilserwartung der beiden grossen*

Exilpropheten, Berlin: W. de Gruyter, 1971; A. Schoors, *I Am God Your Saviour: A Form-critical Study of the Main Genres in Is. XL-LV*, Leiden: E.J. Brill, 1973; R.P. Merendino, *Der Erste und der Letzte. Eine Untersuchung von Jes. 40–48*, Leiden: E.J. Brill, 1981; A. Laato, *The Servant of Yhwh and Cyrus: A Reinterpretation of the Exilic Messianic Programme in Isaiah 40–55*, Stockholm, Almqvist & Wiksell, 1992; P.R. Davies, 'God of Cyrus, God of Israel', in J. Davies, G. Harvey and W. Watson (eds.), *Words Remembered, Texts Renewed: Essays in Honour of John F.A. Sawyer*, Sheffield: Sheffield Academic Press, 1995, 207-225. (C) Ezekiel: E. Kutsch, *Die chronologischen Daten des Ezechielbuches*, Göttingen: Vandenhoeck & Ruprecht, 1985; I.M. Duguid, *Ezekiel and the Leaders of Israel*, Leiden: E.J. Brill, 1994; Th. Renz, *The Rhetorical Function of the Book of Ezekiel*, Leiden: E.J. Brill, 1999. (D) 'New Covenant': B. Gosse, 'La nouvelle alliance et les promesses d'avenir se referant à David dans les livres de Jeremie, Ezechiel et Isaie', *VT* 41 (1991), 419-28; *idem*, 'L'établissement du droit et de la justice et les relations entre les redactions d'ensemble du livre d'Isaie et des Proverbes', *SJOT* 14 (2000), 275-92; N. Lohfink, 'Der Neue Bund im Buch Deuteronomium?', *ZABR* 4 (1988), 100-125; B.P. Robinson, 'Jeremiah's New Covenant: Jer 31,31-34', *SJOT* 15 (2001), 181-204.

6. *The New Theologies.* R.E. Clements, *God and Temple: The Idea of the Divine Presence in Ancient Israel*, Oxford: Oxford University Press, 1965; B. Janowski, ' "Ich will in euer Mitte wohnen". Struktur und Genese der exilischen Schekina-Theologie', *Jahrbuch für Biblische Theologie* 2 (1987), 165-93; T. Mettinger, *The Dethronement of Sabaoth: Studies in the Shem and Kabod Theologies*, Lund: C.W.K. Gleerup, 1982; *idem*, 'The Name and the Glory: The Zion-Sabaoth Theology and its Exilic Successors', *Journal of North-West Semitic Languages* 24 (1998), 1-24; S.L. Richter, *The Deuteronomistic History and the Name Theology*, Berlin: W. de Gruyter, 2002.

7. *The Deuteronomist Historiography and the Babylonian Models.* (A) See §8.6. More specifically, S.L. McKenzie, *The Trouble with Kings: The Composition of the Book of Kings in the Deuteronomistic History*, Leiden: E.J. Brill, 1991; E.T. Mullen, *Narrative History and Ethnic Boundaries: The Deuteronomistic History and the Creation of Israelite National Identity*, Atlanta, GA: Scholars Press, 1993; A. Mayes, 'On Describing the Purpose of Deuteronomy', *JSOT* 58 (1993), 13-33; *idem*, 'Deuteronomistic Ideology and the Theology of the Old Testament', *JSOT* 82 (1999), 57-82. (B) On the use of sources, G. Garbini, 'Le fonti citate nel "Libro dei Re" ', *Henoch* 3 (1981), 26-46; N. Na'aman, 'Royal Inscriptions and the Histories of Joash and Ahaz, King of Judah', *VT* 58 (1998), 333-49; N. Na'aman, 'The Contribution of Royal Inscriptions for a Re-Evaluation of the Book of Kings as a Historical Source', *JSOT* 82 (1999), 3-17; S.B. Parker, 'Did the Authors of the Books of Kings Make Use of Royal Inscriptions?', *VT* 50 (2000), 357-78.

Chapter 12. The Waste Land

1. *The Empty Land.* R.P. Carroll, 'The Myth of the Empty Land', in D. Jobling and T. Pippin (eds.), *Ideological Criticism of Biblical Texts*, Atlanta, GA: Scholars Press,

1992, 79-93; H.M. Barstad, *The Myth of the Empty Land: A Study in the History and Archaeology of Judah during the 'Exilic' Period*, Oslo: Scandinavian University Press, 1996; *idem*, 'On the History and Archaeology of Judah during the Exilic Period. A Reminder', *OLP* 19 (1988), 25-36.

2. *The Flood.* Recently: P.J. Harland, *The Value of Human Life: A Study of the Story of the Flood (Genesis 6–9)*, Leiden: E.J. Brill, 1996.

3. *The Tower of Babel.* Recently: C. Uehlinger, *Weltreich und 'eine Rede'. Eine neue Deutung der sogenannten Turmbauerzählung (Gen 11,1-9)*, Göttingen: Vandenhoeck & Ruprecht, 1990; P.J. Harland, 'Vertical and Horizontal: The Sin of Babel', *VT* 48 (1998), 514-33.

4. *The Garden of Eden.* Annotated bibliography in T. Stordalen, 'Man, Soil, Garden: Basic Plot in Genesis 2–3 Reconsidered', *JSOT* 53 (1992), 3-26; see also L.M. Bechtel, 'Genesis 2.4B–3.24: A Myth about Human Maturation', *JSOT* 67 (1995), 3-26.

5. *The Tripartite World.* Table of Nations: for interpretations which diverge from mine, see B. Oded, 'The Table of Nations (Genesis 10): A Socio-Cultural Approach', *ZAW* 98 (1986), 14-31; J. Vermeylen, 'La "table des nations" (Gn 10): Yaphet figure-t-il l'Empire perse?', *Trans* 5 (1992), 113-32. On Canaan and the curse of Ham, see recently M. Vervenne, 'What Shall We Do with the Drunken Sailor? A Critical Re-Examination of Genesis 9.20-27', *JSOT* 68 (1995), 33-55.

6. *Genealogies and Antiquarianism.* R. Wilson, *Genealogy and History in the Biblical World*, New Haven, CT: Yale University Press, 1977; M.D. Johnson, *The Purpose of the Biblical Genealogies*, Cambridge: Cambridge University Press, 1988. On Greek 'genealogies': S. Mazzarino, *Il pensiero storico classico*, IV, Bari: Laterza, 1966, 58-83. Cruciform monuments: E. Sollberger, 'The Cruciform Monument', *Jaarbericht Ex Oriente Lux* 20 (1968), 50-70.

7. *Nomads of the Mountains and Desert.* Not very useful is T. Staubli, *Das Image der Nomaden im Alten Israel und in der Ikonographie seiner sesshaften Nachbarn*, Göttingen: Vandenhoeck & Ruprecht, 1991. D.I. Block, 'Gog in Prophetic Tradition: A New Look at Ezekiel XXXVIII 17', *VT* 42 (1992), 154-72.

Chapter 13. Returnees and 'Remainees': The Invention of the Patriarchs

1. *The Fall of Babylon and the Edict of Cyrus.* (A) On Cyrus: A. Kuhrt, 'The Cyrus Cylinder and Achaemenid Imperial Policy', *JSOT* 25 (1983), 83-97; E.M. Yamauchi, *Persia and the Bible*, Grand Rapids: Eerdmans, 1990. On the sources, H. Schaudig, *Die Inschriften Nabonids von Babylon und Kyros' des Grossen*, Münster: Ugarit-Verlag, 2001. (B) Edict: J. Briend, 'L'édit de Cyrus et sa valeur historique', *Trans* 11 (1996), 33-44; see the follwing debate: P. Frei, 'Die persische Reichsautorisation: Ein Überblick', *ZABR* 1 (1995), 1-35; J. Wiesehöfer, ' "Reichsgesetz" oder "Einzelfallgerechtigkeit"?',

ZABR 1 (1995), 36-46; U. Rüterswörden, 'Die Persische Reichsautorisation der Thora: Fact or Fiction?', *ZABR* 1 (1995), 47-61.

2. *The Groups of Returnees.* I. Eph'al, 'Changes in Palestine during the Persian Period in Light of Epigraphic Sources', *IEJ* 48 (1998), 106-119.

3. *The 'People of the Land'.* R. de Vaux,' Le sens de l'expression "peuple du pays" et le rôle politique du peuple en Israël', *Revue d'Assyriologie* 58 (1964), 167-72; J.M. Carrière, 'Le "pays" dans le Deuteronome: une notion construite', *Trans* 14 (1998), 113-32.

4. *The Mythical Foundation of the Resettlement.* (A) Promise: N. Lohfink, *Die Landver- heissung als Eid: Eine Studie zu Gn 15*, Stuttgart: Katholisches Bibelwerk, 1967; *idem, Die Väter Israels in Deuteronomium*, Göttingen: Vandenhoeck & Ruprecht, 1991; E. Cortese, *La terra di Canaan nella storia sacerdotale del Pentateuco*, Brescia: Paideia, 1972; S. Boorer, *The Promise of the Land as Oath*, Berlin: W. de Gruyter, 1992. (B) Patriarchs: T. Römer, *Israels Väter: Untersuchungen zur Väterthematik im Deuter- onomium und in der deuteronomistischen Tradition*, Göttingen: Vandenhoeck & Ruprecht, 1990; *idem,* 'Genèse 15 et les tensions de la communauté juive postexilique', *Trans* 7 (1994), 107-121; also J. Vollmer, *Geschichtliche Rückblicke und Motive*, Berlin: W. de Gruyter, 1971.

5. *The Setting of the Patriarchal Narratives.* J. Van Seters, *Abraham in History and Tradition*, New Haven, CT: Yale University Press, 1975; T.L. Thompson, *The His- toricity of the Patriarchal Narratives*, Berlin: W. de Gruyter, 1974; H.M. Wahl, *Die Jakobserzählungen*, Berlin: W. de Gruyter, 1997.

6. *Interethnic Relations.* P.T. Reis, 'Hagar Requited', *JSOT* 87 (2000), 75-109; B. Dicou, *Edom, Israel's Brother and Antagonist*, Sheffield: Sheffield Academic Press, 1994; C.R. Mathews, *Defending Zion: Edom's Desolation and Jacob's Restoration (Isaiah 34–35), in Context*, Berlin: W. de Gruyter, 1995; W.W. Fields, *Sodom and Gomorrah: History and Motif in Biblical Narrative*, Sheffield: Sheffield Academic Press, 1997; W. Oswald, 'Die Revision des Edombildes in Numeri XX 14-21', *VT* 50 (2000), 218-32.

7. *Jerusalem and Shechem.* E. Otto, *Jakob in Sichem*, Stuttgart: W. Kohlhammer, 1979; J.A. Fitzmyer, 'Melchizedek in the MT, LXX, and the NT', *Bibl* 81 (2000), 63-69; L.M. Bechtel, 'What if Dinah Is Not Raped? (Genesis 34)', *JSOT* 62 (1994), 19-36.

8. *The Joseph Story.* D.B. Redford, *A Study of the Biblical Story of Joseph*, Leiden: E.J. Brill, 1970; A. Meinhold, 'Die Gattung der Josephgeschichte und des Estherbuches: Diasporanovellen', *ZAW* 87 (1975), 306-324; *ZAW* 88 (1976), 72-93; G.W. Coats, *From Canaan to Egypt: Structural and Theological Context for the Joseph Story*, Washington: Catholic Biblical Association of America, 1976; J.B. King, 'The Joseph Story and Divine Politics', *JBL* 106 (1987), 577-94; A. Catastini and C. Grottanelli, *Storia di Giuseppe*, Venezia: Marsilio, 1994; A. Catastini, 'Ancora sulla datazione della "Storia di Giuseppe"',

Henoch 20 (1998), 208-224; F.W. Golka and W. Weiss (eds.), *Joseph, Bibel und Literatur*, Oldenburg: Universität Oldenburg, 2000; M.V. Fox, 'Wisdom in the Joseph Story', *VT* 51 (2001), 26-41. Ahiqar: S. Niditch and R. Doran, 'The Success Story of the Wise Courtier: A Formal Approach', *JBL* 96 (1977), 179-93; F.M. Fales, 'Storia di Ahiqar tra Oriente e Grecia', *Quaderni di Storia* 38 (1993), 143-66.

Chapter 14. Returnees and Aliens: The Invention of the Conquest

1. *The Phases of the Return*. For a general framework, see P. Ackroyd in *The Cambridge History of Judaism*, Cambridge: Cambridge University Press, 1984, I, 130-61. Critical analysis of the sources, recently, G. Garbini, *Il ritorno dall'esilio babilonese*, Brescia: Paideia, 2001.

2. *Palestine in the Achaemenid Age*. H. Kreissig, *Die sozialökonomische Situation in Juda zur Achämenidenzeit*, Berlin: W. de Gruyter, 1973; M. Stern, *Material Culture of the Land of the Bible in the Persian Period 538–332 B.C.*, Warminster: Aris & Phillips, 1982; idem, in *The Cambridge History of Judaism*, Cambridge: Cambridge University Press, 1984, I, 70-114; W. Schottroff, 'Zur Sozialgeschichte Israels in der Perserzeit', in *Verkündigung und Forschung* 27 (1982), 46-68; C. Carter, 'The Province of Yehud in the Post-Exilic Period: Soundings in Site Distribution and Demography', in T.C. Eseknazi and K.H. Richards (eds.), *Second Temple Studies*, Sheffield: JSOT Press, 1991, II, 106-145; see also §15.1. On the development of coastal area, see the special number of *Trans* 2 (1990); A.J. Katzenstein, 'Gaza in the Persian Period', *Trans* 1 (1989), 67-105; O. Tal, 'Some Notes on the Settlement Patterns of the Persian Period Southern Sharon Plain', *Trans* 19 (2000), 115-25.

3. *The 'Intruders'*. Canaanites: N.P. Lemche, *The Canaanites and their Land*, Sheffield: JSOT Press, 1991; A.F. Rainey, 'Who is a Canaanite? A Review of the Textual Evidence', *BASOR* 304 (1996), 1-15. Amorites and Hittites: J. van Seters, 'The Terms "Amorite" and "Hittite" in the Old Testament', *VT* 22 (1972), 64-81. Perizzites: N. Na'aman, '*Amarna ālāni pu-ru-zi* (EA 137), and Biblical '*ry hprzy/hprzwt* ("Rural Settlements")', *Zeitschrift für Althebraistik* 4 (1991), 72-75. Traditional interpretation: T. Ishida, 'The Structure and Implications of the Lists of Pre-Israelite Nations', *Bibl* 60 (1979), 461-90.

4. *The Exodus Motif*. M. Liverani, 'Aziru, Servant of Two Masters' in idem, *Myth and Politics in Ancient Near Eastern Historiography*, London: Equinox, 2004, 125-44. Earliest attestations: Y. Hoffman, 'A North Israelite Typological Myth and a Judean Historical Tradition: The Exodus in Hosea and Amos', *VT* 39 (1989), 169-82. Deuteronomistic usage: A. Frisch,' The Exodus Motif in 1 Kings 1-14', *JSOT* 87 (2000), 3-21. In general, Y. Zakovitch, *'And You Shall Tell Your Son...' The Concept of the Exodus in the Bible*, Jerusalem: Magnes Press, 1991; S.E. Loewenstamm, *The Evolution of the Exodus Tradition*, Jerusalem: Magnes Press, 1992; M.S. Smith, *The Pilgrimage Pattern in Exodus*, Sheffield: Sheffield Academic Press, 1997. 'New Exodus': J. van Seters, 'Confessional Reformulations in the Exilic Period', *VT* 22 (1972), 448-59.

5. *Moses, the Desert and the Itineraries.* (A) Moses: H.H. Schmid, *Moses: Überlieferung und Geschichte*, Berlin: W. de Gruyter, 1968; G.W. Coats, *The Moses Tradition*, Sheffield: Sheffield Academic Press, 1993; J. van Seters, *The Life of Moses: The Yahwist as Historian in Exodus-Numbers*, Louisville, KY: Westminster/John Knox Press, 1994. See recently R. North, 'Perspective of the Exodus Author(s)', *ZAW* 113 (2001), 481-504. Egyptian setting: M. Görg, *Die Beziehungen zwischen dem alten Israel und Ägypten*, Darmstadt: Wissenschaftliche Buchgesellschaft, 1997; E.S. Frerichs and L.H. Lesko (eds.), *Exodus: The Egyptian Evidence*, Winona Lake, IN: Eisenbrauns, 1997; historically debatable is J. Assmann, *Moses the Egyptian*, Cambridge, MA: Harvard University Press, 1997. (B) Desert: A. Haldar, *The Notion of the Desert in Sumero-Akkadian and West-Semitic Religion*, Uppsala: Lundequistska bokhandeln, 1950; S. Talmon, 'The Desert Motif in the Bible and in Qumran Literature', in A. Altmann, *Biblical Motifs*, Cambridge, MA: Harvard University Press, 1966, 31-63; idem, 'Har and Midbar', in M. Mindlin, M.J. Geller and J.E. Wansbrough (eds.), *Figurative Language in the Ancient Near East*, London: SOAS, University of London, 1987, 117-42; N. Wyatt, 'Sea and Desert: Symbolic Geography in West-Semitic Religious Thought', *UF* 19 (1987), 375-89. (C) Itineraries: V. Fritz, *Israel in der Wüste*, Marburg: Elwert, 1970; G.W. Coats, 'The Wilderness Itinerary', *CBQ* 34 (1972), 135-72; J.T. Walsh, 'From Egypt to Moab: A Source Critical Analysis of the Wilderness Itinerary', *CBQ* 39 (1977), 20-33; G.I. Davies, *The Way of the Wilderness*, Cambridge: Cambridge University Press, 1979; Z. Kallai, 'The Wandering Traditions from Kadesh Barnea to Canaan', *JJS* 33 (1982), 176-84; M. Har-El, *The Sinai Journeys*, San Diego: Ridgefield, 1983; G.I. Davies, 'The Wilderness Itineraries and the Composition of the Pentateuch', *VT* 33 (1983), 1-13; J.-L. Ska, *Le passage de la mer*, Rome: Biblical Institute Press, 1986; J.M. Miller, 'The Israelite Journey through (around) Moab and Moabite Toponymy,' *JBL* 108 (1989), 577-95. On folkloric motifs see D. Irvin, *Mytharion*, Neukirchen-Vluyn: Neukirchener Verlag, 1978. On rebellions: G.W. Coats, *Rebellion in the Wilderness*, Nashville, TN: Abingdon Press, 1968.

6. *The Difficult Settlement in Canaan*: G. Mitchell, *Together in the Land: A Reading of the Book of Joshua*, Sheffield: Sheffield Academic Press, 1993; R.A. Freund, 'The Land Which Bled Forth its Bounty: An Exile Image of the Land of Israel', *SJOT* 13 (1999), 284-97. On different theories on settlement (conquest/nomadic infiltration/social revolt), see §2.1 and also J.M. Miller, 'The Israelite Occupation of Canaan', in J.H. Hayes and J.M. Miller (eds.), *Israelite and Judean History*, London: SCM Press; Philadelphia: Westminster Press, 1994² [1977], 213-84.

7. *Joshua and the 'Holy War'.* (A) Joshua: J. Sanmartín Ascaso, *Las guerras de Josué*, Valencia: Institución San Jerónimo para la Investigación Bíblica, 1982; G.W. Coats, 'The Book of Joshua: Heroic Saga or Conquest Theme?', *JSOT* 38 (1987), 15-32; A. Malamat, 'Israelite Conduct of War in the Conquest of Canaan', in *Symposia Celebrating the 75th Anniversary of the ASOR*, Cambridge, MA: Harvard University Press, 1979, 35-56; A.G. Auld, *Joshua Retold*, Edinburgh: T&T Clark, 1998; recently, R.S. Hess, 'The Book of Joshua as a Land Grant, *Bibl* 83 (2002), 493-506; W. Brueggemann, *The Land as Gift, Promise, and Challenge in Biblical Faith*, Minneapolis, MN: Fortress Press, 2003. (B) Holy war: G. von Rad, *Holy War in Ancient Israel*, Grand Rapids:

Eerdmans, 1991; M. Weippert, ' "Heiliger Krieg" in Israel und Assyrien', *ZAW* 84 (1972), 460-93; Sa-Moon Kang, *Divine War in the Old Testament and in the Ancient Near East*, Berlin: W. de Gruyter, 1989; M. Weinfeld, 'Divine Intervention in War in Israel and the Ancient Near East', in H. Tadmor and M. Weinfeld (eds.), *History, Historiography and Interpretation*, Jerusalem: Magnes Press, 1983, 121-47; A. Rofé, 'The Laws of Warfare in the Book of Deuteronomy', *JSOT* 32 (1985), 23-44; R. Good, 'The Just War in Ancient Israel', *JBL* 104 (1985), 385-400; J.M. Sprinkle, 'Deuteronomic "Just War" (Deut. 20, 10-20), and 2 Kings 3, 27', *ZABR* 6 (2000), 285-301. See also L.L. Rowlett, *Joshua and the Rhetoric of Violence*, Sheffield: Sheffield Academic Press, 1996. On *ḥērem*: P.D. Stern, *The Biblical Herem*, Atlanta, GA: Scholars Press, 1991; Y. Hoffman, 'The Deuteronomistic Concept of the Herem', *ZAW* 111 (1999), 196-210.

8. *The Landscape and Aetiology*. B.S. Childs,' A Study of the Formula "Until this Day" ', *JBL* 82 (1963), 279-92; *idem*, 'The Etiological Tale Re-examined', *VT* 24 (1974), 387-97; B.O. Long, *The Problem of Etiological Narrative in the Old Testament*, Berlin: W. de Gruyter, 1968. On the case of Jericho, K. Bieberstein, *Josua–Jordan Jericho*, Göttingen: Vandenhoeck & Ruprecht, 1995.

9. *Compromise and Cohabitation*. L. Rowlett, 'Inclusion, Exclusion and Marginality in the Book of Joshua', *JSOT* 55 (1992), 15-23; on Gibeonites: R.K. Sutherland, 'Israelite Political Theories in Joshua 9', *JSOT* 33 (1992), 65-74.

10. *Ideal Borders and Residual Lands*. Y. Kaufmann, *The Biblical Account of the Conquest of Palestine*, Jerusalem: Magnes Press, 1953; M. Saebo, 'Grenzbeschreibung und Landideal im Alten Testament', *ZDPV* 90 (1974), 14-37; N. Na'aman, *Borders and Districts in Biblical Historiography*, Jerusalem: Simor, 1986; *idem*, 'Lebo-Hamath, Şubat-Hamath, and the Northern Boundary of Canaan', *UF* 31 (1999), 417-41.

Chapter 15. A Nation without a King: The Invention of the Judges

1. *The Achaemenid Administrative Organization*. (A) Administrative structure: S. McEvenue, 'The Political Structure in Judah from Cyrus to Nehemiah', *CBQ* 43 (1981), 353-64; H. Williamson, 'The Governors of Judah under the Persians', *Tyndale Bulletin* 39 (1988), 59-82; A. Zertal, 'The Pahwah of Samaria (Northern Israel) during the Persian Period: Types of Settlement, Economy, History and New Discoveries', *Trans* 3 (1990), 9-30; P.R. Davies (ed.), *Second Temple Studies*, I, Sheffield: JSOT Press, 1991; K. Hoglund, *Achaemenid Imperial Organization in Syria-Palestine and the Mission of Ezra-Nehemiah*, Atlanta, GA: Scholars Press, 1992; F. Bianchi, *I superstiti della deportazione sono là nella provincia*, II, Napoli: Istituto universitario orientale 1995; C.E. Carter, *The Emergence of Yehud in the Persian Period: A Social and Demographic Study*, Sheffield: Sheffield Academic Press, 1999. (B) Coinage: J.W. Betylon, 'The Provincial Government of Persian Period Judaea and the Yehud Coins', *JBL* 104 (1986), 633-42; H. Gitler, 'Achaemenid Motifs in the Coinage of Ashdod, Ascalon and Gaza from the Fourth Century B.C.', *Trans* 20 (2000), 73-87; L. Mildenberg, 'On Frac-

tional Silver Issues in Palestine', *Trans* 20 (2000), 89-100. (C) Bullae from antiquarian market: N. Avigad, *Bullae and Seals from a Post-Exilic Judean Archive*, Jerusalem: Institute of Archaeology, Hebrew University, 1976. (D) Urbanization: R. Reich, 'The Beth-Zur Citadel II: A Persian Residency?', *Tel Aviv* 19 (1992), 113-23.

2. *The Context and Chronology of the Book of Judges.* (A) On the Period of the Judges, see the bibliography in A. Mayes, 'The Period of the Judges and the Rise of the Monarchy', in J.H. Hayes and J.M. Miller (eds.), *Israelite and Judean History*, London: SCM Press; Philadelphia: Westminster Press, 1994² [1977], 285-331; then W.J. Dumbrell, *The Purpose of the Book of Judges Reconsidered*, *JSOT* 25 (1983), 23-33. Low chronology: M. Liverani, 'Nelle pieghe del despotismo. Organismi rappresentativi nell'antico Oriente', *Studi Storici* 34 (1993), 7-33; even lower: P. Guillaume, 'From a Post-Monarchical to the Pre-Monarchical Period of the Judges', *Biblische Notizen* 113 (2002), 12-17. (B) Function of the Judges: W. Richter, 'Zu den "Richtern Israels"', *ZAW* 77 (1965), 40-72; K.D. Schunck, 'Die Richter Israels und ihr Amt,' *VT* Supplement 15 (1966), 252-62; A. Malamat, 'Charismatic Leadership in the Book of Judges', in F.M. Cross, *et al.* (eds.), *Magnalia Dei, the Mighty Acts of God: Essays in Memory of G.E. Wright*, Garden City, NY: Doubleday 1976, 152-68; T. Ishida, 'The Leaders of the Tribal League "Israel" in the Pre-Monarchic Period', *RB* 80 (1973), 514-30; A.J. Hauser, 'The "Minor Judges" – A Re-Evaluation', *JBL* 94 (1975), 190-200; Z. Weisman, 'Charismatic Leaders in the Era of the Judges', *ZAW* 89 (1977), 399-411; H.W. Rosel, 'Die "Richter Israels"', *BZ* 25 (1981), 180-203. (C) Elders: G. Bettenzoli, 'Gli "Anziani di Israele"', *Bibl* 64 (1983), 47-73; *idem*, 'Gli "Anziani di Giuda"', *Bibl* 64 (1983), 211-24; J. Bucholz, *Die Ältesten Israels im Deuteronomium*, Göttingen: Vandenhoeck & Ruprecht, 1988; H. Reviv, *The Elders in Ancient Israel*, Jerusalem: Magnes Press, 1989; T.M. Willis, *The Elders of the City: A Study of the Elders-Laws in Deuteronomy*, Atlanta, GA: Scholars Press, 2001.

3. *Historical and Utopian Elements.* B.G. Webb, *The Book of Judges*, Sheffield: JSOT Press, 1987; M. Brettler, 'The Book of Judges: Literature and Politics', *JBL* 108 (1989), 395-418; P.D. Guest, 'Can Judges Survive without Sources?', *JSOT* 78 (1998), 43-61. Political aims: H.W. Jüngling, *Richter 19: Plädoyer für das Königtum*, Rome: Biblical Institute Press, 1981; U. Becker, *Richterzeit und Königtum*, Berlin: W. de Gruyter, 1990. Assembly in Shechem: W.T. Koopmans, *Joshua 24 as Poetic Narrative*, Sheffield: JSOT Press, 1990. Subdivision of the land: A.M. Kitz, 'Undivided Inheritance and Lot Casting in the Book of Joshua', *JBL* 119 (2000), 601-618.

4. *Legendary and Fairy-tale Elements.* R.H. O'Connell, *The Rhetoric of the Book of Judges*, Leiden: E.J. Brill, 1996; C. Grottanelli, *Sette storie bibliche*, Brescia: Paideia, 1998. Most studies are on Samson: J. Crenshaw, *Samson: A Secret Betrayed, a Vow Ignored*, Atlanta, GA: John Knox Press, 1978; S. Niditch, 'Samson as Culture Hero, Trickster, and Bandit: The Empowerment of the Weak', *CBQ* 52 (1990), 608-624; H.J. Meurer, *Die Simson-Erzählung: Erzähltechnik und Theologie von Ri 13-16*, Berlin: W. de Gruyter, 2001.

5. *The Twelve Tribe System.* (A) The theory of the amphictyony was formulated by M. Noth, *Das System der zwölf Stämme Israels*, Stuttgart: W. Kohlhammer, 1928; more recently R. Smend, *Yahweh War and Tribal Confederation*, Nashville, TN: Abingdon Press, 1970; C.H.J. de Geus, *The Tribes of Israel: An Investigation into Some of the Presuppositions of M. Noth's Amphictiony Hypothesis*, Assen: Van Gorcum, 1976; O. Bächli, *Amphiktyonie im Alten Testament*, Basel: Friedrich Reinhardt, 1977; R. Bartelmus, 'Forschungen zum Richterbuch seit Martin Noth', *Theologische Rundschau* 56 (1992), 221-59. (B) Late terminology: A.G. Auld, 'Tribal Terminology in Joshua and Judges', in *Le origini di Israele*, Rome: Accademia Nazionale dei Lincei, 1987, 87-98. (C) Migration of the Danites: Y. Amit, 'Hidden Polemic in the Conquest of Dan: Judges XVII-XVIII', *VT* 40 (1990), 4-20; H.M. Niemann, 'Zorah, Eshtaol, Beth-Shemesh and Dan's Migration to the South', *JSOT* 86 (1999), 25-48; U. Bauer, 'Judges 18 as an Anti-Spy Story in the Context of an Anti-Conquest Story', *JSOT* 88 (2000), 37-47.

6. *Intertribal Space.* M. Liverani, 'Messages, Women and Hospitality', in *idem, Myth and Politics in Ancient Near Eastern Historiography*, London: Equinox, 2004, 160-92; S. Niditch, 'The "Sodomite" Theme in Judges 19-20: Family, Community, and Social Disintegration', *CBQ* 44 (1982), 365-78; S. Lasine, 'Guest and Host in Judges 19', *JSOT* 29 (1984), 37-59; V. Matthews, 'Hospitality and Hostility in Judges 4', *Biblical Theology Bulletin* 21 (1991), 13-21; *idem*, 'Hospitality and Hostility in Genesis 19 and Judges 19', *Biblical Theology Bulletin* 22 (1992), 3-11; K. Stone, 'Gender and Homosexuality in Judges 19: Subject-Honor, Object-Shame?', *JSOT* 67 (1995), 87-107; P.D. Guest, 'Dangerous Liaisons in the Book of Judges', *SJOT* 11 (1997), 241-69. Inner space: J.W. Wright, 'A Tale of Three Cities: Urban Gates and Power in Iron Age II, Neo-Babylonian and Achaemenid Judah', in P.R. Davies and J.M. Halligan (eds.), *Second Temple Studies*, Sheffield: Sheffield Academic Press, 2002, III, 19-50.

Chapter 16. *The Royal Option: The Invention of the United Monarchy*

1. *The Dying Rays of the House of David.* On the *nasi*': I.M.Duguid, *Ezekiel and the Leaders of Israel*, Leiden: E.J. Brill, 1994. On Zerubbabel, K.M. Beyse, *Serubbabel und die Königserwartungen der Propheten Haggai und Sacharja*, Stuttgart: Calwer Verlag, 1972; S. Japhet, 'Sheshbazzar and Zerubbabel', *ZAW* 94 (1982), 66-98; *ZAW* 95 (1983), 218-29; A. van der Woude, 'Serubbabel und die messianischen Erwartungen des Propheten Sacharjas', *ZAW* Supplement 100, Berlin: W. de Gruyter, 1988, 138-56; P. Sacchi, 'L'esilio e la fine della monarchia davidica', *Henoch* 11 (1989), 131-48; F. Bianchi, 'Zorobabele re di Giuda, *Henoch* 13 (1991), 133-50; O. Margalith, 'The Political Background of Zerubbabel's Mission and the Samaritan Schism', *VT* 41 (1991), 312-23; N. Na'aman, 'Royal Vassals or Governors? On the Status of Sheshbazzar and Zerubbabel in the Persian Empire', *Henoch* 22 (2000), 35-44. In general on the history and literature of the period P. Sacchi, *The History of the Second Temple Period*, Sheffield, Sheffield Academic Press, 2000.

2. *The Pro- and Anti-Monarchy Debate.* F. Langlamet, 'Les récits de l'institution de la royauté (I Sam VII-XIII)', *RB* 77 (1970), 121-200; F. Crüsemann, *Der Wiederstand gegen das Königtum*, Neukirchen–Vluyn: Neukirchener Verlag, 1978; G.E. Gerbrandt,

Kingship according to the Deuteronomistic History, Atlanta, GA: Scholars Press, 1986; G. Bettenzoli, 'Samuel und das Problem des Königtums', *BZ* 30 (1986), 222-36; B. Gosse, 'La nouvelle alliance et les promesses d'avenir se referant à David', *VT* 41 (1991), 419-28; A. Moenikes, *Die grundsätzliche Ablehnung der Königtums in der Hebräischen Bibel*, Weinheim: Beltz Athenäum,1995; I. de Castelbajac, 'Histoire de la rédaction de Juges IX', *VT* 51 (2001), 166-85; B.M. Levison, 'The Reconceptualization of Kingship in Deuteronomy and the Deuteronomistic History's Transformation of Torah', *VT* 51 (2001), 510-34. Jotham's fable: R. Bartelmus, 'Die sogenannte Jothamfabel', *Theologische Zeitschrift* 41 (1985), 97-120.

3. *The Mythical Foundations Unity as Archetype*. M. Liverani, 'Telipinu, or: on Solidarity', in *idem, Myth and Politics in Ancient Near Eastern Historiography*, London: Equinox, 2004, 27-52; Near Eastern antecedents: P.A. Ash, 'Jeroboam I and the Deuteronomistic Historian's Ideology of the Founder', *CBQ* 60 (1998), 16-24. Davidic promise: J. Coppens, 'La prophétie de Nathan – sa portée dynastique', in *Von Kanaan bis Kerala: Festschrift J. van der Ploeg*, Neukirchen–Vluyn: Neukirchener Verlag, 1982, 91-100; G.H. Jones, *The Nathan Narratives*, Sheffield: JSOT Press, 1990. 'Israel' as unifying term: J.P. Linville, *Israel in the Book of Kings: The Past as a Project of Social Identity*, Sheffield: Sheffield Academic Press, 1998.

4. *Dynastic Continuity and Stories of Succession.* (A) Dynasty: T.N. Mettinger, *King and Messiah: The Civil and Sacral Legitimation of the Israelite Kings*, Lund: C.W.K. Gleerup, 1976; T. Ishida, *The Royal Dynasties in Ancient Israel*, Berlin: W. de Gruyter, 1977; *idem, History and Historical Writing in Ancient Israel*, Leiden: E.J. Brill, 1999; C. Schäfer-Lichtenberger, *Josua und Salomo: Eine Studie zu Autorität und Legitimität des Nachfolgers im Alten Testament*, Leiden: E.J. Brill, 1995; K.E. Pomykala, *The Davidic Dynasty Tradition in Early Judaism*, Atlanta, GA: Scholars Press, 1995. (B) Stories of succession: still fundamental is L. Rost, *The Succession to the Throne of David*, Sheffield: Almond Press, 1982 [1926]; R.N. Whybray, *The Succession Narrative*, London: SCM Press, 1968; J.H. Grønbaek, *Die Geschichte von Davids Aufstieg*, Copenhagen: Prostant Apud Munksgaard, 1971; K.W. Whitelam, *The Just King: Monarchical Judiciary Authority in Ancient Israel*, Sheffield: JSOT Press, 1979; *idem*, 'The Defence of David', *JSOT* 29 (1984), 61-87; G. Keys, *The Wages of Sin: A Reappraisal of the 'Succession Narrative'*, Sheffield: Sheffield Academic Press, 1996; S. Seiler, *Die Geschichte von der Thronfolge Davids*, Berlin: W. de Gruyter, 1998; A. de Pury and Th. Römer (eds.), *Die sogenannte Thronfolgegeschichte Davids*, Göttingen: Vandenhoeck & Ruprecht, 2000. (C), Imagery and narrative aspects: D. Barthélemy, D.W. Gooding, J. Lust and E. Tov, *The Story of David and Goliath*, Göttingen: Vandenhoeck & Ruprecht, 1986; A.G. Auld and C. Ho, 'The Making of David and Goliath', *JSOT* 56 (1992), 19-39.

5. *Wisdom and Justice*. H.H. Schmid, *Wesen und Geschichte der Weisheit*, Berlin: W. de Gruyter, 1966; G. von Rad, *Wisdom in Israel*, Nashville, TN: Abingdon Press, 1972; R.N. Whybray, *The Intellectual Tradition in the Old Testament*, Berlin: W. de Gruyter, 1974; *idem, The Composition of the Book of Proverbs*, Sheffield: Sheffield Academic Press, 1994; L. Kaligula, *The Wise King*, Lund: C.W.K. Gleerup, 1980; N. Shupak, *Where Can Wisdom Be Found?*, Göttingen: Vandenhoeck & Ruprecht, 1993.

6. *From Royal to Eschatological Messianism.* (A) Kingship in general: K.H. Bernhardt, *Das Problem der altorientalische Königsideologie im alten Testament*, Leiden: E.J. Brill, 1961; J.A. Soggin, *Das Königtum in Israel*, Berlin: W. de Gruyter, 1967; G.E. Gerbrandt, *Kingship according to the Deuteronomistic History*, Atlanta, GA: Scholars Press, 1986. (B) 'Messiah': recently, E-J. Waschke, *Der Gesalbte*, Berlin: W. de Gruyter, 2001; T.L. Thompson, 'The Messiah Epithet in the Hebrew Bible', *SJOT* 15 (2001), 57-82. Keret passage: J. Day, 'The Canaanite Inheritance of the Israelite Monarchy', in J. Day (ed.), *King and Messiah in Israel and the Ancient Near East*, Sheffield: Sheffield Academic Press, 1988, 72-90; (C) Messianic Psalms: still important is S. Mowinckel, *The Psalms in Israel's Worship*, trans. D.R. Ap-Thomas; Sheffield: Sheffield Academic Press, 1992 [Oxford: Blackwell, 1962]; more recently, H.P. Nasuti, *Defining the Sacred Songs*, Sheffield: Sheffield Academic Press, 1999. On the monarchic date of some Psalms: J.H. Eaton, *Psalms of the Way and the Kingdom*, Sheffield: Sheffield Academic Press, 1995; M.D. Goulder, 'Asaph's History of Israel', *JSOT* 65 (1995), 71-81; *idem*, *The Psalms of Asaph and the Pentateuch*, Sheffield: Sheffield Academic Press, 1996 (for post-exilic psalms, see his *The Psalms of the Return*, Sheffield: Sheffield Academic Press, 1998). Cultic foundations: R.J. Tournay, *Seeing and Hearing God with the Psalms*, Sheffield: Sheffield Academic Press, 1991. (D) Messianic expectations: S. Mowinckel, *He That Cometh*, Oxford: Basil Blackwell, 1956; A. Laato, *Joshia and David Redivivus*, Lund: C.W.K. Gleerup, 1992; *idem*, *The Servant of Yahweh and Cyrus*, Lund: C.W.K. Gleerup, 1992; *idem*, *A Star is Rising*, Atlanta, GA: Scholars Press, 1997; W.H. Rose, *Zemah and Zerubbabel: Messianic Expectations in the Early Postexilic Period*, Sheffield: Sheffield Academic Press, 2000.

Chapter 17. The Priestly Option: The Invention of the Solomonic Temple

1. *Palestinian and Babylonian Temples*: see introductory bibliography.

2. *The Myth of the 'First Temple'.* V.A. Hurowitz, *I Have Built You an Exalted House*, Sheffield: Sheffield Academic Press, 1992. On the Jerusalem temple: T.A. Busink, *Der Tempel von Jerusalem*, I-II, Leiden: E.J. Brill, 1970–1980; K. Rupprecht, *Der Tempel von Jerusalem*, Berlin: W. de Gruyter, 1976. On biblical narrative: R. Tomes, ' "Our Holy and Beautiful House": When and Why was 1 Kings 6–8 Written?', *JSOT* 70 (1996), 33-50 (description of the temple still existing in 597–587). Sacred furniture: H. Weippert, 'Die Kesselwagen Salomos, *ZDPV* 108 (1992), 8-41; R.P. Carroll, 'The Temple in the Prophets, in *Second Temple Studies*, Sheffield: Sheffield Academic Press, 1994, II, 34-51.

3. *The Building of the 'Second Temple' and Establishment of Priestly Leadership.* (A) P.R. Bedford, *Temple Reconstruction in Early Achaemenid Judah*, Leiden: E.J. Brill, 2001; O. Lipschits, 'Judah, Jerusalem and the Temple 586–539 B.C.', *Trans* 22 (2001), 129-42; J.M. Trotter, 'Was the Second Jerusalem Temple a Primarily Persian Project?', *SJOT* 15 (2001), 276-94. (B) Haggai and Zechariah: J.E. Tollington, *Tradition and Innovation in Haggai and Zechariah 1–8*, Sheffield: Sheffield Academic Press, 1993; D. Clines, 'Haggai's Temple: Constructed, Deconstructed and Reconstructed', *SJOT* 7 (1993), 51-77; P. Marinkovic, 'What Does Zechariah 1–8 Tell Us about the Second

Temple?', in *Second Temple Studies*, II, 88-103; cf. also G.W. Ahlström, *Joel and the Temple Cult of Jerusalem*, Leiden: E.J. Brill, 1971. (C) Ezekiel's Vision: M. Konkel, *Architektonik des Heiligen: Studien zum zweiten Tempelvision Ezechiels*, Berlin: W. de Gruyter, 2001; also R.K. Duke, 'Punishment or Restoration? Another Look at the Levites of Ezekiel 44:6-16', *JSOT* 40 (1988), 61-81. (D) Lamentations: H.J. Kraus, *Klagelieder*, Neukirchen–Vluyn: Neukirchener Verlag, 1956; F.W. Dobbs-Allsopp, 'Tragedy, Tradition and Theology in the Book of Lamentations', *JSOT* 74 (1997), 29-60. (E) 'Kingdom of priests': H. Cazelles, ' "Royaume de prêtres et nation consacrée" ', in *idem, Autour de l'Exode*, Paris: Gabalda, 1987, 289-94; J.L. Ska, 'Exode 19,3b-6 et l'identité de l'Israel postexilique', in M. Vervenne (ed.), *Studies in the Book of Exodus*, Leuven: Peeters, 1996, 290; more recently G. Steins, 'Priesterherrschaft, Volk von Priestern oder was sonst?', *BZ* 45 (2001), 20-36. (F) On double leadership: A. Sérandour, 'Les récits bibliques de la construction du second temple', *Trans* 11 (1996), 9-32; B. Bosse, 'Le gouverneur et le grand prêtre', *Trans* 21 (2001), 149-73.

4. *Alternative Temples.* (A) Coastal area: J. Kamlah, 'Zwei nordpalästinische "Heiligtumer" der persischen Zeit und die epigraphische Funde', *ZDPV* 115 (1999), 163-90. (B) Samaritan schism: R.J. Coggins, *Samaritans and Jews: The Origins of the Samaritans Reconsidered*, Oxford: Basil Blackwell, 1975; N. Schur, *History of the Samaritans*, Frankfurt: Lang, 1989; A.D. Crown (ed.), *The Samaritans*, Tübingen: Mohr, 1989; I. Hjelm, *The Samaritans and Early Judaism*, Sheffield: Sheffield Academic Press, 2000.

5. *The Temple-City.* C. Schäfer-Lichtenberger, *Stadt und Eidgenossenschaft im Alten Testament*, Berlin: W. de Gruyter, 1983; U. Rüterswörden, *Von der politischen Gemeinschaft zur Gemeinde*, Frankfurt: Athenäum, 1987; J. Blenkinsopp, 'Temple and Society in Achaemenid Judah', in *Second Temple Studies*, Sheffield: Sheffield Academic Press, 1991, I, 22-53; J. Weinberg, *The Citizen-Temple Community*, Sheffield: Sheffield Academic Press, 1992; *idem*, 'Die Mentalität der jerusalemischen Bürger-Tempel-Gemeinde', *Trans* 5 (1992), 133-41; T. Eskenazi and K.H. Richards (eds.), *Second Temple Studies*, II, Sheffield: Sheffield Academic Press, 1994; D. Böhler, *Die heilige Stadt in Esdras α und Esra-Nehemia*, Freiburg: Universitätsverlag and Göttingen: Vandenhoeck & Ruprecht, 1997; J. Blenkinsopp, 'Did the Second Jerusalem Temple Possess Land?', *Trans* 21 (2001), 61-68.

6. *Priests and Levites.* (A) Priesthood in general: A. Cody, *A History of Old Testament Priesthood*, Rome, Biblical Institute Press, 1969; M. Haran, *Temples and Temple Services in Ancient Israel*, Oxford: Oxford University Press, 1978; L.L. Grabbe, *Priests, Prophets, Diviners, Sages: A Socio-Historical Study of Religious Specialists in Ancient Israel*, Valley Forge, PA: Trinity Press International, 1995; U. Dahmen, *Leviten und Priester im Deuteronomium*, Bodenheim: PHILO, 1996. (B) Levites: A. Laato, 'The Levitical Genealogies in 1 Chronicles 5–6 and the Formation of Levitical Ideology in Post-Exilic Judah', *JSOT* 62 (1994), 77-99; A. Taggar-Cohen, 'Law and Family in the Book of Numbers: The Levites and the *tidennūtu* Documents from Nuzi', *VT* 48 (1998), 74-94; R. Nurmela, *The Levites: Their Emergence as a Second-Class Priesthood*, Atlanta, GA: Scholars Press, 1998. (C) Levitical cities: M. Haran, 'Studies in the Account of the Levitical Cities', *JBL* 80 (1961), 45-54, 156-65; A.G. Auld, 'The Levitical Cities:

Text and History', *ZAW* 91 (1979), 194-206; R.G. Boling, 'Levitical Cities', in A. Kort and S. Morschauser (eds.), *Biblical and Related Studies Presented to Samuel Iwry*, Winona Lake, IN: Eisenbrauns, 1985, 23-32; E. Ben Zvi, 'The List of the Levitical Cities', *JSOT* 54 (1992), 77-106; G. Schmitt, 'Levitenstädte', *ZDPV* 111 (1995), 28-48. (D) priestly historiography: still important is M. Noth, *The Chronicler's History*, Sheffield: JSOT Press, 1987; see also R.E. Friedman, *The Exile and Biblical Narrative: The Formulation of the Deuteronomistic and Priestly Works*, Chico, CA: Scholars Press, 1981; P.R. Ackroyd, *The Chronicler in his Age*, Sheffield: JSOT Press, 1991; W. Riley, *King and Cultus in Chronicles*, Sheffield: Sheffield Academic Press, 1993; B.E. Kelly, *Retribution and Eschatology in Chronicles*, Sheffield: Sheffield Academic Press, 1996; M.P. Graham, K.G. Hoglund and S.L. McKenzie (eds.), *The Chronicler as Historian*, Sheffield: Sheffield Academic Press, 1997; M.P. Graham and S.L. McKenzie (eds.), *The Chronicler as Author*, Sheffield: Sheffield Academic Press, 1999; L. Schmidt, *Studien zur Priesterschrift*, Berlin: W. de Gruyter, 1993; D. Murray, 'Retribution and Revival: Theological Theory, Religious Praxis and the Future in Chronicles', *JSOT* 88 (2000), 77-99. (E) Nehemiah and parallels of the same period: U. Kellermann, *Nehemia: Quellen, Überlieferung und Geschichte*, Berlin: W. de Gruyter, 1967; J. Blenkinsopp, 'The Mission of Udjahorresnet and Those of Ezra and Nehemiah', *JBL* 106 (1987), 409-421; N.J. Reich, 'The Codification of the Egyptian Laws by Darius and the Origin of the Demotic Chronicle', *Mizraim* 1 (1933), 178-85. (F) Ezra and the origin of Judaism: H.H. Schaeder, *Esra der Schreiber*, Tübingen: Mohr 1930 (still important); E. Nodet. *A search for the origins of Judaism*, Sheffield: Sheffield Academic Press, 1997; J.L. Berquist, *Judaism in Persia's Shadow*, Minneapolis, MN: Fortress Press, 1995; M.Z. Brettler, 'Judaism in the Hebrew Bible?', *CBQ* 61 (1999), 429-47; D. Janzen, 'The "Mission" of Ezra and the Persian-Period Temple Community', *JBL* 119 (2000), 619-43.

Chapter 18. Self-Identification: The Invention of the Law

1. *The Covenant and the Law, God and the People.* (A) Structure and terminology of the covenant: P. Kalluveettil, *Declaration and Covenant*, Rome: Biblical Institute Press, 1982; M. Weinfeld, 'Covenant Terminology in the Ancient Near East and its Influence on the West', *JAOS* 93 (1973), 190-99. (B) Role of the people: J.B. Wells, *God's Holy People: A Theme in Biblical Theology*, Sheffield: Sheffield Academic Press, 2000; J. Joosten, *People and Land in the Holiness Code*, Leiden: E.J. Brill, 1996. (C) Publicity and secretness: E.W. Conrad, 'Heard but not Seen: the Representation of "Books" in the Old Testament', *JSOT* 54 (1992), 45-59.

2. *The Legendary Foundation: Moses and Sinai.* For a traditional interpretation, see W. Beyerlin, *Herkunft und Geschichte der ältesten Sinaitraditionen*, Tübingen: Mohr, 1961.

3. *The Stratification of the Law:* A recent survey in E. Otto, 'Deuteronomium und Pentateuch: Aspekte der gegenwärtigen Debatte', *ZABR* 6 (2000), 222-84 (and other articles in the same volume).

4. *Social Legislation*: R. North, *Sociology of the Biblical Jubilee*, Rome: Biblical Institute Press, 1954; *idem, The Biblical Jubilee after Fifty Years*, Rome: Biblical Institute Press, 2000; N.P. Lemche, 'The Manumission of Slaves – The Fallow Year – The Sabbatical Year – The Yobel Year', *VT* 26 (1976), 38-59; K. Baltzer, 'Liberation from Debt Slavery after the Exile', in S.D. McBride, *et al.* (eds.), *Ancient Israelite Religion: Essays in Honor of Frank Moore Cross*, Philadelphia, PA: Fortress Press, 1987, 477-85; J.A. Fager, *Land Tenure and the Biblical Jubilee*, Sheffield: Sheffield Academic Press, 1993; H. Ucko (ed.), *The Jubilee Challenge: Utopia or Possibility*, Geneva: WCC Publications, 1997; E. Otto, 'Programme der sozialen Gerechtigkeit: Die neuassyrische (an-)durāru-Institution sozialen Ausgleichs und das deuteronomische Erlassjahr in Dtn 15', *ZABR* 3 (1997), 26-63; C. Carmichael, 'The Sabbatical Jubilee Cycle and the Seven-Year Famine in Egypt', *Bibl* 80 (1999), 224-39.

5. *Matrimonial Legislation*. F. Fechter, *Die Familie in der Nachexilzeit*, Berlin: W. de Gruyter, 1998; C. Pichon, 'La prohibition des mariages mixtes par Néhémie', *VT* 47 (1997), 168-99; H.C. Washington, 'The Strange Woman of Proverbs 1–9 and Post-Exilic Judean Society', in *Second Temple Studies*, I, 217-42; T. Eskenazi and E.P. Judd, 'Marriage to a Stranger in Ezra 9-10', *ibidem*, 266-85; T.L. Thompson, 'Holy War at the Center of Biblical Theology: Shalom and the Cleansing of Jerusalem', in T.L. Thompson (ed.), *Jerusalem in Ancient History and Tradition*, London: T&T Clark International, 2003, 223-57. See also C. Maier, *Die 'fremde Frau' in Proverbien 1–9*, Göttingen: Vandenhoeck & Ruprecht, 1995.

6. *Identity Markers*. (A) In general K. Grünwaldt, *Exil und Identität: Beschneidung, Passa und Sabbat in der Priesterschrift*, Frankfurt: Hain, 1992. (B) Costume: M. Wäfler, *Nicht-Assyrer neuassyrischer Darstellungen*, I-II, Neukirchen–Vluyn: Neukirchener Verlag, 1975. (C) Circumcision: J.M. Sasson, 'Circumcision in the Ancient Near East', *JBL* 85 (1966), 473-76; P. Arata Mantovani, 'Circoncisi e incirconcisi', *Henoch* 10 (1988), 51-68; J. Goldingay, 'The Significance of Circumcision', *JSOT* 88 (2000), 3-18. (D) Sabbath and Passover: H.A. McKay, *Sabbath and Synagogue: The Question of Sabbath Worship in Ancient Israel*, Leiden: E.J. Brill, 1994; T. Veijola, 'The History of Passover in the Light of Deuteronomy 16,1-8', *ZABR* 2 (1996), 53-75.

7. *Purity and Contamination*. M. Douglas, *Purity and Danger*, Harmondsworth: Penguin, 1970; *eadem*, 'The Forbidden Animals in Leviticus', *JSOT* 59 (1993), 3-23; E.V. Hulse, 'The Nature of Biblical Leprosy', *PEQ* 197 (1975), 87-105; W. Houston, *Purity and Monotheism: Clean and Unclean Animals in Biblical Law*, Sheffield: Sheffield Academic Press, 1993; J. Sawyer (ed.), *Reading Leviticus*, Sheffield: Sheffield Academic Press, 1996; R.A. Kugler, 'Holiness, Purity, the Body, and Society: The Evidence for Theological Conflict in Leviticus', *JSOT* 76 (1997), 3-27; T.A. Rudnig, *Heilig und Profan: Redaktionskritische Studien zu Ez. 40–48*, Berlin: W. de Gruyter, 2000; C. Karrer, *Ringen um die Verfassung Judas*, Berlin: W. de Gruyter, 2001.

8. *Proselytism or Exclusivity*. R. Goldberg, *The Nations that Know Thee not: Ancient Jewish Attitudes towards Other Religions*, Sheffield: Sheffield Academic Press, 1997. On the *gēr*: J.E. Ramirez Kidd, *Alterity and Identity in Israel: the* ger *in the Old Testa-*

ment, Berlin: W. de Gruyter, 1999. Love for the 'neighbour': H.P. Mathys, *Liebe deinen Nächsten wie dich selbst,* Göttingen: Vandenhoeck & Ruprecht, 1986. Universalism in Second Isaiah: J. Blenkinsopp, 'Second Isaiah – Prophet of Universalism', *JSOT* 41 (1988), 83-103.

Chapter 19. Local History and Universal Values

The Historiographical Debate. (A) History of Palestinian archaeology in the nineteenth century: N.A. Silberman, *Digging for God and Country: Exploration in the Holy Land, 1799–1917,* New York: Knopf, 1982; in the twentieth century: P.R.S. Moorey, *A Century of Biblical Archaeology,* Cambridge: Lutterworth Press, 1991. (B) On the recent debate, see also W.G. Dever, *Recent Archaeological Discoveries and Biblical Research,* Seattle: University of Washington Press, 1990; *idem,* 'Will the Real Israel Please Stand Up? Archaeology and Israelite Historiography', I, *BASOR* 297 (1995), 61-80; II, *BASOR* 298 (1995), 37-58; K.W. Whitelam, 'The Identity of Early Israel: The Realignment and Transformation of Late Bronze – Iron Age Palestine', *JSOT* 63 (1994), 57-87; W.G. Dever, 'The Identity of Early Israel: A Rejoinder to K.W. Whitelam', *JSOT* 72 (1996), 3-24; *idem, What Did the Biblical Writers Know and When Did They Know It?,* Grand Rapids: Eerdmans, 2001; N.A. Silberman and D.B. Small (eds.), *The Archaeology of Israel: Constructing the Past, Interpreting the Present,* Sheffield: Sheffield Academic Press, 1997 (in particular the articles by W. Dever, 290-310, B. Halpern, 311-40, I. Finkelstein, 216-237); I. Finkelstein and N.A. Silberman, *The Bible Unearthed,* New York: The Free Press, 2001. (C) On the 'minimalist' position – anticipated in Italy by G. Garbini, *History and Ideology in Ancient Israel,* London: SCM Press, 1988 — see D.V. Edelman (ed.), *The Fabric of History: Text, Artifact and Israel's Past,* Sheffield: JSOT Press, 1991; P.R. Davies, *In Search of Ancient Israel: A Study in Biblical Origins,* Sheffield: JSOT Press, 1992; L.L. Grabbe (ed.), *Can a 'History of Israel' Be Written?,* Sheffield: Sheffield Academic Press, 1997; N.P. Lemche, *The Israelites in History and Tradition,* London: SPCK and Louisville, KY: Westminster/John Knox Press, 1998; T.L. Thompson, *The Bible in History: How Writers Create a Past,* London: Jonathan Cape, 1999. (D) Examples of reaction: J. Barr, *History and Ideology in the Old Testament,* Oxford: Oxford University Press, 2000. (E) Hellenistic dating: J. Strange, *The Book of Joshua: A Hasmonean Manifesto?,* in A. Lemaire and B. Otzen (eds.), *History and Tradition of Early Israel,* Leiden: E.J. Brill, 1993, 136-41; *idem,* 'The Book of Joshua: Origin and Dating', *SJOT* 16 (2002), 44-51; L.L. Grabbe (ed.), *Did Moses Speak Attic? Jewish Historiography and Scripture in the Hellenistic Period,* Sheffield: Sheffield Academic Press, 2001. (F) I revealed my own position in M. Liverani, 'Le "origini" di Israele: progetto irrealizzabile di ricerca etnogenetica', *Rivista Biblica* 28 (1980), 9-31; and in 'Nuovi sviluppi nello studio della storia dell'Israele antico', *Bibl* 8 (1999), 488-505.

INDEX

INDEX OF REFERENCES

1. BIBLICAL TEXTS

2. Texts from the Ancient Near East

3. CLASSICAL WRITINGS

1. *Persons*

2. Deities

Made in the USA
San Bernardino, CA
03 November 2017